AF361560

Teaching Film
from the People's Republic of China

Teaching Film from the People's Republic of China

Edited by

Zhuoyi Wang, Emily Wilcox, and Hongmei Yu

The Modern Language Association of America
New York
2024

Options for Teaching 63
ISSN 1079-2562

Library of Congress Cataloging-in-Publication Data

Names: Wang, Zhuoyi, 1974- editor. | Wilcox, Emily, 1981- editor. |
   Yu, Hongmei (College teacher), editor.
Title: Teaching film from the People's Republic of China / edited by
   Zhuoyi Wang, Emily Wilcox, and Hongmei Yu.
Description: New York : The Modern Language Association of America, 2024. |
   Series: Options for teaching, 1079-2562 ; 63 | Includes bibliographical
   references.
Identifiers: LCCN 2023041988 (print) | LCCN 2023041989 (ebook) |
   ISBN 9781603296311 (hardcover) | ISBN 9781603296328 (paperback) |
   ISBN 9781603296335 (EPUB)
Subjects: LCSH: Motion pictures—China. | Motion pictures—Study and
   teaching (Higher)
Classification: LCC PN1993.5.C4 T44 2024 (print) | LCC PN1993.5.C4
   (ebook) | DDC 791.430951—dc23
LC record available at https://lccn.loc.gov/2023041988
LC ebook record available at https://lccn.loc.gov/2023041989

Contents

Part VII: Multidisciplinary Approaches

Zhuoyi Wang, Emily Wilcox, and Hongmei Yu

Introduction

As educators who share with our students today's media-rich world, we can instinctively recognize the potential of film as a powerful pedagogical tool in our classrooms. Compared to written texts, film presents the eyes and ears with ready-made and vividly concrete images and sounds. With its lifelike simulation of space, time, and human interaction, film triggers mental processes and emotional responses such as memory, pain, and anticipation. Especially when dealing with material and social worlds that are unfamiliar to the audience, film can make sense of new vocabulary and information in ways that texts may struggle to do. Film's mechanical forward motion and built-in temporal inertia can make its consumption feel effortless, especially for students who are already accustomed to media-rich methods for learning new information and communicating with others.

These factors, which make teaching with film appealing and effective, also present distinct and often underexplored challenges. The rich aural and visual stimulation that films offer can generate sensory overload. This may leave students with an overwhelming amount of information to process, especially through a critical and analytical lens, without prior training or preparation in reading filmic texts. Similarly, the emotional depth of film experience can necessitate affective labor that may feel alien to students in an academic context, or it may be difficult for students and teachers to link this emotional response to course themes and learning outcomes. The fact that films bring unfamiliar things, places, and people vividly to life on-screen also carries with it the dangerous possibility that students may equate filmic representations, which may be fictional, retrospective, and didactic, with reality or with historical experiences. Likewise, the fact that film moves at its own rapid pace and feels comparatively effortless to consume may provide students a false sense of engagement or rush them through new material that requires more time to digest. The enjoyability of film could risk turning serious, complicated issues into vectors of catharsis or entertainment, potentially diminishing the gravity of these topics or replacing structural concerns with personal narratives.

Teaching Film from the People's Republic of China provides a pioneering and in-depth exploration of these issues by examining the use of film in courses related to China at higher educational institutions. The authors of the essays collected here engage these issues and concerns and address a long-standing need for more attention to the close relationship between research and pedagogy. As Dana Polan points out, "Academic rhetoric frequently invokes a necessary interconnection between research and teaching, but historiographical practices proceed often as if only the former contributed in any substantial ways to defining the contours of disciplines and their practices" (20). The history of teaching film (beginning in the 1910s) is significantly longer than that of the academic specialty of film studies (beginning in the 1950s). However, efforts in film pedagogy have received far less scholarly attention than has analysis of films. This bias obscures the crucial role that classroom practices play in producing, rather than just transmitting, disciplinary knowledge. It has also seriously hindered the development of the study of film pedagogy.

English-language scholarly work in film pedagogy has been ongoing for several decades. In the United States, the Modern Language Association (MLA) made a landmark, book-length contribution to this field by publishing *Film Study in the Undergraduate Curriculum* in 1983 (Grant). However, the second MLA volume dedicated to film pedagogy, *Teaching Film*, in the Options for Teaching series, did not appear until 2012, and by that time the first one was already out of print.[1] During the nearly thirty intervening years, publishers in the United States released just a few film pedagogy books (e.g., Gerster and Zlogar; Polan; Marcus; Brown). British presses somewhat ameliorated this situation in the broader English-speaking world with a publication series by the British Film Series (e.g.,

Quy; Jones; Benyahia) as well as several other books (e.g., Watkins; Eaglestone and Langford; Ritterbusch). But these works were insufficient for the study of film pedagogy to mature. The MLA Options for Teaching series focuses on broad topics in literature or language, and so, as the editors of *Teaching Film* note, their book "has the formidable task of confronting the entirety of the film pedagogical landscape," and they "can only gesture toward broad areas, issues, and questions that [they] trust will receive more detailed consideration in the future" (Fischer and Petro 2). This call for more specification has not yet been adequately answered. The film pedagogy books published since 2012 are still limited in number (e.g., Billsberry; Liston and Renga; Giunta and McCormick; Stoddard and Hicks). Moreover, they generally engage with large pedagogical issues in transcultural film, leaving cultural specificities and national contexts seriously understudied.

Despite the paucity of published research on film pedagogy, instructors' recognition of the potential of film has led to creative uses of films in a wide range of humanities and social science courses in recent years. At the same time, concerns have arisen about the potential pedagogical pitfalls of using films in teaching. Because China is structurally conceived as an other in many English-speaking classrooms, especially in the United States, the use of films in courses about China often epitomizes the intertwined benefits and challenges of employing film as a pedagogical medium. Courses with such titles as China through Film, China on Screen, and China through the Lens are highly popular at North American colleges and universities. The use of films as supplementary or required material is also increasingly common in other humanities and social science courses about China. On the one hand, film can serve as an inviting way into what may be for many students an unfamiliar Chinese linguistic, cultural, societal, historical, and political environment. Film provides a multisensory experience of China for students to discover rich information and engage in enlightening classroom discussions. On the other hand, this pedagogical approach risks mistaking films for "transparent windows" and China for "a signified" behind the windows, in the words of Hongwei Thorn Chen and Aleksander Sedzielarz in their essay in this volume. Teaching Chinese film without adequate pedagogical and epistemological reflections may reify preconceived notions, leading students to further simplify and stereotype China as an other. The twenty-one essays in this volume form a concerted effort for the first time to conduct a critically needed study of teaching Chinese film that addresses these and other related challenges in specific classroom contexts.

Contributions to Chinese Film Studies

English-language research on Chinese film has grown rapidly since the first academic books dedicated to the subject appeared in the 1970s. Today, film is considered a core subfield of modern Chinese language and literature; nearly all Chinese studies programs now offer film courses, and several academic monographs on Chinese film are published annually. Many edited collections have traced the historical evolution of Chinese cinema and its transnational circulations, with a focus on the commonly recognized generations of Chinese film directors, the emergence of major genres such as melodrama and martial arts cinema, and the shifts in theme, style, and consumption habits that have accompanied major changes in Chinese politics and society since the birth of cinema at the turn of the twentieth century.[2] Some collections have also explored particular topics within this larger scope, such as Chinese-language film criticism, women's cinema, ecocinema, independent filmmaking and the New Documentary Film movement, the international reception of Chinese film, the development of Chinese-language cinema outside mainland China, and the relationship between Chinese cinema and Hollywood.[3] Despite the field's enormous expansion in recent years, however, film pedagogy has not yet received significant attention among scholars of Chinese film studies.

Departing from previous studies, this volume aims to reflect in self-conscious ways about how we use film as a pedagogical medium in the classroom. This means using film to teach not only film but also a range of other subjects. The essays in this volume thus consider how to use Chinese film in courses on Chinese history, Chinese language and culture, Chinese society and urbanization, ethnic groups in China, and intercultural and comparative studies. In contrast to teaching Chinese film as film, we consider how to teach these other subjects through Chinese film. In doing so, we shift our focus away from traditional film studies concerns—such as how to apply theories and methods of formal analysis in film studies, where a film fits into the long historical trajectory of Chinese cinema, or how it embodies the characteristics of a specific film genre, period, or director—and instead take up a range of other questions such as the following: What types of reflection can a film elicit in a diverse range of students, and how can such reflection best be transformed into a productive learning moment? What does a film show or obscure about the historical or social issues it addresses, and how might its treatment of Chinese history and society become an opportunity to teach students about historical consciousness, media representation, or research methodology? By starting from positions grounded in classroom experiences, the contributors to this volume pose useful and thought-provoking questions that are relevant not only to the teaching of Chinese film but also to how we employ audiovisual media of all kinds in our day-to-day teaching. The essays in this volume deepen our theorization of film as a pedagogical medium, while urging us all to be more intentional about how we select and utilize Chinese films in our courses. Moreover, they educate scholars outside Chinese film studies about how specific films can be used to teach a wide range of themes and materials.

This book primarily focuses on pedagogical strategies for one particular subset of Chinese cinema, namely, works produced in the People's Republic of China (PRC) from the 1950s to the present. Films from the PRC present special challenges to students in English-speaking universities such as those in North America, Australia, the United Kingdom, and Hong Kong, as well as in other international sites such as Japan and the Philippines, which are the main contexts for teaching Chinese film addressed in this volume. Such challenges arise from the fact that, as a socialist country, China has a sociocultural and political-economic system that may be unfamiliar to students in these learning environments. Films produced since the 1980s during China's reform and opening-up period often contain references to historical events and experiences of the so-called Mao years of 1949–76—typically regarded as the high point of socialist culture in China—and these films tend to offer a critical perspective on the socialist era that reflects contemporary conditions. Instructors require effective pedagogical strategies to prepare students unfamiliar with socialist ideology and cultural production to approach and analyze films that emerge from these contexts.

Another challenge to teaching films from the PRC in English-speaking university settings is that students in these places tend to have minimal basic knowledge about the history and culture of the PRC. What knowledge they do have is often heavily shaped by widespread negative media representations that may lead them to have strong preconceived notions about the country. However, the increasing presence of international students from the PRC in these classrooms creates opportunities for dialogue and mutual learning, making films from the PRC even more valuable as tools that can facilitate meaningful intercultural experiences among students and between students and instructors. Teaching in such contexts is particularly fraught, and thus we contend that using films from the PRC requires even greater levels of care and self-reflection than teaching Chinese-language films from other places and times. For this reason, we have excluded from this volume essays that focus solely on teaching Chinese or sinophone films produced either before 1949 or in places such as Taiwan, Hong Kong, Malaysia, and Singapore, which have significantly different sociopolitical histories from that of the PRC, though some essays in the volume discuss such films for a comparative framework. We feel that these subjects present distinct pedagogical challenges and opportunities and thus deserve dedicated volumes in their own right. This choice reflects the expertise of the three volume editors, who are specialists in PRC culture and have significant teaching experience in this field. For convenience, this volume uses the phrase "Chinese film" to refer to films produced in the PRC, though we acknowledge the phrase's broader meaning in other contexts.

With the increasing availability on video-sharing websites and film-streaming platforms of full-length, English-subtitled films produced in the PRC, these films represent a vast resource for faculty who wish to incorporate authentic international materials into their course syllabi. The fact that students can often stream these films merely by clicking a hyperlink copied into the syllabus makes them attractive options for faculty and students alike.[4] The greater challenge with teaching such films is therefore no longer the technical or linguistic issues of access—as was often the case in the past—but rather the pedagogical questions of how to guide students to engage with and learn from these film-watching experiences.

By widening the scope of Chinese film studies to include film pedagogy, this volume brings a more diverse range of voices into the conversation about Chinese film. In this way, it further enriches the field and introduces new possibilities for how we interact with films, both in and out of the classroom. Most academic research on Chinese film is published by scholars with disciplinary backgrounds in film studies or comparative literature. However, the contributors to this volume possess training not only in film and literary studies but also a variety of additional subjects, including anthropology, communication studies, ethnomusicology, history, linguistics, sociology, theater studies, and urban geography. In adapting films into their courses, these contributors bring their own disciplinary approaches, methods, and specialist knowledge to the interpretation and appreciation of Chinese films. In doing so, they introduce questions and apply frameworks that may be unexpected to scholars whose primary area of research is film studies. By placing these less conventional studies alongside essays by film scholars, this volume stages an interdisciplinary conversation—one that opens new lines of inquiry and provides fresh perspectives on even the most familiar of Chinese films. In some cases, it also introduces film materials that lie outside the traditional canon of films taught in film courses. To address issues of access, availability, and disciplinary contextualization, certain essays include a list of additional resources.

Organization of the Volume

This volume is organized into seven parts according to different themes. Although many connections exist across these clusters, the organization offers a starting point for readers to identify their pedagogical interests and expand them.

The three essays in part 1 form a concerted effort to use Chinese film as a pedagogical tool "to open up learning spaces that privilege multiplicity and connection," according to Chenshu Zhou in this volume. Zhou proposes a rhizomatic approach to the common pedagogical model of teaching "China through film" in order to ride this model's inherent tensions between area studies and film studies; train students to practice empathic close readings of heterogenous, subtle, and changing clues in Chinese films as a simulation of everyday encounters with an unfamiliar culture; help them realize the constructed nature of both China and film; and lead them beyond those totalistic and essentialist generalizations. Drawing from her experiences of teaching an increasingly diverse student body thanks to the upsurge of international students from mainland China, Angie Chau discusses the "delicate balancing act" of using Chinese film as a pedagogical opportunity for instructors and students to reflect on their own relationships to China and its screen representations, create dialogues on such key concepts as authenticity and censorship across diverse positions, and cultivate intercultural understanding and empathic viewership. Zhuoyi Wang points out that the sensitive ideological tensions, contradictions, and gaps among and within Chinese-speaking cultures and societies do not receive adequate attention in the current Chinese curriculum. Through a detailed pedagogical guide on teaching *The Wandering Earth* (流浪地球), he shows how to effectively use a controversial film to help students comprehend not only the multiplicity of the Chinese-speaking world but also the challenges and importance of nuanced cross-cultural and cross-ideological understanding in an increasingly polarized global discursive environment.

Part 2 takes up the question of how film can serve as a tool to teach the history of twentieth-century China, with a focus on using film to rethink conventional narratives of Chinese revolution. Emily Wilcox critiques the tendency of instructors to employ retrospective filmic accounts to introduce students to the early socialist period and instead advocates using films created during that time. Discussing three canonical films from the 1950s and early 1960s, Wilcox argues that these films are especially provocative for stimulating in-depth student explorations of intersections of class, gender, and ethnicity in socialist China. In this way, she suggests, early PRC film can catalyze students' analysis of revolution through an intersectional lens. Turning to films produced during the Cultural Revolution, Angie Baecker offers what she calls "production studies as a pedagogical framework" to teach students to appreciate and understand China's revolutionary culture beyond the simplistic framework of propaganda. She argues that by examining publications written by film directors, cast, crew, and studio employees in conjunction with the organizational sites and practices they inhabit, as well as the exercise of power within those networks, students learn to observe filmmaking in Maoist China as a contested and experimental activity of cultural creation. Moving beyond the Mao era, Ping Zhu shows how films can operate effectively together to teach students that "contemporary Chinese history is fraught with competing historical truths." Using three films from different periods with related narrative structures that unfold in different ways—*Red Detachment of Women* (红色娘子军), *Yellow Earth* (黄土地), and *The Road Home* (我的父亲母亲)—Zhu demonstrates how teaching these films as allegories of China during the socialist period, the reform era, and the postsocialist period can instill in students an awareness of China's drastic social transformations as well as the coexistence of diverse understandings of history. Marjorie Dryburgh continues this historiographical questioning by guiding students to read historical films about early-twentieth-century China through the lens of peripheral female characters. While *1911* (辛亥革命) and *Soul Haunted by Painting* (画魂) are dominated, respectively, by the revolutionary Huang Xing and the painter Pan Yuliang, Dryburgh asks what new understandings of history can emerge when students shift their focus to characters given less attention in the narratives: Huang's wife Xu Zonghan and Madam Pan, Pan Zanhua's wife before Pan Yuliang. Dryburgh shows how this analysis can foster a critical understanding of history and historiography along with the cinematic representation of revolution.

Part 3 addresses the issue of how visual images in film are constructed, generate meaning, and mediate understandings of contemporary social realities in China. With an acute awareness of what the film historian Michèle Lagny argues is the "disarticulated" character of film as a historical object (36), Hongwei Thorn Chen and Aleksander Sedzielarz reflect on "the teaching of Chinese documentary films with the aim of encouraging reflective and ethical thinking in students about the historicity of images." Drawing on an array of widely taught Chinese documentary films, including *West of the Tracks* (铁西区), *Jiang Hu: Life on the Road* (江湖), *River Elegy* (河殇), and *Meishi Street* (煤市街), they show how, through comparative analysis, these films can be used to question assumptions about direct cinema and deepen understandings of images in fictional film. Continuing this exploration of documentary cinema, Jasmine Yu-Hsing Chen, Sydney Pond, and Emma Clawson use the film *Children at a Village School* (村小的孩子) to demonstrate how a documentary can effectively introduce American students to a complex social phenomenon, in this case the issue of left-behind children. The approach they propose encourages students to critically evaluate the reliability of documentaries by analyzing both their narrative and visual aspects, attending to questions such as "what is neglected in the film and how the film may impact the lives of its subjects," in order to make students more critical media consumers. Han Li and Shaolu Yu examine how urban development in contemporary China is remembered, documented, and imagined through cinema. Using a close reading approach to the films *The Postmodern Life of My Aunt* (姨妈的后现代生活), *Beijing Bicycle* (十七岁的单车), and *Last Train Home* (归途列车) in a course on Asian urbanization, Li and Yu illuminate how films provide an important visual portrayal of urban landscapes, while they also work as living artifacts and cultural products of ongoing urban change.

Part 4 deals with the controversial notion of national culture, and the three essays in this section aim to dissect the production of certain cultural traditions. Josh Stenberg examines a distinctive late-twentieth- and early-twenty-first-century film genre called *yinpeixiang* (音配像; "sound matched to image"), in which audio recordings of canonical performances of *xiqu* (戏曲; often known as "Chinese opera") by actors from mid-century were matched to new visual recordings of stage performances by their disciples lip-synching in full costume. The state-initiated *yinpeixiang* project, being explicitly a conservation project, provides a point of entry for students to consider transmission and tradition in Chinese theater and the role of the post-Maoist state in the construction of traditional arts. While Chen Kaige's *Yellow Earth* is often used in classrooms for its notable cinematography, Ho Chak Law approaches this film through the lens of music, and in particular the female singing voice, to unpack "the ways *Yellow Earth* connects music with historical events as well as preexisting cultural practices and discourses." By comparing *Yellow Earth* with some minority films, he also examines how folk songs collected from Han and non-Han communities are part and parcel of the repertoire for national unity. Martial arts cinema, as discussed by Shirley O. Lua, is another important film genre that can be used to investigate the representation and repurposing of layers of cultural tradition in film. By contextualizing Zhang Yimou's *Hero* (英雄) and juxtaposing it with other assassin films, she leads students to a conversation of how certain cultural values often echo anxieties of the era in which a film is produced.

The three essays in part 5 apply intercultural and comparative approaches to examine Chinese films. In tracing the figure of the mermaid in *Suzhou River* (苏州河), Lily Li untwines Hans Christian Andersen's hybrid, intercultural fairy tale "The Little Mermaid," the mythical Chinese carp spirit in the Chinese opera film *Chasing the Carp* (追鱼), and the water nymph Rusalka in the Czech opera film *Rusalka*, thus undertaking a fruitful pedagogical journey into cultural diversity and universality. Furthermore, as Li argues, by "exploring the film and its mythic sources allegorically as the relationship between humanity and nature," *Suzhou River* also provides meaningful sources for an ecocritical study of the love theme. Vincent Casaregola compares *The Red Detachment of Women* with an American film of the Broadway musical *Flower Drum Song*, featuring a group of young Chinese women who each finally find their Mr. Right in Chinatown. Casaregola argues that integration propaganda is a shared strategy of gender construction in both productions despite their ideological differences. His essay creates inspiring conversations with Ping Zhu's cinematic trio, which includes *Red Detachment of Women*, and Emily Wilcox's intersectional analysis of socialist films. Elaine Chung's intercultural and comparative approach takes two Chinese remakes of South Korean films as an important subject of study: *The Big Shot* ("大"人物) and *Twenty Once Again* (重返 20 岁). Using the circuit of culture as a theoretical framework, Chung guides students to discuss the differences between the films and thus to achieve a more holistic and critical understanding of the meaning-making process of culture. Meanwhile, she also emphasizes the importance of developing students' reflexivity when applying Western theories in interpreting Chinese film texts.

Recently, there has been an innovative trend in the field of Chinese language pedagogy: using target-language films to improve students' language skills and cultural literacy and to bridge the conventional divide between the so-called language courses and culture courses. The two essays in part 6 both contribute to this trend. Using *Shower* (洗澡) and *Ip Man* (叶问) as examples, Jin Liu discusses how to effectively integrate the teaching of Chinese language skills and Chinese philosophical concepts in a course on language and film. Jingjing Cai and Su-I Chen provide a critical survey of existing film-based Chinese language textbooks, as well as a thorough report of their yearlong experiment of using film as primary material for teaching Chinese language skills and contemporary social issues.

The three essays in part 7 approach teaching Chinese film through a multidisciplinary lens connecting film studies with such other disciplines as sociology, philosophy, literature, history, and anthropology. Seio Nakajima illustrates how to teach a comprehensive sociological understanding of Chinese independent cinema through class discussions of the cultural-diamond framework. Corey Kai Nelson Schultz deploys the methodology of phenomenology, the analysis of experience, leading students to study Chinese films through an informed and analytic reflection on their individual viewing experiences. Yanshuo Zhang has developed innovative methodologies for teaching Chinese ethnic minority film, in order to push the conventional boundaries of knowledge, including those of academic disciplines, film genres, art forms, ideologies, cultures, ethnicities, and nationalities. Her essay neatly concludes this volume by epitomizing its collective effort to explore the promising pedagogical potential of Chinese film to help students and teachers "tap into the fascinating world of multiculturalism and interdisciplinarity."

Areas of Future Research

This volume is not meant to be comprehensive or prescriptive in terms of what should be taught. Rather, the volume aims to reflect on common challenges when teaching cinema from the PRC and to introduce specific examples, approaches, and strategies that may be applied broadly across a range of disciplines and course content. This volume pays particular attention to the use of film in diverse classroom settings beyond traditional film studies courses, and we recognize that there are important areas that are not adequately covered in the volume. To supplement the themes discussed in the volume, this section shares some of the editors' experiences teaching additional areas that we believe should receive pedagogical research in the future.

Given the possible pitfalls when using film as a pedagogical tool in the classroom, it is more crucial than ever for instructors to cultivate critical visual literacy, a vital concern shared by many essays in this volume. How instructors address this concern at the beginning of students' visual journeys into Chinese film, however, remains a challenging issue when many of them have little knowledge of the Chinese people and their life on-screen. In Introduction to Chinese Cinema, a course for first-year college students, Hongmei Yu selects films that are representative of new Chinese cinema to help students better understand China's history, culture, politics, and aesthetic conventions over the past century. Yu usually starts with *Shadow Magic* (西洋镜) and pairs it with a reading, "*Shadow Magic* and the Early History of Film Exhibition in China," by Xuelei Huang and Zhiwei Xiao. While *Shadow Magic* tells a story of how motion pictures were introduced into China by dramatizing the competition between this Western technological medium and Peking Opera, students can get a more comprehensive sense of early film exhibition in China from the reading, especially Chinese audiences' overall enthusiastic reception of this new entertainment. The discrepancy in the story told in the film and the reading thus sheds light on the issue of representation: Why does the film feature a broke English businessman, Raymond Wallace, despite the fact that Benjamin Brodsky, whom the character was based on, actually made a fortune in China? What's more, how should viewers interpret the gender discourse when the male protagonist Liu pursues a new career and Lord Tan's daughter simultaneously? And what roles do film audiences with different cultural backgrounds play in the circuit of representation and reception?

When discussing national cinema, instructors cannot ignore Hollywood's global influence and the local response. Despite the ideological confrontation between Chinese and Hollywood films, comparative studies of those films could be another effective way to illuminate how cinema works in general, but it is an area not adequately covered in this volume except for Casaregola's insightful comparison between *The Red Detachment of Women* and *Flower Drum Song*. In recent years Yu has also taught the Chinese blockbuster *Wolf Warrior 2* (战狼 2), which serves as a great example of Hollywood visual and narrative style with a Chinese twist. While students can still be drawn to the fast-paced action sequences, the spectacular explosions, and the magnificent (but unidentified) African landscape in the film's long shots, they are quick to identify the overwhelming Chinese nationalist and masculine messages in the film and the negatively stereotypical African characters, in particular the boy whose mouth is always stuffed with food. Gender discussions are often quite productive in helping students read the Chinese American doctor Rachel and the African girl Pasha, who has developed immunity to a deadly endemic disease. However, more could be achieved when the instructor provides some comparative references, such as the Chinese national flag in *Wolf Warrior 2* versus the shield in *Captain America: The First Avenger* that recalls the design of the United States flag, or the plot and setting of *Wolf Warrior 2* versus those of the 2003 Hollywood film *Tears of the Sun*, in which Bruce Willis plays a special operations commander on a mission to rescue an American doctor from the Nigerian jungle. In this sense, *Wolf Warrior 2* works not only as a filmic text for students to examine China's rising nationalist sentiment but also as a mirror for them to reexamine their experience of Hollywood films and the politics of representation in general.

While this volume contains some brief comparisons between films and their literary sources, none of its essays place a pedagogical focus on cinematic adaptations of literary works. But in their own teaching experiences, this volume's editors find that closely examining cinematic adaptation strategies can be effective in helping students understand some key issues in cultural, historical, and political representation. Take, as an example, the widely taught film *To Live* (活着), which depicts a decades-long struggle for the survival of its protagonist Fugui's family from the 1940s to the 1970s. As Chenshu Zhou mentions in the first essay in the volume, *To Live* can be compared with other films to "open up discussions about changing representations of modern Chinese history," making the important point that "China can only be understood by grappling with competing discourses." The fluidity, diversity, relativity, and contradictoriness of the film's representations can also be taught through a comparison between the film and its literary source, Yu Hua's 1992 novel *To Live*, translated into English in 2003.

In his course Remembering Chinese Revolution through Film, Zhuoyi Wang leads students to compare selected parts of the novel *To Live* and the film adaptation to highlight some key changes in the adaptation, including those of temporal framework, point of view, and narrative direction. The novel presents two layers of personal memory, first the narrator's memory of an encounter with Fugui and then Fugui's memory of the painful history of his family. In this backward-looking temporal framework, Fugui vividly recalls the agonies, losses, and deaths that his family suffered, often because of their powerlessness in the social hierarchy of the PRC. Readers are placed in Fugui's helpless position, as the novel is written from the first-person point of view. The traumatic narrative ends in a symbolic, ominous nightfall, which buries Fugui (the lone survivor of his family), the narrator (the lone listener of the story), all the suffering, and the distant memories of it. By contrast, the film discards the two layers of memory, presents the story through a third-person point of view, and often uses long to extremely long shots to give viewers a distant perspective. It structures the story in an onward-looking and two-part temporal framework. The film's first three chapters, titled "The 1940s," "The 1950s," and "The 1960s," depict Fugui and his family's losses but, by changing or omitting incidents in the novel, present those losses as the result of errors rather than of any continuous structural injustice. The film contains no flashback shots, repeats the message in dialogue that the past is not worth mentioning, and keeps its characters hopeful for the future despite all adversities. As the story progresses to "Later . . . ," the fourth and final chapter, the hopefulness reaches a climax. Unlike in the novel, in the film Fugui lives happily with his family and imagines a better future for his grandson. The hopeful future in Fugui's imagination includes the present time of the viewers. All his losses seem to belong to a past that is unfortunate yet forever gone, traumatic yet already corrected and redeemed, and dark yet safely separated from the viewers' world.

This twice-told family story constructs two competing representations of the PRC's history for students to discuss. Compared to the novel, the film much more closely follows the PRC's post-Mao official position. The official discourse declares some chapters of the PRC's history, such as the Great Leap Forward and the Cultural Revolution, as mistakes. However, in the name of *xiangqian kan* (向前看; "looking to the future"; a government slogan), the PRC forbids further public discussions of these periods, especially those that involve accounting of responsibility and the structural injustices shared by the past and the present.[5] Ironically, the film *To Live* was banned from theatrical release in the PRC, while the novel was not censored from publication. Hence, this example can also be used for students to learn and discuss the complexities, contingencies, and contradictions in the censorship system, which may treat different works, authors, and art forms differently for inconsistent and possibly random reasons.

Queer cinema is another area that has significant potential as a means for teaching film from the PRC in a variety of contexts. There is a growing body of scholarly literature on queer Chinese cinema that can serve as a point of reference for instructors seeking to include this theme in their courses (see Lim; Shi; Pecic; Chao). As this scholarship notes, analysis of queer cinema draws our attention to questions of desire, gender, relationships, social norms, and structures of inequality and marginalization, among other subjects. Teaching queer cinema from the PRC also provides an opportunity for instructors and students to engage in critical discussions on heteronormativity as a transnational and cross-cultural phenomenon. In the experience of the volume's editors, LGBTQ issues are often of great interest for students today, and queer cinema allows students to connect experiences of queer people in China as depicted on-screen with concerns they experience in their own lives. For this reason, queer cinema from the PRC can be a useful addition to courses on gender and sexuality in global contexts, as well as courses specifically about China and Chinese cinema.

In her course Introduction to Chinese Cinema, Emily Wilcox starts with a unit on family, gender, and romance, in which she teaches queer films alongside films about heterosexual romance and changing gender roles and family dynamics in Chinese societies. The unit begins with the two films *Eat Drink Man Woman* (饮食男女) and *New Women* (新女性), which each require students to situate discussions of gender and family within a specific historical and social context: globalizing 1990s Taiwan in the former film, and 1920s–30s modernizing Shanghai in the latter. Both films offer examples of Chinese women and men facing difficult social pressures while pursuing their personal and family desires in distinct ways, thereby complicating the idea of a single so-called correct model of gender and family in Chinese contexts. Through discussions of these two films and related readings, Wilcox teaches students to see gender and family in Chinese and sinophone societies as changing and contested, rather than as fixed and monolithic. Students are then introduced to two films that explore heterosexual romance in yet other sociohistorical contexts—*In the Mood for Love* (花样年华), set in 1960s Hong Kong, and *Zhou Yu's Train* (周渔的火车), set in mainland China in the 1990s. Both films employ experimental narrative approaches to the representation of desire and romance, challenging students to move beyond sociological and historical explanations to questions of cinematic expression, sensory experience, storytelling devices, and individual subjectivity.

Building on this foundation, Wilcox then introduces two examples of queer PRC cinema that deal with related themes: *Fish and Elephant* (今年夏天), "the first lesbian film produced in mainland China" (Shi 107), and *Queer China, Comrade China* (志同志), a documentary detailing the history of China's LGBTQ rights movement. To contextualize *Fish and Elephant*, Wilcox assigns Liang Shi's essay "Discovering and Normalizing Lesbians: *Fish and Elephant*," from her book *Chinese Lesbian Cinema: Mirror Rubbing, Lala, and Les* (108–23). The essay offers useful information about the film's production and themes, while also providing detailed scene-by-scene analysis that assists students in interpreting the formal aspects of the film, such as the use of camera angles and framing to convey meaning. As a work of independent cinema, *Fish and Elephant* does not have the high production values of a commercial film, and students are challenged to appreciate its slower pacing and experimental methods, including the use of amateur actors and a scene that captures the lead actress's actual coming out moment with her mother, who plays her character's mother in the film. In addition to centering lesbian romance, *Fish and Elephant* also addresses a variety of family dynamics, from parental pressure to marry and have children, to late-life romance (in the case of the mother), bisexuality, infidelity, parental and sexual abuse, and patricide.

As a documentary, *Queer China, Comrade China* takes a different approach to exploring LGBTQ issues in China but is equally engaging to students. One of the film's strengths is its use of first-person interviews with a wide-ranging group of LGBTQ activists. These individuals have all played central roles in the movement and represent a broad spectrum of ages, genders, sexual identities, professional backgrounds, and viewpoints. In this way, the film provides students with a historical education about LGBTQ activism in China that is precise and vivid while also being multivocal. To deepen students' thinking about the legal issues surrounding LGBTQ rights addressed in the documentary, Wilcox teaches this film together with Tingting Liu and Jingshu Zhu's article "Legislating and Litigating Same Sex Marriage in China," which analyzes two high-profile legal cases for same-sex marriage in China between 2014 and 2016. By reading about the actual legal arguments that have been used to assert claims for marriage equality within China's political and legal context, students not only update their knowledge about how LGBTQ rights have developed in China since the documentary was released in 2008 but also deepen their ability to think comparatively about queer issues in different national contexts. This helps students to gain a critical awareness about the potential problems of universalizing human rights discourse developed in the United States and other Western contexts when addressing LGBTQ activism and other social issues internationally.

Introducing students to a wide variety of filmic genres is also important when teaching film from the PRC. In this volume, such genre variety is explored through Stenberg's essay on *xiqu* film and Lua's essay on *wuxia* film, both of which demonstrate the value of moving beyond realist and documentary styles to engage students. In their own teaching experiences, the editors of this volume find that introducing students to diverse film modalities is not only highly enjoyable but also productive in challenging students' preconceptions about Chinese film culture while further stimulating their interest in allied cultural and artistic practices such as visual art, fashion, music, theater, and dance.

In her course Introduction to Chinese Cinema, Wilcox includes an entire unit dedicated to such genre diversity, which is titled Animation, Musicals, and Martial Arts. The unit begins with the animated film *Princess Iron Fan* (铁扇公主), which productively doubles as an introduction to the history of Chinese animation (including its connections to Chinese ink painting and other visual art traditions as well as animation film history during the Second Sino-Japanese War) and to the classic Chinese novel *Journey to the West*. Students then encounter the Shanghai Yue opera film *Liang Shanbo and Zhu Yingtai* (梁山伯与祝英台), through which they learn about traditional Chinese theater and the use of opera films in Cold War PRC cultural diplomacy. Wilcox also teaches two film musicals set in ethnic minority communities: *Third Sister Liu* (刘三姐), set in Guangxi, and *You Beautify My Life* (你美丽了我的人生), set in Xinjiang. Both films introduce students to local forms of music and dance culture and teach them about China's ethnic and regional diversity. Because the films are made in two very different historical and regional contexts and present different narratives, themes, political messages, and aesthetic styles, teaching the two films side-by-side also challenges students to recognize the range of approaches to representations of ethnic minorities in Chinese film, as well as to think through how these representations intersect with portrayals of class, gender, religion, and place over time. Wilcox has found that students respond particularly well to *Third Sister Liu*, especially to the clever verbal sparring by the Zhuang protagonist sprinkled throughout the film, which one student compared to "rap battles." The expert performances by the renowned Uyghur dancers Yumiti and Gulmira in *You Beautify My Life* also provide opportunities for Wilcox to introduce perspectives from her research on Chinese dance studies and for students with knowledge of contemporary Chinese dance or Turkic, Muslim, or Middle Eastern music and dance cultures to bring this knowledge into class discussion. Students also find it useful to reflect on the culture of music and dance films in other parts of the world (such as India) and to compare representations of minoritized communities through performing arts in different national contexts.

In the context of teaching cinema from the PRC, the essays collected here offer in-depth analyses on a variety of topics: the layers of mediation underlying film production and reception; the historical consciousness that generates and is generated by filmic allegories; the intertwined linguistic, literary, and cultural semiotic systems at work on-screen; the ideological complexity of film that challenges preconceptions about Chinese film prevalent in the United States; the discursive construction of a cultural tradition through modern filming techniques; the multifaceted modernity and modernization process captured and framed by cameras of different perspectives; and how films epitomize intercultural barriers, tensions, connections, influences, and parallels. Drawing on classroom experiences, student assignments, and conversations with students, the contributors to this volume reflect on the epistemological as well as the ethical issues of teaching Chinese film, evaluate films' pedagogical value and risks, consider how to overcome the pedagogical difficulties associated with the otherness of China in classrooms in the United States, and formulate teaching strategies and activities and examine their effects. Together, these essays build "a necessary interconnection between research and teaching" (Polan 20), turning the classroom into a crucial site for knowledge transmission as well as production.

Notes

1. In 2010 the MLA published another book relevant to film pedagogy, *Teaching Italian American Literature, Film, and Popular Culture*, but only five of its thirty-two essays are on film studies (Giunta and McCormick).

2. Collections that trace this history include Berry; Browne et al.; Kuoshu; Kong and Lent; Zhu and Rosen; Khoo and Metzger; Lim and Ward; Zhang; Rojas and Chow; and Peng and Raidel.

3. Collections that explore narrower topics include Fu and Desser; Wang and Barlow; Lu; Lu and Mi; Wang; Rawnsley and Rawnsley; Khoo and Yue; Funnell and Yip; Chan and Willis; Chiu et al.; Yeh; Voci and Hui; and Berry et al.

4. In the PRC, the copyright term of a cinematic work is often fifty years after its first release. Many older films from the PRC have therefore already entered the public domain.

5. The phrase "looking to the future" was used as part of the title of a 1978 talk by Deng Xiaoping that initiated the post-Mao reform era.

Works Cited

Benyahia, Sarah Casey. *Teaching Film and TV Documentary*. British Film Institute, 2008.

Berry, Chris, editor. *Perspectives on Chinese Cinema*. British Film Institute, 1991.

Berry, Chris, et al., editors. *The New Chinese Documentary Film Movement: For the Public Record*. Hong Kong UP, 2010.

Billsberry, Jon, et al. *Moving Images: Effective Teaching with Film and Television in Management*. Information Age Publishing, 2012.

Brown, Kathleen L. *Teaching Literary Theory Using Film Adaptations*. McFarland, 2009.

Browne, Nick, et al., editors. *New Chinese Cinemas: Forms, Identities, Politics*. Cambridge UP, 1994.

Captain America: The First Avenger. Directed by Joe Johnston, Paramount Pictures, 2011.

Chan, Felicia, and Andrew Willis, editors. *Chinese Cinemas: International Perspectives*. Routledge, 2016.

Chao, Shi-Yan. *Queer Representations in Chinese-Language Film and the Cultural Landscape*. Amsterdam UP, 2020.

Chiu, Kuei-fen, et al., editors. *Taiwan Cinema: International Reception and Social Change*. Routledge, Taylor and Francis, 2017.

Deng Xiaoping. "Emancipate the Mind, Seek Truth from Facts, and Unite as One in Looking to the Future." *Marxists.org*, www.marxists.org/reference/archive/deng-xiaoping/1978/110.htm.

Eaglestone, Robert, and Barry Langford. *Teaching Holocaust Literature and Film*. Palgrave Macmillan, 2008.

Eat Drink Man Woman. Directed by Ang Lee, Ang Lee Pictures, 1994.

Fischer, Lucy, and Patrice Petro. "Memories of Underdevelopment." Introduction. Fischer and Petro, pp. 1–12.

———, editors. *Teaching Film*. Modern Language Association of America, 2012.

Fish and Elephant. Directed by Li Yu, Cheng Yong Productions, 2001.

Fu, Poshek, and David Desser. *The Cinema of Hong Kong: History, Arts, Identity*. Cambridge UP, 2000.

Funnell, Lisa, and Man-Fung Yip, editors. *American and Chinese-Language Cinemas: Examining Cultural Flows*. Routledge, 2015.

Gerster, Carole, and Laura W. Zlogar, editors. *Teaching Ethnic Diversity with Film: Essays and Resources for Educators in History, Social Studies, Literature and Film Studies*. McFarland, 2006.

Giunta, Edvige, and Kathleen Zamboni McCormick, editors. *Teaching Italian American Literature, Film, and Popular Culture*. Modern Language Association of America, 2010.

Grant, Barry Keith, editor. *Film Study in the Undergraduate Curriculum.* Modern Language Association of America, 1983.

Huang, Xuelei, and Zhiwei Xiao. "Shadow Magic and the Early History of Film Exhibition in China." Lim and Ward, pp. 47–55.

In the Mood for Love. Directed by Wong Kar-wai, Jet Tone Production, 2000.

Jones, Peter. *Teaching Black Cinema.* British Film Institute, 2008.

Khoo, Olivia, and Sean Metzger, editors. *Futures of Chinese Cinema: Technologies and Temporalities in Chinese Screen Cultures.* Intellect, 2009.

Khoo, Olivia, and Audrey Yue, editors. *Sinophone Cinemas.* Palgrave Macmillan, 2014.

Kong, Haili, and John A. Lent, editors. *One Hundred Years of Chinese Cinema: A Generational Dialogue.* EastBridge, 2005.

Kuoshu, Harry, editor. *Celluloid China: Cinematic Encounters with Culture and Society.* Southern Illinois UP, 2002.

Lagny, Michèle. "Film History; or, History Expropriated." *Film History,* vol. 6, no. 1, 1994, pp. 26–44.

Liang Shanbo and Zhu Yingtai. Directed by Sang Hu and Huang Sha, Shanghai Film Studio, 1954.

Lim, Song Hwee. *Celluloid Comrades: Representations of Male Homosexuality in Contemporary Chinese Cinemas.* U of Hawai'i P, 2006.

Lim, Song Hwee, and Julian Ward, editors. *The Chinese Cinema Book.* Palgrave Macmillan / British Film Institute, 2011.

Liston, Daniel Patrick, and Ian Parker Renga. *Teaching, Learning, and Schooling in Film: Reel Education.* Routledge, 2015.

Liu, Tingting, and Jingshu Zhu. "Legislating and Litigating Same Sex Marriage in China." *Research Handbook on Gender, Sexuality and the Law,* edited by Chris Ashford and Alexander Maine, Edward Elgar Publishing, 2020, pp. 45–59.

Lu, Sheldon H., editor. *Transnational Chinese Cinemas: Identity, Nationhood, Gender.* U of Hawai'i P, 1997.

Lu, Sheldon H., and Jiayan Mi, editors. *Chinese Ecocinema: In the Age of Environmental Challenge.* Hong Kong UP, 2009.

Marcus, Alan S. *Celluloid Blackboard: Teaching History with Film.* Information Age Publishing, 2007.

New Women. Directed by Cai Chusheng, United Photoplay Service, 1935.

Pecic, Zoran Lee. *New Queer Sinophone Cinema: Local Histories, Transnational Connections.* Palgrave Macmillan, 2016.

Peng, Xiaoyan, and Ella Raidel, editors. *The Politics of Memory in Sinophone Cinemas and Image Culture: Altering Archives.* Routledge, 2018.

Polan, Dana. *Scenes of Instruction: The Beginnings of the U.S. Study of Film.* U of California P, 2007.

Princess Iron Fan. Directed by Wan Guchan and Wan Laiming, Cinema Epoch, 1941.

Queer China, Comrade China. Directed by Cui Zien, dGenerate Films, 2008.

Quy, Simon. *Teaching Short Films.* British Film Institute, 2008.

Rawnsley, Gary D., and Ming-Yeh T. Rawnsley, editors. *Global Chinese Cinema: The Culture and Politics of* Hero. Routledge, 2010.

Ritterbusch, Rachel S. *Practical Approaches to Teaching Film.* Cambridge Scholars Publishing, 2009.

Rojas, Carlos, and Eileen Cheng-yin Chow, editors. *The Oxford Handbook of Chinese Cinemas.* Oxford UP, 2013.

Shadow Magic. Directed by Ann Hu, Sony Pictures Classics, 2000.

Shi, Liang. *Chinese Lesbian Cinema: Mirror Rubbing, Lala, and Les.* Lexington Books, 2014.

Stoddard, Jeremy D., and David Hicks. *Teaching Difficult History through Film.* Routledge, 2017.

Tears of the Sun. Directed by Antoine Fuqua, Columbia Pictures, 2003.

Third Sister Liu. Directed by Su Li, Changchun Film Studio, 1960.

To Live. Directed by Zhang Yimou, Samuel Goldwyn, 1994.

Voci, Paola, and Luo Hui, editors. *Screening China's Soft Power.* Routledge, 2018.

Wang, Jing, and Tani E. Barlow, editors. *Cinema and Desire: Feminist Marxism and Cultural Politics in the Work of Dai Jinhua.* Verso, 2002.

Wang, Lingzhen, editor. *Chinese Women's Cinema: Transnational Contexts.* Columbia UP, 2011.

Watkins, Gregory J. *Teaching Religion and Film.* Oxford UP, 2008.

Wolf Warrior 2. Directed by Wu Jing, China Film Group / Bona Films, 2017.

Yeh, Emilie Yueh-yu, editor. *Early Film Culture in Hong Kong, Taiwan, and Republican China: Kaleidoscopic Histories.* U of Michigan P, 2018.

You Beautify My Life. Directed by Yan Qingxiu and Yu De'an, Xinjiang Dasen Culture and Media / Ningbo Film and TV Art, 2018.

Yu Hua. *To Live.* Translated by Michael Berry, Anchor Books, 2003.

Zhang, Yingjin, editor. *A Companion to Chinese Cinema.* Wiley-Blackwell, 2012.

Zhou Yu's Train. Directed by Sun Zhou, Sony Pictures Classics, 2002.

Zhu, Ying, and Stanley Rosen, editors. *Art, Politics, and Commerce in Chinese Cinema.* Hong Kong UP, 2010.

Part I

Pedagogical Methods

Chenshu Zhou

A Rhizomatic Approach to Teaching China through Film

One popular way cinema is brought into the undergraduate curriculum on Chinese culture and society in North American universities is through courses such as China through the Lens, China on Screen, and Modern China through Film and Fiction. As a postdoctoral teaching fellow at Stanford University, I served as a recitation instructor for Understanding China through Film—a course designed and led by Ban Wang for Stanford's first-year liberal education program Thinking Matters. At the time, first-year Stanford students were required to take one course from the Thinking Matters offerings. Being the only course on film and the only one devoted to China, Understanding China through Film, not surprisingly, attracted students interested in both subjects. What I did not expect was how students expressed confusion about the goal of the course. I was asked many times whether this course was supposed to be about China, film, or Chinese films. As we sometimes spent time learning about modern Chinese history and sometimes discussed film aesthetics, some students had a hard time seeing how these different components cohered. Rather, they felt that their attention was being split in different directions. I remember speaking, at the beginning of a quarter, with one student who indicated that he was interested in China but did not particularly care about cinema. He dropped the course the next week.

The problems I observed in Understanding China through Film suggest a need to further reflect on the promises of a popular pedagogical model, which I refer to here as the China-through-film model. This model may be operational not just in courses explicitly claiming to use films to understand China but also in film studies courses, which I now teach at the University of Pennsylvania. In East Asian Cinema, a large lecture course I taught in 2021, many students indicated that their reason for taking the course was to learn about East Asian cultures. Whether or not an instructor intends for them to do so, students look to films to learn about cultures and histories beyond the cinematic world. Despite the impulse to use film in this way, however, questions remain: What about the filmic medium allows it to function as a method for learning about China? How does film compare to other ways of studying China? What version of China is knowable in this manner? What might be the unique contributions of the China-through-film model? To answer these questions, this essay conceptualizes a China-through-film course as a rhizome. Originally a botanical term describing underground stems that can grow horizontally with multiple shoots going out in different directions, *rhizome* has become an influential theoretical concept since the publication of the French philosophers Gilles Deleuze and Félix Guattari's book *A Thousand Plateaus: Capitalism and Schizophrenia*. Borrowing from Deleuze and Guattari, I argue that one unique contribution of the China-through-film model lies in its ability to open up learning spaces that privilege multiplicity and connection. It eschews grand narratives of China and engages students in environments of active learning that simulate real-life encounters with historical or cultural others—individuals from contexts with which students are not personally familiar. In the following sections, I first discuss how a rhizomatic understanding can bring the China-through-film model out of an impasse between competing discourses in the fields of area studies and film studies, allowing for a reimagination of the model's potential. I then describe what a rhizomatic course looks like and make several pedagogical recommendations based on this new conceptualization.

The Window and the Frame

Looking back, I recognize that my students' confusion about the goals of Understanding China through Film mirrored my own unease with the premise of the course and was likely exacerbated by my teaching strategies. The issue can be explained through the metaphor of a window. In the course syllabus, Wang writes: "We will treat films as a window on the ongoing narrative of a people making history and responding to changing circumstances of revolution, reform, political movements, and modernization." I admit that I had conflicted feelings about the word "window" when I first saw it on the syllabus. Would treating films as representations of reality mislead students or discourage them from being critical? Would they forget that film is an art form that can construct different visions of China? I immediately felt the need to strengthen a formal approach to teaching the filmic texts. The antidote to naive readings, I thought, was attention to the medium, a shift of focus from what one can perceive through the window to the window itself, the frame. Treating films as windows into Chinese culture and history and examining the films themselves are not necessarily contradictory activities, but they compete for class time.

I have since realized how this tension between the focus on the window and on the frame is rooted in much broader academic structures. Situated at the intersection of area studies and film studies, the China-through-film model forces instructors to negotiate with the differing priorities and ongoing debates of these adjacent fields. This model is, first and foremost, an offshoot of area studies, which was a product of World War II and the Cold War, initially driven by the American government's need to gather information on so-called enemy states. In this context, the study of literature from foreign areas, and later the study of other forms of representation, was predetermined to treat cultural texts as windows, that is, instruments for knowing the other. And it was the nation-state that served as the basic unit for knowledge production. Research on Chinese cinema became an addendum to studies of modern Chinese literature within the area studies field on China. In contrast to sinology's traditional focus on ancient texts, the study of modern literature was legitimized and marketed through its affinity with modern Chinese reality. The literary historian C. T. Hsia has lamented how, when China has become a subject of intense study, the social scientists of Chinese history and culture have "failed to make use of the literary record" (xiv). The social scientist Ezra Vogel expresses a similar view in his foreword to Donald Gibbs and Yun-Chen Li's *Bibliography of Studies and Translations of Modern Chinese Literature*, stating that "as a vehicle for enhancing Western understanding of China, Chinese literature has a great but as yet almost unexploited potential." Both scholars presume the utility of literature as a historical record, urging other China scholars to take it seriously as such. The China-through-film course model emerged within this context in conjunction with the widespread belief that film is a fun subject that boosts course enrollments. In the China field, the tendency to tie cultural texts to the so-called Chinese reality has since been criticized by scholars like Rey Chow, who has shown how this tendency is upheld by the logics of "ethnic supplement" and "coerced mimeticism" ("On Chineseness" 3, 18) and by beliefs in the instrumentality of language and literature (*Age* 16–17). Yet the expectation that "films can help bring China to life in the classroom" continues to be widely held by students and the general public (Lee 49).

By contrast, under the influence of semiotics, poststructuralism, and psychoanalysis, film studies had for a long time privileged a strategy of foregrounding the frame, or constructedness, of film as an act of politicization against the dominant culture industry. In this discourse, conventional cinematic realism that encourages audience immersion is ideologically suspect. In striving to be windows, to encourage viewers to see through rather than notice traces of their construction, conventional films make ideological use of realism in the Althusserian sense of interpellating spectators into an imaginary relationship with reality. Meanwhile, there is also a so-called window tradition in film studies that can be traced back to theorists such as Siegfried Kracauer, Walter Benjamin, and André Bazin, who place emphasis on film's indexicality—its ability to mechanically reproduce reality without human intervention (Elsaesser and Hagener 13–34). The techniques that Bazin favored on the basis of film's realist ontology, including staging in depth, long shots, and long takes, have come to define the predominant aesthetics of contemporary global art cinema with no signs of abating.

Neither ideological critiques of film's reality effect nor the embracing of film's realism provides a solid ground for treating film as a methodology for learning about China. In the first case, the link between film (signifier) and the real (signified) is essentially severed. There is no looking through the window, because the window is an ideological construction and does not open onto a world out there. The realist tradition, on the other hand, privileges particular kinds of filmmaking. For Kacauer, the establishing of a self-coherent story in film would mean that the film is closed off from reality (Hansen 450). For Bazin, the realization of cinema's realist potential depends on techniques that allow reality to speak for itself (26). Following either theorist, most mainstream fictional films would not bring viewers closer to a reality beyond the film.

The only theoretical tradition in film studies that I have found to be conducive to the China-through-film model is cognitive film theory, which suggests that from the viewer's perspective the skills and procedures involved in the perception of a filmic reality are not that different from how we perceive the real world. According to Torben Grodal, whether a visual stimulation comes from a real-life source, a film, a dream, a memory, or the imagination, it activates the visual cortex and associated areas in the brain in a similar way (21–23). The viewer also brings to the film-viewing experience real-world schemas—"structured knowledge frameworks" that include beliefs, assumptions, and schemes for categorizing and making sense of the world (Rushton and Bettinson 161). From the perspective of cognitive film theory, therefore, it is not that film brings China to life in the classroom but that film transports students from the classroom into the real world and provides training through simulation.

While the tensions between the window and the frame will continue to haunt the China-through-film model, the treatment of film as a simulation and the possibility of focusing on viewers' experiences shift the question for instructors from one of referentiality to one about the internal organization of a course and its overall impact on students. Courses that use the China-through-film model are often organized around individual films and often assign one film per week, in a structure that may seem straightforward and uncreative. Yet by examining how films open up rhizomatic spaces, I show in the next section that the weekly film assignment can be truly innovative and dynamic. If the window-versus-frame debate situates the China-through-film model at an awkward intersection, a rhizomatic revamping of the model will reveal its unique contributions to higher education.

Mapping a Rhizomatic Course

While *rhizome* entered the theoretical vocabulary of humanities and social sciences through the work of Deleuze and Guattari, as a theoretical construct, a structural model, a way of thinking, and a visual metaphor, the rhizome has shown wide applications across academic fields. In education, the rhizome has been invoked to describe a new model of learning. An oft-cited description of rhizomatic learning comes from Dave Cormier:

> The rhizome is [the] stem of [a] plant, like hops, ginger or Japanese bamboo, that helps the plant spread and reproduce. It responds and grows according to its environment, not straight upwards like a tree,

> but in a haphazard networked fashion. As a story for learning, it is
> messy, unstable and uncertain. It is also, as anyone who has ever had
> one in the garden will tell you, extremely resilient. As with the rhizome
> the rhizomatic learning experience is multiple, has no set beginning
> or end,—"a rhizome creates through the act of experimentation."

Because learning is messy, uncertain, and experimental and involves multiple pathways, advocates of rhizomatic education like Cormier emphasize community input as a principle. Rather than having the instructor decide on the learning goals and the syllabus, rhizomatic education prioritizes contributions from members of a learning community and dynamic responses to changing conditions and needs (Sharples et al. 33).

The China-through-film course model does presuppose a learning objective (understanding China) and a method for achieving it (viewing films about China), so the model is not entirely open-ended. But by structuring the syllabus around films (and relevant secondary readings), a course based on this model is poised to spread in different directions, like a rhizome, despite its seemingly linear week-to-week flow. A good contrasting example to a rhizomatic course is Yingjin Zhang's book *Chinese National Cinema*, which typifies a model of knowledge production that fits Deleuze and Guattari's description of a tree in that it has a central through line and a fixed ordering of knowledge based on periodization (Deleuze and Guattari 12). For each period, Zhang attempts a comprehensive discussion of the film industry and of film policy, subject matter, aesthetics, and audiences. The reader is promised an overview of Chinese cinema, a top-down view of what have been predetermined to be major historical facts and issues. In contrast, by starting from individual films, the China-through-film model opens up very different possibilities. In the model, each film functions as a node or point of connection (a "plateau," to use Deleuze and Guattari's term). It is not subsumed under a preconceived argument but invites investigations from diverse angles and may lead the investigator toward different ideas (similar to how a rhizome shoots out in different directions).

Take *To Live* (活着) as an example. A popular film among students, *To Live* is a rich text that opens up multiple conversations and can serve as an entry point into the political history of modern China. The film follows Fugui and his family over a span of four decades, referencing several major political events such as the Chinese Civil War, the Great Leap Forward, and the Cultural Revolution. For students unfamiliar with this history, the film provokes interest in historical knowledge while also providing vivid illustrations that concretize historical narratives. As a representative work of the fifth generation of Chinese cinema, the film can open up discussions about changing representations of modern Chinese history. Instructors can contextualize the film, including its production and reception, in the postsocialist moment in order to highlight its frame, or constructedness, and to encourage students to think about how film techniques are mobilized to present a particular interpretation of history that emphasizes the intrusion of political movements on everyday life. The two readings that Wang selected for the film, one by Chow ("We") and another by Zhaohui Xiong, center on the question of political oppression and resistance, foregrounding a debate about the ethics of surviving at all costs. Other issues that emerged in class discussions included the discourses of communism, modernity, and progress, gendered differences in experiences of trauma, tropes of disability and muteness, and interior decor. One cannot exhaust the exploration of a film's myriad facets.

Moreover, a film is not an isolated event. According to Deleuze and Guattari, the first principle of a rhizome is connection: "any point of a rhizome can be connected to anything other, and must be" (7). The linear temporality of going from one film to the next should not obscure the fact that the films are interconnected. *To Live* can be connected with *Five Golden Flowers* (五朵金花), an earlier socialist film included in the course. Released in 1959, *Five Golden Flowers* offers an exuberant portrayal of the Great Leap Forward movement that contrasts sharply with *To Live*'s bleak emphasis on political coercion and human suffering. Students who took my course also related *To Live* to a later film, *A Touch of Sin* (天注定). In *To Live*, the protagonist, Fugui, remains hopeful for a brighter future even after suffering repeated traumas. *A Touch of Sin* exposes the lie of developmental discourse, showing how beneath the surface of modern prosperity in China there is still violence, ennui, and hopelessness. Connections between films are themselves multiplicities that open up space for further discussions. The comparison between *Five Golden Flowers* and *To Live*, for example, can bring into focus a more nuanced understanding of propaganda. Students may be tempted to assume that since *Five Golden Flowers* is a socialist propaganda film it is less truthful than *To Live*. Instructors should question such an assumption through formal analysis and further contextualization—for instance, by asking students the following questions: What were the goals of socialist cinema? Who were the audiences of *Five Golden Flowers*? What was the social atmosphere at the time of the film's release? Meanwhile, the comparison makes it clear that China can only be understood by grappling with competing discourses and that no film is an unproblematic window into historical truth. By creating a syllabus and developing lesson plans, the instructor necessarily delimits the boundaries of a course. Each film or reading creates a space around it, permitting some topics to be discussed while excluding others. But within these boundaries, a course can grow and expand in unexpected directions through the multiplication of connections.

Conceiving the China-through-film model as a rhizome has several distinct advantages. The first advantage is that it resists totalistic discourses about China. The imaginary coherence of the nation-state has been an object of demystification across humanities and social scientific fields as divisions and connections at both transnational and intranational levels receive more attention. Some students may already be sensitive to the construction of Chineseness; many may hold essentialist understandings of China and Chinese culture. In fact, older scholarship conducted under the national cinema framework, which dominated the study of non-Western cinemas from the 1960s to the early 2000s, often feeds into the tendency to explain diverse phenomena through fixed national traits and identities. Until recently, scholars have felt the need to highlight differences within nominally unified spaces, including China and Asia more broadly. Ani Maitra and Rey Chow, among others, propose a strategy of "disaggregating Asia" by reconceptualizing the local as the assembling of both human and nonhuman actors in uneven, fragmented networks of infrastructure, economic development, governmentality, and livelihood. A rhizomatic pedagogical approach echoes such theoretical interests in assemblage, heterogeneity, and becoming. It embraces the multiplicity inherent in films, which point to assemblages of local, national, transnational, and universal factors. Following this approach, the China-through-film model gains the added benefits of simulating real-life encounters with unfamiliar foreign subjects constituted by different cultures and identities. If my students were to visit China, they would constantly have to decide how to interpret and make intelligible social phenomena. This messy and uncertain process would have to be navigated not through a priori frameworks but through careful and empathic readings of clues. Students can practice such a mode of cross-cultural analysis by watching films precisely because films are complex, rhizomatic entities that simulate everyday situations. Rather than encouraging students to conclude at the end of the course that "China is X" or "China is Y," a rhizomatic approach asks students to grow comfortable with the unknowability of China, which cannot be reduced to facile, and often self-serving, generalizations.

Another advantage of a rhizomatic approach is that it is consistent with the goal of active learning. If a course is an ever-evolving rhizome, then coursework such as in-class discussions, weekly discussion questions, thesis-driven essays, and creative projects are not just a matter of students retaining knowledge or cultivating skills. Instead, students are involved in the active formation of the rhizome through coursework. They are not just travelers on paths predetermined by the instructor but are themselves path builders. In other words, a rhizomatic course has a built-in infrastructure for encouraging active inquiry and research. It validates diverse perspectives and enables students to think of themselves as knowledge producers rather than as mere recipients of knowledge. Moreover, as Internet users, students are already familiar with rhizomatic learning, even if they do not realize it. The Internet is effectively a rhizome. Hyperlinks enable the connection of any two websites, and information on sites like *Wikipedia* can be accessed in many different ways. As Deleuze and Guattari suggest, a "plateau" is "always in the middle, not at the beginning or the end" (21). Browsing on *Wikipedia*, one can move among entries with no prescribed path and with no end in sight. Students practice this mode of browsing and learning on a daily basis. By putting emphasis on multiplicity, connection, and open-endedness, a rhizomatic course thus encourages students to bring in skills of exploration that they have been cultivating outside the classroom and to further develop them.

Teaching a Rhizomatic Course

Based on my experience using this rhizomatic remapping of the China-through-film course model, I make the following pedagogical recommendations.

Explain the rhizomatic structure of the course to students and rethink the role of the instructor.

Students may be familiar with rhizomatic learning as an informal process, but many expect college courses to be different. Since a China-through-film course can attract students from diverse backgrounds, the instructor should be prepared for varying student expectations about learning that they have developed in other disciplinary contexts. It is important, then, that students be informed at the beginning of the course about the kind of work expected of them. Among other things, it is helpful for students to know why the instructor chooses to focus on certain films and themes in the course. On this point, instructors should keep in mind that syllabus design is both political and personal. It is political because a syllabus delimits what can be seen and discussed and because instructors exercise their ultimate agency in a course by deciding what kinds of questions to make time and space for. A syllabus is personal because instructors make individualized choices about what to include and what to leave out. By offering students a rationale for their choices, instructors acknowledge that the syllabus is only one possible path through the material and that it by no means exhausts possible perspectives.

Although students will likely treat the professor as an authority figure who will guide their learning, a rhizomatic approach challenges centralized authority and requires students to take on a more active role in exploring the rhizome. One particularly effective, low-stakes assignment that can help students adopt this role is to have them submit discussion questions before class. A sample prompt for discussion questions I recently used is as follows:

> Compose a paragraph of 150 words or more that includes a discussion question that touches on the film and at least one of the readings assigned for the week. The paragraph should explain the reason you are posing the question, give background information, and identify the issues you would like your classmates to discuss. Whenever possible, you should cite passages in the readings to contextualize your question.[1]

Specified this way, the prompt compels students to engage with textual details and make connections between primary and secondary sources rather than formulate generic questions. After receiving students' questions, I looked over them before class and tried to incorporate as many questions as I could into my lesson plan. When I taught *To Live*, it was from the questions I collected that I realized that many students were interested in issues of gender and in Fugui's wife, Jiazhen. I thereby adjusted my lesson plan to give more class time to discussing Jiazhen and how she relates to political history as a woman. Such an interactive mode of teaching not only boosts student engagement on a day-to-day level, encouraging students to stay invested throughout the course; it is also a great way to bring together various components of the course and make assignments meaningful. My students have mentioned that writing discussion questions helped them brainstorm ideas for their final papers, which became natural offshoots of their earlier work.

Model skills and help students build their skill sets.

If students are to do their own explorations in a rhizomatic course, they need to know how to do it. It is therefore important that the course move beyond merely presenting content and help students develop skills and conceptual frameworks that can enable them to engage with materials on their own. Formal analysis is important for this purpose. It may be tempting for instructors to think that since the focus of the China-through-film model is on China they do not need to pay attention to film form. Yet filmmakers can only express their visions through form, which allows them to construct the particular assemblages of China we see in films. Students need to learn how to analyze a film and parse out its formal elements (editing, mise-en-scène, etc.) to critically reflect on what a film tries to say. One way the instructor can stress the importance of this skill, model it, and have students practice it is to select specific scenes for close analysis in class. A scene analysis exercise can begin with the basic elements ("What do you see or hear in this scene, and what do you feel when watching it?") and then move on to linking formal features with larger themes and questions (e.g., "What is the film suggesting by leaving part of a portrait of Mao outside the film's frame?"). Other useful tools include critical vocabulary used in secondary readings. To undergraduate students, many terms that scholars take for granted, such as *subjectivity, discourse, alienation,* and *realism,* can be alienating. To show how such jargon can empower students to speak their minds, I have found it helpful to demonstrate how a concept can be taken from the original reading and applied to new situations, either by relating it to realities familiar to students or by relating it to a different film. The more skills and concepts students can put in their tool kits, the more likely they will become independent thinkers and investigators.

Create coursework that invites students to expand the syllabus in a dynamic way.

A rhizome can never be complete because it is always growing and expanding. Similarly, a rhizomatic approach to a course on China through film takes the syllabus and the instructor's teaching as an initial framework or an open invitation. The course does not achieve its learning goals unless the students participate in its making. In this context, coursework, including both informal and formal assignments, becomes an extension and diversification of the syllabus, an opportunity for both instructors and learners to adapt to the learning community. For example, in my East Asian Cinema course I recently assigned something I call a rabbit-hole presentation, in which students created a three-minute video presentation that delved into any topic that they could somehow relate to the content of the course. The topic did not need to be significant but did have to genuinely interest the students making the video. The result was a collection of highly original, unexpected, and informative videos, which I then made available for everyone in the class to watch. The students' videos probed into many different topics that were merely touched on in class, showing how films are heterogenous spaces that bring together art, history, social formations, and sometimes natural sciences. Students thus engaged in a kind of collective knowledge production without a center. The knowledge produced was necessarily rhizomatic. Moreover, it was important that students made the videos with the expectation that their classmates would watch them. By having students target classmates, rather than the instructor, as the intended audience, this assignment cultivated horizontal relationships and encouraged peer learning. As part of this shift, I did not grade the videos but asked students to vote for their favorite in several award categories that recognized different kinds of achievements.

From concepts of the window and the frame to the metaphor of the rhizome, my approach to the China-through-film course model shifts the focus from individual films to the overall structure of the course. A rhizomatic approach does not eliminate the tension between viewing a film as a window into Chinese culture and history and viewing it as a frame, or construct, but opens up the film as a unique learning space inviting heterogenous engagements. This opening up may be worrisome for both professors and students because multiplicity may be mistaken for a lack of cohesion. A rhizome, at first glance, is messy. But it is the emphasis on mapping multiplicities within a film and tracing connections across multiple films that will hold the course together. As a result, the subject of the course, China, and the medium of study, film, will cease to pull students in different directions and will instead constitute the broad fields in which connections can be made and questions asked.

A rhizomatic approach to teaching encourages heterogeneous understandings of complex realities and active learning nourished by informal learning strategies that are commonly used in the digital age. As an everyday practice, this approach may not be anything new. But by formalizing it as a conscious pedagogical choice in relation to the rhizomatic potential of film, I hope that the China-through-film course model, reconceptualized as a rhizome, can go beyond being enrollment bait and become a truly innovative model for engaging with the complex assemblage of realities known as China.

Note

1. I thank Hongwei Thorn Chen for generously sharing the original template on which this prompt is based.

Works Cited

Bazin, André. *What Is Cinema?* Vol. 2, U of California P, 2004.

Chow, Rey. *The Age of World Target: Self-Referentiality in War, Theory, and Comparative Work.* Duke UP, 2006.

———. "On Chineseness as a Theoretical Problem." *Boundary 2*, vol. 25, no. 3, 1998, pp. 1–24.

———. "We Endure, Therefore We Are: Survival, Governance, and Zhang Yimou's *To Live.*" *Ethics after Idealism: Theory-Culture-Ethnicity-Reading.* Indiana UP, 1998.

Cormier, Dave. "Trying to Write Rhizomatic Learning in Three Hundred Words." *Dave's Educational Blog*, 13 Dec. 2012, davecormier.com/edblog/2012/12/13/trying-to-write-rhizomatic-learning-in-300-words/.

Deleuze, Gilles, and Félix Guattari. *A Thousand Plateaus: Capitalism and Schizophrenia.* Translated by Brian Massumi, U of Minnesota P, 1987.

Elsaesser, Thomas, and Malte Hagener. *Film Theory: An Introduction through the Senses.* Routledge, 2010.

Five Golden Flowers. Directed by Wang Jiayi, Changchun Film Group, 1959.

Gibbs, Donald A., and Yun-Chen Li. *A Bibliography of Studies and Translations of Modern Chinese Literature.* Harvard U, East Asia Research Center, 1975.

Grodal, Torben. *Moving Pictures: A New Theory of Film Genres, Feelings, and Cognition.* Oxford UP, 1997.

Hansen, Miriam. "'With Skin and Hair': Kracauer's Theory of Film, Marseille 1940." *Critical Inquiry*, vol. 19, no. 3, 1993, pp. 437–69.

Hsia, C. T. *A History of Modern Chinese Fiction.* 3rd ed., U of Indiana P, 1999.

Lee, Tanya. "Ten Top Films for Teaching about China Today." *Social Education*, vol. 74, no. 1, 2010, pp. 49–51.

Maitra, Ani, and Rey Chow. "What's 'In'? Disaggregating Asia through New Media Actants." *Routledge Handbook of New Media in Asia*, edited by Larrisa Hjorth and Olivia Khoo, Routledge, 2015, pp. 17–27.

Rushton, Richard, and Gary Bettinson. *What Is Film Theory?* McGraw-Hill Education, 2010.

Sharples, Mike, et al. *Innovating Pedagogy 2012: Open University Innovation Report 1.* Open University, 2012.

To Live. Directed by Zhang Yimou, ERA International / Shanghai Film Studios, 1994.

A Touch of Sin. Directed by Jia Zhangke, Xstream Pictures / Office Kitano / Shanghai Film Group Shanxi Film and Television Group, 2013.

Xiong, Zhaohui. "*To Live*: The Survival Philosophy of the Traumatized." *Trauma and Cinema: Cross-Cultural Explorations*, edited by E. Ann Kaplan and Ban Wang, Hong Kong UP, 2004.

Zhang, Yingjin. *Chinese National Cinema*. Routledge, 2004.

Angie Chau

Navigating Diverse Viewing Positions in the Film Classroom

Teaching my first undergraduate class at the University of California, San Diego, in the beginning of 2013, I chose what seemed like an exciting topic—controversy in Chinese literature, popular culture, and media—for the course, Readings in Contemporary Chinese Literature. After spending a few weeks on Zhang Yimou's early- to mid-1990s films (labeled "successful filmmaking" on the syllabus), we turned to fiction by the so-called beauty writers Wei Hui, Chun Sue, and Mian Mian, before finishing the term with the work of Guo Jingming, Han Han, and Ai Weiwei in a unit called Celebrity Culture, Blogs, and Political Activism. That spring, *Tiny Times 1.0* (小时代 1.0), the film based on Guo Jingming's eponymous novel, which was on our syllabus, was about to be released in theaters. In class, we watched the movie trailer in eager anticipation after discussing the plagiarism accusations swirling around Guo and Han. Looking back at the syllabus, two impressions strike me. First, it is hard to remember a time before *Tiny Times 1.0* entered mainstream Chinese pop culture consciousness. Second, I was very naive.

Among my numerous awkward teaching firsts, the most memorable occurred during one lecture, after I had spent nearly an hour presenting photographs and essay clips from Ai's blog, loudly proclaiming my enthusiasm and admiration for Ai's critical writing and conceptual art. I could not imagine how anyone could feel differently. But one student raised her hand and, completely outraged, voice breaking, expressed not only her disdain but visible anger at Ai's goal of, in her exact words, 唯恐天下不乱 ("trying to wreak havoc in the world"). Gently cocooned in my cozy world where Ai was an artistic hero, I was shocked by her outburst, and the phrase, which I had previously only encountered when I was scolded as a teenager by my mother, seemed incongruous with the context. At the time, I made a feeble attempt to defuse my student's emotionally charged claim but regrettably failed to recognize the pedagogical value of her valid perspective.

By the following year, when I taught the same class to a different group of students, nearly everyone had seen the first *Tiny Times* movie, and when I asked on the last day of the term which text on the syllabus seemed most realistic, some students vouched for *Tiny Times*, much to my amazement. Because of the course prerequisite of advanced Chinese-language reading skills and an increase in the number of international students on campus, my class in both years consisted of around ninety percent international students from mainland China and a handful of students from Hong Kong and the United States. I assumed (wrongly) that, as recent high school graduates, they would relate more to Han's *Triple Door* (三重门), a novel about the high school education system in China that had inspired a lively in-class debate about the benefits of Chinese- versus American-style education.

Imagine my confusion then, when I later taught *Tiny Times 1.0* in three different courses at Arizona State University—an introduction to Chinese culture, an advanced Chinese-language course, and a study abroad course in China for state scholarship students—and heard the recurring opinion voiced during discussions that *Tiny Times* didn't "look" like a "Chinese" movie. Could this departure from my earlier experience be attributed to the simple fact that the students enrolled in my Arizona State University classes were mostly white American anglophone students, or were there less obvious reasons behind this marked difference in how the same movie was understood?

This essay explores the wide range of student expectations in classes on modern Chinese culture in the university setting, given the noticeable shift in classroom demographics in the last decade, during which an increasing percentage of undergraduate students in Chinese content courses consist of international students from mainland China. Drawing from my experiences teaching Chinese film in public and private universities in the United States, Canada, and China, the essay is organized around three keywords most relevant to the divergence of student expectations: authenticity, censorship, and empathy. My discussion begins with the recognition that any attempt to speak of the diversity of students' viewing positions must challenge the assumption that international Chinese students constitute a homogeneous group. According to China's Ministry of Education, 662,100 students studied overseas in 2018, an increase of 53,700 students from 2017 ("More Chinese"). Although the global pandemic caused a significant drop in international exchange because of limited student mobility, China remained the top source of international students in the United States, and more than 317,000 enrolled in American institutions in the 2020–21 academic year (U.S. Mission China). Given that international students have a diversity of backgrounds and motivations for studying Chinese film, how can instructors best take advantage of the classroom demographics when teaching Chinese film? And what is at stake in the performance of this balancing act of reconciling student expectations with those of the instructor? This essay reveals how film as a medium asks instructors and students to continually adjust their assumptions about their own viewing positions in relation to screen narratives about China. The instructor's recognition of this delicate balancing act, by using film as a way to facilitate dialogue across different groups of students, can lead students to become more receptive and empathetic audiences.

Authenticity

When asked about their reasons for enrolling in Chinese literature and film classes, international students from China will often respond that they take these classes to see how non-Chinese students and instructors respond to and interpret Chinese texts outside of China and to better understand how Chinese culture is taught outside of China. Domestic students in North American classrooms, however, often say that they take these classes to learn about China or Chinese culture. What some of the international students may overlook is that they arrive in classrooms outside China with a set of preconceptions about Chinese film, as do domestic students without prior expertise about China, only the former preconceptions are framed under social pressures that designate Chinese students as cultural insiders. This divergence of student expectations reflects broader dynamics that shape how Chinese culture is viewed outside China, where Chinese film continues to be seen as the marginalized, invisible other in relation to the mainstream, dominant Western (Hollywood) film industry. The use of Chinese films as pedagogical tools highlights the persistent issue of cultural authenticity, as international and domestic students are confronted with images of and stories about China that may not fully conform with what they are familiar with or expected to encounter.

In the light of growing scrutiny over Hollywood's willingness to cater to Chinese censorship demands, Chris Berry's claim that "it is not so much China that makes movies, but movies that help to make China" (131) seems obvious, but Berry's discussion about national agency and collective subjectivity being performative warrants further reflection. In his discussion of the Taiwanese film *City of Sadness* (悲情城市), Berry concludes, "[I]f agency and consciousness are understood as performative, we need only to look to the various mobilizations of this ambiguous text by different audiences and critics to understand how each is a different and specific citation of both the text and, via the interpretations of it, the agency" (150). Along these lines, I would argue that every film or text is as "ambiguous" as *City of Sadness*—even if its subject matter is not as blatantly controversial as the 28 February massacre of Taiwanese people by Kuomintang troops in 1947. This ambiguity is especially important for instructors to consider given the differences in educational and cultural backgrounds of students racialized as Chinese by their institutions, a demographic that includes some Asian American students and students from mainland China, Taiwan, Hong Kong, and other locations. In the classroom setting, as participants who have lived experience in China, international students from China often feel compelled to evaluate the authenticity of a film, such as in the aforementioned debate in my classes over whether the *Tiny Times* series accurately reflects contemporary upper-class youth culture in Shanghai. The obsession with authenticity is directly related to issues of historical accuracy and censorship, especially when it comes to Chinese independent documentary films and contentious historical topics such as the Cultural Revolution and the June Fourth protests in 1989, which are discussed in the next section. To help students move beyond the issue of authenticity, instructors can gently but persistently ask an underlying question: How can literature and film depict history in artistic and creative ways that conventional historical scholarship cannot?

The sense of duty that Chinese students often express about determining a Chinese film's authenticity is tied to the need to publicly claim cultural expertise based on one's relation to China, a version of what Tani

Barlow has called "learning to 'become Chinese'" in reference to the 2006 MIT *Visualizing Cultures* website controversy that I discuss below (123). The concern with historical accuracy and verisimilitude also reveals assumptions about the viewer's cultural identity and relationship to China and the rest of the world. In the film classroom, the performative aspect of interpreting film can manifest for students as proving their Chineseness to fellow classmates and the course instructor, especially if the material on the syllabus does not represent a range of viewpoints and critical perspectives. Providing students with secondary sources written by scholars and critics from mainland China, and the Asian region at large, in addition to the more predictable voices from the sinophone diaspora and Western academia, enables students to situate themselves in more flexible ways to the critical scholarship they encounter.

For example, I frequently teach Lou Ye's film *Summer Palace* (颐和园), most recently in a film class called Screening the Nation. The movie, which follows a group of four young college friends in Beijing from the 1980s to the 2000s, includes graphic sexual content that can be disturbing for students, plus it tackles head-on the emotional trauma of the June Fourth protests, a nationwide series of demonstrations that was suppressed by the Chinese government and that remains a politically sensitive historical topic. Depending on their educational backgrounds, students arrive with different knowledge about what happened during the 1989 protests, and I present a range of archival images, documentary clips, newspaper headlines, and history textbook accounts in English and Chinese so that the class will begin from a shared understanding of how the protest movement has been documented. I then introduce the film by foregrounding critiques of its sexual content, presenting review blurbs from mainstream American media, such as Derek Elley's claim that the movie panders to Western audiences: "Lou is deliberately pressing hot buttons to cater to Western aud[ience]s. If the pic does end up being banned in China, that will only add to its prestige in some Western critical circles." Yes, the movie was banned in mainland China, and yes, Lou used documentary news footage to depict the political changes occurring in the aftermath of the Tiananmen Square massacre, including the fall of the Berlin Wall and the 1997 handover of Hong Kong from the United Kingdom to the People's Republic of China, so the issue of historical accuracy is indeed an important aspect of the movie. But pairing the film with a secondary reading by the contemporary writer Yan Lianke on mainland China's efforts to erase historical memory highlights the importance of freedom of speech in literature and art. Yan's essay explores how individual and collective memory, combined with voluntary and involuntary forms of forgetting, are shaped by and also inform the ways that history is rewritten by the state, which allows us in class discussion to draw comparisons between different national institutions and history textbook writing practices.

In the case of how memory functions in *Summer Palace*, students can look closely at the main character, Yu Hong, and her diary writing, focusing on scenes that depict the ways in which she and her friends struggle to remember and to forget in order to overcome trauma. These film clips can generate ways to talk about how the deeply personal (including the private and sexual) can become political. Elley's and Yan's respective viewpoints on *Summer Palace* can effectively challenge students' assumptions about what an authentic American or Chinese perspective looks like and can open up alternative ways of thinking critically and engaging with the film. Whereas focusing on historical authenticity forces students to choose sides about whether what the Chinese government did during the protests to maintain social stability was morally justified, the thematic shift to memory encourages them to think about how artistic renditions of history are appealing to particular social or political groups and can also be powerful tools in shaping national memory.

Another way to offset students' frequent obsession with authenticity is to focus on the translation of humor, borrowing approaches from literary and translation studies to have students reflect on why particular forms of humor do or do not travel well. A movie suited for this kind of exercise is Feng Xiaogang's comedic blockbuster *Big Shot's Funeral* (大腕), which was released days after China's 2001 admission to the World Trade Organization and follows the adventures of a Beijing cameraman enlisted to help with a remake of *The Last Emperor*. A satirical clip that has been deleted in some DVD versions but is available on *YouTube* (unfortunately, without English subtitles) features patients chatting at a psychiatric ward about luxury apartments and the real estate market; the scene seems completely illogical yet eerily resembles the social reality during China's economic boom at the turn of the twenty-first century. One mental patient's rambling monologue states the socially accepted philosophy of financial prosperity— "Do you know what indicates a successful person? A successful person always buys what's most expensive, not what's best"—and culminates in his climactic declaration, "So in the real estate industry, our motto is, 'Don't strive for the best, strive for the most expensive!'" (Dawan *zui jingdian de dubai*).[1] Why was this scene, widely appreciated by most Chinese audiences and perceived as one of the most hilarious scenes in the entire movie, deleted from the English subtitled versions released on DVD in the United States? The clip's absence suggests that Feng's humor might be lost on American viewers not familiar with the profit-driven business discourse in present-day China. Students of all backgrounds may already be familiar with some of the social status indicators referenced in the clip, like luxury cars, but for those less aware of contemporary Chinese societal trends added context about Chinese housing complexes with foreign-inspired architectural details and names can illuminate the movie's broader critique of the obsession with Western cultural capital. Without this added context, the critical edge of Feng's humor can easily be overlooked. Considering the erasure of this scene enables students to think about the difficulties of translating humor, in a way that complicates the concept of cultural authenticity but also connects it back to the film's themes of fluency and commodity in the era of globalization.

Censorship

China and the West may be heading toward what some have called a new Cold War (Karl and Lanza), but the current tension in relations between China and the United States is nothing new. Although the issue of censorship may appear to be increasingly fraught in the classroom, this change is only a sign that the "growing pains" of American institutions hosting Chinese international students, as observed in the early aughts (Monaghan), have not receded in the last decade. In 2015, the journal *Positions* published a special issue revisiting the Chinese student protests that took place in 2006 over a digital exhibit on *Visualizing Cultures*, an MIT website, which featured violent images of Japanese soldiers executing Chinese prisoners. In the editors' introduction, Jing Wang and Winnie Won Yin Wong raise the issue of how expertise gets tied to censorship: "[W]hat is the boundary that separates the protestors from the censors, and how do we prevent debates over freedom and dissent from becoming a casualty of the dichotomizing Sino-US competition over political righteousness?" (Wang and Wong 8). This question remains a pressing one today, when many faculty members and students persist in viewing mainland Chinese students as "products of the party-state narrative of victimization, disruptive and hostile, devoid of humanistic aspirations and whose politics need to be treated with suspicion" (10). In Chinese film classes, instructors must strike a balance between focusing narrowly on politically controversial films that may seem to cater to non-Chinese students and using the opportunity to make censored films accessible to students from the People's Republic of China who would otherwise only have limited exposure to them.

In the field of world literature, Yingjin Zhang has highlighted the two-way mapping of geopolitics when it comes to viewing positions on centers and peripheries in a configuration that situates mainland China as the center to its sinophone peripheries, resulting in a "double marginalization": "what China is to the rest of the world, the Sinophone is to the Chinese" (5). Government censorship in mainland China adds another layer of complexity to the country's relation to world cinema, as mainstream Chinese film occupies the ambivalent position of being hegemonic in relation to independent (often banned) Chinese film, yet marginal to its more established counterparts in Hong Kong and Taiwan film, two sinophone filmic traditions that have already received global critical acclaim. Outside China, the Chinese movies that non-Chinese audiences are familiar with may also not align with the box-office hits seen by Chinese domestic audiences, and Hollywood productions continue to constitute a substantive portion of movies released in mainland China.

In contemporary Chinese literary studies, marketing that draws attention to the banning of a literary work is frequently characterized as a gimmick used to entice domestic and international readers alike. If instructors discuss the labeling of banned movies, they should begin with an explanation of the fundamental differences between independent filmmaking in China and in Hollywood, which boil down to issues of funding, production, and how movies are released, all aspects of the wider film industry that have undergone dramatic changes in recent years because of streaming media technology and new viewing practices. Just because a movie is banned in China does not mean it is not seen or circulated by Chinese viewers, though consumers cannot purchase a ticket to see a banned movie at a conventional theater box office. Just because a film is banned at a particular moment does not mean that the film will always be banned, and the careers of Lou Ye and Jia Zhangke, for instance, reveal that just because a filmmaker's film is banned does not mean that subsequent movies by the filmmaker will also be banned. Movies get banned in China for a range of reasons—not all of which are glamorous, sexy, or violent—and these reasons are constantly changing. Clarifying these points can help students avoid fetishizing banned movies and the censorship process.

A creative filmic mode that gives voice to marginalized forms of truth telling, documentary films can be especially effective in challenging student expectations about banned films. Hu Jie's somber *Though I Am Gone* (我虽死去) tells the story of Wang Jingyao and his deceased wife, Bian Zhongyun, a middle school vice principal in Beijing who was beaten to death by Red Guards in 1966 during the start of the Cultural Revolution. Hu combines family photographs with interview footage and other archival materials, some painstakingly preserved over the years by Wang. The film's understated and balanced tone, presented through Hu's detached perspective, stands in stark contrast to the horrific violence documented in the film. This kind of truth-telling film can be difficult for students to watch. Some students may choose to look up Chinese-language sources (sometimes during lecture) to point out historical inaccuracies or flaws in this film's version of history. Using some impromptu online research, one student pointed out that Wang and Bian had committed acts of violence during the Land Reform movement. This unexpected objection raised in class led to further discussion about what this additional context provides: Whether it's true or verifiable, does it make Wang and Bian less sympathetic? Does it mean that Bian deserved to be murdered? The line of questioning reveals to students that cycles of persecution during the Cultural Revolution are a key pattern in modern Chinese history that can be traced to the decades leading up to 1949 and that continues to reverberate. In this case, the defensive stance of a Chinese student concerned with an overly sensational depiction of the Cultural Revolution (especially as presented in the North American classroom environment in the face of non-Chinese viewers) can be an instructive opportunity to teach about collective trauma.

Themes of historical veracity, memory making, and the search for justice have broader implications and can be tied to the ongoing issue of public apologies that extends beyond modern Chinese history into specific North American and Asian cultural contexts. *Though I Am Gone* contributes to a longer ongoing conversation about personal accountability during social movements, and additional readings are crucial. For instance, Song Binbin, one of the leaders of the Red Guards responsible for Bian's murder, wrote an apology that was published in the journal *Remembrance* (记忆) and then mocked in cartoons critiquing her public performance of her apology (Henochowicz). This piece, along with other related readings, could be especially provocative for class discussion and can elicit new understandings about performance and forgiveness, to show how Hu's film, although banned in mainland China, nonetheless actively engages with lively and critical discussions about history that continue to take place in China.

The documentary films in Wu Wenguang's *Memory Project* series are also useful in survey classes on Chinese film or classes with a thematic focus on history and memory in Chinese film.[2] Initially conceived as a project providing young filmmakers with the tools and skills to make films in their family villages in the countryside, the films feature interviews with elderly relatives of the filmmakers about their memories of the Great Famine. Many of the *Memory Project* films, like Zhang Mengqi's *Self-Portrait* series about the filmmaker's home village outside of Suizhou in northern Hubei province, have gradually evolved into vibrant works documenting the process of community building and creative experimentation. In the age of social media, especially *TikTok* (also known as *Douyin*), and live streaming, students may not fully appreciate how revolutionary independent documentary filmmaking was at its roots. Wu Wenguang's early essay "DV: Individual Filmmaking" is a reminder of the technological changes that have given young people the mobility and flexibility to film what they want. Wu's discussion of independent filmmaking as personal filmmaking can help students move beyond purely commercial or political understandings of government censorship.

Empathy

Encountering Chinese film in the college classroom makes it possible and necessary for students and instructors to reflect on their place in the world and their relationship to the making of China. Film offers its viewers an immersive experience that enables changes in their thoughts and actions; drawing attention to diverse viewing positions can be an effective way of fostering empathy in the humanities classroom. Empathy can inform how we as viewers relate to the characters on-screen, but also how we relate to the filmmaker and appreciate or make sense of the film as a work of art. While the films discussed in the previous two sections (with the exception of *Tiny Times*) may appear overtly political, including some light-hearted films can help balance the otherwise serious course materials.

One film that students respond to enthusiastically is Stephen Chow's blockbuster hit *The Mermaid* (美人鱼). This is a deceptively lighthearted movie, which is to say that partly because of the comic charm of its superstars, Deng Chao and Show Lo (Luo Zhixiang), and partly because of Chow's signature nonsensical humor, students hope to avoid analyzing the movie. However, the theme of environmental degradation, coupled with the movie's pointed critique of children of the nouveau riche (referred to as the *fuerdai* [富二代; "rich second generation"]), offer ways to conceptualize the relationship between humans, animals, and their environment. The film also critiques real estate development, human greed, science, and mythology, and it illustrates Chow's transition from being a Hong Kong director to a Chinese director (a process that has been called *daluhua* [大陆化; "mainlandization"]). If students find the mermaid, Shanshan (played by Lin Yun), too fantastical to relate to, they might empathize with other characters in unexpectedly funny ways, such as Deng's playboy character, Liu Xuan, when he tries to describe the mermaid to the policemen for their sketch and is ridiculed—viewers can feel his frustration and relate the scene to their own experience of being disbelieved when sharing what they know to be the truth—or Show's Octopus, when he pretends not to feel his tentacles being prepared for teppanyaki. Packaged as a crowd-pleasing comedy, *The Mermaid* offers students the opportunity to come together over pressing global concerns about environmental conservation and media technologies through the lens of ecocinema. Students from different backgrounds may agree that the film demonstrates some degree of ecological consciousness, but when asked to think critically about how it challenges the label of ecocinema—particularly whether the film proposes any solutions to ecological problems or assigns blame to particular social groups and institutions—students can draw on their diverse backgrounds to generate an open discussion that considers multiple perspectives. International students, likely already aware of the complicated relationship between Hong Kong and mainland China, can be encouraged to think about the power dynamics related to place, while domestic students should attain a basic understanding of how the popular film market in China operates and of Chow's role within that market. Both groups of students can also examine the movie's pointed message about the tendency for digital media to document and exhibit sensational, violent, and even destructive moments in order to question assumptions about public engagement versus governmental action.

An arguably less accessible film that invites the audience's empathy in surprising ways is Jia Zhangke's *24 City* (二十四城记). The partly fictional documentary, which has been called "docufiction" (Deppman), presents the oral histories of former employees of the Chengfa Corporation's former military factory as it gets demolished to make way for construction of a new residential complex in Chengdu, Sichuan. Combining the oral testimonies of actual state workers with the testimonies of workers performed by professional actors, the movie features another unusual practice—scenes of stillness in which the camera rests on individuals for extended periods of silence, which recall Paul Schrader's analysis of time-image manipulation in what Schrader calls "transcendental style" (6). As a complement to the interview footage, these scenes allow for a moment of introspection that permits viewers to reflect on the workers' relationship to the physical space of the factory and the passage of time depicted. After screening a series of six clips in class, I ask students to reflect on what is unexpected about these scenes: What does the camera capture when we take away words? Why are silence and immobility uncomfortable, but how can they also establish intimacy and human connection?

The theme of human connection can also be related to circulation and audience, and Jiwei Xiao's article "The Quest for Memory: Documentary and Fiction in Jia Zhangke's Films" aptly points out the contradictory impulses in Jia's "quest for memory" and the director's "search for an audience." In the essay prompt below, I encourage students to think about this tension, particularly in relation to the role of empathy.

> In *24 City*, Zhao Tao plays the character Su Na, who is described as being born in 1982 in Chengdu (1:38:42). In a former classroom in the local middle school, Su discusses her educational experience and relationship with her parents, why she decided not to work in the factory, and her current position as a buyer of luxury goods in Hong Kong.
>
> Write a three-to-four-page film commentary (double spaced) that considers how Su's story of visiting her mother in the factory (1:45:00–47:35) illustrates Jia Zhangke's powerful technique of selecting "more common or generic" stories and the director's "implicit pact with his ideal domestic audience, his appeal to their common knowledge and experience of the past." Indicate in your commentary whether you agree that this scene is an example of what Jia imagines viewers "can most easily understand, identify with, and relate to" (Xiao), and explain your reasoning.

This prompt is designed to give students space to explore a range of potential topics, from Jia's choice to use the famous actor Zhao to depict the down to earth Su, to the film's heartrending stories about the trauma that migrant labor inflicts on family bonds, to why the film ends with Su's story. Students might also make the valid argument that Su's story is unconvincing, that she represents a generational obsession with commercial consumer culture, and that Jia's quest for audience fails in this regard to foster empathy. Regardless of the approach students take, the prompt requires them to first think carefully about their own positions as viewing subjects and how those positions can produce a range of responses to the same story.

The diversity of viewing positions and student expectations in Chinese film classes allows for the realization of two learning objectives: for students to share and be exposed to new perspectives and for them to learn about Chinese culture. Getting students to recognize cultural differences in the classroom and to acknowledge their subjective viewing positions is an essential first step in achieving these objectives. This requires that we as instructors not assume all international students have the same expectations or experiences and that we more deeply unsettle the binary between international students and domestic students, whom we might be tempted to think of as "our" students: international students are also our students. Ultimately, we should treat student diversity in any humanities classroom—but especially in those featuring contemporary Chinese film—as an opportunity for practicing critical self-reflection, developing intercultural understanding, and ideally, cultivating empathy for all individuals.

The potential impact of this humbling process may not be immediately obvious to all involved parties. During spring 2013, after I had recovered from my initial disbelief about my student's anger toward Ai Weiwei, I still didn't take the student's reaction seriously and instead shared the incident as a humorous anecdote at an academic conference, receiving one sparse chuckle from the sleepy audience. Nearly a decade later, I see that I had overlooked the possibility of students' having more emotionally varied responses to creative work that I appreciated—and only in hindsight can I better understand and empathize with this former student's frustration, though it's also a reminder for me to be more attentive to diverse viewpoints in the future.

Notes

1. Translations in the essay are mine unless otherwise indicated.

2. Selected *Memory Project* films with English subtitles are available for purchase through the vendor China Classics. See "Memory Project" for some of the films without subtitles.

Works Cited

Barlow, Tani. "How Chinese Are You? or, It Could Have Been Me." *positions: asia critique*, vol. 23, no. 1, Feb. 2015, pp. 121–29.

Berry, Chris. "If China Can Say No, Can China Make Movies? or, Do Movies Make China? Rethinking National Cinema and National Agency." *Boundary 2*, vol. 25, no. 3, autumn 1998, pp. 129–50.

Big Shot's Funeral. Directed by Feng Xiaogang 冯小刚, Sony Pictures, 2001.

City of Sadness. Directed by Hou Hsiao-hsien 侯孝贤, 3H Films, 1989.

大碗最经典的独白 [Dawan *zui jingdian de dubai*; *All-Time Classic Monologue from* Big Shot's Funeral]. *YouTube*, uploaded by Jason Z, 14 Jan. 2009, www.youtube.com/watch?v=l2nm6b1UaLo.

Deppman, Hsiu-Chuang. "Reading Docufiction: Jia Zhangke's *24 City*." *Journal of Chinese Cinemas*, vol. 8, no. 3, 2014, pp. 188–208.

Elley, Derek. "Summer Palace." *Daily Variety*, vol. 291, no. 35, 19 May 2006, variety.com/2006/film/markets-festivals/summer-palace-1200516187/.

Han Han 韩寒. *Triple Door*. Writers Publishing House, 2000.

Henochowicz, Anne. "Drawing the News: Apology Not Accepted." *China Digital Times*, 21 Jan. 2014, chinadigitaltimes.net/2014/01/drawing-news-apology-accepted/.

Karl, Rebecca, and Fabio Lanza, editors. "Introduction: A New Cold War?" *Positions Politics*, no. 5, Apr. 2021, positionspolitics.org/episteme-5/.

"The Memory Project." *Duke University Libraries*, repository.duke.edu/dc/memoryproject.

The Mermaid. Directed by Stephen Chow 周星驰, Sony Pictures, 2016.

Monaghan, Peter. "Open Doors, Closed Minds?" *The Chronicle of Higher Education*, vol. 53, no. 37, 19 May 2006, www.chronicle.com/article/open-doors-closed-minds/.

"More Chinese Study Abroad in 2018." *Xinhua*, 30 Mar. 2019, www.xinhuanet.com/english/2018-03/30/c_137077465.htm.

Schrader, Paul. *Transcendental Style in Film: Ozu, Bresson, Dreyer*. UC Press, 2018.

Song Binbin 宋彬彬. 四十多年来我一直想说的话 ["Sishi duo nian lai wo yizhi xiang shuo de hua"; "What I Have Wanted to Say for Forty Years"]. *Remembrance* [记忆], no. 80, 31 Jan. 2012, pp. 3–15.

Summer Palace. Directed by Lou Ye 娄烨, Laurel Films / Dream Factory / Fantasy Pictures / Rosem Films, 2006.

Though I Am Gone. Directed by Hu Jie 胡杰, dGenerate Films, 2006.

Tiny Times 1.0. Directed by Guo Jingming 郭敬明, Edko Films, 2013.

24 City. Directed by Jia Zhangke 贾樟柯, Cinema Guild, 2008.

U.S. Mission China. "China Remains the Top Sender of International Students to the United States in 2020/2021." *U.S. Embassy and Consulates in China*, 17 Nov. 2021, china.usembassy-china.org.cn/china-remains-the-top-sender-of-international-students-to-the-united-states-in-2020-2021/.

Wang, Jing, and Winnie Won Yin Wong. "Unpacking a Controversy: National Histories, Visual Cultures, and Digital Dissent." *positions: asia critique*, vol. 23, no. 1, Feb. 2015, pp. 1–14.

Wu Wenguang. "DV: Individual Filmmaking." Translated by Cathryn Clayton. *The New Chinese Documentary Film Movement: For the Public Record*, edited by Chris Berry et al., Hong Kong UP, 2010, pp. 49–54.

Xiao, Jiwei. "The Quest for Memory: Documentary and Fiction in Jia Zhangke's Films." *Senses of Cinema*, no. 59, June 2011, www.sensesofcinema.com/2011/feature-articles/the-quest-for-memory-documentary-and-fiction-in-jia-zhangke's-films/.

Yan Lianke. "On China's State-Sponsored Amnesia." *The New York Times*, 1 Apr. 2013, www.nytimes.com/2013/04/02/opinion/on-chinas-state-sponsored-amnesia.html.

Zhang, Yingjin. "Mapping Chinese Literature as World Literature." *CLCWeb: Comparative Literature and Culture*, vol. 17, no. 1, 2015, https://doi.org/10.7771/1481-4374.2714.

Zhuoyi Wang

Teaching Ideology through a Controversial Chinese Film: The Case of *The Wandering Earth*

The complex history of the Chinese-speaking world has produced closely interconnected yet distinct cultures and societies. Students often find it difficult to comprehend the tensions between and within these multifaceted cultures and societies. Courses on Chinese language and culture, however, seldom focus on this sophisticated aspect of the Chinese-speaking world, often leaving unchallenged the common totalistic view of Chinese culture.

Narrative films can be an effective tool to overcome this pedagogical challenge. Their storytelling can present diverse views and values in a palpable way. Their audiovisual nature can immerse students in an unfamiliar sociocultural environment more effectively than text can. Often symptomatic of ideological complexity and conflicts, controversial films are particularly useful in provoking in-depth political discussions in class.

This essay focuses on *The Wandering Earth* (流浪地球) as an example to illustrate how to use a popular and controversial Chinese film to teach this ideological complexity and diversity. Primarily thanks to its box-office windfall of 4.65 billion yuan (nearly $700 million) in mainland China, this science fiction film was the second-highest-grossing Chinese film of all time (Suixin). It also generated substantial media attention in Taiwan, despite not being theatrically released there, and in Hong Kong.[1] As discussed in the essay, *The Wandering Earth* has the potential to move beyond the individualistic heroic fantasy films typical of Hollywood as well as the nationalistic heroic fantasy films typical of China. However, this potential is often overshadowed by the film's diverse and controversial receptions, which are symptomatic of the tensions, contradictions, and communication gaps in and between the various Chinese-speaking societies. In debates about the film, conflicting sides often ironically share the same tendency to reduce the film to a simple piece of nationalist propaganda for the People's Republic of China.

The three sections of this essay focus on *The Wandering Earth*'s narrative, style, and reception, respectively, and provide a step-by-step guide for an in-depth class discussion of the film's potentially sophisticated message and how the message gets lost. The discussion can be pedagogically effective in helping students understand not only the ideological complexity and diversity shaping the production and reception of this film in Chinese-speaking societies but also, more generally, the importance and challenges of taking a nuanced position on polarizing issues.

Narrative

The neoformalist approach to film narrative offers a useful differentiation between plot and story. Plot, in this approach, refers to "everything visibly and audibly present in the film before us," whereas story refers to "the viewer's imaginary construction of all the events in the narrative" based on what the viewer sees and hears in the plot (Bordwell and Thompson 76, 481).

In an article that offers a historicized close reading of *The Wandering Earth*, I argue that the film's ideological complexity lies in its iceberg-shaped narrative. Revealing just a "tiny tip of the story" (Z. Wang 221), the film's affirmative and entertaining plot seems to endorse Chinese nationalism and follows the formula of Hollywood individualist monomyths. However, "a much larger portion of the story is dark, cold, ridden with unfathomable problems, and hidden from the plot" because of "a double-layered restraint imposed on it by the state and the market" (222). At the center of the underwater portion of the narrative iceberg lies an ethical dilemma of whom to rescue and whom to sacrifice. Struggling with this dilemma, the film "attempts to imagine a new kind of united fight for [a] human future, taking an important step toward the planet-based totality and away from individualistic and nationalistic heroic fantasies." However, it "eventually fails to make a convincing call for hope" (228). This section provides advice on teaching three film sequences that can serve as entry points for students to approach the ethical dilemma and delve into the film's ideological complexity.

A teacher may begin class discussion on *The Wandering Earth* after screening its opening sequence, which sets the story in a future when the aging sun is about to explode (0:00:00–0:05:40). Cooperating in a consortium called the United Earth Government, the nations of the world have initiated a Wandering Earth project, which uses planetary thrusters to put Earth on a voyage away from the sun. During the exodus, people need to live in subterranean cities to survive the disasters on Earth's surface. But they must draw lots to enter the cities, which can only accommodate half of the world population.

This sequence features one family: a Chinese astronaut Liu Peiqiang (Wu Jing); his terminally ill wife, Han Duoduo (Wang Zhi); his young son Liu Qi (Guo Hexuan); and his father-in-law, Han Ziang (Ng Mantat). Chosen by the Chinese state to serve on a United Earth Government pathfinder space station that will guide Earth on its voyage, Liu Peiqiang says to Han Ziang: "After I leave, you'll be Liu Qi's only guardian and can get subterranean city residency without drawing lots" (0:01:55–0:02:05).[2]

The teacher may ask this question about the sequence: Why can Han Ziang accompany Liu Qi to get subterranean residency (and therefore survival rights) without drawing lots? The film does not clearly explain this in its plot. As a result, many viewers, including possibly many students, may imagine a story where Han Ziang and Liu Qi have are exempt from the lottery because they are family members of an astronaut chosen by the Chinese state. Some critics have furiously derided the film based on this understanding of its story. In a social media article sensationally titled "*The Wandering Earth* Is a Frenzied Attempt to Bring Earth to Destruction," one mainland Chinese critic takes the film simply as a shameless propaganda piece for the Chinese government's authoritarian, hypocritical, and corrupt rule (Hu).

It is unclear, however, how this story of privilege can explain other plot turns in the film. For example, observant students may note that a child gains subterranean residency without drawing lots in the film's second sequence (0:52:30–0:53:20). It is likely that the child, who is an orphaned infant girl, is brought to a subterranean city after all the lots have been drawn. At this point, Earth is about to escape its orbit around the sun, the doors to the subterranean cities are apparently already shut, and people left on Earth's surface are dying in great floods. The subterranean cities are sending out rescue teams, one of which includes Han Ziang as a member. In a relay effort, some of the adults struggling in the water lift the girl and push her to the boat of Han Ziang's team. Han Ziang then brings the girl to his subterranean city and adopts her as his granddaughter.

Students may discuss the following questions about this sequence: Why do the subterranean cities send out rescue teams when all the lottery winners are probably already underground? Whom do these teams attempt to rescue on Earth's surface? Why do the adults dying in the water help the infant onto the rescue boat? Why is Han Ziang willing and able to bring this orphan, who has no relationship to him, into the subterranean city at this late stage?

This discussion provides a good chance for the teacher to introduce Liu Cixin's novella "The Wandering Earth" (1–48), which inspired the film, because the novella clearly presents an age-based rule for survivor selection that can help answer the questions. According to this rule, subterranean city residents must line up according to their age when evacuating in an emergency. Robot nurses holding infants are at the head of the line while the oldest people wait at its end (24). The film subtly reflects this rule in the third sequence that the teacher may use for this discussion: a scrolling TV news ticker reads that minors have all evacuated from an ongoing emergency while adults are still evacuating (*Wandering Earth* 0:04:50–0:04:58).

Students should find it easy to understand that the age-based rule aims to maximize the human race's chance to survive. Following the logic of this rule, they should now be able to imagine a story where children are all exempt from the lottery and entitled to subterranean residency because their lives are the most important for continuing the human race. This child-first principle can explain the rescue teams' mission and the dying adults' selfless behavior: The teams are searching for those children who are still missing outside, and the adults who help the infant girl know that she can still enter a subterranean city while they themselves have lost their chance at survival. This can also explain why Han Ziang says in the second sequence: "Everyone under the water is [the infant's] parent" (0:52:51–0:52:57).

With Han Ziang's mention of "parent," the teacher may lead students to contemplate the terrifying implications of the novella's age-based rule. One consequence of the rule is that all children are separated from their parents in an evacuation line and will likely become orphans in the event of disaster. In fact, it is in precisely such a scenario that the protagonist of the novella loses his mother. For Liu Cixin, who proudly describes his works as featuring a "cruel but sober rationality" (Liu and Jiang), robots' caregiving would be good enough for children. But students may take a different view on the necessity of human nurturing and should now understand why Han Ziang is exempt from the lottery as "Liu Qi's only guardian" (*Wandering Earth* 0:01:57–0:01:59). Departing from the novella, the film exempts from the lottery one and only one guardian for each child to avoid orphaning the children.

The discussion of these three sequences should enable students to imagine a story where neither Liu Qi nor Han Ziang is above the rules: Liu Qi enters the subterranean city as a child, and Han Ziang enters as the child's only guardian. Rather than granting anyone privileges, this story establishes a set of fair and even sensitive rules for survivor selection. However, in the same moment that the film presents a possibility for this seemingly positive story, it also leaves plot clues to a dark one.

The teacher can guide students to delve into the dark story through an incomplete line in the opening sequence: With tearful eyes, Liu Peiqiang says to Han Ziang: "This is the only choice . . . Father, sorry!" (0:02:16–0:02:33). As he speaks, the camera briefly cuts to Liu Peiqiang's hospitalized wife, Han Duoduo, who lies in a coma. Later, the film shows that "the only choice" refers to Liu Peiqiang's decision to end Han Duoduo's treatment shortly before Han Ziang and Liu Qi enter the subterranean city and that Liu Qi remains angry at his father for this decision for many years.

Here, a group role-playing activity can be organized for students to think through each character's perspective in this situation. Those who play Han Duoduo can give this silent character a voice, expressing her feelings about the decision made about her life. Those who play Liu Qi can elaborate on his anger. One question that may be asked by either character is if Liu Peiqiang indeed has no other choice. Of course, he may not have the choice to designate Han Duoduo as the guardian taking care of Liu Qi underground because she is terminally ill and in a coma. However, if he did not terminate her treatment and drew lots on her behalf, she could still have a fifty percent chance of entering the subterranean city and having her life extended as long as possible. She is deprived of this chance by Liu Peiqiang's decision, which Han Ziang reluctantly accepts. Students who play Liu Peiqiang and Han Ziang may also ask if they indeed have any other choice.

This question points to a dilemma inherent in the age-based rule. To help reveal this dilemma, the teacher may guide students to review the film's evacuation scenario once again and to discuss this question: Should a terminally ill thirty-year-old wait in the line before or after a healthy thirty-one-year-old? Those who want to maintain the age-based order would find that in this scenario the order defeats its own rational purpose of maximizing the human race's chance of surviving. Those who want to change the order would open Pandora's box: If a terminally ill person should be sent to the back of the line, then how about the mentally ill, the disabled, the physically weak, the infertile, and, eventually, whomever is deemed inferior for continuing the human race by whoever has the power to make that assessment?

In the context of this systemic dilemma, students should better understand the pressure on Liu Peiqiang and Han Ziang. Technically, they can indeed draw lots for Han Duoduo and give her the same chance for survival that others have. However, a ticket to the subterranean city for Han Duoduo would be a lost opportunity for another, probably healthier, person and might require the city to spend limited medical resources on extending Han Duoduo's life. It is not difficult to imagine the unbearable moral burden attached to such an outcome, which would also incur furious attacks from those people trying to increase the human race's chance of survival.

Rather than persuade students to side with any specific character among the four, this roleplaying activity serves to help them understand the systemic dilemma at the center of the film. The dilemma is not present in the original novella, in which subterranean cities can accommodate the entire world population and there is no need to draw lots. The film, by contrast, sets a lottery system and adds a terminally ill character in its plot. As a result, its story may vacillate between a dystopian vision of the future and a hopeful call for a new kind of fair and caring global collective beyond individualist and nationalist interests.

Adding another layer to the ideological complexity, the film's plot almost conceals the dilemma of the age-based rule behind a family problem: The adolescent Liu Qi (Qu Chuxiao) blames his father, and only his father, for his mother's death. Seemingly the only issue in the film, the father-son relationship is restored when the father eventually sacrifices his own life to save the son and the entire population on Earth. While the dilemma of the age-based rule is hidden in the film's narrative, like the part of an iceberg that lies underwater, the Chinese heroes' Hollywood-style individual deeds are very much visible. This is why the film may give viewers an impression that it endorses Chinese progressivist nationalism and follows the conventional formula of Hollywood science fiction monomyths, which grant a few and eventually just one world savior unquestionable authority to decide whom to rescue. The next section provides advice on helping students further understand such ideological complexity through the film's style.

Style

Neoformalism defines film style as the "repeated and salient uses of film techniques" that can be divided into four major categories: mise-en-scène, cinematography, editing, and sound (Bordwell and Thompson 481). This section provides pedagogical suggestions for discussing the style of *The Wandering Earth* through two sequences in the film. The suggestions concern such mise-en-scène elements as colors, props, lighting, setting, and performance; such cinematographic elements as shot angles and distance; and many editing and sound choices.

The first sequence takes place when the film introduces the Wandering Earth project. It begins with a shot of a line of people entering the gate of a subterranean city. These people are lottery winners who have gained a precious chance at survival. However, this sequence's style shows no celebrative atmosphere except for a banner that reads: "Moving to a subterranean city, building a new home together." The banner is red, a festive color in Chinese culture, yet the concrete and metal gate where it is hung are a gloomy gray. Moreover, snowy wind is blowing the banner hard and has begun to tear it. An off-screen television newscaster reads in a dull voice: "The lottery result cannot be transferred, borrowed, or gifted." The voice continues when the camera cuts to a giant warning sign: "Those who do not win the lottery are strictly forbidden to enter subterranean cities." Underneath the sign, the people move slowly with their heads lowered. The following shots, all in depressing low-key lighting, show mounted loudspeakers, armed riot police, and electric fences. Extreme high-angle shots taken from the loudspeakers and the warning sign make the people below appear particularly powerless and vulnerable. Among them there are

Han Ziang and Liu Qi, whose distressed faces are clearly visible in several medium and medium close-up shots (0:05:09–0:05:40).

Class discussion on the style of this sequence may begin with the question why the setting resembles a prison more than a haven. There is obviously no need to force people to stay inside the subterranean city, the only place they can survive. The real function of the police and the fences, as the television newscaster and the warning sign should remind students, is to keep out those who did not win the lottery. The prison, therefore, is outside the fences rather than inside. Completely invisible in this sequence and barely visible in the entire film, dying inmates of this giant prison appear only briefly in the scene where a few of them selflessly save the infant orphan. Yet, as implied by the stern warnings and the heavy guards, their untold stories may not uniformly be ones of willing self-sacrifice.

The discussion may then move to another element implied in the style of this sequence: the connection between those left on Earth's surface and the subterranean survivors. The only such connection that the film explicitly presents is between Han Duoduo and the other members of Liu Peiqiang's family. Although Han Duoduo is already terminally ill, leaving her behind is still an unbearable trauma for the family. What would happen, then, to all those families who have to sacrifice more members or members who are not terminally ill? The sequence's dismal atmosphere, comprehensively rendered by its stylistic choices, should remind students that each desolate person walking inside the fences may be connected to family members kept outside.

Moreover, the teacher may direct students' attention to the authoritative figures unromantically presented in the sequence, the television newscaster and the police, and ask if these people should be exempt from the lottery. If they should, then would the lottery system still be fair? If they should not, then could the United Earth Government still maintain order? By extension, what of the army, the upper echelons of the government, large companies, major organizations, and various other powerful forces and figures in the social hierarchy?

By now, students should realize that *The Wandering Earth*'s style is rich with subtle clues to all sorts of dark questions. A further exploration of such questions would easily lead to a dystopian vision of the future. Here, a class focusing on Chinese film history may review the political troubles that science fiction films have experienced in mainland China.[3] Even without the context of film history, however, students should still understand that it is impossible for a dystopian film to pass the strict censorship of the Chinese government, which defines itself as not only leading a great nationalist rejuvenation but also creating a "bright tomorrow" for a global "community with a shared future for mankind" (Xi 55, 7). Therefore, the film's dystopian vision can only exist as dark clues hidden in an idealistic plot focusing on Chinese heroes. This dismal vision is so well hidden, in fact, that the Chinese state has used the film for propagandistic purposes.

It may not be as easy for students to realize that the so-called free market can be nearly as restrictive as governmental censorship. To discuss this point, the teacher may invite students to present their stylistic observations about another film sequence, which takes place in a subterranean school classroom seventeen years after Han Ziang adopts the infant and names her Han Duoduo after his deceased daughter. Using what they have learned from the discussion of the first sequence and facilitated by the teacher, students should be able to provide the following observations.

At the beginning of the sequence, lighting, setting, and sound work together to create a warm atmosphere. The classroom features large windows viewing a sunny springtime campus. Students are reading aloud a work of prose, which praises the spring season as a hopeful time for a new beginning. Among the students, however, the adolescent Han Duoduo does not fit into the atmosphere. Close-ups of her hand and face show that she is not reading but playing with her pen, chewing gum, and looking around with boredom. She even sighs with an annoyed look when a student affectedly recites a textbook description of hope: "Hope is precious like a diamond in our time! Hope is the way to guide us home!" Shortly after this recital, the classroom suddenly plunges into darkness. It turns out that the windows are actually large screens displaying a virtual campus and that the power has been cut off by Liu Qi, who comes to help Han Duoduo escape from the school for a forbidden trip to Earth's surface (0:08:05–0:08:59).

After students present their observations, the teacher may ask why this sequence, which features Han Duoduo, stylistically presents the preaching of hope almost as a deception. The question should direct students' attention to Han Duoduo's deep connection to those left outside the subterranean cities: She is saved by people dying in the flood and named after a patient deprived of her chance at survival. Indeed, for all the people abandoned aboveground, "precious" hope was nothing but a cruel illusion that guided them to a "home" underwater.

The teacher may then inform students that an earlier version of *The Wandering Earth* intended to further explore this plotline leading to the "home" of the dead: The original purpose of Han Duoduo's adventure on Earth's surface was to look for her parents' remains, and in this earlier version of the film the girl eventually finds them among a great number of other deceased people, who maintain their struggling gestures in frozen water (Yujunzhumengjiu). The devastating weight of death on her shoulders serves as a dramatic contrast to the efforts people make to save her life during the dangerous adventure, including two characters who sacrifice their own lives to maintain hope for children like her. This experience eventually turns Han Duoduo from an innate doubter to a firm believer in hope. Toward the end of the film, she successfully makes a global call for a crucial effort to save Earth at the darkest moment.

However, under a prevailing uncertainty about the chances of success for a Chinese film in the science fiction market, a market dominated by Hollywood films, this plotline was later changed and shortened to reduce the film's length in order to increase the possible number of screenings per day, make it easier to consume for general audiences, and thereby improve its box-office prospects. As a result, Han Duoduo's part was significantly diminished, and she becomes a naive girl who wants to go to Earth's surface simply because she is bored by her underground life. Disastrous to Han Duoduo's characterization and plotline, this change was the most important reason that many viewers across the Chinese political spectrum found the performance of her global call, which was meant to be a touching climax, pretentious and unconvincing.

The discussion of *The Wandering Earth*'s narrative and style should give students a better sense of how the film's critical and imaginative potential was restrained by both the state and the market. They should now be ready to proceed to a discussion of the film's reception, which is symptomatic of the ideological gaps in the Chinese-speaking world.

Reception

When discussing *The Wandering Earth*'s reception, the teacher may begin with the Liaowang Institute's data analysis of 210,000 comments that viewers of the film posted on mainland Chinese websites. The analysis found that the comments overwhelmingly focus on elements of the film that were appealing and comparable to elements in Hollywood films, such as fast-moving plot and decent visual effects, and on how the film is a hopeful signal for a rise in the quality of Chinese-made science fiction films.[4] Some comments do praise the film for nationalist reasons, seeing it as a promotion of Chinese heroism and patriotism, the spirit of the Chinese nation, or a so-called Chinese value of preserving home soil (despite the fact that using the Earth as a spaceship is not a Chinese idea in the film or in the history of science fiction). But these comments are far fewer than those on the film's blockbuster elements.

Having thoroughly discussed the film, students should understand why these comments do not reflect much propagandistic effect. Rather than delivering a nationalist message that China saves all, the film leaves open the question of who should save whom. Although the film's plot focuses on Chinese heroes, it does not diminish the important roles of other nations, including Russia, France, Korea, Japan, and the United States, in the international cooperation to save Earth.[5]

The teacher may then review *The Wandering Earth*'s reception in Chinese state media, which overwhelmingly focuses on the abovementioned nationalist interpretations of the film, even praising the film as a gift to the seventieth Chinese national day for promoting the idea of the "community with a shared future for mankind" (Song and Zhao). Ironically, it was precisely the Chinese state media's appropriation of *The Wandering Earth*'s success that triggered a wave of fierce criticism of the film as nationalist propaganda. This wave of criticism appeared in both social and traditional media in Hong Kong and Taiwan, while it appeared only in social media articles in mainland China because of state censorship (e.g., Hu; Wang X.; Wu; "Zhiyou gongchandang").

The media of these three Chinese-speaking societies have also produced more thoughtful and nuanced reviews of *The Wandering Earth* and its reception. The teacher may summarize the reviews for students or, in an advanced Chinese language class, have them read one such review, which can give them a vantage point from which to see the political battle fought over the film. For example, the Taipei-based news website *The News Lens* published Yang Buhuan's article "Does *The Wandering Earth* Mark the Beginning of the 'First Year for Chinese Sci-Fi' or Is It Just '*Wolf Warrior* in Space?'" Yang answers no to both questions in the title, accurately pointing out that the film's worldview "is beyond nationalism and [is instead] a product of generations of development" of Chinese science fiction. The article also reviews how the ideological conflicts in the Chinese-speaking world reduced the film to "a battlefield of advocates and opponents of [Chinese] nationalism."

Debates about *The Wandering Earth* are also symptomatic of other political cleavages. A long-running thread about the film on *PTT*, the largest terminal-based bulletin board system in Taiwan, can serve as a good pedagogical example. The original poster watched the film in mainland China, shared a largely positive review of the film, and was soon attacked by a follow-up poster as an unwelcomed "Chinese person" posting a "Chinese-style" promotion of a "Chinese film" on a Taiwanese bulletin board. The original poster counterattacked, vowing that they were a "true Taiwanese." The conflict soon escalated into a heated debate among many, including radical participants on both sides. Some attacked defenders of the film as prodictatorship Chinese or pro-China Taiwanese with such offensive labels as "fifty cents" (a pejorative term referring to Internet commentators working for the PRC's government), "Shina" (an archaic Japanese name for China now viewed as offensive), "26" (a pejorative homophonic pun for "mainlanders" in Taiwanese Hokkien), and "Chinese Taiwanese." And the attackers were counterattacked as naive followers of Taiwan's pro-independence Democratic Progressive Party with equally pejorative terms like "green woke" and "Taiwanese bumpkins." At the same time, some participants tried to lead the debate beyond simple-minded antagonism and into a rational discussion of not only the film but also the cross-strait relationship (eagleleo). The debate presents a microcosm of Taiwan's diverse politics with vivid examples of authentic argumentative rhetoric as well as language commonly used on the Internet, which are a vital asset for learning to communicate in the modern Chinese-speaking world that can seldom be found in any language textbook.

With a sophisticated comprehension of *The Wandering Earth* and its reception, students should see that much of the controversy was not based on an in-depth understanding of the film's narrative and style, but a result of a multipartite competition to appropriate the film for preexisting and conflicting political agendas. The competition not only reflects the ideological complexity and diversity in the Chinese-speaking world but also reveals the challenges and importance of nuanced cross-cultural and cross-ideological understanding, which is a lifelong pursuit worthy of all students, especially those of Chinese language and culture.

Notes

1. In Hong Kong, the film had just a one-week run and grossed $270,895, ranking as the third among the four newly released films that week ("Hong Kong").

2. Translations of Chinese-language quotations in the essay are mine.

3. For more discussion of this history, see Z. Wang; Yang.

4. The film does reflect a strong influence from Hollywood blockbusters. However, it also departs, crucially and in a restrained manner, from the Hollywood science fiction model. For more discussion of this point, see Z. Wang.

5. A significant number of viewers, including some of my students in the United States, suspect that the film embodies anti-US attitudes because it seems to exclude the United States from the global effort to save Earth. In fact, however, the film recognizes the United States as the first nation in the United Earth Government by showing its national flag before or above those of the other nations in multiple shots. American English is also the default language of computer interfaces and automated voice commands throughout the film. The uncomfortable suspicion is rather symptomatic of a biased expectation cultivated by Hollywood that global disaster movies must give the United States and American heroes nothing less than a central focus. If students raise this suspicion, the teacher may use this chance to help them critically reflect on their cultural expectations shaped by Hollywood-dominated media.

Works Cited

Bordwell, David, and Kristin Thompson. *Film Art: An Introduction*. 8th ed., McGraw Hill, 2008.

eagleleo. [超好雷]《流浪地球》["[Chaohaolei] *Liulang diqiu*"; "[Highly Recommended, Spoiler Alert] the Wandering Earth"]. 批踢踢實業坊 [*Pi ti ti shiye fang*; *PTT*], 15 Feb. 2019, www.ptt.cc/bbs/movie/M.1550216358.A.509.html.

"Hong Kong 2019 Week 9." *Box Office Mojo*, www.boxofficemojo.com/weekly/2019W09/?area=HK&sort=rank&sortDir=asc&ref_=bo_wl___resort#table

Hu Tianyao 胡天遥.《流浪地球》是丧心病狂地带着地球去毁灭 ["*Liulang diqiu* shi sangxinbingkuang de daizhe diqiu qu huimie"; "*The Wandering Earth* Is a Frenzied Attempt to Bring Earth to Destruction"]. 微信 [*Weixin*], 12 Feb. 2019, mp.weixin.qq.com/s/JAiOOyiJELQEN78LJ5kImg.

Liaowang Institute 瞭望智库.《流浪地球》靠"太空战狼"才火起来? 我们分析完 21 万条评论后发现真相 ["*Liulang diqiu* kao *Taikong zhanlang* cai huo qilai? Women fenxi wan ershiyi wan tiao pinglun hou faxian zhenxiang"; "*The Wandering Earth* Gained Popularity as a Science-Fiction Version of *Wolf Warrior*? We Have Found the Truth through an Analysis of 210,000 Online Comments"]. 微信 [*Weixin*], 16 Feb. 2019, mp.weixin.qq.com/s/kGwxWTiTRY8mxkdWvI1Zcg.

Liu Cixin 刘慈欣. *The Wandering Earth*. Translated by Ken Liu et al., Tor Books, 2013.

Liu Cixin and Jiang Xiaoyuan 江晓原. 为什么人类还值得拯救? ["Weishenme renlei hai zhide zhengjiu?"; "Why Is the Human Race Still Worth Saving?"]. 知乎 [*Zhihu*], 26 July 2019, zhuanlan.zhihu.com/p/75329053.

Song Xinrui 宋心蕊 and Zhao Guangxia 赵光霞. 影片《流浪地球》研讨会摘编 ["Yingpian *Liulang diqiu* yantaohui fayan zhaibian"; "Selected Discussions at the Colloquium on *The Wandering Earth*"]. 人民日报 [*Renmin ribao*; *People's Daily*], 21 Feb. 2019, p. 16.

Suixin 随心. 《流浪地球》上映 90 天 国内总票房今日定格 [“*Liulang diqiu* shangying 90 tian, guonei zong piaofang jinri dingge”; “Box Office Number of *The Wandering Earth* Is Set Ninety Days after Its Release”]. *Mydrivers*, 6 May 2019, news.mydrivers.com/1/625/625740.htm.

The Wandering Earth. Directed by Frant Gwo, China Film Group, 2019.

Wang Xinyu 王心妤. 惨! 救了地球救不了票房 强国科幻片只卖 7 张票 [“Can! Jiule diqiu jiubuliao piaofang: ‘Qiangguo’ kehuanpian zhi mai qi zhang piao”; “Pathetic! It Can Save Earth but Not the Box Office: A Sci-Fi Film from the ‘Powerful Nation’ Sold Only Seven Tickets”]. 自由时报 [*Ziyou shibao*; *Liberty Times*], 3 Mar. 2019, ent.ltn.com.tw/news/breakingnews/2714602.

Wang, Zhuoyi. “Between the World Ship and the Spaceship: Planetarianism, Hollywood, Nationalism, and the Iceberg-Shaped Story of the Wandering Earth (2019).” *Prism: Theory and Modern Chinese Literature*, vol. 18, no. 1, 2021, pp. 210–34.

Wu Duan 无端. 从《战狼2》到《流浪地球》, 为什么吴京屡遭差评? [“Cong *Zhanlang 2* dao *Liulang diqiu*, weishenme Wu Jing lü zao chaping?”; “From *Wolf Warrior 2* to *The Wandering Earth*: Why Are Wu Jing’s Films Often Criticized?”]. 搜狐 [*Sohu*], 15 Feb. 2019, www.sohu.com/a/294891099_427962.

Xi Jinping. “Secure a Decisive Victory in Building a Moderately Prosperous Society in All Respects and Strive for the Great Success of Socialism with Chinese Characteristics for a New Era.” 18 Oct. 2017, www.xinhuanet.com/english/download/Xi_Jinping’s_report_at_19th_CPC_National_Congress.pdf.

Yang Buhuan 杨不欢.《流浪地球》开启了“中国科幻元年”抑或只是“太空版战狼”? [“*Liulang diqiu* kaiqi le ‘Zhongguo kehuan yuannian’ yihuo zhishi ‘Taikong Ban Zhanlang?’”; “Does *The Wandering Earth* Mark the Beginning of the ‘First Year for Chinese Sci-Fi’ or Is It Just ‘*Wolf Warrior* in Space’”?]. 關鍵評論網 [*Guanjian pinglun wang*; *The News Lens*], 11 Feb. 2019, www.thenewslens.com/article/113521.

Yujunzhumengjiu 娱菌主梦九. 流浪地球: 删减情节曝光 [“*Liulang diqiu*: Shanjian qingjie baoguang”; “*The Wandering Earth*: A Disclosure of Deleted Scenes”]. *KK News*, 8 Feb. 2019, kknews.cc/entertainment/rjz6myv.html.

只有共产党可以救地球, 中国科幻片票房破十亿 [“Zhiyou gongchandang keyi jiu diqiu, Zhongguo kehuanpian piaofang po shi yi”; “Only the Communist Party Can Save Earth: The Box-Office Revenue of a Chinese Sci-Fi Film Exceeds One Billion”]. 批踢踢實業坊 [*Pi ti ti shiye fang*; *PTT*], 9 Feb. 2019, www.ptt.cc/bbs/movie/M.1549674213.A.4F8.html.

Part II

Reexamining
Revolutionary Narratives

Emily Wilcox

Gender, Class, and Ethnicity in *Li Shuangshuang, The White-Haired Girl,* and *Five Golden Flowers*

Teaching films from China's early socialist era in classrooms in the United States can be a difficult undertaking for a number of reasons. On the one hand, the long-established Cold War discourse about China in the United States has conditioned most students in American universities to regard Chinese socialist culture with skepticism. For this reason, students tend to assume that socialist films are inauthentic propaganda that lack representational honesty and artistic value, making them problematic as a medium for either historical lessons or film appreciation. On the other hand, the social worlds that inspire and are depicted in films from China's early socialist period are often alien to contemporary university students in the United States. Whether in terms of the specific social problems addressed in such films or the larger ideological values the films aim to espouse, these films may pose difficulties for students at the level of both basic comprehension and relatability. As a result, more work falls onto the instructor to help students understand and appreciate such films.

To lessen this work, when teaching about socialist China through film, many instructors will choose to assign films that offer retrospective accounts of socialist life rather than films actually produced in the socialist era. Canonical works by fifth-generation filmmakers such as *To Live* (活着),

Yellow Earth (黃土地), and *Farewell My Concubine* (霸王別姬) are common choices for this purpose. While such films also require a large amount of historical contextualization for students to grasp and meaningfully interpret them,[1] they nevertheless present fewer challenges in terms of their ideological messages. This is because such films share with US Cold War discourse a basic skepticism about the social experiments and ideological values of China's early socialist culture. Rather than presenting socialist culture as a complex and legitimate project that one can seek to understand, relate to, and even learn from, they treat it as a failure and something to be criticized and exposed as fraudulent by those outside it.

In my teaching, I have shifted away from using fifth-generation films to teach about early China's socialist era retrospectively and instead have adopted films produced in the era. To my pleasant surprise, I have found students to be extraordinarily receptive to early Chinese socialist films; they often comment on how much they learned from the films and, indeed, how much they enjoyed watching them, in large part because they were not what the students initially expected them to be. By pairing films with appropriate readings that illuminate the social problems and historical issues they represent as well as the artistic strategies of cultural production that informed early socialist filmmaking, I have found that students relish the excitement of interpreting early socialist films on their own terms. Through their contributions to class discussions and written responses, students demonstrate a strong capacity to understand and analyze these films once they have the appropriate intellectual scaffolding to do so. The learning they gain from this experience is greater than that of learning from retrospective accounts because it challenges students to develop a new frame of reference rather than rely on ones they already have. In some cases, students also reflect on the differences between early socialist-era films and contemporary films, developing a critical engagement with current ideological assumptions and filmmaking practices that they may have previously taken for granted.

In this essay, I discuss my experience teaching films from the early socialist period in a first-year seminar on Chinese socialist history and culture titled Revolution in Life: How Communism Changed China. The seminar presumes no prior knowledge of Chinese language, history, or culture, and it is open equally to students intending to major or minor in Chinese studies and to those taking the course only for a general education credit. In this class and others in which I teach films from China's early socialist period, I have found that using these films to inspire student learning around intersectionality is particularly effective. The films *The White-Haired Girl* (白毛女), *Five Golden Flowers* (五朵金花), and *Li Shuangshuang* (李双双) present compelling depictions of intersecting class, gender, and ethnic identities that students can understand and analyze. These and other films from China's early socialist period, when paired with appropriate readings, assignments, and discussion questions, can be a useful medium for thinking through issues of intersectionality in China and potentially beyond it.

Intersectionality as Concept and Analytic Frame

Intersectionality is a nexus of concerns that, in its most basic formulation, points to the need to consider multiple identity categories together when analyzing the interface between individual experience and social structures.[2] Intersectionality highlights problems of compounding inequities and structural violence around issues of race, gender, and class, but it also extends to similar concerns around sexual orientation, ability, ethnicity, nationality, religion, education, and so on. In the United States, the academic concept of intersectionality grew out of a particular history of Black feminist thought as a way to recognize the compounding pressures faced by Black women and others whose identities make them vulnerable to multiple forms of discrimination, structural inequities, and violence.[3]

Intellectual and social historians have pointed to the ways in which early Chinese feminists advanced complex analyses of their own social worlds that anticipated, and at times went beyond, contemporary conceptions of intersectionality. Lydia Liu, Rebecca Karl, and Dorothy Ko argue that the concepts of *nannü* (男女; "man and woman" or "male-female") and *shengji* (生计; "livelihood"), theorized in a series of 1907 essays by the Chinese feminist woman writer He-Yin Zhen, offer fundamental critiques of the social operations of patriarchy that are more comprehensive and enabling than the notions of sex, gender, and class in contemporary US intersectional discourse. Using historical archives of the Shanghai Women's Federation, Wang Zheng examines the intellectual, cultural, and activist work of Chinese feminists who advanced intersectional agendas from their positions within organs of the Chinese Communist Party during the early years of the People's Republic of China, when the films I examine in this essay were produced. Liu and colleagues and Wang show the value of bringing questions of intersectionality into studies of twentieth-century China. In my work on Chinese dance in the early People's Republic of China, I have shown how the concept of intersectionality is useful for interpreting the political messages in China's socialist performance culture, including dance films (Wilcox, *Revolutionary Bodies*).

In this essay, I focus on two relationships that are especially salient in films from early socialist China: between gender and class and between class and ethnicity.[4] When teaching intersectionality through Chinese films from the early socialist era, I guide students to attend to these two relationships as both historical problems and cinematic themes. Below I outline strategies and approaches to this pedagogical objective through the discussion of specific films and assignments.

Gender and Class in *Li Shuangshuang* and *The White-Haired Girl*

In my course Revolution in Life: How Communism Changed China, I use the films *The White-Haired Girl* and *Li Shuangshuang* to deepen students' thinking about the intersecting issues of gender and class in China's socialist revolution. Because *The White-Haired Girl* is set during the period of land reform, and *Li Shuangshuang* during the period of rural collectivization, the films also help students see how women and men experienced these significant social movements and how messages about gender and class struggle were handled differently in different periods.

The class is divided into three units: (1) Comparative Trajectories—Communist Revolution from Marx to Lenin to Mao; (2) Communism at the Ground Level—Revolution as Lived Experience; and (3) Revolutions of Thought—The Communist Media Sphere. *Li Shuangshuang* is assigned in the last week of unit 2, and *The White-Haired Girl* is introduced at the beginning of unit 3. Thus, before students watch either film, they spend about eight weeks learning about communist thought and the histories of socialist revolution in Russia and China.

As part of their preparation for interpreting films from the early socialist era, students learn about the ideological underpinnings of socialist cultural production as well as the historical contexts represented in each film. We begin the first unit with a class session devoted to discussing retrospective accounts of the Cold War from opposing political perspectives. This discussion achieves two goals: to offer a general overview of the period and its global significance and to introduce the idea that the history of anti-communism shapes understandings of socialist China in the United States. Next we spend two weeks learning the basics of Marxist thought and the history of the Russian Revolution. Then we spend five weeks learning about the historical development of communist political thought and the Communist revolution in China. Students learn about the evolution of the Chinese Communist Party (CCP) and Mao Zedong as a political, intellectual, and cultural leader. They also engage in in-depth readings on land reform, women's experiences of rural transformation in the 1950s, and, to prepare them to watch *The White-Haired Girl*, the development of revolutionary culture in Yan'an. Because the readings are challenging and sometimes dense, I provide in-class quizzes to ensure students have read and processed the readings before we discuss them. As a result of this in-depth study, students gain a strong grounding in both the major concepts in international communist thought and the concrete historical challenges of applying these ideas in practice in the Soviet Union and the People's Republic of China.

An important goal throughout the course is for me to help students think through the relationship between abstract political ideology, on the one hand, and its concrete transformation and adaptation in social praxis, on the other. Because this first-year seminar doubles as a writing course, students engage with these questions through in-class discussions and a series of three-to-five-page analytic papers, which require students to synthesize their learning at the end of each of the three class units. The prompt for the paper assignment in the first unit is as follows: "Karl Marx's ideas set up a theoretical basis for communist revolution, but the Bolsheviks in Russia and the CCP in China were the first to put those ideas into practice. Given the Soviet and Chinese examples, identify what you believe are the three defining features of a communist revolution and discuss whether Marx predicted them, based on what you've read so far in the course." Through writing this paper, students learn to differentiate between communism as a set of ideas and its application in practice. Furthermore, they learn to distinguish between the communism of Marx and Friedrich Engels and that of leaders such as Vladimir Lenin and Mao, who adapted it to their local contexts.

The prompt for the paper assignment in the second unit, in which *Li Shuangshuang* is assigned, asks students to think about how individuals in China experienced the revolutionary movements of the late 1940s and 1950s, including those relating to land reform, the marriage law, new approaches to women's labor and health, and rural collectivization. The main text that students read to prepare them to interpret *Li Shuangshuang* is a book about the lives of rural women in 1950s China, Gail Hershatter's

2011 *The Gender of Memory: Rural Women and China's Collective Past.* As a feminist historian, Hershatter centers the voices of rural women by employing oral history as a key research methodology. In this unit I require students to conduct their own interview with a person who grew up in China, as a way for them to gain a personal connection to the subject matter and think through questions about what individual stories can tell us about history. Since each student gives a ten-minute presentation on the life of their interviewee to the class during unit 2, students have this additional context when they encounter their first socialist film, *Li Shuangshuang.*

With all of this preparation, students are able to engage in sophisticated discussions about the intersectional relationship between class and gender in *Li Shuangshuang,* a film about a rural couple struggling to adjust to women's changing social and economic roles on a collective farm. Students watch the film independently. To prompt discussion during class, I offer the following straightforward question: "What parts of the film do you see connecting with the readings we've done?" Because of the close connection between the film's content and the readings, students are able to quickly make incisive observations about the complicated ways new policies affected women's and men's lives and how individuals navigated their gender and class identities in this period. In less than ten minutes of open discussion, my students came up with the following insights:

> The subplot in which Guiying clashes with her parents over whom she should marry demonstrates how the Chinese government's new marriage law allowing women to choose their spouses was sometimes difficult to enforce and illuminates how class affects gender dynamics: Guiying wants to marry a lower-class man from the countryside whom she loves, but her parents pressure her to pursue an arranged marriage with a higher-class stranger from the city.
>
> The conflict between Li Shuangshuang and her husband over gender inequality in the distribution of work points in the village illuminates the historically documented imbalance in gender-based expectations about labor: women were expected to complete domestic tasks such as childcare and cooking while also laboring in the fields to earn work points.
>
> The conflict between Li Shuangshuang and her husband over Li's active participation in village politics and her public criticism of men who shirked their responsibilities illuminates the struggle over

changing expectations about appropriate gendered behavior and women's roles in rural society.

The conflicting responses to Li Shuangshuang's capability and public leadership—Li is praised for being intelligent and having good ideas but then demeaned and told that she is incapable of certain tasks—reflects a lingering double standard as well as the pervasive sexism faced by rural women even at a time of official state support for gender equality.

The film's depictions of women bringing their sewing to political meetings reflects the reality that women were expected to carry out domestic labor while also engaging in new kinds of work: these expectations were exhausting and unrealistic for rural women but were part of the national drive for productivity and collectivization.

In the film, the receptivity of conservative and powerful men to legitimate criticisms from women in the village seemed more optimistic than realistic, reflecting more what was supposed to happen than what actually did happen.

The fact that Li Shuangshuang's husband abandons Li and their daughter several times during the film yet faces few consequences from the other villagers reflects the continued greater mobility of men during this period and the looser expectations about men's family obligations compared to the mobility of women and expectations about the obligations of women of the same economic status.

The film uses comedy to point out serious problems in a light-hearted and accessible way, serving effectively as an educational medium for rural Chinese audiences of the period.

In their papers for this unit, students also identified additional themes. For example, one student observes that the film warns of the possibility for new social classes to develop in a socialist society, by showing how male village leaders abused their status and homosocial friend networks to evade work. Another student writes about the film's critique of the limitations of the work point system in collective farming, such as incentivizing the pursuit of speed over quality in farm labor. One student, Linda Li, nicely demonstrates intersectional thinking in the following passage in her essay for unit 2, where she analyzes *Li Shuangshuang* in conversation with Hershatter's work:

In tandem with the general peasant population advancing towards financial security, women's lives were specifically impacted by the communist revolution in the labor force. Women were actively encouraged to work in the fields by the central Party commission, to the extent that "[agriculture] gradually became the major content of women's work" (Hershatter 130). With married and unmarried women working alongside men, formerly isolated women were granted the chance to expand their social ties vastly. Although female labor participation rates were uneven across rural areas, women who did leave their domestic chores during the day forged unique bonds with other women and experienced livelier atmospheres (137). The Party's mission to mobilize women paved the path for reshuffling women's duties compared to the pre-liberation period when it was taboo for women to spend too much time outside the home. Women were recognized as capable of contributing to the local economy; they integrated work schedules into their domestic lives and earned work points for their labor. Many women utilized their newfound roles to clinch leadership positions, teach themselves and others necessary skills, and get paid under their names—all of which were breakthroughs from the previous feudal traditions (137–39). Undoubtedly, women's active participation [was] critical to agricultural co-operatives' success. On the flip side, the Party's rush to add women to the labor force left little room to debate the gender wage gap, biological differences between men and women, and women's health issues. As the desire to earn work points consumed the peasants' lives, the stress was multiplied for women as they had to work the same amount as men while attending to childcare duties. In the film *Li Shuangshuang* (1962), the protagonist Li Shuangshuang, a diligent and charismatic mother and agricultural laborer, tells her husband that she earned four work points that day. Her husband retorts that a male villager Sun You earned ten points in less time than her. This scene sheds light on the deep-seated inequality that persisted throughout the liberation era, as women themselves did not necessarily see the wage gap as a structural problem—in Hershatter's interviews, the real life women said that biological differences justified their lower pay (141).[5]

Students have offered similarly nuanced readings of the imbrication of gender and class in the film *The White-Haired Girl*, which they watch one week after seeing *Li Shuangshuang*. Whereas students are mainly prepared to analyze *Li Shuangshuang* in terms of the film's narrative content, I prepare them to think critically about both the content and the aesthetic strategies in *The White-Haired Girl*. The main textual reference for analyzing *The White-Haired Girl*'s content—peasant-landlord conflict as a pretext for class struggle during the period of land reform—is selections from William Hinton's 1966 classic *Fanshen: A Documentary of Revolu-*

tion in a Chinese Village.[6] Students read the Hinton selections and write about them in the second unit. However, whereas the second unit focuses on how individual lives were shaped by the revolution, the third and final unit turns students' attention to the role that culture played in this process and the strategies of cultural production that were advocated in early socialist China to make culture and art serve revolutionary transformation. Before students watch *The White-Haired Girl,* I also have them read Ellen Judd's 1985 essay "Prelude to the 'Yan'an Talks': Problems in Transforming a Literary Intelligentsia" along with Mao Zedong's epoch-making 1942 "Talks at the Yan'an Forum on Literature and Art," a canonical text determining official policy for cultural production in socialist China.

With these readings as background, students engaged in intersectional analysis of *The White-Haired Girl* by identifying the pivotal role that sexual violence played in advancing a narrative that was primarily intended to represent and encourage class struggle in the context of land reform. Students noted how the scene in which the landlord's son Huang Shiren rapes the young peasant heroine, Xi'er, conveys viscerally the harshness of class exploitation in prerevolutionary rural China. They also pointed out that the scene produces empathy in viewers for the peasants and antipathy for landlords and that it could easily have incited anger among audiences when it was initially released. Students noted that the film was heartbreaking and difficult to watch because it reveals the dynamics of absolute power and exploitation and that they could see how the film would be effective in glorifying the Communist movement in peasants' eyes.

To encourage students to think about formal elements of the film, I reminded them of the readings we had done about the use of folk forms in literature and art in Yan'an and explained that the film was adapted from an opera that had been developed in Yan'an shortly after Mao's talks of 1942. With this prompt, students quickly identified folk singing as one of the creative elements the filmmakers had incorporated into the film to popularize it and help it appeal to rural audiences. While a few students found the singing difficult to appreciate, they still understood how it served strategically to instill a rural aesthetic sensibility in the film and how this strategy reflected the efforts of CCP intellectuals to incorporate rural folk forms into their literary and art works and make them enjoyable and understandable to rural viewers. Students noted that the singing conveyed both anguish and resolution, pain as well as power. Apart from the singing, the students also noted the cinematic use of extended close-ups on characters' faces to emphasize emotion and encourage empathetic viewing. They further identified scenes of beautiful countryside and crops as appealing to the idea that the land was a precious resource and the center of life and meaning for rural communities.

Finally, by thinking of this film as a form of socialist education, students also identified its potential shortcomings. One student, for example, commented that having the female lead be rescued in the end by a group of men undermines the message of gender equality, which was supposed to be part of CCP values. Others noted that the film's portrayal of Xi'er's father being physically forced to sell his daughter discounts the normalization of child selling in prerevolutionary society, which itself attested to the dire economic situation in rural communities. Students further observed that the film presents peasants as highly united, glossing over the internal divisions and fear that arose among peasants during the period of land reform as well as the gradations within peasant-landlord relations that made class struggle and land reform a complex affair. Students felt that by reducing these complexities the film gains accessibility, which was one of Mao's stated goals for socialist culture. However, in gaining accessibility the film elides issues that would have been relevant to audiences at the time, such as teaching class consciousness and allaying fears of retribution when encouraging peasant revolt.

In sum, when students are prepared to understand and appreciate the complex issues at work in China's early socialist cinema, films from the period can serve as a powerful vector animating intersectional analysis that is both historically grounded and far-reaching.

Gender and Ethnicity in *Five Golden Flowers*

Five Golden Flowers is the last early-socialist-era film I show in my first-year seminar, and it serves as a way to introduce considerations of ethnic diversity. Although the film is set in an ethnic-minority context, students identify clear continuities between *Five Golden Flowers* and the other two films. They note the use of folk songs in all three films as a way to connect to rural audiences, and they also identify the shared elements of comedy and portrayals of marital strife in *Li Shuangshuang* and *Five Golden Flowers* as reflecting on social change and women's new roles in society. They also see in all three films strong endorsements for collective action, enthusiasm for work, and celebration of those who willingly help others. Because of these strong commonalities, some students argued that *Five*

Golden Flowers conveys the message that Han and non-Han peoples in China are not different from one another.

I find this reaction from students striking and significant given how often China's ethnic minority films are described in scholarly writing as markedly distinct from other films of the socialist period.[7] As Yanshuo Zhang discusses in her essay in this volume, students lacking prior familiarity with China often require guidance to identify non-Han cultural markers in ethnic minority films. Students who possess greater knowledge of Chinese ethnic representation, including international students from China, are often able to discern these differences. However, they still notice that the markers of ethnicity in *Five Golden Flowers* are relatively superficial—or as one student put it, "decorative"—and are limited largely to costume, music, and festivals. From this perspective, students noted, *Five Golden Flowers* conveys a message that all of China's ethnic groups, regardless of cultural differences, are expected to contribute equally to China's socialist national construction. In the film, Bai women and men are shown contributing in ways similar to their Han counterparts, such as to steel ore production, the collectivization of agriculture, and the promotion of gender equality in areas such as marriage choice, political leadership, and professional work.

A clear opportunity for students to connect *Five Golden Flowers* with the course readings and engage in intersectional analysis appears in the film's treatment of Han urban intellectuals who visit ethnic minority regions to study and collect folk materials. In the film, two men from the Changchun Film Studio—one a musician collecting folk songs and the other an artist collecting ethnic scenes and visual designs—visit the Bai village and contribute to the film's comedy of errors through their lack of local knowledge and misunderstandings of local customs. While students typically cannot recognize these characters on their own, with guidance they can realize that these characters are representations of the CCP intellectuals discussed in Judd's essay and Mao's Yan'an talks. The film's portrayal of these two characters as benign and well-intentioned is an official endorsement of the rural-to-urban and minority-to-majority transfers of cultural knowledge that were normalized in Chinese socialist cultural production. At the same time, the humorous depiction of these characters as somewhat bumbling and naive also indicates a space within Chinese socialist films for self-reflection and even light self-mockery, since the characters can be seen as stand-ins for the makers of *Five Golden Flowers*, which was a product of the real Changchun Film Studio.

In their essays for unit 3, students are asked to identify common elements that run through China's socialist culture from the pre-1949 era, through the first seventeen years of Communist rule (1949–65) and the Cultural Revolution (1966–76), and into the post–Cultural Revolution era. One theme that many students identify, in *Five Golden Flowers* and other socialist period films, is the presence of strong female protagonists who exemplify new ideals and models for socialist identity formation. In these films, leading characters often inhabit several social identities that were oppressed in prerevolutionary society. Thus, the heroines Xi'er and Li Shuangshuang identify as women and are of rural, lower-class status in *The White-Haired Girl* and *Li Shuangshuang*, respectively, and the heroine Jinhua identifies as a woman and has an ethnic minority identity in *Five Golden Flowers*.

The exploration of intersectional identity and experience is a key driver of much of the early socialist cinema in China. Overcoming one source of oppression would not have been enough to make a character in these films truly inspiring or educational to the films' original audiences; rather, the compounding of oppressions is what contributes to their memorable and moving impact. When they are given the necessary background to appreciate the messages in these films and the strategies through which they are communicated, students learn to challenge their preconceived notions about socialist culture.[8] At the same time, they gain skills of intersectional analysis that they can apply in other courses as well as in their own lives.

Notes

1. For more on teaching *To Live* and *Yellow Earth*, see the essays in this volume by Chenshu Zhou, Ping Zhu, and Ho Chak Law.

2. Discussions of intersectionality have extended into more complex terrain. However, in the context of a first-year seminar, I employ this more basic understanding as a way to introduce students to the larger conversation.

3. Crenshaw coined the term *intersectionality* in 1991, but Collins and Bilge identify key principles of intersectional thought in the intellectual production and activism of Black women, Chicanas, Asian American women, and Native women in the United States during the 1960s; for an example of this production, see Beal. Since the 1990s the work of Crenshaw and others have led to a blossoming of intersectionality studies in the US academy, a field that has also joined international discourses in feminist scholarship and social activism.

4. For more on gender and ethnicity, see Yanshuo Zhang's essay in this volume.

5. Reproduced with permission by Li.

6. Selections are Hinton xxi–xxv, 1–68, 128–56, 198–209, 243–58.

7. For more on how ethnic minority–themed cultural production during the early socialist period often bears a strong resemblance to Han-themed cultural production of the time, see Wilcox, "Beyond Internal Orientalism." For a reading of *Five Golden Flowers* that challenges standard claims made about the exoticization of ethnic minorities in the film, see Ban Wang.

8. For more on strategies for teaching about PRC history, see DeMare and Meyskens.

Works Cited

Beal, Frances. *Double Jeopardy: To be Black and Female.* Third World Women's Alliance, 1969.

Collins, Patricia Hill, and Sirma Bilge. *Intersectionality.* Polity Press, 2016.

Crenshaw, Kimberlé. "Mapping the Margins: Intersectionality, Identity Politics, and Violence against Women of Color." *Stanford Law Review,* vol. 43, 1991, pp. 1241–99.

DeMare, Brian, and Covell Meyskens, editors. *Teaching the PRC,* special issue of *PRC History Review.* Vol. 6, no. 4, 2021, prchistory.org/review-october-2021.

Farewell My Concubine. Directed by Chen Kaige, Tomson Films / China Film Co-production / Beijing Film Studio, 1993.

Five Golden Flowers. Directed by Wang Jiayi, Changchun Film Studio, 1959.

Hershatter, Gail. *The Gender of Memory: Rural Women and China's Collective Past.* U of California Press, 2011.

Hinton, William. *Fanshen: A Documentary of Revolution in a Chinese Village.* Monthly Review Press, 2008.

Judd, Ellen. "Prelude to the 'Yan'an Talks': Problems in Transforming a Literary Intelligentsia." *Modern China,* vol. 11, no. 3, 1985, pp. 377–403.

Li Shuangshuang. Directed by Lu Ren, Haiyan Film Studio, 1962.

Liu, Lydia He, et al., editors. *The Birth of Chinese Feminism: Essential Texts in Transnational Theory.* Columbia UP, 2013.

Mao Zedong. "Talks at the Yan'an Forum on Literature and Art." *Modern Chinese Literary Thought: Writings on Literature, 1893–1945,* edited by Kirk Denton, Stanford UP, 1996, pp. 458–84.

To Live. Directed by Zhang Yimou, ERA International / Shanghai Film Studio, 1994.

Wang, Ban. "Laughter, Ethnicity, and Socialist Utopia: *Five Golden Flowers.*" *Maoist Laughter,* edited by Ping Zhu et al., Hong Kong UP, 2020, pp. 19–36.

Wang Zheng. *Finding Women in the State: A Socialist Feminist Revolution in the People's Republic of China, 1949–1964.* U of California P, 2017.

The White-Haired Girl. Directed by Wang Bin and Shui Hua, Northeast Film Studio, 1950.

Wilcox, Emily. "Beyond Internal Orientalism: Dance and Nationality Discourse in the Early People's Republic of China, 1949–1954." *Journal of Asian Studies,* vol. 75, no. 2, 2016, pp. 363–86.

———. *Revolutionary Bodies: Chinese Dance and the Socialist Legacy.* U of California P, 2018.

Yellow Earth. Directed by Chen Kaige, Guangxi Film Studio, 1984.

Angie C. Baecker

Cultural Revolution Films and Their Production History

One of the biggest challenges faced by instructors of modern Chinese culture is the perception among students that Chinese cultural production from the Maoist period amounts to propaganda. This assumption—that the meaning of a cultural text from Maoist China is self-evident—has a reductive effect in the classroom, stripping away notions of artistic merit and creative agency while flattening the historical specificity and complexity of cultural production into a space of predetermined meaning. This effect is especially compounded in the study of the Cultural Revolution, conventionally defined as lasting from 1966 to 1976, a period whose culture is so closely associated with its failed revolutions that it may seem impossible for any distance to exist between the period's twin projects of culture and revolution.

Nonetheless, artistic products of the Cultural Revolution constitute some of the most visible domestic and international representations of the People's Republic of China during the Maoist era, from performances of the revolutionary ballet *The Red Detachment of Women* (红色娘子军) to screenings of the film based on the ballet, and of films such as *The White-Haired Girl* (白毛女) and *The Red Lantern* (红灯记). Yet although the period is named after its culture, some scholars display a surprising reluctance to explore the nature of the role played by culture during the period, instead treating films or operas produced during the decade as disputed political texts.[1] Thus, the widespread assumption that all Maoist cultural production was propaganda and that the Cultural Revolution in particular was devoid of culture has the effect of rendering the culture of the late 1960s to mid-1970s something of an ontological impossibility.

This essay proposes that the culture of the Cultural Revolution can and should be taught in the classroom through a more critical perspective, specifically through the use of production studies as a pedagogical framework for introducing undergraduate students to films from the period. Production studies uses what John Caldwell calls "an integrated cultural-industrial method of analysis" to present film and television as an industrial practice (Caldwell 4). Within this practice, "authorship [is] inherently protracted, collective, and contested" by the workers involved in a film's production (201). Production studies rejects an understanding of film solely through the final product and isolated from the systems and circumstances of filmic production. Instead, it treats "production communities themselves [as] cultural expressions and entities involving all of the symbolic processes and collective practices" of any meaning-producing cultural practice (2). I argue that an emphasis on the film production process can productively challenge students' assumptions regarding films as propaganda and complicate the direct causal relationship presumed between the form of a work and its message.

To provide insight into how a film was made, I suggest that instructors assign primary source reading materials published during the Cultural Revolution in English alongside films from the period (see the appendix for materials in English; Chinese-language sources may also be assigned, as appropriate). These materials are written by film producers, directors, screenwriters, actors, cinematographers, score composers, dancers, and musicians, among others, who reflect on creative decisions they faced during the production process. By exploring the decisions made by a film's cast and crew, students begin to see cultural production in Maoist China as an inherently contested, collective, and experimental site of creative cultural production. By establishing basic familiarity with the industrial production processes of Maoist filmmaking, students can contextualize Chinese films from the period not as an aberrant and isolated form of cultural production but within a greater context of global industrial film history. I conclude this essay with reflections on how a deeper engagement with the culture of the Cultural Revolution not only renders propaganda an active, complex, and multisited process of contextualization but may also challenge some of the implicit assumptions instructors and students bring to the idea of culture itself.

Production History as a Pedagogical Framework

In an essay on approaches to teaching the Cultural Revolution, the historian Denise Ho identifies two existing pedagogical frameworks for teaching the Cultural Revolution in the classroom: the affective and cognitive approaches. The affective approach relies on exposing students to "personal stories and their ability to move" (24); such stories might include Jung Chang's memoir *Wild Swans* and revisionist films depicting the period, such as *To Live* (活着). The cognitive approach supplies students with substantive qualitative research and theoretical frameworks for understanding the Cultural Revolution.

Ho advocates for teaching the Cultural Revolution through a combination of the affective and cognitive approaches, however difficult that balance may be to strike in practice. "No classroom introduction to the Cultural Revolution is complete without some reference to its place in memory, or to its legacies," she writes, but she notes that the affective approach can be misleading when students are not given a greater context for understanding individual stories. On the other hand, an overreliance on the cognitive framework can result in distanced engagement, which Ho sees as a lost opportunity for harnessing the strong emotional animus students often bring to studying the period. If these frameworks are so fraught, then why do they remain necessary? Ho's answer is that they are necessary because we cannot always "examine historical subjects on their own terms" (26). In other words, primary sources from the period are not honest brokers of historical knowledge, nor are students likely to see them as such. Indeed, as Ho points out, "[m]any students will believe that materials from the Cultural Revolution . . . are inherently untrue" and will "focus on seeking some kind of absolute truth behind the veil" (25).

Even when students bring to the classroom the assumption that primary sources from the period intend to communicate a didactic message about the Cultural Revolution, they do not necessarily know what the Cultural Revolution was intended to signify. This is because the purpose and meaning of the Cultural Revolution was deeply contested within its own time (Wu 9). Examining art and culture from the Cultural Revolution can help students and scholars to approach the values that cultural creators believed the Cultural Revolution was intended to embody, or to better understand the ideals of the period. In this regard, no film, or other single work of art, can provide access to the entire political signification of the Cultural Revolution, no matter how prominently it was associated with the political project of the period.

Instead, filmmaking, including filmmaking during the Cultural Revolution, should be presented as an inherently collective industrial creative process. Indeed, what may be historically specific about films from the period are the cultural precepts operative in those films' releases, which may be surprisingly parallel to precepts operative in the release of a major film today. A film made in the PRC during the 1960s and 1970s was neither a work of art made by a visionary auteur nor a work of capitalist corporate entertainment; films of the time were instead made to shape and reflect national mass culture, to showcase socialist culture and entertainment, and to defend national policies. This is an insight echoed in production studies, which sees the communities producing films and television programming as "cultural expressions and entities involving all of the symbolic processes and collective practices that other cultures use: to gain and reinforce identity, to forge consensus and order, to perpetuate themselves and their interests, and to interpret the media as audience members" (Caldwell 2).

Instead of understanding the centralized production apparatuses for Cultural Revolution films as a monolith, instructors can break down the socialist film industry into its component parts and present it as something more akin to Bruno Latour's actor-network, in which the creative process (or "cognition") is distributed across the group's industrial practice (46). Indeed, as Timothy Cheek has written, films produced in Maoist China were not intended to be interpreted in isolation (or as art for art's sake) but as exemplars of a new mass culture that participated in contemporary grassroots mobilization campaigns (14–15). Films were thus contextualized in a variety of ways, as Laurence Coderre demonstrates in her reading of the 1976 film *Counterattack* (反击). While some of that interpretative framing would have been implicitly understood by the films' intended viewers because of their lived historical experience, the publication of a host of different types of writing on each film was also an essential component of the overall meaning-making process for each film.

Coderre calls these publications the constitutive "contextualization" of a filmic text and considers them as part of a larger interpretative project (212), while Tina Mai Chen understands these writings as attempts to define the permissible boundaries of discourse around a film and its content and to construct a film's ideal audience through the modeling of appropriate responses. The contextualization of a film can also be understood as industrial reflexivity, a creative process where human agency and critical, interpretative competence manifest at the level of the individual encounter, distributing the creative agency across social registers. Exposing students to different accounts of a film's production process exposes them to different registers of this process of contextualization and signification, demonstrating how multisited the filmmaking process is.

Contextualizing Film Publications

In hindsight, it's clear that filmmaking during the Cultural Revolution left behind an inconsistent record. The history of filmmaking during the decade overlaps with much of the political periodization of the Cultural Revolution, but this periodization should not be adopted wholesale for the Cultural Revolution's film history: cultural histories are not equivalent to political histories, and the periodization of the Cultural Revolution is highly contested.[2]

Instructors may briefly characterize the film production of the period: during the height of Red Guard activity, from 1966 to 1967, no new films went into production with the exception of newsreels (Zhuoyi Wang 171–82; Clark, *Chinese Cinema* 125–53).[3] During this period, institutions of cultural production halted activities or were significantly reorganized. Following the military suppression of the Red Guard movement in late 1968, filming activity began cautiously with the Beijing Film Studio's film adaptation of a staged Peking opera performance, *Taking Tiger Mountain by Strategy* (智取威虎山). Nearly without exception, films released from 1970 to 1973 were cinematic stagings of revolutionary operas and ballets written and adapted during the Cultural Revolution: *wutai yishu pian* (舞台艺术片; "theatrical stagings"), such as *Shajiabang* (沙家浜) and *On the Docks* (海港). Jiang Qing played a large role in developing the distinctive styles and formal languages of these productions (Gu).[4] In 1974, a drive to increase production of original *gushipian* (故事片; "feature films") resulted in a marked increase in the number of new films released year to year: according to Paul Clark, only four films were released in 1973, compared to seventeen in 1974, twenty-five in 1975, and thirty-seven in 1976 (*Chinese Cinema* 185). This trend was hampered by the political watersheds of 1976 (Mao Zedong's death and the arrest of the Gang of Four and six high-ranking military leaders), but by 1978 the film industry had recovered, and in the early 1980s more than one hundred films were being released every year.

Publications from the socialist period that comment on major films fall roughly into the following categories: screenplays, narrative synopses, film reviews, essays on new genres and performance formats (such as the revolutionary ballet and revolutionary Peking opera), reflections by screenwriters or screenwriting collectives on the process of adapting different media into film, accounts by performers of their preparation for prominent roles, directors' commentaries, essays by cinematographers, and responses to films by audience members, in particular members of the *gongnongbing qunzhong* (工农兵群众; "worker-peasant-soldier masses"). There is considerable variation in the substance of individual responses to or accounts of a film's production, although the political language used is quite consistent.

For example, in first-person essays, performers such as actors, dancers, and singers reflect on the pressures of being cast in nationally prominent roles. Young and relatively unknown actors were often cast in leading roles, especially in feature films from late in the Cultural Revolution, such as *Spring Shoots* (春苗), *Red Rain* (红雨), and *Sparkling Red Star* (闪闪的红星). Chu Xinyun was cast as Pan Dongzi (Winter Boy) in *Sparkling Red Star* at the age of twelve. In addition to lacking professional experience, these young actors sometimes came from vastly different backgrounds than their characters did. As performers, they often belonged to professional performance groups and came from urban, educated backgrounds, whereas the characters they depicted tended to be rural, uneducated proletarians.

Performers took different approaches to the challenges of getting into character. Shi Zhongqin, one of two dancers playing Xi'er, the eponymous protagonist in *The White-Haired Girl*, writes that as "a young ballet dancer enjoying the happiness of life in New China," she had never "experienced the hardships of the old society" (Shih 103). For Shi, understanding the traumatic experiences of an older generation was the key to understanding Xi'er. Other actors created an entirely different affect for their roles. Yang Chunxia, an actor in *Azalea Mountain* (杜鹃山), discusses violating the taboos of traditional Peking opera for her role. "When I played feudal young ladies it was a rule that 'the wrists should not project from the sleeves, the teeth must not be revealed when smiling, the skirts must not be ruffled when walking.' It would be quite impossible to portray our workers, peasants, and soldiers with such conventions" (Yang Chun-hsia 122). For Li Xiuming, an actor in *Spring Shoots*, a physical transformation was necessary to look the part. "During rehearsal, when I saw how white and smooth my hands were, I felt ashamed," she writes. But after embedding herself in a rural Jiangxi rice-growing community, her hands became "strong and callused. I felt I could carry the role" (Li Hsiu-ming 39). In an even more extreme case, *Sparkling Red Star*'s child star describes finding the motivation to drop pounds for his role as the undernourished preliberation Pan Dongzi (Chu Hsin-yun). The actors took these varied approaches to performance in order to create a credibly textured performance that achieves the overall aesthetic principles of combining revolutionary realism with revolutionary romanticism.

In the classroom, one film can be taught in tandem with first-person accounts of its production to illustrate the multisited nature of filmmaking as a creative process. Students can, for instance, watch *Sparkling Red Star* while consulting its script and then discuss the film alongside written comments about the production by the film's lead actor, screenwriter, cinematographer, and codirector. The actor Chu Xinyun describes his understanding of the film's lead character and his process for getting into character, which involved performing the same physical activities as those performed by Pan Dongzi, such as chopping wood and transporting kindling on shoulder poles (Chu Hsin-yun). The screenwriter Lu Chuguo offers extensive remarks on how he isolated key narrative elements from the film's source novel while writing the film's script. Lu's script cuts away nearly fifteen years from the novel, axing extraneous antagonists and adding scenes highlighting the material scarcity and provisional nature of guerilla warfare in order to zero in on the main character's experience of the Second Sino-Japanese War (Lu Chu-kuo). The cinematographer Cai Zhiwei describes his decision to create a distinctive tonal landscape for the film through the use of forest green spiked with pops of bright red. The colors become "linked dialectically" through the invocation of red at moments of revolutionary passion, while green underscores depictions of "the Winter Boy and the revolutionary people. . . . A dot of red in the ocean of green conveys a deeper meaning to the saying 'living things depend on the sun for their growth'" (Tsai 103). The codirector Li Jun describes how he sought to create a visual language for the film to illustrate its central narrative of the heart-rending experiences that lead a chipper young child to a political awakening. Li's overarching goal was to create a film with "evocative power" (Li Chun 94), and his comments on how he constructs an evocative "sublime" through the combination of sounds, images, and the direction of the actor helps students unpack the formal and affective choices that go into making a film (95).

Another guiding principle of Cultural Revolution filmmaking was to turn "the stage over to workers, peasants, and soldiers" in order to redress their long-standing exploitation (Chu Lan 91). But if film narratives were meant to center the stories of the proletarian underclasses, how exactly should the agency of the downtrodden be portrayed? Performers and producers alike struggled with this question. The dancer Mao Huifang describes performing Xi'er's dramatic escape from her village by swaying and tottering "to show her difficulty in fording a stream" (Mao Hui-fang 102). But after receiving feedback from a former peasant, who found Mao's demeanor unlike those of existing peasant women, Mao changed her interpretation to focus less on Xi'er's frailty and more on the character's capacity for enduring hardship. Qian Haoliang and Liu Changyu, vocalists of *The Red Lantern*, adapted the film's musical score to highlight the agency of the central character even while he is incarcerated: "What formerly was an instrumental passage between two verses, we have expanded into a long piano solo showing that although Li's body is confined to jail, his mind embraces the entire world" (Chien and Liu 23).

Ideally, the filmmaking process itself would reflect the collective, democratic ideals of the film. Narratives were streamlined around proletarian heroes who were intended to typify and embody a higher truth that was rooted in the people. Thus, when adapting prerevolutionary narratives to revolutionary contexts or works in one medium to another, creators like the screenwriter Lu Chuguo worked by starting "from the real life of the masses, [typifying] the conflicts and struggles . . . , and [re-creating them]. Our principle was to adhere faithfully to the spirit of the original, but not to be restricted by its details" (Lu Chu-kuo 87–88). Film executives like Sang Hu, director of *The White-Haired Girl*, challenged the hegemony of above-the-line creatives by discarding the typical hierarchies of decision-making on a set: "In the past filmmaking the director's word was law. . . . But during the cultural revolution we debunked this lack of democratic discussion and adopted the system of democratic centralism. . . . We consulted [cast and crew] at every stage, sometimes making alterations or additions on the base of their suggestions." This practice was also adopted on the set of the director Li Wenhua's *Breaking with Old Ideas* (决裂).

Ultimately, the pursuit of the "unity of revolutionary political content and the highest possible perfection of artistic form" resulted in the perception that performance works from the Cultural Revolution successfully unified function with form (Chu Lan 90).[5] Thus, scenes were blocked to highlight "the positive character among all the roles," "the heroic characters among the positive," and "the principal hero, that is, the chief character among the heroic characters" (Shen 109). These points of emphasis were visually signified by the lead character anchoring the most central and elevated spot on a set, a practice characteristic of film and stage productions of the time. Ironically, the assumption of a supposed unity between medium and message obscures the extent to which the formal language of filmmaking was itself a key site of experimentation during the Maoist period.

The Cultural Revolution challenges the typical frameworks instructors and students bring to the study of Chinese culture. Whether or not students see Maoist film as propaganda, my hope is that by the end of a unit on the production history of Cultural Revolution films, they will understand filmmaking in socialist China as a complex process of experimentation and contextualization that asks to be actively read in order for its meaning to become legible. Indeed, precisely because the autonomy of culture during the period is so fraught, instructors and students must question what exactly they understand culture to be. Is culture to be thought of primarily as an artistic practice? If so, should the emphasis be on the final product or the process of its making? Or should culture be understood anthropologically as the formation of a "whole way of life" (Williams 13) and as manifested in the learned and shared symbolic codes that govern our lives?

In fact, the Cultural Revolution rejected adherence to either sense of culture, for it aimed explicitly to create a specifically socialist fine arts and culture that could compete with the fruits of capitalist civilization, even while it embraced culture as an Althusserian ideological state apparatus of persuasion and reproduction. Recognizing this tension allows us to shift the questions that we ask students about culture: What constitutes a strong and vibrant culture? What resources are necessary to foster the growth of a national culture, and is the vitality of culture predicated on the presence of a robust commercial market for culture? Are other distributions of cultural resources and arrangements of cultural infrastructure possible, and what role should the state play in their allocation? With greater attention to the particulars of representation as a discrete and embodied process, students and scholars can begin to answer these questions through the filmic texts and production publications of the Cultural Revolution.

Notes

1. For more on the reluctance of historians to address the cultural legacies of the Cultural Revolution see Clark's comments on MacFarquhar and Schoenhals's

authoritative survey of the Cultural Revolution (Clark, *Chinese Cultural Revolution* 2).

2. For a prominent alternative political periodization of the Cultural Revolution, see A. Chen.

3. The few films released in 1966 were productions that had begun prior to the start of the Cultural Revolution.

4. For additional accounts of Jiang Qing's role in filmmaking, see Wang Zheng 199–220; Inouye.

5. Chu Lan is a pen name believed to represent the views of the State Council Cultural Creation Leadership Small Group, which included Jiang Qing.

Appendix: Primary Source Readings in English

Culture of the Cultural Revolution

Ah Wen. "Three Young Artistes in the Revolution in Peking Opera." *Chinese Literature*, no. 9, 1974, pp. 95–103. Profiles of three performers who starred in films from the period.

Chiang Ching. "On the Revolution in Peking Opera." *Chinese Literature*, no. 8, 1967, pp. 118–24. July 1964 speech to theater workers on Peking opera.

Chu Lan. "A Decade of Revolution in Peking Opera." *Chinese Literature*, no. 9, 1974, pp. 85–94. Essay on the reinvention of Peking opera during the Cultural Revolution.

Hsin Hua. "Mass Debate on Revolution in Literature and Art." *Chinese Literature*, no. 6, 1976, pp. 102–08. Summary of a mass debate among workers, peasants, and soldiers about the direction of the arts.

Shen Hung-hsin. "Models in Depicting Proletarian Heroes." *Chinese Literature*, nos. 11–12, 1969, pp. 103–14. Transcript of a speech on the development of heroic and model characters in theater and film.

Tao Chu. "Some Problems Concerning Dramas on Revolutionary Modern Themes." *Chinese Literature*, no. 6, 1966, pp. 104–18. Report on the development of new and existing dramas with revolutionary themes.

Wen Hsiao. "China's Revolution in Literature and Art." *China Reconstructs*, no. 8, 1976, pp. 2–8. Overview of the most prominent cultural activity during the Cultural Revolution.

Yen Feng. "Continue to Advance along Chairman Mao's Line on Literature and Art." *Chinese Literature*, no. 8, 1976, pp. 85–94. Reflective comments on the decade of art and culture produced during the Cultural Revolution.

Azalea Mountain

Chu Lan. "*Azalea Mountain*, a Modern Revolutionary Peking Opera." *China Pictorial*, vol. 1, 1974, pp. 6–11. Film summary accompanied by color photographs.

"In Praise of the Proletarian Line in Army Building—about the Modern Revolutionary Peking Opera *Azalea Mountain*." *Peking Review*, vol. 4, 1974, pp. 8–12. Commentary on the historical significance of the film's plot.

Wang Shu-yuan. "Azaleas Bloom Red over the Mountains." *Chinese Literature*, no. 1, 1974, pp. 114–19. Dramatist's comments on stage and screen versions of *Azalea Mountain*.
Wang Shu-yuan et al. "*Azalea Mountain* (a Revolutionary Modern Peking Opera)." *Chinese Literature*, no. 1, 1974, pp. 3–69. Script.
Yang Chun-hsia. "What the Revolution in Literature and Art Has Taught Me." *Chinese Literature*, no. 7, 1976, pp. 116–23. Comments by the lead performer on her performance.

Breaking with Old Ideas

Breaking with Old Ideas. Directed by Li Wenhua, Voyager Press, 1986. VHS. With English subtitles.
Chun Chao and Chou Chieh. "Breaking with Old Ideas." *Chinese Literature*, no. 6, 1976, pp. 6–80. Script.
Li Wen-hua. "Strive to Depict Heroic Characters of the Proletariat." *Chinese Literature*, no. 10, 1976, pp. 111–14. Director's comments.
Tien Shih. "New Film: Breaking with Old Ideas." *Chinese Literature*, no. 10, 1976, pp. 91–98. Short summary of the film.

On the Docks

"*On the Docks* (a Revolutionary Model Peking Opera)." *Chinese Literature*, no. 1, 1969, pp. 3–53. Script.
On the Docks Group of the Peking Opera Troupe of Shanghai. "On the Docks." *Chinese Literature*, no. 5, 1972, pp. 52–98. Revised script.
Wen Chun. "An Opera on Proletarian Internationalism." *Chinese Literature*, no. 6, 1972, pp. 101–10. Review of the filmed production of the revised opera.
Wu Feng-chien et al. "Dockers Hail the Performance of 'On the Docks.'" *Chinese Literature*, no. 1, 1969, pp. 73–80. Commentary by three dock workers.

The Red Detachment of Women

China Ballet Troupe. "Red Detachment of Women." *Chinese Literature*, no. 1, 1971, pp. 3–80. Revised version of the script.
Chinese Literature editor. "The Film 'The Red Detachment of Women.'" *Chinese Literature*, no. 9, 1971, pp. 99–111. A review of the film based on interviews with the Filming Group of the Beijing Studio.
Hsueh Ching. "The Birth of the First Ballet with a Modern Revolutionary Theme." *Chinese Literature*, no. 3, 1967, pp. 9–12. Commentary by a ballet company member.
"A New Road for Chinese Ballet." *Chinese Literature*, no. 1, 1971, pp. 81–95. An editorial on the revised film staging of the ballet.
"Red Detachment of Women (A Revolutionary Model Ballet)." *Chinese Literature*, no. 5, 1969, pp. 3–14. Script.
Wu Hsiao-ching. "A Great Victory in 'Making Foreign Things Serve China.'" *Chinese Literature*, no. 5, 1969, pp. 78–86. A review of the ballet.

The Red Lantern

Chien Hao-liang and Liu Changyu. "Fight to Create New and Glorious Proletarian Arts." *Chinese Literature*, no. 9, 1968, pp. 18–23. The lead vocalists's commentary on the score and its performance.

Kao Cheng-en et al. "On 'The Red Lantern.'" *Chinese Literature*, no. 2, 1969, pp. 99–104. Workers' and soldiers' responses to the film.

Kao Liang. "'The Red Lantern' which Cannot Be Put Out." *Chinese Literature*, no. 3, 1967, pp. 19–23. Comments on Jiang Qing and military involvement in the production.

Kuo Fu-yu et al. "Sunlight and Dew Nourish New Flowers." *Chinese Literature*, no. 9, 1968, pp. 24–31. Responses to the film from workers, peasants, soldiers, and performers.

The Red Lantern Group of the China Peking Opera Troupe. "Struggle for the Creation of Typical Examples of Proletarian Heroes—an Appreciation of the Portrayal of Li Yu-ho's Heroic Image." *Chinese Literature*, no. 8, 1970, pp. 53–69. Article on the development of the film's main character.

Wen Ouhong and A Jia. *The Red Lantern.* Revised by the China Peking Opera Troupe, translated by Brenda Austin and John B. Weinstein. *The Columbia Anthology of Modern Chinese Drama*, edited by Xiaomei Chen, Columbia UP, 2010. Script.

Workers and PLA Soldiers. "On 'The Red Lantern.'" *China's Cultural Revolution, 1966–69: Not a Dinner Party*, edited by Michael Schoenhals, 2nd ed., Routledge, 2015, pp. 228–32. Audience commentary on the film.

Yin Cheng-tsung. "Be Revolutionary Cultural Workers always Loyal to Chairman Mao." *Chinese Literature*, no. 9, 1968, pp. 11–17. Comments on the film's score by the pianist and composer.

Shajiabang

Hai Chen et al. "Peking Opera 'Shachiapang—the Screen Version.'" *Chinese Literature*, no. 12, 1971, pp. 101–06. Responses to the film by a worker, a peasant, and a soldier.

Huo Chu. "'Shachipang'—a Beacon Fire." *Chinese Literature*, no. 3, 1967, pp. 13–18. Comments on Jiang Qing's involvement by a member of the Number 1 Peking Opera Company.

Liu Yun-kuei et al. "Workers, Peasants, and Soldiers on 'Shachiapang.'" *Chinese Literature*, no. 3, 1969, pp. 85–91. Responses by a commune member and members of the People's Liberation Army.

Peking Opera Troupe of Peking. "Shachiapang." *Chinese Literature*, no. 11, 1970, pp. 3–62. Revised script.

"*Shachiapang*: A Revolutionary Peking Opera." *Chinese Literature*, no. 11, 1967, pp. 3–53. Script.

"Strive to Portray Proletarian Heroes of People's War." *Chinese Literature*, no. 11, 1970, pp. 63–75. Editorial including comments on differences between the opera and its film adaptations.

Tan Yuan-shou. "Create Heroic Images by Applying Mao Tse-tung's Thought." *Chinese Literature*, no. 11, 1967, pp. 98–102. Opera company member's commentary on adapting the opera.

Sparkling Red Star

Chu Hsin-yun. "As I Acted Winter Boy I Learned from Him." *Chinese Litera-ture*, no. 2, 1975, pp. 97–101. Lead actor's comments.
Li Chun. "Creating the Image of a Winter Boy." *Chinese Literature*, no. 2, 1975, pp. 92–96. Codirector's comments.
Lu Chu-kuo. "Adapting a Novel for the Screen." *Chinese Literature*, no. 2, 1975, pp. 87–91. Screenwriter's comments on adaptation.
Tsai Chi-wei. "From a Cameraman's Notebook." *Chinese Literature*, no. 2, 1975, pp. 102–06. Cinematographer's comments.
Wang Yuan-chien and Lu Chu-kuo. "*Sparkling Red Star* (a Film Scenario)." *Chinese Literature*, no. 2, 1975, pp. 3–58. Script.

Spring Shoots

Chao Chi-chiang et al. "Spring Shoots." *Chinese Literature*, no. 10, 1976, pp. 3–78. Script.
Li Hsiu-ming. "Acting a Barefoot Doctor on the Screen." *China Reconstructs*, vol. 25, no. 6, June 1976, pp. 39–40. Comments from the lead actor on developing her performance.
Shu Hsin. "A Song in Praise of the Cultural Revolution." *Chinese Literature*, no. 10, 1976, pp. 88–92. Analysis of the film's narrative.

Taking Tiger Mountain by Strategy

China Reconstructs. Vol. 19, no. 2, Feb. 1970. Special issue on *Taking Tiger Mountain by Strategy*, including the abridged script, production stills, and commentary.
"Drawing Heroes." *Chinese Literature*, no. 12, 1970, pp. 105–09. Essay on adaptation of the film to picture-book format.
Musical workers of the Comrades-in-Arms Art Troupe of the Peking Garrison Forces. "Brilliant Example of the Revolution in Peking Opera Music." *Chinese Literature*, no. 2, 1970, pp. 93–104. Musicians' comments on the score.
Peking Opera Troupe of Shanghai. "Taking Tiger Mountain by Strategy." Translated by R. E. Strassberg. *The Red Pear Garden: Three Great Dramas of Revolutionary China*, edited by John D. Mitchell, D. R. Godine, 1973. Script.
Taking Tiger Mountain by Strategy Group of the Peking Opera Troupe of Shang-hai. "Drawn from Life, but on a Higher Plane." *Chinese Literature*, no. 2, 1970, pp. 81–92. Collective comment on creating heroic dance roles.
Yu Chou-hung. "The Colour Film 'Taking Tiger Mountain by Strategy.'" *Chinese Literature*, no. 2, 1971, pp. 86–94. Film review.

The White-Haired Girl

Chiang Ling-chih et al. "Comments on the Ballet 'The White-Haired Girl.'" *Chinese Literature*, no. 8, 1966, pp. 133–40. Responses to the film from a factory worker, an agronomist, a commune member, and a member of the People's Liberation Army Air Force.

Ling Kuei-ming. "Taking Up Arms." *Chinese Literature*, no. 7, 1972, pp. 106–08. Comments by a dancer on his portrayal of the character Wang Dachun.

Mao Hui-fang. "Hsi-erh's Indomitable Spirit." *Chinese Literature*, no. 7, 1972, pp. 100–02. Reflections by one of the two dancers who performed the lead role; Mao danced the role of Xi'er (Hsi-erh) with dark hair.

Pei Ping-tien et al. "An Appreciation of the Ballet 'The White-Haired Girl.'" *Chinese Literature*, no. 4, 1969, pp. 75–86. Comments by commune members, People's Liberation Army soldiers, and a member of the Shanghai School of Dance.

Sang Hu. "About the Film 'The White-Haired Girl.'" *Chinese Literature*, no. 7, 1972, pp. 96–99. Director's comments.

Shih Chung-chin. "A Heart Burning with Revenge." *Chinese Literature*, no. 7, 1972, pp. 103–05. Reflections by one of the two dancers who performed the lead role; Shih danced Xi'er (Hsi-erh) with white hair.

Tung Hsi-lin. "Three Blows with the Shoulder Pole." *Chinese Literature*, no. 7, 1972, pp. 109–11. Comments by a dancer on his portrayal of the character Yang Bailao.

Yu Lu-yuan. "The Revolutionary Ballet 'The White-Haired Girl.'" *Chinese Literature*, no. 8, 1966, pp. 117–40. Commentary on the adaptation of the folktale to stage.

Works Cited

Azalea Mountain. Directed by Xie Tieli, Beijing Film Studio, 1974.

Breaking with Old Ideas. Directed by Li Wenhua, Beijing Film Studio, 1976.

Caldwell, John. *Production Culture: Industrial Reflexivity and Critical Practice in Film and Television*. Duke UP, 2008.

Chang, Jung. *Wild Swans: Three Daughters of China*. Touchstone, 2003.

Cheek, Timothy. *Propaganda and Culture in Mao's China: Deng Tuo and the Intelligentsia*. Clarendon Press, 1997.

Chen, Anita. "Dispelling Misconceptions about the Red Guard Movement: The Necessity to Re-examine Cultural Revolution Factionalism and Periodization." *The Journal of Contemporary China*, vol. 1, Sept. 1992, pp. 61–85.

Chen, Tina Mai. "Propagating the Propaganda Film: The Meaning of Film in Chinese Communist Party Writings, 1945–1965." *Modern Chinese Literature and Culture*, vol. 15, no. 2, fall 2003, pp. 154–93.

Chien Hao-liang and Liu Changyu. "Fight to Create New and Glorious Proletarian Arts." *Chinese Literature*, no. 9, 1968, pp. 18–23.

Chu Hsin-yun. "As I Acted Winter Boy I Learned from Him." *Chinese Literature*, no. 2, 1975, pp. 97–101.

Chu Lan. "A Decade of Revolution in Peking Opera." *Chinese Literature*, no. 9, 1974, pp. 85–94.

Clark, Paul. *Chinese Cinema: Culture and Politics since 1949*. Cambridge UP, 1987.

———. *The Chinese Cultural Revolution: A History*. Cambridge UP, 2008.

Coderre, Laurence. "Counterattack: (Re)contextualizing Propaganda." *Journal of Chinese Cinemas*, vol. 4, no. 3, Jan. 2010, pp. 211–27.

Gu, Yizhong. "The Three Prominences." *Words and Their Stories: Essays on the Language of the Chinese Revolution*, edited by Wang Ban, Brill, 2011, pp. 283–303.

Ho, Denise. "Teaching China's Cultural Revolution." *The PRC History Review*, vol. 4, no. 2, Aug. 2019, pp. 24–26.

Inouye, Karin Mei Li. *Performing Jiang Qing (1914–1991): Gender, Performance, and Power in Modern China*. 2020. Stanford U, PhD dissertation.

Latour, Bruno. *Reassembling the Social: An Introduction to Actor-Network-Theory*. Oxford UP, 2005.

Li Chun. "Creating the Image of a Winter Boy." *Chinese Literature*, no. 2, 1975, pp. 92–96.

Li Hsiu-ming. "Acting a Barefoot Doctor on the Screen." *China Reconstructs*, vol. 25, no. 6, June 1976, pp. 39–40.

Lu Chu-kuo. "Adapting a Novel for the Screen." *Chinese Literature*, no. 2, 1975, pp. 87–91.

MacFarquhar, Roderick, and Michael Schoenhals. *Mao's Last Revolution*, Belknap Press, 2006.

Mao Hui-fang. "Hsi-erh's Indomitable Spirit." *Chinese Literature*, no. 7, 1972, pp. 100–02.

On the Docks. Directed by Xie Tieli and Xie Jin, Beijing Film Studio, 1972.

The Red Detachment of Women. Directed by Pan Wenzhan and Fu Jie, Beijing Film Studio, 1971.

The Red Lantern. Directed by Cheng Yin, August First Film Studio, 1971.

Red Rain. Directed by Cui Wei, Beijing Film Studio, 1975.

Sang Hu. "About the Film 'The White-Haired Girl.'" *Chinese Literature*, no. 7, 1972, pp. 96–99.

Shajiabang. Directed by Wu Zhaodi, Changchun Film Studio, 1971.

Shen Hung-hsin. "Models in Depicting Proletarian Heroes." *Chinese Literature*, nos. 11–12, 1969, pp. 103–14.

Shih Chung-chin. "A Heart Burning with Revenge." *Chinese Literature*, no. 7, 1972, pp. 103–05.

Sparkling Red Star. Directed by Li Jun and Li Ang, August First Film Studio, 1974.

Spring Shoots. Directed by Xie Pu et al., Shanghai Film Studio, 1975.

Taking Tiger Mountain by Strategy. Directed by Xie Tieli, Beijing Film Studio, 1970.

To Live. Directed by Zhang Yimou, Shanghai Film Studio / ERA International, 1994.

Tsai Chi-wei. "From a Cameraman's Notebook." *Chinese Literature*, no. 2, 1975, pp. 102–06.

Wang Zheng. *Finding Women in the State: A Socialist Feminist Revolution in the People's Republic of China, 1949–1964*. U of California P, 2017.

Wang, Zhuoyi. *Revolutionary Cycles in Chinese Cinema, 1951–1979*. Palgrave Macmillan, 2014.

The White-Haired Girl. Directed by Sang Hu, Shanghai Film Studio, 1971.

Williams, Raymond. *Keywords: A Vocabulary of Culture and Society.* Oxford UP, 1983.

Wu, Yiching. *The Cultural Revolution at the Margins: Chinese Socialism in Crisis.* Harvard UP, 2014.

Yang Chun-hsia. "What the Revolution in Literature and Art Has Taught Me." *Chinese Literature,* no. 7, 1976, pp. 116–23.

Ping Zhu

Chinese History and the Cinematic Trio

The Chinese sociologist Fei Xiaotong once commented that America is a land without ghosts. Fei was suggesting that Americans live only in the present moment and have no reverence for the past. For Fei, the vision of ghosts represented a historiography in which "the past, the present, and the future are blended together, becoming an unending string of happenings" (138; my trans.). Instead of viewing history as a singular, continuous, and ascending process, the ghost vision of history calls for the recognition of the radical heterogeneity of history and its nonlinear mode. It is noteworthy that the heterogeneity of history does not simply mean the inclusion of different actors and events; more crucially, it means that the same actor or event can be radically transformed in new historical narratives without erasing the apparition of the past. In this way, there are different historical truths coexisting in one historical narrative, some of them visible, others repressed or overlooked. History is such an ongoing, unresolved process of incessant happenings.

One of the biggest challenges of teaching Chinese cinema in American classrooms, however, is teaching students to view films with an awareness of the heterogeneity of history. I've had my moments of frustration when some students interpreted the Chinese films as if the diegesis had just happened the previous week or when students appeared oblivious to the nonindividualistic notions that have suffused modern Chinese history, such as nation, community, class, and culture as a collective project. The tumultuous history of the People's Republic of China is especially difficult for students to grasp when they have no background knowledge, as contemporary Chinese history is fraught with competing historical truths that contest and contradict each other at an accelerated pace.

In my Chinese Cinema class at the University of Oklahoma, I help students understand the heterogeneity and complexity of contemporary Chinese history through a cinematic trio: *The Red Detachment of Women* (红色娘子军), *Yellow Earth* (黄土地), and *The Road Home* (我的父亲母亲). These three films cover three important periods in the history of the People's Republic of China: the socialist period, from 1949 to 1976; the new era, from 1977 to 1989; and the postsocialist period, from 1990 to the present, respectively. They offer illuminating, albeit radically different, representations of the changing historical trajectory, national identity, and subjectivities of the Chinese people in the second half of the twentieth century.

I normally ask my students to approach the three films from the point of view of plot and to perform a structural analysis of their narratives. Despite the cultural differences, students who lack in-depth knowledge of China can still understand the basic plot of a Chinese film without too much difficulty. The film theorist Christian Metz suggests that "the narrative force of a plot . . . will always be understood too well—since it communicates with us in images of the world and of ourselves" (41). Metz's words not only affirm the approachable nature of a film's narrative but also hint at a potential problem of film viewing and film analysis: no matter how foreign a film appears, we as viewers tend to project our own reality into the diegesis of the film because of "our constant impulse to invest [the film] with the 'reality' of fiction . . . a reality that comes only from within us, from the projections and identifications that are mixed in with our perceptions of the film" (10). This tendency can seriously hamper the ability of viewers to appreciate the foreign and heterogeneous elements in a film.

If we look at the basic narratives of *The Red Detachment of Women*, *Yellow Earth*, and *The Road Home*, we will find that all three films revolve around a plot that starts with a male protagonist's arrival in the female protagonist's hometown. Things happen from there. This basic plot has a broad appeal that resonates with audiences worldwide because its gendered characterization of an active male character and a passive female character appears in narratives from other cultures. The Western fairy tale "Sleeping Beauty," for example, has a similar plot: a princess is trapped in her castle, waiting to be rescued by a mobile prince who comes from elsewhere. It would be easy for students to establish an emotional connection with the characters in these Chinese films by projecting onto them a romanticized imagining of gender that they are already familiar with. However, although having an emotional investment in the films will motivate students to watch them more attentively, the projection that enables this emotional investment overlooks the specific historical contexts of those films. The professor, therefore, should dissipate this ahistorical projection by juxtaposing the three films as contrasting narratives from different historical periods.

Claude Lévi-Strauss performs a structural analysis of myth in which he organizes a myth in a three-dimensional order (diachronically, synchronically, and transversally) and observes how all the variants of the myth differ in these dimensions. According to Lévi-Strauss, "any difference to be observed may be correlated with other differences, so that a logical treatment of the whole will allow simplifications, the final outcome being the structural law of the myth" (436). The three-dimensional observation is necessary because mythological time "is both revertible and non-revertible, synchronic and diachronic" (431). I employ Lévi-Strauss's approach to structural analysis in my Chinese cinema class to teach history. My students are given multiple historical positions from which to look at the variations of the basic plot in the three films. With this approach, even though initially they cannot articulate the concrete historical differences between the films, they realize that the present is not an absolute or permanent state but rather a transient and contingent moment within the long, ongoing process of history and that the ghosts of the past persistently coexist in a state of tension with the present.

Inspired by Lévi-Strauss's structural analysis of myth, I have designed a few interactive writing exercises that can be given to students in the discussion session on the three Chinese films. The professor can ask students to fill out a table by describing the identities of the male and female protagonists and their relationship to one another (see table 1); in this way students can quickly grasp the different historical agents during different stages of modern Chinese history. The professor can also ask students to fill out the table by comparing the spatial movements of the male and female protagonists in order to establish more tangible parameters for discussing gender differences and women's agency in the three films (see table 2).

Table 1. The protagonists' identities and relationships

Film	Male protagonist	Female protagonist	Their Relationship
The Red Detachment of Women	Hong Changqing is a party representative in the Chinese Red Army.	Wu Qionghua is an enslaved peasant who later became a soldier in the Red Army.	Hong Changqing is the savior, teacher, role model, disciplinarian, forbidden lover and "symbolic creditor" for Qionghua (Chi 190).
Yellow Earth	Gu Qing is a cultural soldier in the party's Eighth Route Army.	Cuiqiao is a peasant.	Gu Qing is a potential savior for Cuiqiao.
The Road Home	Luo Changyu is an intellectual.	Zhaodi is a peasant.	Changyu is Zhaodi's infatuation.

Table 2. The protagonists' spatial movements

Film	The male protagonist's spatial movements	The female protagonist's spatial movements
The Red Detachment of Women	Hong Changqing comes to Coconut Village then returns to the Communist-controlled area.	Wu Qionghua leaves Coconut Village and arrives at the Communist-controlled area thanks to Hong Changqing's help.
Yellow Earth	Gu Qing comes to a village in northern Shaanxi province from Yan'an then returns to Yan'an.	Cuiqiao dies while leaving the village
The Road Home	Luo Changyu comes to Sanhetun from the city and stays.	Zhaodi lives in Sanhetun all her life.

The Red Detachment of Women was made during the socialist period, but the story is set in the 1930s. The male protagonist, Hong Changqing, is a Chinese Communist Party representative in the Red Army, who eventually sacrifices his life for the party. Directed by Xie Jin, the film is a masterpiece of socialist realism, a style that was originally developed in the Soviet Union and was adopted as the official art style in China between 1953 and 1965. *Yellow Earth*, directed by Chen Kaige, was a pioneering piece of the fifth generation of Chinese directors, who received their college education right after the Cultural Revolution and took the opportunity to reflect on socialist history as soon as they were able to make films. As an avant-garde film, *Yellow Earth* is the most ambiguous and enigmatic film among the three. However, it should not be too hard for students to tell that the male protagonist, Gu Qing, is an ordinary Eighth Route Army soldier who has limited agency. The fact that he fails to accomplish the goal of his trip (to collect folk songs) indicates the decline of the party's political authority in postsocialist China. The cinematographer of *Yellow Earth*, Zhang Yimou, directed *The Road Home*, a fin de siècle nostalgic tale about the past. Its male protagonist is an intellectual and a schoolteacher. The film includes a long flashback, which, ironically, is set in the socialist period of the 1950s, when intellectuals were persecuted by various political movements. Intellectuals were rarely protagonists in films produced in the socialist period; however, they are everywhere in postsocialist films, including *The Road Home*. An interesting question arises: what was attractive in the socialist period for Chinese people living in the fin de siècle? Zhang Yimou seems to suggest that China's embrace of capitalism in the late twentieth century was more detrimental for the country than was class struggle in the socialist period.

The female protagonists in the three films are peasant girls. Only one of them, Wu Qionghua, in *The Red Detachment of Women*, manages to leave home, in this case Coconut Village (Yelinzhai), where she was trapped and enslaved, and later acquires a new identity as a Communist soldier in the Red Army. Qionghua also enjoys a more complex relationship with the male protagonist, Hong Changqing. As Robert Chi points out, "Hong Changqing dominates Qionghua's trajectory as saviour, teacher, role model, disciplinarian, forbidden lover and symbolic creditor" (190). After Changqing's death, Qionghua takes his place; at this moment, she is "politically sublime but not gender specific" (Cui 79–80). Qionghua's life is a remarkable story of female empowerment, affirming the socialist policy of gender equality. However, it must be pointed out that Qionghua's freedom and power were given to the exploited and oppressed class that she belonged to and not to her as an individual. Qionghua is doubly qualified for this oppressed class because she is a peasant and a woman. During the socialist period, the party believed that the gender problem was subordinate to the class problem, so it viewed all Chinese women as an oppressed class to be liberated from the clutches of feudalism and imperialism. Xie Jin's film faithfully represents this belief. Hong Changqing, on the other hand, is an avatar of the party. The relationship between the male and female protagonists in this film is thus symbolic of the relationship between the Chinese Communist Party and the oppressed Chinese people, conveying the strong political message that the Chinese people can only be liberated under the leadership of the party. Before showing this film to students, the professor can ask them to read excerpts of Mao Zedong's "Talks at the Yan'an Forum on Literature and Art" to better understand the creative premise of Chinese socialist films.[1]

This familiar socialist tale, in which the party saves a peasant girl in distress, has been completely rewritten in Chen Kaige's *Yellow Earth*. The male protagonist, Gu Qing, is a disempowered party representative who fails to connect with the peasants. He is unable to strike up a conversation with the crowd of peasants during a wedding in the beginning of the film, and later his irreverent attitude toward nature offends the father of Cuiqiao. When Gu Qing stays with Cuiqiao's family, he succeeds in painting in Cuiqiao's mind a better outside world for women like Cuiqiao but cannot take her with him when he leaves for Yan'an, as bringing her would violate the Eighth Route Army's rules. Just as the local villagers follow rigid traditional rules, a Communist soldier must obey the rules in the Eighth Route Army. Cuiqiao and Gu Qing are thus both different and similar: they live in two incompatible systems (the Communist and feudal systems, respectively), yet both systems are patriarchal and inflexible. Cuiqiao and her younger brother Hanhan are the only two individuals in the film who are striving to break away from the collective. Cuiqiao's escape comes at the cost of her life; Hanhan's destiny is not revealed in the film.

The 1980s were a period when the Chinese elites eagerly bid farewell to the revolution and looked forward to rejoining the capitalist world system. By representing the disconnect between the party and the peasants, *Yellow Earth* embraces this zeitgeist. Whereas *The Red Detachment of Women* treats women's liberation as a natural consequence of the liberation of the oppressed class, *Yellow Earth* eschews the rhetoric of class struggle. There exists only one class—the peasants—in the northern Shaanxi village represented in the film, yet the people there suffer without a personified oppressor. The women suffer more than the men, which suggests that the gender problem is real and can exist independently from the class problem. What's more, in contrast to how they are frequently represented in socialist films, the miserable peasants in *Yellow Earth* are not enthusiastic supporters of the Communist revolution; on the contrary, they appear utterly indifferent to it. Their bitter songs are not indications of their revolutionary consciousness but rather a way for them to come to terms with their bitter lives.

In addition to presenting an antithesis to socialism, *Yellow Earth* also shows a strong desire to acknowledge China as a subaltern nation in the world system. Chen Kaige says in an interview with George Semsel in 1985: "We were working with the idea that life in Shaanbei, the northern region of Shaanxi Province, could be equated to the position that China occupies in the contemporary world. I want to express how Chinese have lived for many, many years. The location is a microcosm. That place is one of the most backward places I know, and China is backward" (Semsel 136). The northern region of Shaanxi province, with its yellow earth and the Yellow River that runs through it, is the cradle of Chinese civilization, and it remains a location most impervious to the influences of modernity. The yellow earth and the Yellow River both sustain and occasionally claim the lives of the peasants living in this area. They constitute "a place in dire need of reform, . . . also stubbornly resistant" (Yau 26). The film thus not only represents the party's disconnection from the peasants but also a backward China's disconnection from the modern world. Who can be the savior of those miserable Chinese peasants living at the mercy of the earth? The film offers no clear answer.

From the 1980s to the 1990s, China underwent seismic changes as a result of its integration into the global system. Globalization, however, has come with dire consequences. Massive urbanization deprived millions of Chinese of their homes, communities, and familiar ways of life; the market economy has allowed many Chinese to get rich quickly yet also produced millions of laid-off workers and landless peasants, creating a highly polarized society. A nostalgia for the bygone socialist period emerged when the disprivileged Chinese laboring class yearned for the equality and community they had once had. *The Road Home* was produced in such a historical context.

The story of *The Road Home* is told through a *mise en abyme* structure. Students should be alerted to this special feature before viewing the film, otherwise they risk being easily absorbed in the fairy-tale-like flashback in the film. The main story is told from the point of view of Luo Yusheng. The film starts when Yusheng returns to Sanhetun, a village in North China, from the city upon the death of his father, Luo Changyu. Yusheng's old mother, Zhaodi, insists on carrying Changyu's corpse home from the hospital in the traditional way. Yusheng tries to persuade her to use a car, but the mother refuses. Later, Yusheng asks his mother to move to the city to live with him, and she refuses again. In between the opening and ending scenes, which occur in the present and are filmed in black and white, the audience is presented with the love story of Zhaodi and Changyu, which happened forty years earlier, in a fifty-six-minute flashback filmed in brilliant colors.

Unlike *The Red Detachment of Women* and *Yellow Earth*, *The Road Home* reverses the gender stereotypes of the active male and the passive female protagonists as well as the relationship between the village and the outside world. The male protagonist in *The Road Home* takes a passive role in his relationship with the female protagonist: It was Zhaodi who fell in love with Changyu at first sight, who did him lots of small favors, who created opportunities for many "chance" encounters with him, and who waited for him when he had to go to the city to be repudiated as a rightist. In *The Road Home*, the village is no longer a place of violent class struggles (like Coconut Village in *The Red Detachment of Women*) or an extremely harsh environment (like the northern Shaanbei village in *Yellow Earth*) but a heavenly place, sheltering people from the political turmoil and commodity culture of the outside world.

The film does not tell us why Zhaodi fell in love with Changyu; it seems that she merely loved listening to him teaching his pupils. It is noteworthy that Zhaodi was attracted by Changyu's voice rather than the content of his teaching. This point explains why Changyu's knowledge has left virtually no imprint on Zhaodi, who remains an illiterate peasant woman after forty years of marriage. Therefore, although the film has an intellectual protagonist, it does not exalt knowledge. What is exalted in this film are two seemingly contradictory commitments embodied by the two protagonists: Changyu's commitment to educating the kids in the village, and Zhaodi's commitment to tradition. Education is linked with the project of modernization and can help people leave the village to live a modern life in the city (as Yusheng does). Tradition, however, involves retaining beliefs and repeating practices that allow the continuation of the past in the present. These two incongruent commitments are symbolic of China's dilemma as the country joined the global system in the postsocialist period. Changyu and Zhaodi's love and marriage, therefore, is imbued with the director's romanticized desire to bring tradition and modernity together in harmony in contemporary China.

Toward the end of the film, when Changyu's body is being carried back home on a snowy day, more than one hundred people show up, all of whom are Changyu's former students. Many of them have returned to the village from the cities they now live in. The homecoming of Changyu's body is thus simultaneously the homecoming of those modernized Chinese, who once again experience solidarity, equality, community, and devotion under the auspices of tradition, symbolized by Zhaodi. In the film, the village of Sanhetun, hemmed in by mountains, is rendered as a spiritual home for the Chinese people in the age of globalization. This spiritual home's past is represented by a young woman who allures and nurtures her husband and then waits for his return. Later in her life she still adheres to the tradition and waits for her son's homecoming. Considering the role of women in the Indian colonial context, Partha Chatterjee argues that nationalism stresses the spiritual and cultural value of its domestic traditions in order to resist the material superiority of the West: "The home was the principal site for expressing the spiritual quality of the national culture, and women must take the main responsibility of protecting and nurturing this quality" (626–27). In *The Road Home*, Zhang Yimou chose to fetishize a woman in response not to nationalism but to the bleak contemporary social realities brought about by global capitalism.

After viewing the three films in chronological order, students can get a concrete understanding of why the same core narrative is written in radically different ways during the different historical periods. All three films are allegories of their corresponding historical periods—namely, the socialist period, the new era, and the postsocialist period—and can offer illuminating insights into the social structure, collective mentality, aesthetics, social taboos, and gender norms in each period. However, this is by no means the end of teaching history through this cinematic trio. If history is an ongoing and unresolved process, as I mentioned in the beginning of this essay, then students must be encouraged to critically assess what has been buried or repressed in the film narratives—to look for, in Herbert Marcuse's words, "the unhappy consciousness of the divided world, the defeated possibilities, the hopes unfulfilled, and the promises betrayed" (64). The past, in other words, remains part of the inconsistent multiplicity lying beneath a particular historical narrative, waiting to be summoned and reactivated.

It can be said that *The Road Home* summons and reactivates one historical truth—the importance and beauty of tradition—that is repressed in *The Red Detachment of Women* and *Yellow Earth*. Toward the end of *The Road Home* the ghostly image of the young Zhaodi is repeatedly superimposed on the image of the village forty years later, a scene that blends the past and present while calling for a better future. The specter of the past, which represents the radical heterogeneity of history, also appears in *The Red Detachment of Women* and *Yellow Earth*. In the former, the past refers to the suffering of the oppressed Chinese, which must be grieved over in the film, and again through public rituals, to show the solidity of the proletarian class and the legitimacy of the party's revolutionary cause. In the latter, the past has turned into bitter songs the peasants sing; however, their lives are nothing more than the reenactments of what those songs describe. We are not only seeing different representations of the past in these three films but also different historiographies: *The Red Detachment of Women* depicts history's upward trajectory driven by dialectical materialism; in *Yellow Earth*, history moves slowly and cyclically in a self-contained fashion; in *The Road Home*, history is a redeeming angel coming from the remote past to salvage the present.

At this stage, students compare any two of the films and identify one or more historical truths presented in the earlier film that have been repressed in the latter film but are nonetheless useful to illuminate the latter film's historical period. For example, if we compare *The Red Detachment of Women* and *The Road Home*, we can see that the notion of gender equality has been totally repressed in the latter film, where sexual stereotypes are unapologetically naturalized: women are assigned to manual labor (cooking and weaving), while only men can do the intellectual work (teaching). Compared with Qionghua's movements from Coconut Village to the liberated area, from the old to the new society, and from being a slave to being a party leader in *The Red Detachment of Women*, Zhaodi's lack of freedom in *The Road Home* can be appalling. In addition, although Zhaodi is endowed with the divine power of tradition in the film, as a fetishized object of the male gaze (represented by the camera that gazes voraciously at her beautiful face), she, as well as the tradition she represents, exists as a commodity for global spectatorship. If we compare *Yellow Earth* with *The Road Home*, then we may ask why the patriarchal nature of tradition is not interrogated in the latter film, and why the film romanticizes the fraught history of Chinese socialism as a fairy tale.

Of course, plot is but a fragment of the expansive world of cinema. As Metz asserts, "One will never be able to analyze film by speaking directly about the diegesis." It is necessary for students to realize, as Metz suggests, that the meaning of a film as a whole is produced by the seesaw between the semiotics of the narrative (the signified) and the audiovisual semiotics of cinema (the signifiers; 143). The latter is the vehicle of the former, although they both have some autonomy. Throughout the discussions of the three films, the professor should encourage the students to take note of how the act of narrativity is achieved through cinematic language. When the primacy of representations is identified by students, it becomes relatively easier for them to coordinate the seesaw of the semiotics of the narrative and the audiovisual semiotics of cinema. Choices for color schemes, lighting, camera movements, editing, mise-en-scène, symbolic objects, and music will no longer appear to students as isolated elements; instead, these elements can provide exciting supporting evidence to the structural analysis of the narrative. In this way, they are signifiers of history. At this stage, students can answer the full range of questions as to what historical truth is represented in a given film, why it is represented, and how it is represented. For example, students can be tasked with discovering different symbols of the patriarchy in the three films or discussing the development (or nondevelopment) of a character by analyzing the mise-en-scène of a particular film.

This pedagogical model of teaching Chinese history through the cinematic trio invites students to reflect on each film's deliberate use of an allegorical narrative of China during a unique period in the second half of the twentieth century. Viewed together, these films not only help my students understand the multiple dimensions of contemporary Chinese history but also show them that history contains inconsistent and multiple possibilities that will always haunt and rupture the present.

Note

1. Excerpts from Mao can include the introduction and sections 1 and 2 of the conclusion.

Works Cited

Chatterjee, Partha. "Colonialism, Nationalism, and Colonialized Women: The Contest in India." *American Ethnologist*, vol. 16, no. 4, 1989, pp. 622–33.

Chi, Robert. "*The Red Detachment of Women*: Resenting, Regendering, Remembering." *Chinese Films in Focus II*, edited by Chris Berry, British Film Institute, 2008, pp. 189–96.

Cui, Shuqin. "Gender Politics and Socialist Discourse in Xie Jin's *The Red Detachment of Women*." *Women through the Lens: Gender and Nation in a Century of Chinese Cinema*, edited by Shuqin Cui, U of Hawai'i P, 2008, pp. 79–96.

Fei Xiaotong. 美国人的性格 [*Meiguoren de xingge*; *American characteristics*]. Lianhe Chubangongsi, 2018.

Lévi-Strauss, Claude. "The Structural Study of Myth." *The Journal of American Folklore*, vol. 68, no. 270, 1995, pp. 428–44.

Mao Zedong. "Talks at the Yan'an Forum on Literature and Art." *Marxists Internet Archive*, www.marxists.org/reference/archive/mao/selected-works/volume-3/mswv3_08.htm.

Marcuse, Herbert. *One-Dimensional Man: Studies in the Ideology of Advanced Industrial Society*. Routledge, 2002.

Metz, Christian. *Film Language: A Semiotics of the Cinema*. Translated by Michael Taylor, U of Chicago P, 1974.

The Red Detachment of Women. Directed by Xie Jin, Shanghai Film Studio, 1961.

The Road Home. Directed by Zhang Yimou, New Pictures, 1999.

Semsel, George Stephen. "Chen Kaige and Zhang Yimou: Fifth Generation Director and Cinematagrapher." *Chinese Film: The State of the Art in the People's Republic*, edited by Semsel, Praeger, 1987, pp. 134–41.

Yau, Esther C. M. "*Yellow Earth*: Western Analysis and a Non-Western Text." *Film Quarterly*, vol. 41, no. 2, 1987–88, pp. 22–33.

Yellow Earth. Directed by Chen Kaige, Guangxi Film Studio, 1984.

Additional Resources

Berry, Chris, and Mary Ann Farquhar. "Post-socialist Strategies: An Analysis of *Yellow Earth* and *Black Cannon Incident*." *Cinematic Landscapes: Observations on the Visual Arts and Cinema of China and Japan*, edited by Linda Erlich and David Desser, U of Texas P, 1994, pp. 81–116.

Chow, Rey. "Sentimental Returns: On the Uses of the Everyday in the Recent Films of Zhang Yimou and Wong Kar-wai." *New Literary History*, vol. 33, no. 4, 2002, pp. 639–54.

Farquhar, Mary Ann. "The 'Hidden' Gender in *Yellow Earth*." *Screen*, vol. 33, no. 2, 1992, pp. 154–64.

Harris, Kristine. "Re-makes/Re-models: *The Red Detachment of Women* between Stage and Screen." *The Opera Quarterly*, vol. 26, nos. 2–3, 2010, pp. 31–42.

Leung, Helen Hok-sze. "*Yellow Earth*: Hesitant Apprenticeship and Bitter Agency." *Chinese Films in Focus II*, edited by Chris Berry, British Film Institute, 2008, pp. 258–64.

McGrath, Jason. "Communists Have More Fun! The Dialectics of Fulfillment in Cinema of the People's Republic of China." *World Picture*, vol. 3, 2009, www.worldpicturejournal.com/WP_3/McGrath.html.

Marjorie Dryburgh

Not Watching Jackie Chan: Historical Film and Marginal Women

The history of twentieth-century China is richly represented in mainland Chinese film. The experiences of China's recent past are explored in a lineage of works from 1956 to the present that includes *Railway Guerrillas* (铁道游击队), *Wreaths at the Foot of the Mountain* (高山下的花环), and *The Opium War* (鸦片战争); films by fifth-generation directors, such as *Red Sorghum* (红高粱) and *To Live* (活着); and more recent works such as *Youth* (芳华) and *The Eight Hundred* (八佰). These sit beside films that more closely align with state-sponsored narratives and that explore recent history or contemporary society, from *The East Is Red* (东方红) to, most recently, anthology films such as *My People, My Hometown* (我和我的家乡). Across these films we find different frames of gender: while female characters are at the core of some stories—notably, *To Live* and *Youth*—others offer highly male-centered understandings of China's past. This gender imbalance is not confined to older works or to works such as war stories, which are central to Chinese film histories generally, where the setting may make the inclusion of female characters implausible. An appraisal of the critically acclaimed 2021 television drama *The Age of Awakening* (觉醒年代), which charts China's path to revolution through the activities of "New Culture" progressive intellectuals, laments that, "[i]n a show brimming with rich, well-developed male characters, the women who helped spark China's revolution are portrayed as little more than wallflowers" (Qi).

The two films discussed below reflect a similar gender imbalance: the commemorative blockbuster *1911* (辛亥革命) retells the fall of imperial China and the country's transition to a republic; the biopic *Soul Haunted by Painting* (画魂) recreates the personal, emotional, and artistic life of one of China's first modern female artists. On one level, audiences may read these works as straightforward public histories: as reappraisals of the birth of the Chinese republic and the social change and conflict that marked the first decades of that new order. On another level, the choices involved in the centering of characters and narrative strands may marginalize other characters—notably, women—and draw the viewer's attention away from other possible histories.

Robert Rosenstone's study of history on film and film as history offers a guide to reading work of this kind. Historical film explores the experience of the past through the lives of individuals, reworking national myths or familiar stories that "dramatize, personalize and emotionalize the past" (47) and thereby making that past intelligible and meaningful to present audiences. Rosenstone notes the familiar criticisms of inaccuracies and other misrepresentations in history on film but argues that the possibilities of the medium and the value of the other truths it can reveal outweigh these criticisms. More recently, historical dramas such as Netflix's *Bridgerton* have sparked conversations about the ways in which fictional historical dramas can reframe our understandings of the past, not by faithful reproduction but—for example—by the creative use of anachronism (Thorpe).[1]

At the same time, we should be wary of drawing too firm a line between the truth claims of conventional, particularly archive-based, histories and the histories represented on film: on one hand, we are increasingly alert to the silences and evasions of some orthodox histories, and on the other, discussions of method that are designed to address the silences and omissions in the archive itself underline the creative and critical crafting that underpins some social histories. Susan Mann addresses this process of crafting as she describes the writing of her book *The Talented Women of the Zhang Family*, in which she builds a social history and a collective biography of a family through an investigation of the fragmentary historical record and the application of informed, critical imagination ("Scene-Setting" 637–39). Mann notes the centrality of biography to Chinese historiography and observes that traditional biography requires a degree of inventiveness: "life stories were supposed to convey history's great moral lessons. The historian's job was to make sure the lessons were crystal-clear, and so most biographies were recorded in dramatic scenes, sparked with verbatim dialogue. It is impossible, as a historian working today, to resist the appeal of these stories" (631). In her work on the Zhang women, Mann eschews the moral mission of traditional biography while adapting its "scene-setting" methods to new purposes, building on the fragmentary written record to reimagine the experiences of family life, including marriage, widowhood, family separation, and collaboration or competition between siblings (633).

Thus Rosenstone and Mann offer a range of possible approaches to reading historical film for a range of audiences. In the two films discussed here, moral lessons can be derived from the lives of the historical figures Huang Xing and Pan Yuliang, though these lessons depend on careful selections from an imperfect historical record. I propose, rather, that we take these films as a starting point for the exploration of alternative narratives that set aside the demands of commercial film and return to the possibilities offered by historical inquiry.

This is not a retreat from Rosenstone's insistence that we "stop expecting films to do what (we imagine) books do. Stop expecting them to get the facts right, or to present several sides of an issue, or give a fair hearing . . . to all the characters and groups represented in a particular situation, or to provide a broad and detailed historical context for events" (37). It is, however, a modification of Rosenstone's approach, and unapologetically so. This modification is not because Rosenstone's approach to historical film is inherently flawed. As Rosenstone observes, "Film offers us history as the story of a unitary, closed and completed past . . . [which typically] provides no alternative possibilities to what is happening on-screen, admits no doubts and promotes each historical assertion with confidence" (47). We can, I suggest, readily accept this as a legitimate mission of the historical film, while nonetheless assuming that all historical work, broadly conceived, must be founded on a recognition of alternative possibilities, doubt, and a generous skepticism toward every confident assertion and that the emotional truth gaps—so to speak—in historical film are as legitimate a call to new inquiry as the empirical or analytical gaps in the formal historical literature.

This approach is potentially very fruitful. In a first-year undergraduate class on twentieth-century Chinese history, for students who generally had little prior knowledge of the subject, I found that the use of Chinese feature films added depth to more conventional methods. There were of course challenges to this approach: first, in identifying films that were both sufficiently engaging for students and purposeful enough in their engagement with the past to be academically useful, and second, in developing a productive conversation on the uses of fictionalized or dramatized work in this context. The original rationale here was to prompt discussions about films as public or popular history and to use specific films to generate questions that might be researched in more conventional ways. In many iterations of the course, the films prompted students to raise questions about the accuracy of stories, about the extent to which any one story can be considered representative of wider Chinese experience, and about the reworking of a complex past to fit a relatively short entertainment form. Assigning readings from Rosenstone's work before showing the films did not entirely prevent these questions from recurring but did direct students more purposefully toward the metaphorical or emotional truths that the films offered.

The films *1911* and *Soul Haunted by Painting* suggested a new approach to this work. These films connect more directly, through historical figures, to documented events than films such as Zhang Yimou's *To Live*; they therefore challenge viewers to consider the work of packaging the past into drama while they offer a range of routes for further research and discussion. Each film centers on a single, powerful character: the revolutionary Huang Xing (played by Jackie Chan) and the painter Pan Yuliang (played by Gong Li), respectively. However, both films allow screen time to figures—as foils to those central characters—who raise other compelling historical questions. Repeated in-class viewings of these films increased the time I spent not watching Jackie Chan or Gong Li but instead wondering how the action on-screen—and its imaginary off-screen hinterland—looked to the more peripheral characters, what we might find if we looked more closely at their lives and how their marginality in academic history, as well as on-screen, reflects the necessarily multiple or partial nature of historical analysis and storytelling.

This alternative approach demands a shift in reading strategies. We, as instructors, work hard to persuade students of the importance—as intellectual exercise and time-management device—of identifying a core argument or central contribution in the readings we assign. Here, rather, we must ask them to read the films purposefully against the grain, taking the scenes set by directors and performed by actors and recentering them on characters who are decidedly peripheral to the film as delivered, taking seriously the experience and subjectivity of these characters either to locate new evidence on which new scenes may be set or at least to formulate new, critical questions. As discussed below, the two films present different challenges on this front.

1911 is unambiguously a Jackie Chan vehicle, and his character Huang Xing—action hero to Wilson Chan's earnest and rather pale Sun Yat-sen—takes center stage. Beside Huang Xing, however, is the figure of Xu Zonghan. Xu Zonghan should be interesting in her own right. Born into the family of a tea merchant in Guangdong province, Xu was educated at home with her sisters. Married at eighteen and widowed soon after, she had two children. An active philanthropist, even as a young woman, Xu converted to Christianity and joined Sun Yat-sen's Revolutionary Alliance in the early 1900s. She became first an assistant, in early 1911, then partner to Huang Xing, and they had two children together. After Huang's death in 1916, Xu concentrated on social reform work, running the Nanjing Poor Children's Home before spending the war years—her last years—in Chongqing ("Xu Zonghan"). Xu Zonghan, therefore, led a publicly visible and documented life—albeit one less documented than Huang Xing's.

The film *1911* reflects almost none of this history. It should not surprise us that a film released on the centenary of the transition from the Qing dynasty to the republic should center on the high politics and military drama surrounding the year of revolution: in Sun Yat-sen's struggle to raise funds and rally support overseas and in the imperial court's increasingly desperate efforts to survive. However, although the film opens with the execution of another female revolutionary, Qiu Jin, it shows strikingly little interest in Xu Zonghan as a political actor, and how she has been repositioned in that grand narrative is instructive. When Sun Yat-sen first mentions her name to Huang Xing in the film, he recommends her as a political collaborator and mentions her experience in coordinating underground revolutionary organizations in Guangzhou. However, with the exception of an early sequence where she transports ammunition for the failed Guangzhou uprising in early 1911, she appears most often in domestic roles, as a helpmeet to the revolution, and not as a revolutionary in her own right. Thus, we see her finding the last letters written by young (male) revolutionaries to their families as she does their laundry and comforting dying soldiers in a field clinic; her political contribution is limited to supporting Huang Xing, as she amputates an infected finger to save his hand and berates him when he appears to lose faith in the revolution.

Soul Haunted by Painting is a very different film: it tells the life of the painter Pan Yuliang, who was orphaned as a child and sold to a brothel, where she met a progressive official, Pan Zanhua. After leaving the brothel and becoming Pan's second wife, she studied painting in Shanghai and, from 1921, in Europe. She lived in China between 1928 and 1937 and taught in the Art Department of the National Central University in Nanjing, but persistent scandalmongering about her past and her colleagues' resistance to Western-style art prompted her to return to France in 1937, where she lived until her death in 1977 ("Pan Yuliang"). The peripheral figure here, Pan Zanhua's first wife, leaves strikingly little trace in the historical record.

Soul Haunted by Painting is therefore most sympathetic to Yuliang's struggles as a woman in a conservative society, where the painter's art and past are judged by traditionally minded men. However, these conflicts intersect with tensions within the Pan family, notably in Yuliang's relationship with Zanhua's first wife, who is not named in the film but is identified as Fang Shanyu in the Asia Art Archive's chronology of Yuliang's life (Pan Yuliang materials). Fang Shanyu appears in the film as a traditional first wife who is outgrown by her self-consciously modernizing husband. She is first mentioned on Zanhua and Yuliang's wedding night, when Zanhua tells Yuliang, "I have never seen her whole body"; she appears in the film only when Yuliang, unable to conceive a child with Zanhua, writes to her in Zanhua's name to summon her to Shanghai. The film encourages viewers to sympathize with Yuliang (while recognizing the embarrassment that her art causes Zanhua) but shows Fang Shanyu primarily as determined to preserve her own status over Yuliang's, as when she complains that Zanhua has taught his concubine to read. As the film progresses, though, the stresses and humiliations of Fang Shanyu's position come to the fore, first in Zanhua's visible reluctance to leave Yuliang in order to impregnate his wife, and later in the competition between the two women for the attention and affection of Fang Shanyu's son, who was born in 1921, after Yuliang's departure for Europe.

Although Xu Zonghan and Fang Shanyu inhabit the edges of the onscreen narratives, and neither character is well developed, both are potentially more interesting, and raise more interesting questions, than their status in the films suggests. I suggest three approaches to analyzing these films: we might describe these approaches as primarily empirical, positional, and historiographical, respectively. As Mann's "scene-setting" formulation suggests, there is a dynamic relation between the three, and the answers produced through one approach often raise questions that can best be addressed through another. Notably, while setting scenes for the two films depends on students' repositioning or reimagining of the past in critically and empirically informed ways—combining the first two approaches—a recognition of the limits to the scenes that we can set in this way points to historiographical lacunae in the sources or in the scholarly literature.

This listing of empirical, positional, or historiographical approaches suggests an ascending order of difficulty, but the challenges of these approaches can depend on the scaffolding provided by instructors and the resources that students bring to the work, in their familiarity with Chinese history and histories of gender and their competence or confidence in the use of Chinese-language materials. The critical input of international students, who have grown up within different audiences and may identify other readings of the films, and particularly the input of Chinese students, who may have learned other histories of China, can further enrich the discussion. In addition to works on the historical contexts of these two films and on the currents of reform that surrounded the end of the Qing dynasty and the long May Fourth era, instructors may also direct students toward a growing body of historical work on women and gender in China. Works by Gail Hershatter and by Paul Bailey offer critical overviews of this scholarship, and research essays, monographs, and translated primary sources offer insights into the changing experiences and mentalities of (mostly elite) women.[2] On this basis, students may begin to formulate questions from what they see on-screen.

The first, empirical approach requires further research into the two films' peripheral characters and into the lives of women in early-twentieth-century China, reframing Xu Zonghan and Fang Shanyu as subjects in their own right or as representatives of neglected groups of women but not simply as context for the stories of prominent figures such as Huang Xing and Pan Yuliang. Students may first notice the different paths that these two women of similar ages took across the unstable historical landscape of the early twentieth century. Xu's biography shows Xu as a revolutionary and, later, a social reformer, and her early life points to the social changes that predated the last-gasp Qing reforms of 1905 and the highly visible changes associated with the May Fourth era. Fang Shanyu's life—or what we can see of it—underlines the durability of a more traditional family order.

Beginning with Xu, we may ask how the education of girls changed in the late nineteenth century, how this change equipped Xu and her contemporaries for contact with new ideas and opportunities, and how far Xu's exceptional engagement with the revolutionary movement was enabled by broader, more commonplace social changes. What, practically speaking, were the objectives of girls' education at this time? Who had access to education beyond the routine requirements of letter writing and contribution to family businesses, and in what types of school? What factors governed that access? How did schools extend or reinforce family and other social networks for women? Did these networks continue to depend on the associations of fathers, brothers, or husbands, or did women now enjoy greater autonomy? How were young women expected to use their education after graduation? Who populated the networks of teaching and philanthropic work that Xu Zonghan and her sisters engaged in? How far did these networks overlap with more purposefully political or activist networks, with commercial interests, or with missionary associations? Was the establishment of the republic in 1912 followed by wider shakeouts in revolutionary associations, or more widely in public life, and a movement of former revolutionaries to more gradualist reform work? And to what extent were those developments governed by approaches to politics and revolution, by gender attitudes, and by other influences?

Turning to Fang Shanyu, we find a subgeneration of women who were apparently left behind by the changes of the early twentieth century and who figure only in passing in the biographies of husbands—the more famous examples including Lu Xun, Mao Zedong, Sun Yat-sen (and indeed Huang Xing, who first married in 1892). These men, we are told, chafed against early arranged marriages and later settled down with younger, more apparently modern wives. Their stories draw our attention to changes in marriage and family arrangements that may predate the familiar objections to traditional marriage and family hierarchies by participants in the May Fourth movement: How did shifting attitudes affect marriage practices across the first decades of the twentieth century? Did other social or economic changes (e.g., in education, communications, or public discourse) add to the intangible resources—in personal cultural capital, social networks, and reinventions of the relatively traditional family—available to women within their marital families? When Fang Shanyu first arrives in Shanghai in *Soul Haunted by Painting* and hands the family account books to Pan Zanhua, does this action point to her economic dependence on him? Or was she responsible for managing family property (that in part may have funded Zanhua's life in Shanghai with Yuliang)? Comparing the two women, we may further ask where their lives, or the lives of women like them, were recorded. How much did they figure in records of their own activities, such as Xu Zonghan's charitable work? And to what extent are they confined to relational accounts, such as the biographies or writings of relatives?

The second, positional approach is to recenter the narrative on our marginal characters and to consider how the developments shown in the films and—for a further challenge—the wider context of those developments look from their perspectives. In addition to the formal shift in narrative perspective, this approach requires also a shift in our understanding of individual values and experiences of historical change: that we step aside from our own positionality, and from the positionality of central characters such as Huang Xing or Pan Yuliang, and take seriously the preoccupations and subjectivity of the peripheral figures. If we take either film at face value, it is reasonably straightforward to reassemble a relational narrative for either Xu Zonghan or Fang Shanyu. Working only with the evidence in *1911*, we may take the collapse of the Qing dynasty as a background against which Xu Zonghan's personal investment in the revolution and revolutionaries—as an organizer, practical supporter, and field nurse—is complicated by Xu's relationship with Huang Xing, and we may explore the insights that this offers into the uncertainties and frustrations that afflicted the revolutionary movement. Similarly, we might draw on *Soul Haunted by Painting* to recreate Fang Shanyu as the author of a tale of conservative woe, in which her husband neglects her emotionally and expects her to play second fiddle to a concubine who was taken without her approval, despite her status as Pan Zanhua's primary wife and, later, as mother of his only son.

The risk here, of course, is that we produce narrowly ventriloquistic stories that reproduce Xu Zonghan's and Fang Shanyu's marginal status and fail to take seriously the concerns and experiences that these women—as individuals or as members of a generation—brought to the developments shown on-screen. We might consider that these were the wrong stories to tell or that we have somehow failed in our efforts at recentering the narratives. Alternatively, it could be more productive to take this as a first step in a more critical, reflective process. The framing of their stories appears to assume that a notional audience would find Huang Xing's story more compelling than Xu Zonghan's and would more readily empathize with Pan Yuliang than with Fang Shanyu. Discussions with students suggested that this assumption was often correct, and we should ask why this was so. Do we see differences here of time, space, or culture, and if so, how do we articulate these? To what extent are our responses to these specific pasts shaped by our understandings of the present? And how can we draw on empirical understandings of their context to rethink our positionality relative to theirs?

The third approach is to consider the historiographical dimension of the problem and the challenges involved in understanding the lives of women born in the late 1800s. On one hand, while research into the cultural and social histories of the early twentieth century has deepened scholarly understandings of the context of China's revolutions, the connections between revolutionary processes and actors and other strands of change—such as the welfare work later pursued by Xu Zonghan—have been less fully explored. On the other hand, as Dorothy Ko has observed, early research on women and gender in Chinese history was squeezed between Orientalist assumptions in the Western academy of social and political stasis in imperial China and the claims of the Chinese Communist Party to have liberated women from an unvaried state of prerevolutionary oppression (1–5). The conventional narratives of revolution and of gender thus tend to obscure the more complex territory that both Xu Zonghan and Fang Shanyu inhabited.

While these conventional narratives can appear persuasive to student readers, recentering the narratives on marginal characters such as Xu Zonghan and Fang Shanyu allows us to rethink history from new angles. It demands that we consider what historiographical lacunae a study of either woman might fill and what existing bodies of work we might draw on to attempt a study of this kind. For this consideration, we may draw on the empirical and positional questions sketched above and on a recategorization of Xu and Fang: if their categorization in the films as revolutionary wife and first wife, respectively, relegates them to the margins of the story, how should we characterize them as subjects in their own right? And having done so, how do we conduct our new inquiry?

Histories of women and gender in China published in recent decades suggest the kind of work involved here. Bret Hinsch's list of ten highly influential books on Chinese women's history that were published between 1993 and 2013 acknowledges the political barriers to social history research in China in the earlier socialist period but shows both the dramatic later shifts within the Chinese scholarship and the possibilities offered by creative research methods. Hinsch's discussion emphasizes the critical reappraisal by social historians of conventional understandings of Chinese society in earlier periods and a number of recurring themes that can apply also to work on more recent periods. For example, there is much to learn from the gaps between the classics that represent elite, generally male, efforts to define and enforce behavioral norms and those sources that claim to record the activities of individual women, and while the available sources most commonly record the experiences of elite women, accounts of women of lower status can reveal both the effects of class on gender norms and the specifics of some women's engagement in the family economy and the impact of changes in marriage finances. In the English-language literature on women's work in China since the seventeenth century, from textile to literary production, a wealth of research published since the 1990s has added depth and texture to our understanding of gender and women's experience through the sophisticated use of newly available sources and—crucially—a skeptical approach to earlier assumptions about the status and experiences of women.[3]

Fang Shanyu and Xu Zonghan were members of an underresearched generation of women whose lives spanned the 1911 revolution and the New Culture era but who enjoyed neither the new freedoms that resulted for some nor the recognition accorded to others. While Xu's positioning in *1911* is jarring, given her work, Fang's treatment in *Soul Haunted by Painting* appears emblematic of the experiences of a wider generation of women whose acceptance—willing or otherwise—of earlier social conventions left them stigmatized once those conventions were discarded. Whether or not we feel immediate sympathy for Xu and Fang, however, we should recognize that their marginalized status on-screen is to some extent a proxy for gaps in current historical scholarship and is therefore a call to further inquiry. In asking students to recenter their reading of the films on these peripheral characters, we redirect their attention toward relatively neglected strands of past experience and place at center stage the question of whose stories get told.

Notes

1. See, in particular, the remarks by Madeleine Pelling quoted in Thorpe.

2. This is a growing field, which includes work such as Judge and Hu; Liu et al.; Hershatter and Wang; Ko and Wang; and Glosser.

3. Key works here include, among others, Bray; Ko; and Mann, *Precious Records*.

Works Cited

Bailey, Paul J. *Women and Gender in Twentieth-Century China*. Macmillan International Higher Education, 2012.

Bray, Francesca. *Technology and Gender: Fabrics of Power in Late Imperial China*. U of California P, 1997.

Glosser, Susan L. *Chinese Visions of Family and State, 1915–1953*. U of California P, 2003.

Hershatter, Gail. "State of the Field: Women in China's Long Twentieth Century." *The Journal of Asian Studies*, vol. 63, no. 4, 2004, pp. 991–1065.

Hershatter, Gail, and Wang Zheng. "Chinese History: A Useful Category of Gender Analysis." *The American Historical Review*, vol. 113, no. 5, 2008, pp. 1404–21.

Hinsch, Bret. "Ten Chinese Books That Changed Our View of Women's History." *Nan nü: Men, Women, and Gender in Early and Imperial China*, vol. 20, no. 1, 2018, pp. 153–67.

Judge, Joan, and Hu Ying. *Beyond Exemplar Tales: Women's Biography in Chinese History*. U of California P, 2011.

Ko, Dorothy. *Teachers of the Inner Chambers: Women and Culture in Seventeenth-Century China*. Stanford UP, 1994.

Ko, Dorothy, and Wang Zheng. "Introduction: Translating Feminisms in China." *Gender and History*, vol. 18, no. 3, 2006, pp. 463–71.

Lee, Lily Xiao Hong. *The Twentieth Century, 1912–2000*. Routledge, 2015. Vol. 2 of *Biographical Dictionary of Chinese Women*, Lily Xiao Hong Lee and A. D. Stefanowska, editors in chief.

Liu, Lydia He, et al., editors. *The Birth of Chinese Feminism: Essential Texts in Transnational Theory*. Columbia UP, 2013.

Mann, Susan. *Precious Records: Women in China's Long Eighteenth Century*. Stanford UP, 1997.

———. "Scene-Setting: Writing Biography in Chinese History." *The American Historical Review*, vol. 114, no. 3, 2009, pp. 631–39.

———. *The Talented Women of the Zhang Family*. U of California P, 2007.

1911. Directed by Zhang Li, Mega Star, 2011.

"Pan Yuliang." Lee, pp. 417–20.

Pan Yuliang materials. Cdn.aaa.org.hk/_source/John_Clark_Archive/4-2-pan-yuliang-materials-1.pdf. Accessed 30 Oct. 2021.

Qi Haiyan. "China's Missing Women Revolutionaries." *Sixth Tone*, 18 June 2021, www.sixthtone.com/news/1007772.

Rosenstone, Robert. *History on Film, Film on History*. Pearson Longman, 2006.

Soul Haunted by Painting. Directed by Huang Shuqin, Facets Video, 1994.

Thorpe, Vanessa. "Rewriting History: How Imperfect Costume Dramas Make the Past Relevant." *The Guardian*, 27 June 2021, www.theguardian.com/tv-and-radio/2021/jun/27/rewriting-history-how-imperfect-costume-dramas-make-the-past-relevant.

"Xu Zonghan." Lee, pp. 606–08.

Part III

Image and Reality of a Changing China

Hongwei Thorn Chen and Aleksander Sedzielarz

Chinese Documentaries: A Series Approach

The historical real haunts the teaching of Chinese films. Despite our resistance as scholars to understanding films as transparent windows onto China, this is precisely the structural expectation in most classrooms in the United States, where films perform the double duty of serving as texts of creative production and representations of Chinese culture and history. The questions of historicity—namely, of how films from a certain national context signify national history and culture—cast their shadows over all national cinema courses. They are acute and unavoidable when teaching documentary, the mode of filmmaking that is most expected to make claims to historical and social verisimilitude. This essay examines the problems that emerge out of such a context and discusses strategies for using documentary to guide students' reflections on how China is mediated through cinematic images. As we argue, concepts emerging out of film historiography—in particular, the concept of the historical series—can serve as an effective principle for situating Chinese documentary films in various syllabi. Rather than taking for granted existing narratives of historical change and teaching films as exemplars of these narratives, we argue that Chinese documentaries can be used in a number of settings to break apart reified understandings of both documentary history and Chinese history.

For professional historians, the document series is an essential intermediary between the archive and its narrativization. Consisting of a set of documents with relatively consistent qualities (for example, grain prices ascertained by similar means), the series enables researchers to isolate and build narratives about differences within a homogenous set. Michèle Lagny argues that such methods are difficult to apply to film history, insofar as films are "disseminated" and "disarticulated" objects, containing traces of multitudinous historical processes: artistic, material, industrial, economic, cultural, political, and others (36). This plurality of historical series, and hence possible historical narratives, is for Lagny a generative possibility. As a document in a disarticulated set of historical series, films can be used to answer a variety of historiographic questions beyond self-contained "film history." By treating individual films as "symptoms"—that is, collections of "signs related to other signs"—films can be studied as "open fields where different forces . . . come into being and confront each other" (41).

Lagny's series approach has been taken up in contemporary film and media scholarship, which has mapped film's coeval development with other technological, political, social, and cultural tendencies. In the classroom, the time constraints of syllabi and film screenings, as well as the need to introduce students to touchstone works, often makes it efficacious to resort to relatively fixed narratives of film or national history in order to frame the significance of individual film texts. Individual films must be allowed to stand as representatives of broader movements and trajectories. We propose, nonetheless, that Lagny's insights be applied to teaching, and in particular, the teaching of Chinese documentary films with the aim of encouraging reflective and ethical thinking in students about the historicity of images. The historical series can be taken as a principle that is reflected in the design of syllabi, the preparation of lectures and discussions, and the creation of assignments that enable multivalent storytelling possibilities. Applied to the teaching of Chinese films, this principle aims to guide students to resist their impulse to take China as a signified that the films represent—a tendency determined both by Orientalist cultural formations and by the structural position of national cinemas in curricula—and instead to relativize their understanding of the relationship between films and their contexts.

As Philip Rosen argues, documentary films pose acute questions of historicity because the procedures they employ are remarkably akin to those of professional historiography: they assemble fragmentary source documents that they then interpret to create a narrative about the real (234). These narratives of the real, in turn, achieve authority through professional institutions and stabilized generic conventions and hence take on the function of social and political mediation. All these levels of documentary production, distribution, exhibition, and reception have their own multivalent histories: they at once belong to a globally recognized institution and mode of spectatorship while splintering off into other more localized and non-film-related series. With this dynamic in mind, we discuss in this essay the use of Chinese documentaries in two course contexts: a standard course on documentary and a Chinese national cinema survey course. Although we attempt to generalize, we base our remarks on specific courses that we have taught. The section "Documentary and Comparative Method" is based on an introductory composition and communications course previously taught by Aleksander Sedzielarz at the Georgia Institute of Technology. This section details how Chinese documentaries can be used to relativize the dominant Euro-American narrative about the direct-cinema approach also known as cinema verité. The section "Documentary as an Auxiliary Text" is based on an intermediate Chinese cinema course, Politics of Chinese Cinema, first taught at Brown University and later adapted for teaching at Tulane University by Hongwei Thorn Chen. Organized around politicized debates about the relationship between cinema and the Chinese nation, the course focuses primarily on fiction films. This section explores how to use specific clips from Chinese documentaries to clarify the historical signification of fiction film images.

The films that are discussed below serve as particular examples of how our design principle can be utilized. For instructors seeking to use these films in the classroom, we have included an appendix with information on accessing subtitled versions. *River Elegy* (河殇) and *West of the Tracks* (铁西区) present logistical difficulties for the classroom on account of their lengthy run time. The only version of *River Elegy* available with English titles is a shortened fifty-minute satellite television broadcast of the original three-and-a-half-hour series, although auxiliary texts, such as the readers guide by the series creators Su Xiaokang and Wang Luxiang, can help instructors teach the other segments. The sections below include a discussion of strategies for working with these logistical hurdles.

Documentary and Comparative Method

Films from mainland China provide instructors in documentary cinema courses a way of intervening in two interrelated problems: first, the preconception among students that the documentary film is, a priori, a representation of historical reality, and second, the universalizing Euro-American narrative of documentary history. This section suggests that the use of Chinese *zhuanti pian* (专题片; "special topics films") from the 1980s and *xianchang* (现场; "on the spot") films of the Chinese New Documentary Film movement can be used to relativize the historical narratives of documentary's relationship to truth, manifested, in particular, in debates around direct cinema and cinema verité.[1] By complicating universalizing periodizations of documentary history—surmised, for example, as a historical trajectory from the work of Robert Joseph Flaherty to voice-over government documentaries, direct cinema or cinema verité, and reflexive or performative approaches—such films can be used to highlight the relationship between documentary modes and sociocultural context.

Before screening New Documentary films, the instructor provided background readings from the anthology *The New Chinese Documentary Film Movement: For the Public Record* and a lecture that frames cinema's historical relationship to politics and the economy in mainland China.[2] Nonetheless, the urge to know often overtakes the process of learning: many students inevitably impose onto films a generalized ideological notion of China based in Western-biased projections of China as either a communist state or a developing nation. Documentary films from China are thus most effective when taught in a way that creates what Elizabeth Cowie calls the "irreconcilable gap" between film images and the historical forces that give rise to them (186). Students face, on the one hand, the clearly mediated nature of films (even those that take a direct approach to their subjects) and, on the other, a disruption in which images perceived as historical reality refuse to fit within students' assumptions about Chinese history. In the gap, students build on what is unknown by attending in detail to the art and rhetoric of documentary—as mimetic works of art composed of fragments of reality or as rhetorical situations driven by an audience's desire for the real within a localized sociocultural context.

Throughout the course, students revisited the origin of the term *documentary* in a way that led into particularities of the history of documentary in the United States and Europe: the course began with John Grierson's attribution of "documentary value" to Robert Flaherty's films (Grierson). Students tracked the use of continuity editing and narrative realism in *Nanook of the North* to draw into question the film's empirical connection to the Itivimuit peoples of northern Canada.[3] Drawing on Bill Nichols, who describes phases of documentary-film form articulated from within more general historical processes in which "the success of every form breeds its own overthrow: it limits, omits, disavows, represses" ("Voice" 18), the class surveyed a series of polemics that question cinema verité as a telos for treating documentary as cinematic truth telling and the achievement of an unmediated documentary reality in the post-1960s period.[4] Rather than categorically defining vérité within film history, these intellectual exchanges help bring students to question film styles perceived as natural or nonideological in a given historical context. Versions of vérité offered by polemicist accounts against it serve a pedagogical aim by mirroring students' conflicting perceptions of reality and history in cinematic representation.

Organizing a syllabus around polemics over verité precludes having one single or authoritative historical account of verité and thus situates films within a plurality of historical documents, a set of series that provide fertile ground for rethinking assumptions about documentary truth and the constructedness of historical truth. However, despite the convenience of unity that such a design provides, through it the syllabus becomes a parochial version of film history with an extremely limited and biased account of vérité. This approach leads students to develop an understanding of stylistic innovation in contemporary documentary films based on a narrow periodization. To avoid this outcome, instructors can introduce verité-style films from mainland China to create productive dialectical breaks and help students think of the syllabus series in plural and heterodox terms. Not only are these films irreconcilable with what students might presume to be a unified Euro-American film history, intricacies of form and style that arise from the Chinese New Documentary Film movement's use of film to expose the contingency of local historical processes are irreducible to a generalized historical narrative of China.

The earliest iteration of the documentary course included a screening of *Jiang Hu: Life on the Road* (江湖), in which the filmmaker travels with a countryside art troupe, which was paired with Wu Wenguang's essay "DV: Individual Filmmaking." In the essay, Wu recounts the influence of direct cinema and describes the filmmaker as active within the social and historical context of the film. Wu's film and text deepen students' understanding of the contingency of events on film as a constructed marker of truth formed in an ongoing relationship with the subjects of the documentary. Because students understood Wu's film solely in relation to the brief but influential contact that Wu and other New Documentary filmmakers had with direct cinema approaches, which Lü Xinyu explains were a seminal part of a first phase of New Documentary filmmaking in the

1990s, later versions of the course featured units on the controversial *zhuanti pian* documentary *River Elegy* and Wang Bing's independent documentary *West of the Tracks* to map the emergence and diverse uses of *xianchang* aesthetics from 1980s state documentary production to New Documentary films ("Ruins" 24–25). This history presents the possibility of an alternative periodization of cinema verité. Rather than understanding verité as an embrace of a perceived ideal of unmediated documentary sound and image—or through the withering criticism made by advocates of reflexive modes of post-1960s documentary film that cinema verité makes naive presumptions of having privileged access to the real— students came to understand the debate plurally as they viewed verité techniques deployed within a localized historical series by filmmakers working against the grain of *zhuanti pian* television broadcasts. *Zhuanti pian* and *xianchang* films break up familiar historical series from which a given film might be read or within which a given film might be inserted as a document. The films thus returned the class to critiques of documentary representation encountered earlier in the course, but made representation personal by asking students to question global and Western frames of reference.

With a run time of 555 minutes, *West of the Tracks* invites students' interest because it so far exceeds the limits of temporality and structure that students might assume pertains to film production. Often considered a monument of the New Documentary Film movement, *West of the Tracks* offers a paradigmatic and peculiar case of the *xianchang* approach: although it is shot on location in the declining industrial plants of Shenyang, its overwhelming run time and focus on contingent everyday details give it a poetic, dreamlike quality, complicating claims that on-the-spot shooting yields direct and unmediated representations of reality. Although instructors may decide to only screen sections of *West of the Tracks* that are relevant to lectures, assignments, and readings, encouraging students to review the entire film in some form is necessary to demonstrate the filmmaker's relationship to the profilmic—that is, to a range of contingent objects and events captured by the film—that is characteristic of the New Documentary Film movement.

The most effective approach to screening New Documentary films with long run times is to put the entire film on reserve or upload the film to a learning management system and then direct students in individualized or group screening assignments (see the appendix for films available on *YouTube*). If the film is covered in one or two weeks, students can be assigned to self-report which sections of the film they watched and why they chose a specific section of the film to watch. If a longer part of the term is devoted to the New Documentary Film movement, students can be assigned to keep a viewing journal to gather observations and note what sections of the film they watched each day. Assigning a plot segmentation exercise encourages students to more closely watch one section of the film. In the segmentation exercise, students are given a choice to watch one part of the film and are later given a numbered list of narrative events in each part of the film. They are then asked to identify and organize the narrative events within the section of the film that they watched. Another way of viewing the entire film, or long sections of the film, as a class is by pairing group screenings with plot segmentation activities that students complete after watching in groups and later present to the class. Student groups can be assigned one of the three parts of the film to watch and given an assignment sheet on which they number and break down sections of the film's narrative into segments that they define as major plot events. Students then present their segmentations to the class with screenshots as illustrations that also exemplify the visual and formal symmetries of each segment of the film.

Short writing assignments based on Wu's essay, as well as on a reading by Lü Xinyu ("Ruins") that places Wang Bing's *West of the Tracks* within China's political, social, and economic conditions at the end of the twentieth century, prompted students to determine how relationships between the documentary filmmaker and members of the performance troupe and the factory workers depicted in *Jiang Hu* and *West of the Tracks*, respectively, are mediated in the films by recording, editing, and captioning. Students were also asked to reflect on connections between *xianchang* documentary filmmaking and ethical problems presented by new technologies. One way of doing this is to have students brainstorm the parallels between the contemporary proliferation of cell phone cameras and the New Documentary Film movement's self-reflexive involvement in profilmic events recorded on digital video. In their writing assignments, students raised questions about the concept of liveness (and thus contingency) in the film, about the filmmaker's ultimate control over the narrative, and about the social responsibility entailed in the relationship between filmmaker and documentary subject. While these open-ended questions launched abstract ethical debates, they sometimes closed what Cowie refers to as the "gap" between film images and historical forces (186): students interpreted films through discourses of political and economic liberalism that undergird everyday life in the United States and thereby erase difference within the films. They derived a picture of a China progressing toward the total freedom of a market economy and only held back by vague forces of totalitarianism, censorship, and state control—as one student described it, quoting directly from *River Elegy*, "oriental despotism." In closing the gap, students entered into what Daniel Vukovich has described as a Western sinological knowledge that produces China as a form of dubious knowledge (8–9). The task then in articulating these films within their immediate historical context was to put under scrutiny this urge to make filmic images representative of a China perceived as commensurate with the United States in terms of globalized political and economic power and to develop a break.

Presenting the New Documentary Film movement's uses of verité alongside the People's Republic of China's television broadcasts of earlier *zhuanti pian* documentaries, which *River Elegy* is both a variant on and a subversion of, allows for an even more focused and historically situated analysis of how documentary filmmaking practices evolve in a complex relationship with other media in a market economy. In teaching *River Elegy* and *West of the Tracks*, instructors may link verité techniques with, for example, the availability of consumer recording technologies in China's growing market economy under Deng Xiaoping and Jiang Zemin (Berry and Rofel). At the same time, introducing students to the dynamic Chinese intellectual debates over market economies in the late 1980s underscores *River Elegy*'s explicit positioning of audience vis-à-vis hegemonic master narratives (Su and Wang). Concluding the semester by comparing *West of the Tracks* with Steven Bognar and Julia Reichert's films *American Factory* and *The Last Truck: Closing of a GM Plant* stimulates students to challenge their assumptions about documentary, China, and the United States while anchoring class discussions in the specific conditions of each society's political economy as experienced by the working class. Encouraging students to comparatively investigate verité and direct-cinema approaches in order to raise questions of self, public, and political apparatus in the context of post-1989 China both expands their view of verité and illuminates Chinese cinema from within multiple complex historical series. For some students, the meditative ruminations on history presented in *River Elegy* complicated stereotypes of communist media: by not presenting the party-line political views that they expected to find in the film, *River Elegy* taught them the significance of the *zhuanti pian* documentary within a historical moment of mediation and dialogue between party intellectuals and a growing class of media consumers. Responding to *West of the Tracks*, students stated that the film's prolonged shots and the reflexive presence of the filmmaker revealed intricacies of economic change through what they viewed as the interconnectedness of media and labor. Students noted the intrinsic contradiction in on-the-spot filmmaking technologies being both a visible and material sign of economic advance and a mode for documenting localized crises surrounding deindustrialization.

Documentary as an Auxiliary Text

Beyond being used in a general class on documentary film, Chinese documentaries can be made to serve an auxiliary function in a national cinema survey course, where the focus is on narrative fiction. Due to the structural demands of coverage in national cinemas courses (see Majumdar), Chinese national cinema courses often do not have the space for a stand-alone unit on documentary through which a nuanced discussion of this mode of filmmaking could be developed. The Politics of Chinese Cinemas course mentioned earlier provided a survey of post-1949 filmmaking, with a focus on film as a medium of political claim making in China. The course took up narrative films such as *To Live* (活着), *Song of Youth* (青春之歌), and *The Founding of a Republic* (建国大业) to explore, in particular, how the narrativization of historical memory serves present political functions. In addition to short writing assignments throughout the semester, students wrote two papers in which they used formal film analysis to elaborate how certain political themes or debates surfaced in a particular film and how they were in turn complicated by the particulars of film form, aesthetics, and spectatorship. In this context, a documentary can be used effectively as an auxiliary text, shown either in whole or in selected clips, to situate and pose research questions about the landmark fiction films that are usually the main attractions. With their built-in yet notably partial claims to historical reality, documentaries can function here not to establish context but to produce historical series, offering a sense of how particular images from fiction films take on variable meanings.

Consider, for example, the pairing of *River Elegy* with *Yellow Earth* (黄土地), a key text of fifth-generation filmmaking and an exemplar of the root-seeking tendencies of the 1980s cultural debates. Taken on its own, *Yellow Earth* is a self-conscious and stylistically provocative film, capable of sustaining complex discussions about the politics of style (Zhu), the revaluation of Yan'an as the cradle of the communist revolution, theoretical investigations into the representation of subalterns (Chow), and a site for ethnomusicological analysis.[5] In the film, the Yellow River and the titular earth of the Loess Plateau are saturated with historical symbolism, which can be established through supplementary readings and examples from other media. To open the historicity of the iconic images to examination by students, however, a larger sample size is needed. Here, *River Elegy* offers an ideal auxiliary text, presenting its own discursive interpretation of the river and earth as symbols of China's five-thousand-year-old agricultural civilization in need of radical change. There is no question of taking the argument in *River Elegy* at face value as describing a historical reality to which the director Chen Kaige and the cinematographer Zhang Yimou responded in *Yellow Earth*. Instead, the documentary, which draws on archival images from the fifth-generation film *Yellow Earth*, among others, uses them to illustrate a historiographical argument that took a radical position on prevailing intellectual debates (Wang 118–36; Su and Wang). While the *zhuanti pian* televisual format of *River Elegy* is a far cry from the art-house-oriented *Yellow Earth*, the two texts maintain consistency in terms of how they work with certain symbolically charged images, and on this basis they can be put into conversation.

In this setting, the six-part documentary series does not need to be viewed in toto and can be broken into smaller semantic units, particularly those that feature images akin to or taken directly from *Yellow Earth* (e.g., the enigmatic scene of praying for rain, which becomes used to emphasize the dependence of civilization on water). In discussion, instructors might ask students how *River Elegy* reframes these images through montage (e.g., repeated shots of Egyptian pyramids). They may also ask students to identify lines of dialogue and cinematographic strategies from *Yellow Earth* that might fit the narrative advanced in the documentary as well as aspects of *Yellow Earth* that break from the argument in the documentary or render its conclusion ambiguous. Such exercises are not meant to establish a definitive historical argument about *Yellow Earth*'s statement on reform in 1980s China or the proximities and distances between fifth-generation filmmakers and the makers of *River Elegy*. Rather they encourage students to think about film images historically as taking on determinate yet variable meanings depending on the social milieu of viewers, and moreover, they frame a set of historically situated debates on which students can build focused formal analyses.

A similar unit could be taught on the connection between so-called sixth-generation (or urban-generation) filmmaking in the 1990s and 2000s and the New Documentary Film movement. Scholars such as Jason Mc-Grath and Luke Robinson (*Independent Chinese Documentary*) have established clearly the historical links between the two cinematic movements. Here, instructors might focus on a particular set of questions pertaining to the role of the *xianchang* aesthetic in picturing postsocialist transformation, utilized in sixth-generation films such as *Xiao Wu* (小武) and *Suzhou River* (苏州河) and documentaries such as *Meishi Street* (煤市街). In this course, claims of on-the-spot realism are made to speak not to the global history of cinema verité but to the specific conjuncture of independent films made in the 1990s and 2000s in China. Such films have often been praised by critics for providing unofficial and hence unfiltered images of Chinese reality compared to the films of the allegorically inclined fifth generation and the institutionalized ideological discourse of the *zhuanti pian* documentary form. Without rejecting this dualistic formulation, the class can explore how the pairing of fiction film with documentary can put pressure on claims of realism that are based on the indexical effect of the cameraperson being on the spot of social phenomena.

Being on the spot appears to establish an authoritative connection between the filmmaker and social reality, but in *Meishi Street* the filmmakers' decision to distribute digital camcorders to the film's subjects raises questions about the relationship between on-the-spot images and narrative authority. Students might be asked to debate whether Zhang Jinli, an activist against the demolition of his Beijing neighborhood and the main subject of the film, could shape how his footage would be used or whether the narrational authority lay with Ou Ning and his filmmaking team. Beyond raising questions about documentary ethics, such debates allow for students to develop variable interpretations of the signification of on-the-spot footage. Such concerns are refigured in *Xiao Wu*, where, as McGrath argues, the director expertly straddles the line between the documentary-indebted procedures of on-location, handheld-camera work and a more refined arthouse long-take style, showing how the real in independent cinema is institutionally mediated (89–95). The opening documentary shots of the eponymous river in *Suzhou River* cite the roots of sixth-generation cinema in *xianchang* aesthetics, but the ensuing narrative, framed by the perspective of a cameraman for hire who dreams up variations of a love story concerning two lovers, takes a further turn on the New Documentary slogan that "the camera does not lie," questioning, precisely, the relationship between indexical footage and narrative.[6] The fact that all three films use images of urban ruins as indexes of the postsocialist transformation allows us to establish a set of questions similar to those we raised with *River Elegy*. For example, in their final essays, students might compare the representation of urban ruins in the noir-like dreamscape of *Suzhou River* and the depiction of urban struggle in *Meishi Street*. As with our selection of *River Elegy*, the aim of juxtaposing these two films is neither to teach rarified film history nor to use documentaries to establish facts about a historical milieu but rather to show how a particular set of images can be used to make and question claims to historical reality.

Possessing the seductive glimmer of historical reality, documentary films in any course risk prompting students to see film as a record of the world rather than a representation. Incorporating documentary films from mainland China in a college classroom in the United States poses a pedagogical challenge for the instructor, who must separate students' desire to understand China as a whole from the specific and localized problems that film brings under discussion. Taught as part of diverse historical series, documentary films allow students to come face-to-face with the discrete functioning of artistic, material, industrial, economic, and cultural processes before these processes are reified into master narratives of history. Although the two courses were vastly different, the learning outcomes for each course required a rethinking of methods of film history in such a way that allowed for films' status as "disarticulated" objects to come into view (Lagny 36). For an educator, reflecting on the seriality involved in creating screenings, assignments, and lectures on a syllabus can lead to a critical understanding of the classroom as a site of meaning making that happens from within polymorphic sets of historically interconnected and intersecting texts or objects. For students, aiming to loosen these unities can be a learning outcome that encourages different ways of looking at assigned texts but also centers students' agency in questioning rigid structures of meaning.

We suggest designing independent research projects that ask students to explore films by which they might reorder the historical series of the course syllabus or to create presentations or videographic essays on historical documents discovered in the archive that challenge presumed historical seriality. Such projects can interrupt the institutional and authoritative development of course materials as much as they can deepen inquiry into the sociocultural contexts of film technologies, film production and reception, or cinema style or approach. Inspiration for these pedagogical moves ultimately arises from the open field that film brings into view—and the further demands that documentary film puts on students and educators to interpret mediation from within multiple networks of local and global media, politics, and entertainment. Considering documentary films from mainland China as narratives of the real about China, and as self-reflexively signifying a presumably real time and place in history that touches on students' everyday experiences, invites desire but ultimately defers unified interpretation. This suspension of desire, as we have demonstrated, makes the classroom a place where students can freely conjecture, hypothesize, and loosen master narratives of history while actively becoming better analysts of film who can unsettle a public discourse in which historical reality becomes fixed through visual representation.

Notes

1. Debates around direct cinema and cinema verité describe two tendencies in post-1960s documentary filmmaking in Europe, the United States, and Japan that eschewed voice-over commentary in favor of the camera's seemingly unmediated presentation of events. While direct cinema and cinema verité are now frequently taught as part of the dialectical development of documentary through modernist, reflexive, and postmodern techniques and modes, they remain a point of reference—and contention—for documentary theory and production techniques that deploy sound and image recording to capture events as they happen and in which the filmmaker appears in the middle of the events on film. Mamber and other early advocates of direct cinema and cinema verité in the United States and Europe expressed a zeal for ostensibly unmediated styles that would "strip away the accumulated conventions of traditional cinema in the hope of rediscovering a reality that eludes other forms of filmmaking" (4).

2. Background readings include Lü Xinyu, "Rethinking"; Robinson, "From 'Public.'"

3. Here we were guided by Russell, who writes that Flaherty represents "native culture as outside of history, stuck in an eternally present tense" (110).

4. Although Nichols later observes that verité is "amorphous" rather than one single tendency—while subdividing it into "observational" and "interactive" styles (*Representing Reality* 38–39)—the seminal essay "The Voice of Documentary" sketches successive "phases" (18) that later crystalize into a polemical engagement with verité in the work of critics like Linda Williams. See also Rabinowitz's overview of critiques of verité and direct cinema (124–28).

5. For an ethnomusicological analysis of *Yellow Earth*, see the essay by Ho Chak Law in this volume.

6. For more on *Suzhou River*, see the essay by Lily Li in this volume. For a discussion of the slogan "my camera doesn't lie," see Braester.

Appendix: Annotated Filmography

This filmography was compiled to help researchers and teachers locate complete original versions of documentary films from mainland China, which often circulate outside of mainstream commercial channels. Dialogue in the films is in Mandarin. It is highly recommended that instructors secure a copy of a film and not rely on *YouTube*.

Jiang Hu: Life on the Road

The full, 130-minute version of *Jiang Hu* is available from Wu Wenguang Caochangdi Workstation. A 120-minute DVD version has English subtitles.

Meishi Street

Meishi Street was produced by Alternative Archives and has a run time of eighty-five minutes. In the United States, it is distributed by dGenerate Films. The film is available for institutional DVD and streaming purchase from dGenerate and is available with an institutional subscription to *Alexander Street*. With English subtitles.

River Elegy

The full, six-episode, 219-minute version of *River Elegy* was produced by China Central Television (Zhongyang Dianshi Tai). In the United States, it was distributed by Meiguo Nanhai Limited in Millbrae, California (Meiguo Nanhai You Xian Gong Si), on VHS.

   A condensed fifty-eight-minute version of the film was broadcast by Direct Broadcast Satellite Deep Dish TV. This version was part of a 1990 series called "Will Be Televised: Video Documents from Asia," which also included segments on Korea, the Philippines, Taiwan, and Hong Kong. Available on *YouTube* (*River Elegy* [*YouTube*]) with English subtitles.

West of the Tracks

West of the Tracks was produced by the Wang Bing Film Workshop and the Rotterdam Film Festival Hubert Bals Fund and has a 555-minute run time. An eight-disk set of the film on DVD is distributed by Documentary Educational Resources. A four-disk set is also available from Tiger Releases. The film is also available on *Kanopy* and *Alexander Street* for those with a subscription. All the versions listed here have English subtitles. The full version is available on *YouTube* ("*West of the Tracks* Part 1 Disk 1"; "*West of the Tracks* Part 1 Disk 2"; "*West of the Tracks* Part 1 Disk 3"; "*West of the Tracks* Part 1 Disk 4"; "*West of the Tracks* Part 2 Disk 1"; "*West of the Tracks* Part 2 Disk 2"; "*West of the Tracks* Part 2 Disk 3"; "*West of the Tracks* Part 3 Disk 1"; "*West of the Tracks* Part 3 Disk 2").

Works Cited

American Factory. Directed by Steven Bognar and Julia Reichert, Higher Ground Productions / Participant Media, 2019.

Berry, Chris, and Lisa Rofel. "Alternative Archive: China's Independent Documentary Culture." Berry et al., pp. 135–54.

Berry, Chris, et al., editors. *The New Chinese Documentary Film Movement: For the Public Record.* Hong Kong UP, 2010.

Braester, Yomi. "Excuse Me, Your Camera Is in My Face: Auteurial Intervention in PRC New Documentary." Berry et. al., pp. 195–216.

Chow, Rey. *Primitive Passions: Visuality, Sexuality, Ethnography, and Contemporary Chinese Cinema.* Columbia UP, 1995.

Cowie, Elizabeth. *Recording Reality, Desiring the Real.* U of Minnesota P, 2011.

The Founding of a Republic. Directed by Han Sanping and Huang Jianxin, Shanghai Film Studio, 2009.

Grierson, John. "Flaherty's Moana, a Poetic South Sea Film Comes to the Rialto." *The New-York Sun,* 8 Feb. 1926.

Jiang Hu: Life on the Road. Directed by Wu Wenguang, Wu Wenguang, 1999.

Lagny, Michèle. "Film History; or, History Expropriated." *Film History,* vol. 6, no. 1, 1994, pp. 26–44.

The Last Truck: Closing of a GM Plant. Directed by Steven Bognar and Julia Reichert, HBO Films, 2009.

Lü Xinyu. "Rethinking China's New Documentary Movement: Engaging with the Social." Translated by Tan Jia and Lisa Rofel. Berry et al., pp. 15–48.

———. "Ruins of the Future: Class and History in Wang Bing's *Tiexi District.*" *New Left Review,* no. 31, 2005, pp. 125–36.

Majumdar, Neepa. "Teaching Indian Cinema." *Teaching Film,* edited by Lucy Fischer and Patrice Petro, Modern Language Association of America, 2012, pp. 163–79.

Mamber, Stephen. *Cinema Verite in America: Studies in Uncontrolled Documentary.* MIT Press, 1974.

McGrath, Jason. "The Independent Cinema of Jia Zhangke: From Postsocialist Realism to a Transnational Aesthetic." *The Urban Generation: Chinese Cinema and Society at the Turn of the Twenty-First Century,* edited by Zhang Zhen, Duke UP, 2007, pp. 81–114.

Meishi Street. Directed by Ou Ning, Alternative Archive, 2006.

Nanook of the North. Directed by Robert J. Flaherty, Les Frères Revillon, 1922.

Nichols, Bill. *Representing Reality: Issues and Concepts in Documentary.* Indiana UP, 1991.

———. "The Voice of Documentary." *Film Quarterly,* vol. 36, no. 3, 1983, pp. 17–30.

Rabinowitz, Paula. "Wreckage upon Wreckage: History, Documentary and the Ruins of Memory." *History and Theory,* vol. 32, no. 2, 1993, pp. 119–37.

River Elegy. YouTube, uploaded by Tetley Bildungsroman, 24 Apr. 2012, www.youtube.com/watch?v=39j4ViRxcS8&t=6s.

River Elegy. Directed by Su Xiaokang et al., China Central Television, 1988.

Robinson, Luke. "From 'Public' to 'Private': Chinese Documentary and the Logic of *Xianchang.*" Berry et al., pp. 177–94.

———. *Independent Chinese Documentary: From the Studio to the Street.* Palgrave Macmillan, 2013.

Rosen, Philip. *Change Mummified: Cinema, Historicity, Theory.* U of Minnesota P, 2001.

Russell, Catherine. *Experimental Ethnography.* Duke UP, 1999.

Song of Youth. Directed by Chen Huaiai and Cui Wei, Beijing Film Studio, 1959.

Su Xiaokang and Wang Luxiang. *Deathsong of the River: A Reader's Guide to the Chinese TV Series* Heshang. Translated by Richard W. Bodman and Pin P. Wan, Cornell UP, 1991. Cornell East Asia Series.

Suzhou River. Directed by Lou Ye, Dream Factory, 2000.

To Live. Directed by Zhang Yimou, Shanghai Film Studios, 1994.

Vukovich, Daniel F. *China and Orientalism: Western Knowledge Production and the P.R.C.* Routledge, 2012.

Wang, Jing. *High Culture Fever: Politics, Aesthetics, and Ideology in Deng's China*. U of California P, 1996.

West of the Tracks. Directed by Wang Bing, Wang Bing Film Workshop, 2002.

"*West of the Tracks* Part 1 Disk 1." *YouTube*, uploaded by David Griffith, 13 Sept. 2021, www.youtube.com/watch?v=7V3XKriMdPo.

"*West of the Tracks* Part 1 Disk 2." *YouTube*, uploaded by David Griffith, 13 Sept. 2021, www.youtube.com/watch?v=tUE9mWSQg7o.

"*West of the Tracks* Part 1 Disk 3." *YouTube*, uploaded by David Griffith, 13 Sept. 2021, www.youtube.com/watch?v=Re5xG1A6wuw.

"*West of the Tracks* Part 1 Disk 4." *YouTube*, uploaded by David Griffith, 13 Sept. 2021, www.youtube.com/watch?v=YCo7YTh3Leg.

"*West of the Tracks* Part 2 Disk 1." *YouTube*, uploaded by David Griffith, 13 Sept. 2021, www.youtube.com/watch?v=2Ep--ieo214.

"*West of the Tracks* Part 2 Disk 2." *YouTube*, uploaded by David Griffith, 13 Sept. 2021, www.youtube.com/watch?v=C-7gkFGsQak.

"*West of the Tracks* Part 2 Disk 3." *YouTube*, uploaded by David Griffith, 13 Sept. 2021, www.youtube.com/watch?v=y07o2L_iJe4.

"*West of the Tracks* Part 3 Disk 1." *YouTube*, uploaded by David Griffith, 13 Sept. 2021, www.youtube.com/watch?v=7WQgU78E7H0.

"*West of the Tracks* Part 3 Disk 2." *YouTube*, uploaded by David Griffith, 13 Sept. 2021, www.youtube.com/watch?v=OdLmWIGOgyE.

Williams, Linda. "Mirrors without Memories: Truth, History, and the New Documentary." *Film Quarterly*, vol. 46, no. 3, 1993, pp. 9–21.

Wu Wenguang. "DV: Individual Filmmaking." Translated by Cathryn Clayton. Berry et al., pp. 49–54.

Xiao Wu. Directed by Jia Zhangke, Hu Tong Communications, 1997.

Yellow Earth. Directed by Chen Kaige, Guanxi Film Studio, 1984.

Zhu, Ying. *Chinese Cinema during the Era of Reform: The Ingenuity of the System*. Praeger, 2003.

Additional Resources

Herzog, Werner. "The Minnesota Declaration: Truth and Fact in Documentary Cinema." *Ferocious Reality: Documentary according to Werner Herzog*, edited by Eric Ames, U of Minnesota P, 2012, pp. ix–x.

Sherman, Sharon R. *Documenting Ourselves: Film, Video, and Culture*. UP of Kentucky, 1998.

**Jasmine Yu-Hsing Chen,
Sydney Pond, and Emma Clawson**

Teaching Contemporary China through Documentary

Documentaries can be powerful pedagogical tools in teaching about contemporary China and supporting educators' classroom practices in general. This film genre is particularly useful in helping students explore and reflect on cultures new to them and providing perspectives that are often unrepresented in policy debates, academic discussions, and textbooks. When covering debatable issues and marginalized populations, documentaries can build empathy among different groups by providing a unique type of cross-cultural contact. As such, these films help educators tackle the daunting task of teaching about issues of culture and difference. However, most research on the pedagogical usefulness of documentaries is social science–oriented, and only a few sources are oriented toward the humanities. Additionally, despite the medium's proven learning benefits, its inclusion is not highly evident in the books and supplementary materials assigned in Chinese film courses. The teaching of Chinese films in North America has centered on feature films, leaving Chinese documentaries sidelined. Thus, this essay contributes to the literature on cultural education with a discussion on how to use documentaries to teach about contemporary China and enrich students' global awareness and sensibility.

Drawing on interdisciplinary film scholarship and classroom experience, the authors combine film analysis with pedagogical evaluations of using documentary films in classrooms. This essay centers on teaching the topic of China's *liushou ertong* (留守儿童; "left-behind children")[1]—children who are left behind in rural regions by parents who work in urban areas. The documentary *Children at a Village School* (村小的孩子) is used to demonstrate how a documentary can effectively introduce American students to the multifaceted issues of contemporary China. This documentary is directed by the Hunan-based filmmaker Jiang Nengjie. Jiang's filming of this documentary allowed him to capture a rare level of depth and feeling that can enrich the viewer's understanding of the topic. Additionally, Jiang targets audiences in China and worldwide with the main aim of raising their awareness of left-behind children. At the same time, this work contains English subtitles, giving American and other English-speaking college students access to the issue through Jiang's camera.[2]

The topic of left-behind children reflects numerous issues in contemporary China. Discussing this topic through documentaries motivates students to consider how globalization affects local communities and rural families. This essay provides instructors with topic-based analysis for group discussion and personal reflection. Strong discussion questions can guide students to debate various aspects of the topic covered in the documentary, including the uneven distribution of educational resources, power imbalances within social structures, sensational representation of the issue in public media, and the dangers of creating stereotypes of left-behind children as passive. The lesson plan can also be structured to encourage students to question the generalizability and reliability of documentaries, as recommended by the sociologist John Scott, who prompts a critical inquiry into whether documentary may be deemed fully authentic, credible, and representative. In a film the camera frames and guides the viewer's vision, and the director can select and edit the narrative; educators should discuss these elements as they help students become informed media consumers. Instead of treating documentaries as transparent and objective representations of real life, educators can further extend learning by exploring what is neglected in the film and how the film may impact the lives of its subjects. The analysis in this essay demonstrates how a documentary can create a space for diverse discussions and critical thinking. Thus, it contributes to the development of globally conscious viewers who can understand contemporary China from multiple perspectives.

Documentary as a Pedagogical Tool

Documentaries are utilized by educators in many fields as pedagogical tools to support their teaching practices. Documentary films are "perspective-laden narratives" that expose students to a variety of issues, events, and people that they might not encounter in their textbooks (Hess). As a teaching resource, they are particularly useful in helping students explore and reflect on new cultures because they can open "inaccessible places" to students (Hay 563). Scholars have noticed that the medium can help them teach about cultural diversity and ethics by introducing students to how people of minority cultures have contributed to specific fields (González et al.). Other studies demonstrate the effectiveness of documentaries as a teaching resource in various disciplines, including social work (Shdaimah), education (Brown), language (Yamada), and history (Marcus et al.). As shown above, many educators use documentary films to teach about culture. However, current academic publications on Chinese documentaries mainly focus on either historical contextualization or formal analysis (e.g., Robinson; Cui; Berry et al.), and there is little discussion in the literature about how this medium can be used in teaching about contemporary China.

Documentaries are especially effective as a teaching tool in culture courses. This medium is visually stimulating, engaging, and well-suited for capturing emotions in subjects' raw and vulnerable moments and telling broader overarching stories (Shdaimah). Students can see and hear the subjects in documentaries, making them more accessible than other written or verbal classroom resources. A documentary not only gives students access to a place that they may otherwise never see but also offers them the opportunity to reflect on issues that they may not have known existed (Ruggiero). Their unique capacity to provide engaging visuals, first-person accounts, reflective information, and vivid depictions of faraway places also makes them ideal for teaching sensitive and potentially triggering topics in a way that is inspiring and representative.

The Importance of Teaching about China's Left-Behind Children

Unlike traditional lectures, documentaries can introduce students to difficult subjects in a visual and intercultural manner. The issue of left-behind children is highly related to the Chinese government's strict household registration policy. This policy controls internal migration, as each citizen is registered at birth as belonging to a rural or urban household. Without an urban household registration or residency status, migrant workers from rural areas cannot access education, health care, and other public welfare programs, and so they are socially excluded from the urban mainstream (Zhou and Cheung). An insufficient income from farming, which is the main livelihood in rural regions, forces parents to leave their children behind to continue learning in rural schools while the parents migrate to cities to work for higher wages. This places families in a heartbreaking position; left-behind children commonly only see their parents once a year.

In 2017, the United Nations Children's Fund reported that over sixty million children in China were left behind (1). Despite this being an ongoing, massive problem, most students in the United States are unfamiliar with it, and it is not mentioned in many college courses related to Chinese culture or contemporary China. In the 2019 and 2020 fall semesters, Jasmine Yu-Hsing Chen introduced this topic to college students at Utah State University in the course Culture of East Asia, a depth humanities and creative arts course that is cross-listed in the history, anthropology, and language departments. Except for five international students from China, only three of the forty-nine students (total enrollment for the two semesters) had prior knowledge of China's left-behind children before taking the class, whereas all of them recognized the importance of learning about it after the discussion. Educators need to help students become informed about complicated intercultural and global issues because global awareness is crucial for developing students who strive to understand different perspectives and are well-informed decision-makers (Picardo). The issue of left-behind children is an apt one for these learning aims, as it is not only a result of the Chinese household registration policy but also a concrete reflection of the impact of globalization on local communities and rural families in China.

The issue of left-behind children points to numerous serious challenges in contemporary China, including mental and developmental health risks. Researchers have studied worrisome emotional and behavioral problems developing in China's left-behind children, including an increase in depression rates, greater levels of loneliness (Ling et al.), and developmental risks due to changes in family structure (Ding and Bao). Further, the issue of left-behind children reflects the uneven quality of China's education system (Ding and Bao; Zhang and Yang), the social price of China's economic boom (Ye), and the internal migration of rural labor and the mobility and immobility of children (Ye and Pan). From a wider perspective, these issues can indicate how China's large-scale migration and rapid urbanization are at unprecedented rates globally (Chen et al.) and how family separation has reconfigured parenting relationships in the Global South, including in China (Guan and Deng). Class discussions can cover various cultural and social issues related to left-behind children, including education, household policy, population movement, the urban-rural inequality gap, and globalization.

The alarming number of left-behind children in China has caught the attention of several news outlets and directors, leading to the production of several short news reports and documentaries such as *Hopeless: A Chinese Girl's Journey from Left-Behind Child to Migrant Worker*, a ten-minute segment produced by the *South China Morning Post*. However, not all of these documentaries would fit the needs of a college classroom in the United States. Some examples, such as *Down from the Mountain*, by Max Duncan, and *The Young Generation Left Behind in China*, by ABC News, tend to only encompass a short time period in rural China. These films cover briefly what a left-behind child's life is like. Some documentaries produced in China also come with challenges. For instance, the Chinese director Zeng Fuhu's documentary *The Childhood* is an impressive work that contains interviews of left-behind children across seven provinces in China and incorporates an insider perspective, but it does not have English subtitles. The various Chinese vernaculars used in Zeng's film create a level of difficulty in understanding, even for Mandarin speakers. The lack of English subtitles makes this and other Chinese documentaries that cover the appropriate topic poorly suited for use in some classrooms.

Children at a Village School is well-suited for students in the United States. The director, Jiang, has filmed several documentaries on left-behind children in his hometown Xinning, a rural village in Hunan province. *Children at a Village School* is unique because it follows the lives of a group of children over six years. Because of Jiang's insider perspective and long-term work on the project, the director was able to fully capture the figures and develop personal relationships with each of the families. This documentary is a beneficial teaching tool because it allows the viewer to see from the perspective of the children themselves. Jiang states that he was a left-behind child and wanted to create these documentaries as a tribute to his own childhood and to highlight the lives of these children, along with their challenges, feelings, and desires (Jiang).

Instructors can articulate that an insider's perspective has both strengths and limits. At times, an insider may feel conflicted over their multiple roles, and some people may treat an insider as an advocate rather than an unbiased observer of an issue. However, Jiang focuses more on the children's daily lives than on dramatic events, so the documentary rather shows more of the benefits of his insider perspective. The children trusted and valued him, and they viewed him as an older brother rather than a strange man with a camera. They even call him "Brother Jie" (*Children* 00:35:22). In building these relationships, Jiang could help the children feel comfortable at extremely vulnerable moments. For example, when a bird belonging to Jiang Yunjie dies, she secretly arranges a thoughtful funeral with her friend. The camera moves from a middle shot showing the snowy valley to a couple of close-ups showing how the children carefully bury the bird. Yunjie asks the director not to tell anyone where the bird is buried because she is afraid that someone may remove it, and then she cannot see the bird anymore. Yunjie is unwilling to share this secret with her family, but she invites the director to the funeral and humbly requests that he give her a photo that he took of the bird. This scene is a simple example of how these left-behind children face loss in the remote village. They keep their sadness a secret to avoid further loss. With such touching content, this documentary gives students a space to experience and connect with the depicted problems and subjects in a more personal way than would traditional lectures or readings.

Topic-Based Analysis of *Children at a Village School*

Students at Utah State University used topic-based analysis to study the documentary. This analysis directed students' attention to specific issues related to left-behind children that have implications beyond the scope of the documentary. More than just consuming the information presented in *Children at a Village School*, students were able, through discussion, to analyze possible reasons for the children's situations. The teaching goal was to facilitate students' critical thinking by comparing diverse opinions, thereby helping them avoid generalizing individual cases and forming stereotypes. To achieve these goals, discussions directed students to consider the following aspects.

Uneven Educational Resources in Rural and Urban China

The uneven distribution of resources in rural and urban China is not limited to materials but includes human resources as well. *Children at a*

Village School depicts the poverty experienced by left-behind children and their families. Viewers can see that the families' homes and the village school's classrooms are very humble. Even in the snowy winter, the classroom does not have a heater. Jiang Yunjie does not even have rain boots, so she wears sandals when walking to school, which takes over an hour on the muddy mountain road in sleet. Economic deficiencies are the main reason many parents leave their rural hometowns and work in major cities. Such poverty leaves rural children at a disadvantage in terms of their competitiveness with children living in urban China. Since parents leave for work opportunities elsewhere, children must take care of chores and even help with farming, which further limits their time and energy for learning. Their schoolteachers earn a meager wage that barely sustains them. In the film, one teacher in the school is not paid and leaves; the replacement teacher struggles with the desire to teach because of these conditions, which affect the quality of the students' education. To parse such sentimental and complex content, instructors can guide students to draw a tree diagram as a visual tool to analyze how insufficient human and educational resources lead to poverty and reproduce it in a vicious cycle. Poverty also forces parents to make the hard decision to leave their young children home while they work elsewhere for a better wage. Students can further enrich their tree diagrams by examining comparable cases of left-behind children in the Philippines (Madianou and Miller; Asis), Vietnam (Hoang and Yeoh), and other Asian countries (Nguyen et al.). Examining these cases can give students a more in-depth understanding of how labor issues and movements cross regions and borders because of discrepancies between income levels and human resource development in the era of globalization.

Power Imbalances within Social Structures

The documentary, which covers six years, raises a thought-provoking issue: the problematic nature of quick-fix solutions. After the village petitioned the government for years to rebuild the school, the government finally decided to do it. The camera captures the town mayor giving a speech dedicating the brand-new school and requesting all students to show their gratitude to the government, while the children are standing outside freezing in the cold weather. The scene visually symbolizes the uneven power relationship between the local officials and the children. The mayor's high-sounding words are in stark contrast with the following scenes that show the new school to be poorly made and in need of repairs within the first month. The new schoolhouse lacks heating and many other amenities typically found in other schools. A close reading of this scene can help students analyze how the documentary shows the local government's window-dressing solutions that cannot decrease the urban-rural inequality gap. Students might note that at the opening ceremony children raise a long red ribbon that covers the view of their freezing faces while the local governor passionately emphasizes how the new school building reflects the government's support for education in rural areas and how it can cultivate future talents. The children are treated like decorations because the governor does not really care about them; the children look like political pawns to make him look good. This formal analysis shows that to solve resource and power imbalances within social structures, a far more complicated approach is needed than simply using government funds to build a good-looking yet shoddy school building.

Sensational Media Representations

The misleading aspects of media depictions of poverty are another important issue found in *Children at a Village School*. The documentary captures how another media group notices the children's need for a school bus and then invites a few of the children to appear on a live television fundraiser. The TV show dramatically reports on the children's plight in order to gather donations for the purchase of a school bus. The short clip that shows the fundraiser is a good example that instructors can use to guide students' close reading; students may notice how the TV show preys on peoples' emotions by incorporating melancholy background music and close-ups to depict the children as helpless rather than strong and brave, as they are shown to be in the documentary. On the show two well-dressed hosts with bow ties and suits stand in front of a big screen introducing how left-behind children in the rural village cry and walk through muddy mountain streets and dangerous, busy roads to the school downtown. The narrator in a prefilmed segment sentimentally explains how having a school bus take them to school could make numerous children's dreams come true and bring them a bright future. The contrast between the hosts' well-kept and polished appearance and the children's lower quality of life can be read as the epitome of the gap between urban and rural China. The dramatic TV program does bring in enough funds for the purchase of a school bus, but the audience can only see this achievement on TV. The public media does not report on the fact that children actually only ride the bus for a couple of months because the narrow, unkempt roads in the village are impassable for a bus. After being pitifully portrayed on the TV program, the children are quickly back to their regular, long walk to school. This is another example in the documentary, along with the new schoolhouse, of a generous contribution that comes with no prior consideration of what the children really need and no follow-up support. This situation was easily exploited to bring good publicity to this media group but did not fundamentally improve the plight of the left-behind children. Rather, it turned them into objects of consumerism. These examples can spark important classroom discussions about the difference between aid that is designed to attract media publicity and deep, systemic change.

The Dangers of Generalizing and Stereotyping

One important goal of the class discussions on left-behind children is to cultivate students' awareness of the pitfalls of generalizations and how they can reinforce stereotypes. *Children at a Village School* portrays the variety of circumstances and challenges faced by left-behind children and their families. While there may be similarities in their cases, it is essential that students closely examine them to avoid overgeneralizations. Instructors should facilitate a classroom discussion about the stereotype that these children are passive and about examples of the children playing active roles in their own lives. In the film, some children maintain positive attitudes and build strong relationships with their grandparents. Others deal with harsher circumstances, such as the Fan children, whose mother died and whose father is in jail. However, in contrast to the stereotype that left-behind children live with no hope, Fan Yuyuan works during the summer to earn tuition for her middle and high school education. She even becomes one of a handful of students in the village accepted to college. Stories like this can help college students in the United States understand the diversity and agency that exist within a group that may be otherwise stereotyped as passive and hopeless.

Instructors need to emphasize that a documentary often only reflects select perspectives on a topic. Thus, students should not view the depicted children and their families as a monolith or as representative of all left-behind children, because either view can lead to developing stereotypes about them. For example, students' first impression of left-behind children may be that they live lonely childhoods, lacking love. Conversely, statistical research has shown that only a small percentage of left-behind children live completely alone. Among left-behind children, fifty-three percent live with one parent, thirty-three percent live with grandparents, and eleven percent live with others (All-China Women's Federation). While it is still tragic that some children do live entirely alone, most of these children live with family, which is crucial because a child's quality of life can largely be determined by living arrangements and family relationships (Wen and Lin).

In discussions, it is important that students recognize the diversity of left-behind children and their circumstances and not simply assume that every aspect of being left behind is negative. One study, for example, found that children who were left behind by both parents demonstrated greater altruistic economic preferences than children who had one or both parents in the home. This finding runs counter to assumptions, based on some popular opinions, that these children would develop these preferences at a slower rate (Cadsby et al.). Such preferences have been linked to the fact that children whose parents leave to earn higher wages benefit from the resulting increased financial stability (Benenson et al.). The gap between urban and rural household incomes in China is large, thereby worsening the inequalities between the two spheres (Sicular et al.). Hence, parents who migrate to work in big cities for higher pay can substantially increase their household income and thus achieve financial stability for their families. Several studies also suggest that some left-behind children may gain an expanded worldview from their parents, who learn more about the world by working in cities and share this new information with their children (Toyota et al.; Wen and Lin). Educators should approach the topic of migrant parents carefully by promoting thoughtful, nuanced conversations and avoiding stereotyping.

Major Reflections on Students' Responses

After viewing the film, the twenty-one students in the 2020 fall semester course completed a response assignment outside of class, which gave them space to reflect on what they learned and conduct further research. Overall, students showed a substantial increase in their knowledge about China's left-behind children. Many students described how the documentary enriched or changed their understanding of contemporary China. One of the most prevalent similarities in student responses was the surprise of learning about the stark difference in quality between education in rural and urban China. Several students expressed that this inequality differed greatly from their prior perception of China's educational system based on media representations. Before watching the film, they thought that the Chinese educational system provided rigorous training to produce highly competitive students, but the documentary's stark contrast between urban and rural education overturned this perception. Thus, in viewing the documentary, students had the opportunity to interrogate their own internally held stereotypes about Chinese education and allow space for a more nuanced understanding of a complicated system (nine of the twenty-one students mentioned this point in their responses). Some students further linked the Chinese government to these inequalities, stating that it fails to act despite being aware of the inequalities within the Chinese education system. Thinking about the role of government in the education system added another piece to the puzzle, as students worked to gain a detailed understanding of the causes and effects of the issues facing left-behind children (eleven student responses mentioned this point).

One discussion question asks students to think about how poverty can affect people not only materially but also mentally. Students mentioned that, with the help of a close reading of the clip highlighting children's long walks to school and heartbreaking talks with their parents by phone, viewing the documentary helped them recognize specific details in the challenges that left-behind children face in pursuing an education and social class mobility. These details included the physical barriers, such as the distance between the children's homes and schools, and the conditions of the classrooms. They also discussed details likely to affect the children emotionally, including being yelled at by adults or experiencing immense pressure to succeed in school so that in the future they can secure a job that will not require them to leave their own children behind. Because the documentary format focuses on these details, it is unsurprising that students remembered them. Students even mentioned that seeing, rather than reading about, left-behind children changed the way they viewed the issue and caused the details to stand out to them (two student responses mentioned this point).

To expand their understanding, students were required to explore in their written responses potential issues that were not included in the documentary. The instructor taught students how to use various resources to conduct the research, including library collections, academic data, and videos of expert interviews on social media. Knowing these resources became especially important when many students noticed that the documentary explains the economic difference between the city and rural areas but omits details and explanations as to why the parents had to leave in the first place. Subsequently, students conducted research and learned more about the household registration system and how it affects families in rural areas (as noted in eight student responses). Students also deepened their knowledge of some topics that are hard to visually represent in one documentary, such as left-behind children's mental and emotional health challenges (seven responses), the lack of transparent policies in China (one response), the diversity of China's left-behind children in various rural areas (four responses), and the parents' decisions to leave (two responses). Interestingly, students' research reports in their written responses highlighted how Internet-based technology, especially social media, has increased awareness of China's left-behind children (two responses). However, students found that left-behind children are more likely to develop Internet addictions because of loneliness and their grandparents' use of cell phones as electronic babysitters (one response). Incorporating a research section in the response form pushed students to develop a more comprehensive interpretation of social dilemmas, words, and pictures. This assignment motivated students to challenge their understanding by connecting multiple disciplines to the course content.

The topic of China's left-behind children is highly suited for college settings because it can give students an informed perspective on a current global issue that they otherwise might never learn about. Exploring topics through Chinese documentaries can introduce college students to the influence of media and its effects on current issues. Observing real-life issues through the lens of a documentary increases students' understanding of contemporary issues in China and around the globe. However, educators must emphasize that documentaries merely offer one perspective and do not always strictly or accurately mirror reality. It is essential to consider not only what is presented in a documentary but also what is omitted. Through follow-up research, students can realize such omissions and thereby effectively enlarge their understanding of the topic. After all, there is only so much a director can show and say in one documentary. By being aware of such concerns, students can avoid standardizing and oversimplifying perceptions of groups based on assumptions derived from prior media experiences. Students can vocalize their new understanding of the topic gained through documentaries by writing a reflection assignment that incorporates a miniresearch project. In tandem, educators can engage students in classroom discussions and activities using documentaries and help them understand some of the real-life experiences of the subjects. Together, these assignments and discussions allow students to gain a nuanced, compassionate awareness of contemporary China and its evolving issues, thus becoming better global citizens.

Notes

1. These children are commonly described as poor, left-behind, or abandoned, and the essay encourages instructors to challenge the stereotype that these children are passive by highlighting the active roles they play in their own lives.

2. The film is available on DVD, published by Mian Hua Sha Studio and Yihui Media, and may be streamed on *Orient Indie Films*. See "Children at a Village School" for online rental options.

Works Cited

All-China Women's Federation. "Report on Rural Left-Behind and Rural-Urban Migrant Children in China." *Reform Data*, 2013, www.reformdata .org/2013/0510/22228.shtml.

Asis, Maruja M. B. "Living with Migration." *Asian Population Studies*, vol. 2, no. 1, Mar. 2006, pp. 45–67.

Benenson, Joyce F., et al. "Children's Altruistic Behavior in the Dictator Game." *Evolution and Human Behavior*, vol. 28, no. 3, May 2007, pp. 168–75.

Berry, Chris, et al. *The New Chinese Documentary Film Movement: For the Public Record*. Hong Kong UP, 2010.

Brown, Tony. "Using Film in Teaching and Learning about Changing Societies." *International Journal of Lifelong Education*, vol. 30, no. 2, Mar. 2011, pp. 233–47.

Cadsby, C. Bram, et al. "Are 'Left-Behind' Children Really Left Behind? A Lab-in-Field Experiment Concerning the Impact of Rural/Urban Status and Parental Migration on Children's Other-Regarding Preferences." *Journal of Economic Behavior and Organization*, vol. 179, Nov. 2020, pp. 715–28.

Chen, Yiwen, et al. "To Migrate with or without Ones' Children in China—That Is the Question." *Annals of Economics and Statistics*, no. 135, 2019, pp. 69–88.

"Children at a Village School." *Orient Indie Films*, www.orientindiefilms.com/content/documentary/children-at-a-village-school/.

Children at a Village School. Directed by Jiang Nengjie, Mian Hua Sha, 2014.

Cui, Shuqin. "Alternative Visions and Representation: Independent Documentary Film-Making in Contemporary China." *Studies in Documentary Film*, vol. 4, no. 1, Jan. 2010, pp. 3–20.

Ding, Guodong, and Yixiao Bao. "Editorial Perspective: Assessing Developmental Risk in Cultural Context: The Case of 'Left Behind' Children in Rural China." *Journal of Child Psychology and Psychiatry*, vol. 55, no. 4, 2014, pp. 411–12.

González, E. L., et al. "Classroom Use of Narrative and Documentary Film Leads to an Enhanced Understanding of Cultural Diversity and Ethics in Science." *Bioscene*, vol. 42, no. 1, 2016, pp. 40–42.

Guan, Shanshan, and Guosheng Deng. "Whole-Community Intervention for Left-Behind Children in Rural China." *Children and Youth Services Review*, vol. 101, June 2019, pp. 1–11.

Hay, Iain. "Moving Pictures: From Ethnographic to Autoethnographic Documentary in the Internationalization of the Geography Curriculum." *Journal of Geography in Higher Education*, vol. 41, no. 4, Oct. 2017, pp. 562–73.

Hess, Diana. "From Banished to Brother Outsider, Miss Navajo to an Inconvenient Truth: Documentary Films as Perspective-Laden Narratives." *Social Education*, vol. 71, no. 4, 2007, pp. 194–99.

Hoang, Lan Anh, and Brenda S. A. Yeoh. "Sustaining Families across Transnational Spaces: Vietnamese Migrant Parents and Their Left-Behind Children." *Asian Studies Review*, vol. 36, no. 3, Sept. 2012, pp. 307–25.

Jiang, Nengjie. "The Dream of Left-Behind Children under My Camera Is to Get a Part-Time Job." *Ifeng*, 1 Mar. 2023, sd.ifeng.com/c/8No54XpMcRJ.

Ling, Hui, et al. "Peer Relationships of Left-Behind Children in China Moderate Their Loneliness." *Social Behavior and Personality*, vol. 45, no. 6, Mar. 2016, pp. 901–14.

Madianou, Mirca, and Daniel Miller. "Mobile Phone Parenting: Reconfiguring Relationships between Filipina Migrant Mothers and Their Left-Behind Children." *New Media and Society*, vol. 13, no. 3, May 2011, pp. 457–70.

Marcus, Alan S., et al. *Teaching History with Film: Strategies for Secondary Social Studies*. 1st edition, Routledge, 2010.

Nguyen, Liem, et al. "Migration and the Well-Being of the 'Left Behind' in Asia." *Asian Population Studies*, vol. 2, no. 1, Mar. 2006, pp. 37–44.

Picardo, José. "Why Students Need a Global Awareness and Understanding of Other Cultures." *The Guardian*, 25 Sept. 2012, www.theguardian.com/teacher-network/2012/sep/25/students-global-awareness-other-cultures.

Robinson, Luke. *Independent Chinese Documentary: From the Studio to the Street*. Palgrave Macmillan, 2013.

Ruggiero, Diana M. "'Más Allá del Fútbol': Teaching Highland Afro-Ecuadorian Culture and Engaging Race and Racism through Documentary Film." *Hispania*, vol. 98, no. 3, 2015, pp. 594–606.

Scott, John, editor. *Documentary Research*. 1st ed., SAGE, 2006.

Shdaimah, Corey. "The Power of Perspective: Teaching Social Policy with Documentary Film." *Journal of Teaching in Social Work*, vol. 29, no. 1, Jan. 2009, pp. 85–100.

Sicular, Terry, et al. "The Urban-Rural Income Gap and Income Inequality in China." *Understanding Inequality and Poverty in China: Methods and Applications*, edited by Guanghua Wan, Palgrave Macmillan, 2008, pp. 30–71.

Toyota, Mika, et al. "Bringing the 'Left Behind' Back into View in Asia: A Framework for Understanding the 'Migration–Left Behind Nexus.'" *Population, Space and Place*, vol. 13, no. 3, 2007, pp. 157–61.

United Nations Children's Fund. *UNICEF Annual Report 2017: China*. 2017, www.unicef.org/about/annualreport/files/China_2017_COAR.pdf.

Wen, Ming, and Danhua Lin. "Child Development in Rural China: Children Left Behind by Their Migrant Parents and Children of Nonmigrant Families." *Child Development*, vol. 83, no. 1, 2012, pp. 120–36.

Yamada, Racquel-María. "Integrating Documentation and Formal Teaching of Kari'nja: Documentary Materials as Pedagogical Materials." *Language Documentation and Conservation*, vol. 5, Apr. 2011, pp. 1–30.

Ye, Jingzhong. "Left-Behind Children: The Social Price of China's Economic Boom." *The Journal of Peasant Studies*, vol. 38, no. 3, July 2011, pp. 613–50.

Ye, Jingzhong, and Pan Lu. "Differentiated Childhoods: Impacts of Rural Labor Migration on Left-Behind Children in China." *The Journal of Peasant Studies*, vol. 38, no. 2, Mar. 2011, pp. 355–77.

Zhang, Lufa, and Fan Yang. "Food Insecurity and School Performance among the Left-Behind Children in Rural China: Depression and Educational Expectation as Mediators." *School Psychology International*, vol. 40, no. 5, Oct. 2019, pp. 510–24.

Zhou, Shu, and Monit Cheung. "*Hukou* System Effects on Migrant Children's Education in China: Learning from Past Disparities." *International Social Work*, vol. 60, no. 6, Nov. 2017, pp. 1327–42.

Additional Resources

Lijia Zhang. "The Orphans of China's Economic Miracle." *The New York Times*, 27 Mar. 2018, www.nytimes.com/2018/03/27/opinion/china-left-behind-children.html.

"Liu Feiyue's Family Photos for Left-Behind Children." *China Development Brief*, en2020.cdb.org.cn/reports/liu-feiyues-family-photos-for-left-behind-children/.

"Liu Feiyue's Village of Left-Behind Children." *China Development Brief*, 3 Aug. 2015, chinadevelopmentbrief.cn/reports/liu-feiyues-village-of-left-behind-children/

Han Li and Shaolu Yu

Teaching Asian Urbanization through Cinema

Many Asian countries have experienced transformative urbanization since the beginning of the twentieth century. Huge waves of rural-to-urban migration in Asian countries have not only led to the largest human migration flows in history but also given birth to the world's major metropolises, such as Tokyo, Hong Kong, Beijing, Shanghai, Mumbai, and Jakarta. Urbanization leads to significant changes in the demographic, social, economic, cultural, and environmental landscapes. As a result, the topic of urbanization and its transformative impact provide compelling opportunities for examining human life and the societal phenomena driven by economic and sociopolitical forces in Asian countries, especially over the past few decades.

As faculty members based in Modern Languages and Literatures and Urban Studies, respectively, at Rhodes College, we coteach an interdisciplinary course, Asian Urbanization through Cinema. Approaching Asian urbanization through both sociological and cinematic lenses, the course combines the strengths of the two fields. On one hand, the course equips students with major concepts, methodologies, and tools in urban studies and explores the evolving status of the massive urbanization processes in Asian countries. On the other hand, the course examines how these transformations shape human experiences and how they are represented in contemporary cinema. The use of film provides a humanistic and visual portrayal of urban landscapes, lifestyles, and human relations and shows how these urban changes are documented, memorialized, and imagined. In other words, the sessions on urban studies contextualize the films, while the films serve to humanize the sociological understandings of urbanization with audiovisual materials.

The course is organized thematically and regionally, running a total of fifteen weeks during one semester, with two seventy-five-minute meetings per week. The first weekly meeting introduces students to various urban studies concepts, theories, and issues involving one particular Asian city, region, or country. In the week's second meeting, the class discusses the cinematic representations of the aforementioned ideas and part of Asia. While the selected films usually substantially reflect the urban studies topics for that week, the two sessions may not entirely overlap. Together, they offer a stimulating interdisciplinary experience in approaching the history, reality, and artistic interpretation of Asian urbanization.

Below we show how the class uses two Chinese films to examine urbanization issues in mainland China. Since our course also examines other parts of Asia and Asian diasporas, we provide in an appendix the weekly films, topics, and readings discussed in the course. Films adopted in this course are intentionally selected from different countries, periods, genres (including drama, comedy, thriller, romance, and documentary), and directorial oeuvres. In addition to *Last Train Home* (归途列车) and *The Postmodern Life of My Aunt* (姨妈的后现代生活), we include *Shower* (洗澡), *Beijing Bicycle* (十七岁的单车), *Echoes of the Rainbow* (岁月神偷),[1] *Parasite* (기생충), *Like Father, Like Son* (そして父になる), *Slumdog Millionaire, Ladda Land* (ลัดดาแลนด์), and *Saving Face.*[2] Instructors can select themes and films according to the length, focus, and purpose of their courses.

Teaching *The Postmodern Life of My Aunt*

The course begins with a session introducing students to some fundamental urban studies concepts such as social-spatial differentiation and an overview of urbanization history in mainland China. Then the course uses *The Postmodern Life of My Aunt* to examine the changes in urban landscape, socioeconomic space, and interpersonal relationships during the postsocialist era in China.

Before the second class meeting each week, students watch the film (either in a group or individually, depending on the instructor's pedagogical choice and on practical constraints) and must answer the following two prompts in a discussion thread in the course's online learning management system: "What do you observe in the film that is related to the topic of urbanization or urbanism in general and to the particular region under discussion this week?" "Please select one sequence from the film that interests you the most and analyze it in detail." Students are also required to comment on at least one other student's post. Our experience shows that students find their classmates' posts inspiring and that they benefit considerably from each other's insights. This practice also enables the instructors to gauge the class's understanding of the film and incorporate some of the students' comments during the in-class lecture.

The discussion in the seventy-five-minute film studies session closely relates to the two discussion prompts—one about the filmic representation of the weekly urban issues, the other about the detailed visual techniques used by the film. In *The Postmodern Life of My Aunt*, socialist urbanization is seen through flashbacks about Aunt Ye's sent-down days in Anshan, a northeastern city that is known for its heavy industry and where viewers catch glimpses of the relics of the socialist industrialization heyday. While viewing these scenes, students are constantly reminded to pay attention to visual details and cinematic techniques such as the use of color, camera angles, frame composition, and so on. In these flashbacks, the harsh winter setting, which has a pale, grayish tone, and the long POV take of Aunt Ye's cold back in the center of the frame as the character heartlessly abandons her Anshan family demonstrate how determined she is to leave Manchuria. At the same time, her red suitcase and pink scarf externalize her excitement and eagerness to return to Shanghai. When it isn't depicting the socialist past, the film serves as a kaleidoscope showing a fast-changing, postsocialist urban modernity through Aunt Ye's chance encounters with urban dwellers and drifters of various socioeconomic backgrounds in metropolitan Shanghai.

The film well illustrates the key urban studies concept introduced in the week's first meeting, social-spatial differentiation. In Shanghai, Aunt Ye lives in a box-shaped work-unit apartment building next to an alleyway market, which certainly reflects her background and social status. Ye's love interest, Pan, lives in a colonial-style mansion, alluding to both Shanghai's semicolonial history and his purported aesthetics-seeking lifestyle. Among the strangers Aunt Ye encounters, the girl who scams Aunt Ye (in coordination with Kuankuan, Ye's grade school nephew) lives in a *shikumen* (石库门; "stone-gate house") neighborhood where Shanghai locals cluster, and the nouveau riche family that turns Ye down for an English tutoring job because of her old-fashioned British accent takes viewers inside a modern apartment complex.[3] Additionally, it is worth examining the "nonspace" and "homeless" characters such as Kuankuan and Niu Jinhua (a female migrant worker), who separately stay with Ye temporarily. Though both homeless, Kuankuan and Niu represent two ends of the spectrum of China's neoliberal urbanization—while Niu's drifting is due to the socio-economic disparity between rural and urban China, Kuankuan is able to wander around because of the transnational resources of his mother, who works as an expatriate in Australia.

Beyond discussing the visualization of the urban issues discussed earlier in the week, we also conduct in class a close analysis of sequences from the film to stress the effects that cinematic techniques can achieve. The selected sequences are usually one to three minutes long, and the students are gradually introduced to film studies techniques and terminology regarding mise-en-scène, cinematography, editing, sound, and so on. The class views a particular sequence multiple times, and students share their observations after each viewing. We found that a progressive method of describing, observing, and interpreting was highly effective in propelling students to delve deeply into the scene's artistic aspects.

After first viewing the sequence where Aunt Ye interviews for the job as an English tutor (13:30–14:00), students see that the sequence begins with a still shot of an urban apartment complex exterior. They are reminded that a statement like the previous sentence is a description of what happens in this shot and is something that can be derived directly from the frame. When prompted to pay more attention to how things in the frame are presented, they see that the apartment complex is filmed with a low-angle shot and that the look of the modern, radish-colored, and mixed-height buildings suggests vibrancy. Students then realize that these visual details, while still in the frame, require keen observations to see and articulate (and therefore might not be noticed by every viewer). Moreover, the fact that this building contrasts sharply with Ye's faded and box-shaped Soviet-style apartment building, which is made to look smaller through a high-angle shot, is an interpretation that requires analytical association that goes beyond the given frame.

Another example in this thirty-second sequence is when Aunt Ye tutors the boy in the room (description). When asked to spell out the details in the mise-en-scène, students see that the room is luxuriously decorated and brightly lit and has contemporary furniture (observation). While Aunt

Ye and the boy sit at the table (description), the lamp and its wire visually divide the space evenly between the two characters (observation). This division symbolizes their equal status in stark contrast to the conventional hierarchical teacher-student relationship, as the status of the boy is boosted by his family's capital (interpretation). Observations and interpretations of the film scenes are often closely knit together and do not necessarily need to be articulated separately. In this scene the boy is dressed in formal attire—a suit and black leather shoes—which might be considered too mature for his age or too formal for a daily tutoring occasion. Both the desk and the chair seem to be too large for the boy, creating a sense of imbalance between him and his surroundings, suggesting the eagerness of the newly rich to accelerate their children's (English) education and participate in the global neoliberal structure.

Many sequences in this film merit close reading, and we selected ones that prominently illustrate the relationship between the characters and their physical and social space. Another telling example is the two streetview scenes that should be read in juxtaposition. The first scene is when Aunt Ye visits the alleyway market and proudly engages in Shanghai's vibrant local urban life (9:02–9:55). In this one-minute sequence, the camera's distance and dynamic movement send a strong message regarding Ye's optimism and vitality at this stage of the narrative. The sequence begins with a bird's-eye view of Aunt Ye and Kuankuan walking through the alleyway market (description and observation). As the shots change from long shot to medium and medium close-up, students see how Aunt Ye, striding in brightly colored clothing, becomes increasingly prominent in the composition, and the fresh groceries she carries symbolize liveliness and vitality (observation and interpretation). Coming from a socialist background, Aunt Ye lectures Kuankuan about her life wisdom and planning strategy with enthusiasm and confidence, while Kuankuan, crippled, seems to need assistance (description). As they walk down the market, the camera cruises the streetscape: the jumpy fish, busy food stalls, and numerous customers engaged in communal, mundane life all contribute to an energetic and lively feeling (observation and interpretation). The sequence ends with Aunt Ye's remark "Life is all about planning ahead," which reflects not only the historical impact that the planned-economy period has had on her but also her optimism in being able to control her life, though this control later proves to be an illusion (interpretation). The whole sequence is accompanied with swirls of diegetic sounds in the market and a lively and joyful nondiegetic tune (observation).

As students see how this scene's elements work together to convey Aunt Ye's relationship to the vernacular urban space, it then becomes quite clear what kind of effects are achieved in the second street-view scene, where everything in the mise-en-scène is the opposite to that in the market scene. The scene is about how Aunt Ye, after losing her economic, social, and physical mobility, leaves Shanghai (1:35:07–1:36:56). The sequence starts with Aunt Ye, her daughter, and her son-in-law sitting in a taxi on a dark winter evening (description). Aunt Ye's daughter smokes, looking impatient and indifferent, while Aunt Ye takes her last gaze at her apartment building—her last attachment to this city (observation). This shot exemplifies for students that though description and observation can be similar, observations—such as about the dark lighting and atmosphere and the different expressions of Aunt Ye and her daughter—go beyond what plot summary can convey. As the taxi departs, the camera produces a distanced view, often mediated through the windshield glass, of Shanghai's cosmopolitan cityscape (observation). As in the market scene, the camera pans through the urban space, this time illustrating the city's metropolitan splendors, such as dazzling festival lights, fancy shopping malls, illuminated landmark architecture, and huge rooftop billboards. As students meticulously list these splendors, they realize that their inclusion in the scene is deliberate. Using this observation, some students interpret the illuminated urban scene as a foil for Aunt Ye's disillusionment with her Shanghai dream: the distanced nature of the shots suggests Aunt Ye's emotional distance from the city at this point. The sequence ends with an aerial view of the taxi disappearing into the dark Shanghai night (observation). Students note that the camera movement in this scene is exactly the opposite of that in the earlier street market scene—while the camera in the earlier scene takes viewers closer and closer to the space, the camera here takes viewers further and further away (interpretation).

As students examine various scenes more critically, they are increasingly able to unpack the rich cinematic elements that a plot summary cannot convey. The observations made regarding the filmic techniques then become the foundation for student interpretation of the meanings of each scene. The progress students made in this regard is clearly demonstrated in their answers to the second prompt: at the beginning of the semester, many of the students were still retelling the plot of the sequence they chose, whereas toward the second half of the semester, their scene reading became significantly more analytical.

Teaching *Last Train Home*

Since rural-urban migration is another prominent topic in this course, we choose the feature film *Beijing Bicycle* (十七岁的单车) and the documentary *Last Train Home* to illustrate this phenomenon.[4] While *Beijing Bicycle* explores migrant workers' identity, mobility and immobility, and urban displacement, *Last Train Home* showcases gendered migration experiences, migrant enclaves, villages in cities, and the clear juxtaposition between rural hometowns and temporary city homes. In addition, this film also documents the far-reaching issues resulting from China's decades-long urbanization, including abandoned villages, left-behind children, family disintegration, and the institutional barriers such as the *hukou* (户口; "household registration") system.

This week of the course focuses on the urban-rural dichotomy, home-making, left-behind children, and their experience with the neoliberal economy. One of the central themes in *Last Train Home* is the making of "home" (or rather, the failure to make it), and the documentary shows this on both ends of the workers' annual migration—their workspace home in the city and their rural home. It is fruitful for students to examine the representation of physical and social homes as well as the narrative and cinematic strategies (such as the use of dialects and cinematography) in both settings. The parents featured in the film have a dormitory home in Guangzhou that is a claustrophobic room attached to their workspace, offering no distinction between their work and private lives. This home, as an extension of their workplace, is a residence "designed essentially for the (re)production of daily manual labor" (Wang 54). Outside the room, their displacement and isolation in the city is further illustrated in the film by smoggy and noisy cityscapes, gloomy lighting, and the depressing atmosphere through which their environment is portrayed. In stark contrast, their home back in the countryside (or rather a utopian image of their home) is often shown in the film as offering lush green fields, beautiful sunsets, a slow-paced lifestyle, and a peaceful and relaxed atmosphere. However, this fantasy of rural tranquility and harmony is eventually shattered by a father-daughter confrontation when the parents return to the countryside for Chinese New Year. The daughter Qin's identity as a left-behind child and a second-generation migrant worker is worth a close reading as well. As a left-behind child, Qin suffers from emotional estrangement from her parents because of their long-term separation. A good portion of the documentary records the life she and her younger brother have with their elderly grandmother in the rural home and the tension she has with her parents when they come back for their annual Chinese New Year visit. Later, when she enters the city, she is enchanted with the urban views and neoliberal ideals that seem to promise freedom and mobility through work and consumption. However, the film suggests that because of the alienating capitalist mode of production and the institutionalized *hukou* system that segregates the rural and urban population, Qin's urban dream remains nothing but a fantasy of the neoliberal reformation (Wang 65–67).

As with each film, we select a few sequences from *Last Train Home* for close reading. Following the Zhang family for three years, the film foregrounds its authenticity and truthfulness in using a zero-degree style (a purportedly neutral and objective aesthetic stance). So when reading the selected sequences, we ask a series of questions that go beyond the ones regularly asked about feature films and that include the following: Does this scene employ cinematic techniques? If so, what kinds of techniques are used? What effects do they achieve, and how do the effects influence viewers' perception of this scene? Do the techniques violate the documentary's claim to being objective and truthful? If so, is it ethical for the documentary to use them?

Though many scenes can be used for this purpose, the opening sequence, in which a crowd of migrant workers rushes to board a train, is quite effective. Instead of showing the train station crowd directly, the film actually begins with a dark screen and sounds of rain and a crowd hustling (description). Thus, even before students see the crowd, they get a feeling of the scene's tension and urgency (interpretation). As the train station fades into view, the camera first shows a relatively vacant area of the square and then slowly pans to the left, where a gigantic space is filled with passengers waiting impatiently; the view of the crowd may induce a feeling of awe in the audience (observation and interpretation). The camera continues to pan, and the frame stays filled with tumultuous crowds of migrant workers dressed in shades of gray and essentially indistinguishable from one another (observation). The duration of this panning shot is so long that it creates a sense of despair (interpretation). As the camera drops to eye level, it gets uncomfortably close to the passengers as they push their way forward and suddenly zooms in on individuals yelling or crying (observation). Eventually, the screen shows the underground tunnel connecting the square to the platforms, and the camera waits at one end of the tunnel. The cramped space with dim light and depressing silence can only invoke a sense of claustrophobia. Within seconds the silence is broken by the sounds of running steps and heavy gasps of migrant workers as they dash expressionlessly toward the camera (description and observation). Although the sequence seems to comprise raw and unfiltered images of what is known as the world's largest human migration, students find that the scene's cinematography amplifies their sense of chaos and dysfunction in the situation. Then we pose the following questions to students: Is it ethical to exaggerate an effect in a documentary? To what extent is the exaggeration justified?

If the cinematic techniques used to enhance the effect of the train station scene seem reasonable, then the techniques used in the scene where Qin visits a hairdresser could be considered more controversial. Quitting school against her parents' wishes, Qin enters the city and becomes a migrant worker like them. In this scene (36:50–37:50), after Qin and her workmates stroll in a fancy mall, she goes to a hair salon (description). Instead of directly filming her in the seat, the camera focuses for an unusually long duration on a wall poster featuring a modern girl with a fancy hairstyle and dyed hair (observation), suggesting this is an image that Qin is pursuing (interpretation). As she gets her hair treated and asks the hairdresser about her look, the camera films her gazing contentedly, if not narcissistically, into the mirror and appreciating the hairdresser's compliment, "Like a barbie doll. Foreigners all look like that" (observation). At last when Qin exits the hair salon, the camera first catches her from a low-angle position, conveying her happiness and excitement, then follows her closely as she walks down the city street in her new fashionable look. Meanwhile, the sequence also includes a nondiegetic, upbeat pop song featuring the lyrics "cute little bunny opens the door and is ready to date," which externalize Qin's juvenile longings (observation and interpretation).

Students see that compared to the scene when Qin fights with her father, where the camera is explicitly acknowledged,[5] the use of the camera in this scene is much subtler. But they acknowledge that the cinematography, editing, and sound in this scene, despite being subtler, amplify Qin's apparently naive excitement as she is first exposed to consumer culture in cities. Given that at other moments the film suggests that the freedom and mobility that Qin thinks urban living will offer her are just illusions, the exaggeration of her naivety about the urban dream seems cruel. Viewing this scene, students inevitably wonder, Is the camera exploiting her and her emotions? Is it ethical for a documentary director to do that? Therefore, in addition to its cinematic elements, this sequence provides an opportunity to discuss the ethics and politics of documentary filmmaking.

Films on other Asian countries, regions, and cities are studied in a similar mode to the one described above. Since the course can reasonably accommodate just ten to eleven films (a list of which is provided at the end of this essay), many Asian regions and issues are inevitably omitted. Therefore, the students' final papers and presentations serve to significantly expand the course scope. For the final paper, students select a film about an Asian geographic area of their interest and discuss urban studies issues concerning the chosen place or places as well as their cinematic representations. For the presentation, which students deliver before they complete their final paper, they discuss with the class the primary themes in their selected films and their own major observations. This activity allows students to receive peer and instructor feedback while staying on track with completing the paper, and it significantly expands the range of course content in regional and thematic areas selected by the students themselves.

Overall, the strength of the course comes from its rich integration of urban studies and film studies themes, concepts, and techniques. As a reflection of this interdisciplinary approach, the course's learning objectives include gaining basic factual knowledge (e.g., concepts, methods, and theories) about Asian urbanization; developing an understanding of Asian (including Asian diasporic) cultures, diverse perspectives, and global awareness; and developing a critical appreciation of intellectual and artistic products such as films.[6]

Notes

1. Given the limited room in this course, we alternate between teaching Hong Kong and Taipei as urbanization sites. *Echoes of the Rainbow* provides a valuable text to examine Hong Kong's 1950s urban history. For Taipei, Edward Yang's *Yi Yi* (一一) provides a telling text to study the portrayal of a millennial urban family and the legibility of the cityscape. Hao sheds light on how characters in *Yi Yi* perceive, inhabit, and move around the urban landscape and how urban signature spaces (such as "path," "node," and "district," according to Kevin Lynch's five mental map elements [47]) are used for cinematic storytelling. When examining mainland China, the course also uses *Chungking Express* (重庆森林), under the theme of globalization, Disneyfication, and floating identity, because the film's flaneur-like characters take viewers to the dazzling heart of the metropolis of Hong Kong and expose its urban dwellers' isolation. In addition, Ann Hui's *The Way We Were* (天水围的日与夜) and *A Simple Life* (桃姐) each open a window to the

clustered public housing on the city's periphery along with the humble and mundane way of life there.

2. We use *Saving Face* to discuss the issue of model minorities, but instructors could also use the documentaries *My Life in China* and *Reunification* and the fictional film *Wedding Banquet*, which portray Chinese American families' immigration history and legacy.

3. British English was taught in China in the 1960s through 1980s, but later American English became more popular and was viewed as more modern and global.

4. Jia Zhangke's *The World* (世界) and *A Touch of Sin* (天注定) can also be considered for this topic, as both films take an intimate look at the migration, exploitation, and powerlessness that migrant workers experience in China's rapid modernization and urbanization in the age of global capitalism.

5. This is another scene worth close reading. Qin, who feels neglected and distanced from her parents, confronts her father, who believes that the only way for his children to escape poverty is through education. As the confrontation escalates, Qin dashes to the camera and yells: "You want to film the real me? This is the real me!" (*Last Train Home* 01:06:02). In this scene, not only is the camera acknowledged, but its presence seems to intensify the verbal and physical altercation.

6. These objectives are modified from the learning objectives in the IDEA student ratings system.

Appendix: Weekly Films, Topics, and Readings

Week	Films	Topics	Readings
1	*The Postmodern Life of My Aunt*	Postsocialist urbanization	Xiao
2	*Shower*	Urban renewal and gentrification	Proctor-Xu
3	*Beijing Bicycle*	Rural-urban migration and citizenship	Gladwin
4	*Last Train Home*	Rural-urban dichotomy, migration, and migrant enclaves	Wang
5	*Echoes of the Rainbow*	Postcolonial urbanization and heritage preservation	Lee
6	*Parasite*	Wealth disparity, dual city, and social (im)mobility	Rife
7	*Like Father, Like Son*	Gendered space, fatherhood, and family	Ehrlich 165–72
8	*Slumdog Millionaire*	Slums and slumification	Mendes
9	*Ladda Land*	Middle-class suburbanization, global expatriates, the space of consumerism	Ancuta
10	*Saving Face*	Asian diasporas; intersectionality of immigration, race, and sexuality; model minorities	Yu

Works Cited

Ancuta, Katarzyna. "Spirits in Suburbia: Ghosts, Global Desires and the Rise of Thai Middle-Class Horror." *Horror Studies*, vol. 5, no. 2, 2014, pp. 233–47.

Beijing Bicycle. Directed by Wang Xiaoshuai, Sony Pictures Classics, 2001.

Chungking Express. Directed by Wong Kar-wai, Jet Tone Films, 1994.

Echoes of the Rainbow. Directed by Alex Law, Sil-Metropole Organization, 2010.

Ehrlich, L. C. *The Films of Kore-eda Hirokazu*. Palgrave Macmillan, 2013.

Gladwin, Derek. "No Country for Young Men: Chinese Modernity, Displacement, and Initiatory Ritual in Chinese Sixth Generation Cinema." *Asian Cinema*, vol. 23, no. 1, 2012, pp. 31–44.

Hao, Xiaofei. "*Yi Yi*: Nostalgia upon Diaspora." *Motion Pictures and the Image of the City*, Springer, 2016, pp. 77–132.

Ladda Land. Directed by Sopon Sukdapisit, Sahamongkol Film International, 2011.

Last Train Home. Directed by Fan Lixin, Eyesteelfilm, 2009.

Lee, Vivian Pui-yin. "Contested Heritage: Cinema, Collective Memory, and the Politics of Local Heritage in Hong Kong." *East Asian Cinema and Cultural Heritage*, edited by Kinnia Yau Shuk-ting, Palgrave Macmillan, 2011, pp. 53–68.

Like Father, Like Son. Directed by Hirokazu Kore-eda, Fuji Television Network / Amuse / Gaga, 2013.

Lynch, Kevin. *The Image of the City*. MIT Press, 1960.

Mendes, Ana Cristina. "Showcasing India Unshining Film Tourism in Danny Boyle's *Slumdog Millionaire*." *Third Text*, vol. 24, no. 4, 2010, pp. 471–79.

My Life in China. Directed by Kenneth Eng, 2014.

Parasite. Directed by Bong Joon Ho, Barunson E&A / CJ Entertainment, 2019.

The Postmodern Life of My Aunt. Directed by Ann Hui, Cheerland Entertainment / Polybona Films, 2006.

Proctor-Xu, Jani. "Sites of Transformation: The Body and Ruins in Zhang Yang's *Shower*." *Embodied Modernities: Corporeality, Representation and Chinese Cultures*, edited by Fran Martin and Ari Larissa Heinrich, U of Hawai'i P, 2006, pp. 162–75.

Reunification. Directed by Alvin Tsang, 2015.

Rife, Casey. "Parasitic Poverty." *Aegis: The Otterbein Humanities Journal*, vol. 17, 2020, pp. 46–53.

Saving Face. Directed by Alice Wu, Destination Films, 2004.

Shower. Directed by Zhang Yang, Laurel Films, 1999.

A Simple Life. Directed by Ann Hui, Bona Entertainment, 2012.

Slumdog Millionaire. Directed by Danny Boyle, Celador Films / Film4, 2008.

A Touch of Sin. Directed by Jia Zhangke, Office Kitano / Xstream Pictures, 2006.

Wang, Yanjie. "Trauma, Migrant Families, and Neoliberal Fantasies in *Last Train Home*." *Concentric: Literary and Cultural Studies*, vol. 42, no. 1, 2016, pp. 49–72.

The Way We Were. Directed by Ann Hui, Film Workshop / Sil-Metropole Organization, 2008.

Wedding Banquet. Directed by Ang Lee, Good Machine / Central Motion Pictures, 1993.

The World. Directed by Jia Zhangke, Xstream Pictures / Office Kitano / Lumen Films, 2000.

Xiao, Hui Faye. "Getting Married to Shanghai." *Family Revolution: Marital Strife in Contemporary Chinese Literature and Visual Culture.* U of Washington P, 2014, pp. 147–65.

Yi Yi. Directed by Edward Yang, Atom Films / Omega Project, 2000.

Yu, Shaolu. "'I Am Like a Deaf, Dumb and Blind Person': Mobility and Immobility of Chinese (Im)migrants in Flushing, Queens, New York City." *Journal of Transport Geography*, vol. 54, 2016, pp. 10–21.

Recontextualizing National Culture

Josh Stenberg

Yinpeixiang Films in the Theater Classroom

Xiqu (戏曲; often known as "Chinese opera") has been recorded on film since the beginnings of Chinese-language cinema. Indeed, the first efforts to create sound film in China as well as in colonial Hong Kong and Taiwan were based on *xiqu* productions (Yeh 78).[1] Over the century-long history of Chinese film, *xiqu* has appeared in various forms. These forms include full-length *xiqu* feature films, performer biopics, and narrative documentaries as well as cameo uses of *xiqu* for local color or interpolated vignettes, not to mention stage-performance captures and pedagogical videos. Different forms have fulfilled various functions (e.g., entertaining, teaching, archiving).

In the 1950s and 1960s, *xiqu* cinema had a mass audience and was a major genre in the People's Republic of China, Hong Kong, Taiwan, and among the Southeast Asian diaspora. These *huangmeidiao* (黄梅调) films were hugely popular on either side of the Cold War in Asia. A few years later, *yangbanxi* (样板戏; "revolutionary opera") movies became among the most iconic and enduring cultural products of the Cultural Revolution and today retain broad though often conflicted recognition. In the last half-century, however, *xiqu* has become much less central to Chinese cinema and Chinese arts in general. *Xiqu* popularity on stage and screen waned by the 1980s throughout the Chinese-speaking world, and the era of large-scale film productions dedicated to *xiqu* tapered off.

One can perhaps speak of *xiqu* film since then as a niche rather than a presence in mainstream cinema. In feature films, *xiqu* has been reduced to serving an important thematic role or providing a visually attractive setting (such as in *Peking Opera Blues* [刀马旦] and *Farewell My Concubine* [霸王别姬]). It also appears as an emblematic cameo (*East Palace, West Palace* [东宫西宫]) or an element of local color (*A Touch of Sin* [天注定]). *Xiqu* has continued to represent an important element of television programming, and its audiovisual dissemination was bolstered by the establishment of a dedicated *xiqu* national broadcaster (CCTV-11) in the PRC in 2001. Meanwhile, in the pedagogical space, especially for *xiqu* amateur performers, students, and connoisseurs, the "hybrid form of 'filmed theatre' continues as a viable and valued stream of access to *xiqu* performance in contemporary China" (Evans 21). Archival projects have sought to create a reliable representation of the *xiqu* canon.

Most ways of incorporating *xiqu* into screen arts have fairly clear Euro-American, Soviet, or other East Asian counterparts—for instance, the filmed performance, the cinematic adaptation, and the musical biopic. But it does not seem to be an exaggeration to call one *xiqu* genre unique to China: *yinpeixiang* (音配像). The genre emerged through a particular way of apprehending *xiqu* repertoire and technique and the development of a strategy to conserve it. In *yinpeixiang* films, well-known actors lip-synch to audio recordings made decades earlier. Those recordings are typically of their own teachers, the disciples using stage actions and full costumes.[2] The teacher-student connection generates a claim to faithful transmission of repertoire based on the legitimacy of artistic lineage. *Yinpeixiang* means "sound matched to image": the previously recorded teacher's sound is matched to the closest available image of their performance: since the masters (mostly deceased) are no longer available to perform, their students are offered as an approximation for a reliable, apparently traditional account of repertoire.

In theater history courses, the use of video materials is inevitable, but instructors must consider the awkward circumstance that the media they are using illustratively is not the same media that is being studied. Students are too often left with no context to mediate this dissonance. Considering examples of *yinpeixiang* allows instructor and class to broach the essential questions of modern and contemporary theater in China—conservation, transmission, modernization, the role of the state, censorship, and audience—with a genre conceived of as a repository for theatrical practice. This essay focuses on how *yinpeixiang* can be incorporated into university teaching in courses on world theater, contemporary China, or heritage and culture. It uses a single *yinpeixiang* film titled *Single Sword Meeting* (单刀会) to illustrate this multifaceted issue (*Hou Yongkui*).

Nearly an hour long, this recording was released in 2000 and matches the physical performance of that period with a 1957 audio recording. This film recommends itself for use in the classroom because it has three features that accentuate the capacity for *yinpeixiang* to illustrate historical processes: First, the actor Hou Yongkui, who performs on the audio recording, was the father of the actor Hou Shaokui, who performs on the video recording of the film and was his chief disciple in this role and indeed across his repertoire in the northern branch of the *kunqu* (昆曲) tradition. Second, the genesis of this famous scene from *kunqu* repertoire allows for an exploration of contemporary Chinese theater as one module in a much longer chain of storytelling (in this case, Three Kingdoms narratives). And third, the contents of the scene themselves constitute a meditation on history and the passage of time.[3]

Yinpeixiang as a Conservation Genre

The post–Cultural Revolution period saw the resumption of traditional *xiqu* performances throughout the PRC. As the era of reform and opening up progressed, however, the delayed effects of the persecution of artists and the alienation of audiences during the Cultural Revolution were becoming increasingly apparent in the *xiqu* sphere, after a brief euphoria of performance resumption during the early Deng Xiaoping period (Mackerras 83–84). Li Ruihuan, a protégé of Deng, was a successful mayor from 1982 to 1989 and party secretary of Tianjin from 1987 to 1989 before becoming a politburo member from 1989 to 2002 and chairman of the Chinese People's Political Consultative Conference from 1993 to 2003—and an ardent *xiqu* enthusiast. A moderate, he played a major role in fostering a return to pride in the Chinese classical tradition and a liberalization of cultural policy (Keane 249; Rahav 1088, 1092). Generally, he is thought to have played a major role in the development of a new cultural nationalism, toward which support and control of the arts—explicitly including *xiqu*—was intended to contribute. As a result, arts and culture projects he supported emphasized tradition rather than foregrounding state socialist ideology. To date, Li has been the last of senior PRC leadership to show a personal investment in the future of traditional stage arts (Rolston 61).

In the 1990s, *jingju* (京剧; "Peking opera"), long officially designated as the national form of theater, became "the chief target of government inspired attempts at revival of traditional arts" partly because its decline in popularity had "aroused enormous concern among those who care about the survival of Chinese traditional culture in the context of the modern world" (Mackerras 83). By the 1990s video recording technology had become more widespread and cheaper, but the high-status culture bearers—mid-century stars such as Mei Lanfang and Yu Zhenfei—were by then either elderly or deceased. For this reason, *yinpeixiang* was a solution particular to the time and genre: combining the audio from historic performances (overwhelmingly *jingju*) with an attempted facsimile of the performance's choreography and technical practices, and representing a claim of being this repertoire's canonical, authentic, and original performance practice. The solution derived from connoisseur narratives, according to which earlier performers' renditions of repertoire necessarily represent a higher grade of authenticity and technical execution than later ones (including renditions by those performers' students). Those narratives were and are furthermore predicated on the claim that *xiqu* performance is determined by fixed versions of performance maintained (albeit in increasingly attenuated form) through student-teacher transmission in an exclusive lineage. Since the younger generation of actors was deemed "not nearly big or good enough to bring about a truly effective revival" (84), the point of *yinpeixiang* was to archive canonical repertoire using the skills of the older generation. Since an actor is performing according to an existing recording, one could say that the performance constitutes "body-synching" (Rolston 61).

As a powerful party figure, Li had the influence and funds to initiate *yinpeixiang*, at first trialing it in Tianjin, as an "urgent rescue mission for *jingju* repertoire after the devastation of the decade-long Cultural Revolution" (Liu, "Quantitative Visualisation" 457). The project initiated by Li ultimately lasted from 1994 to 2006, involved seventy *jingju* troupes and thirty thousand people, and led to the production of 460 audiovisual recordings. Of these recordings, fifteen were of *kunqu*, while the rest were of *jingju* (Liu 456).

The project was from first to last explicitly archival, aiming to "salvage the 'embodied memory' . . . of classical *jingju* repertoire before it became 'archival memory'" (Liu, "Theatre Reform" 387).[4] It was mandated top-down from the party-state bureaucracy, and more or less the entirety of the *jingju* institutional and the academic *xiqu* establishment was at some point invited to signal approval of the project. The titles of essays collected in a volume in honor of the project give an idea of the discourse surrounding it: for instance, "For the People of Today and Those of Tomorrow" (Li Shiji), "Historical Recording and Transmission" (Zhou), and "On the Unlimited Achievement of the *Yinpeixiang* Project" (Ye). In the essay she contributed, Sun Yumin, a well-known performer and at the time the director of the Beijing School of *Xiqu* Arts, directly addressed the combination of patriotism and filial piety implicit in the project. Giving a speech at an event celebrating the successful completion of the project, Li Ruihuan described the project as using "contemporary work" to ensure "profit for centuries" (1). Though intending to protect tradition, Li simultaneously conceived of the project as "brand-new, unprecedented" (2).

On the one hand, the *yinpeixiang* project can be conceived of as an unspoken renunciation of repeated PRC efforts to reform and modernize *xiqu* repertoire. In the era of reform and opening up, "[r]ecognition of such consequences of the reforms has led to concerted efforts . . . to restore some of the classic repertoire and techniques" (Liu, "Theatre Reform" 405), an agenda that obliquely acknowledged the damage that theater reform had done to traditional repertoire. Any conception of the *yinpeixiang* recordings as an archive of tradition is necessarily complicated not only by the straightforward representation of disciples as reproducing their teachers' performances but also by the fact that early recorded PRC *xiqu* performances, which furnished most of the audio material for the *yinpeixiang* project, already reflect the major changes wrought in *xiqu* repertoire by the extensive program of drama reform in the 1950s (Wang, "Jingju"; Liu, *Transforming Tradition* 326–28). *Yinpeixiang* therefore produces an uncritical and quite monolithic representation of a traditional repertoire, even as its archiving project remains of enormous value for facilitating access to important historical performances and revealing the mechanics of *xiqu* transmission.

Lord Guan and the River of History

The exceptionality of the *yinpeixiang* genre and its initiation at the highest levels of the state make it useful for teaching aspects of theater theory and PRC cultural history in Chinese and Asian theater classes, especially in conjunction with *xiqu* films and stage-performance capture. The example of the *Single Sword Meeting yinpeixiang* film, with Hou Shaokui furnishing the physical performance to accompany the voice of his father, Hou Yongkui, illustrates the interplay between *xiqu* teaching lineage and state-led conservation. The example is given added poignancy by the fact that this *kunqu* scene's plot and lyrics also operate as a reflection on the passage of time—interpretable as evoking the futility of human endeavors and the necessity nevertheless to honor and pursue such endeavors. This emotional intensity provides a point of entry for students to consider a number of features of *xiqu* that contributed to creating the unique genre of *yinpeixiang*: the relationship between the audio and visual elements (Are they more integral in *yinpeixiang* than in Western forms?); the construction of canon and tradition in the recent PRC (Why did the state initiate and support such a project, and why in this period?); and the importance of lineage (Why and how are teacher-student relationships fundamental for the project?). These questions can help students understand that tradition in modern and contemporary *xiqu* practice is not an absolute or a given but a discursive construction built on technical foundations and aesthetic practices entailing considerable state involvement.[5]

The content of the film is also conducive of a discussion of the construction and meaning of history. The film is ultimately derived from the *zaju* (杂剧; "variety play") drama *The Great Prince Guan Attends the Single Sword Meeting Alone*, by one of the most famous Yuan dramatists, Guan Hanqing. The plot's main role is the Three Kingdoms warrior Guan Yu, also known as Lord Guan. As Lord Guan crosses a river to attend a banquet, at which he suspects that he will be ambushed, he contemplates the flowing river and conceives of it as a metaphor for war and its sacrifices. He recites, 这也不是江水 / 这是那二十年流不尽的英雄血! ("This is no river water; / [*Singing*] this is twenty years of heroes' blood unending"; *Hou Yongkui* 17:43). The war has gone on for twenty years, much blood has flowed, and yet it seems peace is no nearer—in some ways, Lord Guan seems to lament perpetual war, providing something of a Homeric moment in Guan Hanqing's script and on the *xiqu* stage—the death of soldiers being the ultimate alteration, which nevertheless produces no (political) change but on the contrary leads only to more rivers of gore. At the same time, the carnage of war is integrated into a narrative that by and large vaunts military glory and loyalty as the chief objects of human (or at least male) striving.

Drawing on assigned readings and the *yinpeixiang*, the instructor can assign students to work in groups of three or four to create a genealogy, flowchart, or illustrated poster that shows how the various iterations of the historical figure Lord Guan compares or relates to the *yinpeixiang* character as performed by Hou Shaokui. These charts are then presented to the full class or in tutorial sessions, allowing students to work through various ways of modeling the relationship between history and fiction, stage and screen, and tradition and innovation. A partial genealogy might look something like this:

> Lord Guan, a historical figure from the Three Kingdoms period who
>> died around 220, is transformed in the Sui dynasty into
> a deity of popular worship[6] that enters into a complex of fictional and
>> theatrical representations, among which is
> *The Great Prince Guan Attends the Single Sword Meeting Alone*, a *zaju*
>> script written by Guan Hanqing in the early fourteenth century,
>> roughly contemporaneous with, and no doubt interacting with, the
>> *Romance of the Three Kingdoms* novels (the most famous of which
>> also appears in the fourteenth century), which also feature Guan
>> Yu, and for generations
> Guan's *Sword Meeting* script continues to be adapted and performed
>> on stage in various performance genres, including *kunqu*,[7] while
>> such adaptations also interact with other stage depictions of Lord
>> Guan. The best-known twentieth-century *kunqu* interpreter of that
>> repertoire is
> Hou Yongkui (1911–81), whose son
> Hou Shaokui (born 1939) produced in 2000, with government sup-
>> port, a version in which Hou fils (whose name, Shaokui, echoes his
>> father's name, Yongkui, but with the character 少 [*shao*] indicating
>> his later position in the lineage) provides the image to Hou père.

This exercise should help students understand how *xiqu* is not only intertextual—referring always to past performances by teachers, or by the same actor in other roles—but also self-conscious and metatheatrical. In the *yinpeixiang* format, other avenues open up for thinking through the performance. The Three Kingdoms soldiers mourned by Lord Guan are remote to the audience because of multiple mediations and a historical distance of nineteen centuries. The Lord Guan whom we see is therefore not only a singular instance of a particular performance but also an amalgam, reanalysis, and descendant of the various fictionalized Lord Guans who have come before him and who have generated both the Lord Guan on stage and the Lord Guan in the audience's mind. *Yinpeixiang* Lord Guan, appealing to tradition by the way in which he is assembled from sound and image, can lead the viewing student to metatheatrical interpretations, making the homage to the dead heroes exceed its literal referent (the soldiers who contributed to the "twenty years of heroes' blood" in a far-removed past), but can also suggest, to the audience and performers, the actors who suffered through the vicissitudes of twentieth-century China to hand down to us this particular iteration of Lord Guan. After all, the rationale for *yinpeixiang* was the traumatic break of the Cultural Revolution—the attack on traditional culture, the damage it did to the arts, and the many artists who suffered persecution or worse during that time. As such, the mourning that Hou the son performs, while perhaps not intended to operate in that direction, is available for such an interpretation, including in classroom discussion.

Guan Hanqing's Lord Guan (reinscribed multiple times by means of script changes, performance practices, and audiovisual mediation), like Herodotus and many a Chinese writer, conceives of the river as history, as the passage of time, and also as a river of blood. But blood is never only a symbol of violence, and Chinese shares with English the close association captured in phrases such as "blood, sweat, and tears," to which *xinxue* (心血; "heart's blood") is a near analogue. If we consciously read against the grain of the archival project, then the unending river of heroes' blood would suggest not only the widespread persecution of actors during the Cultural Revolution but also the heart's blood, the millions of hours of training, teaching, and performing that generated and maintained the lines of transmission for the *xiqu* performance tradition, which forms one of the world's great theater traditions.

Yinpeixiang also offers a complication to conceptions of the craft and duty of the actor, who is ordinarily conceived of as performing a role or a character, because in this case Hou the son is simultaneously performing his own father and Lord Guan, or rather he is performing his father as Lord Guan. Of course, in a biopic one may very well find sequences of performance when, for instance, performers' lives are dramatized and sequences represent them on stage (Mario Lanza as Enrico Caruso as Rodolfo, for instance, in *The Great Caruso*), but such sequences usually function diegetically—that is, these performances can be shown because they occur within the narrative world. In *yinpeixiang* the doubling of roles is nondiegetic, insofar as the two roles (Hou the father and Lord Guan) are indistinguishable and coterminous. The teacher and the father are conflated, and this already multiple figure is associated to a character who is both divine and generated by the innumerable layers of Chinese tradition that take us from the flesh-and-blood Lord Guan to the endlessly reflected, remodeled, and reproduced versions of him.

Charting the genesis and logic of *yinpeixiang* should stimulate fruitful classroom conversation on the following three topics. First, how does the genre conceive of tradition, and how does it represent lineage? Can theater be preserved, and what does preservation mean for an artistic practice? Does *xiqu* regard movement, costume, vocal production, and so on, as being part of tradition—can the claim of *xiqu* to being a comprehensive art be retained, against a Western theater model that is flexible on items of production, such as movement, sets, props, and lighting and that defines a piece of theater principally as a drama text? The overt positioning of the *yinpeixiang* as conserving traditional masterpieces offers an illustration of a wide but perhaps not hugely flexible image of tradition and authenticity. This image in turn can lead to a question of archiving and fixing performance and to broader questions of national and international cultural policy such as intangible cultural heritage.

Second, what is the role of the state in *yinpeixiang*, and who is the audience for *yinpeixiang* videos? Students may be unfamiliar with the idea of theater as a project of the state, as an important carrier of national tradition, not least because the anglophone world is increasingly ambivalent about a state role in supporting cultural institutions such as theater. *Yinpeixiang* poses the question of the state's responsibility to tradition, including theater traditions. This conversation can be approached in potential connection with the Cultural Revolution and revolutionary operas, when state control of PRC theater reached its peak (and which is likely also to be taught in classes on modern Chinese theater, film, or culture). In a class on world theater, the idea of *yinpeixiang* might be considered in comparison with other forms of state theater, ranging from the Soviet model to Western state subsidy for prestige forms to Cold War state uses of theater in cultural diplomacy.

And third, what are the distinguishing features of *xiqu*? What are the elements that constitute performance in the Chinese conception of theater that produced *xiqu*? What makes *yinpeixiang* a phenomenon that appeared in *xiqu* but seemingly has no analogy? In other words, why do we not find this type of record in other genres, either in China or in the West? Could it be transferred for Western opera or into popular music? For instance, one could ask students whether they can imagine Madonna dressed up as Marilyn Monroe and lip-synching Monroe's film lines in order to conserve certain dance routines. Why might this read as parody or homage rather than as conservation? Would a leading stage soprano today lip-synch a Maria Callas recording? Why or why not?

It is probable that at this juncture more contemporary PRC valorization of the Chinese artistic heritage will come up in class discussion. Despite curation and the politically necessary "blind spots" of the *yinpeixiang* project (Wang, "Yinpeixiang"), its materials remain among our best audiovisual sources for performances of the late republican era and the early PRC, by a generation of performers of whom video footage is sparse. Attributing tradition to these recordings is a complex matter, not least because the person emitting the voice is not the person whose body is presented. There are other such matching processes—ghost singers, dubbing, dialogue replacement to correct errors in the sound—but none of these are intended archivally, and in such cases it is the body that precedes the voice, whereas in *yinpeixiang* it is the voice being supplied with a body. Put another way, the voice (identified as the most authentic source) requires a body to host tradition.

Using films to teach about the past requires teachers to "ensur[e] that students possess the historical film literacy skills to learn from, interpret, and evaluate the creations" (Marcus 66). Films can, however, purvey misleading or incorrect views of the past as easily as they can lead students to a solid understanding of past events and critical attitudes toward historiography. For this reason, as with other areas of teaching about the past, it can be useful to use film to teach not only about the past per se but also about how the past is constructed. In the case study presented in this essay, seeing and comprehending the historical context and basic structure of *yinpeixiang* allows students to grasp not only how theater transmission and tradition are conceptualized in China but also how archival recording and state involvement might create and fix as well as preserve tradition.

This understanding is pertinent particularly in a class dealing with genres such as *xiqu*, which exist in the present but stake their claim on being meaningfully from the past, both in terms of their content (in this case, a Three Kingdoms narrative) and in terms of their representation (the heritage of a particular genre, in this case *kunqu*). Using *yinpeixiang* can help students to learn to be reflective about the constantly mediated nature of what is called tradition in Chinese theater, the role of the state in fostering and shaping *xiqu*, and the ways and means by which the stories and practices of the Chinese past reach the present. In particular, the alienating, ventriloquizing effect of *yinpeixiang* recordings, intended to serve a greater authenticity, reveals structures that are often hidden. For those without a background in Chinese literature or periodization, the general principles of the construction of tradition are rendered visible by the simple facts about this project of conservation. Students with background knowledge in Chinese history can improve their understanding of the finer-grained chain of representation of Lord Guan over a 1600-year period, from history to story to canonical drama to later genre convention to Hou Yongkui to Hou Shaokui.

Through film viewing and class discussion, students should become aware that the "products of [*xiqu*] archivism" such as *yinpeixiang* "cannot be regarded simply as objective records to be mined to uncover a historical Kunqu" (Hunter Gordon 5). The same holds true for any other form of traditional theater since the recording is equally a process of creation by the organizers of the archive. The interplay of tradition and alteration allows students to consider what one scholar of Chinese dance has called "dynamic inheritance" even as they begin to evaluate whether such state archiving of tradition is being used to elide the novel, creative, and ephemeral nature of actors' performances (Wilcox 77). Having been introduced to the heritage logic of rescue and conservation through the archive, students can either endorse such strategies of conservation (which they can apply to other traditions, whether high-status practices such as calligraphy and papermaking, tangible heritage sites such as Lijiang or Pingyao, or so-called minority arts such as *muqam* and Tibetan opera) or decide that the shortcomings of such an approach outweigh the benefits.

The past is constructed not once but repeatedly, incessantly, and in every medium. Any given episode or any account of the past is thus a palimpsest of other pasts, of potentially endless recessions of representations. The *yinpeixiang* project was overtly and regularly conceived of as a matter of "rescuing" or "recovering" or "attempts at repair[ing]" pieces of repertoire whose authenticity was guaranteed by the teacher-student chain (Lei 62). Watching and discussing *yinpeixiang* should show students how this chain is conceived and revered and allow them to investigate how, why, and whether it functions—and what purpose it serves—for a contemporary state and a traditional art.

Notes

1. Historians of Chinese film consider the 1905 film *Dingjun Mountain* (定军山), a lost silent recording of the *jingju* (京剧; "Peking opera") star Tan Xinpei in a Three Kingdoms role, to be the first Chinese film.

2. The fact that stage movement is considered equally canonical with vocal production (singing as well as recitative) in certain genres of *xiqu*, especially *kunqu* (昆曲), perhaps does the most to explain why the *yinpeixiang* genre

emerged to conserve *xiqu* but does not have a direct equivalent in Euro-American traditions.

3. For a translation of an account by Hou Shaokui of how he performs this scene, including a discussion of some differences between Hou Yongkui and Hou Shaokui's performances of the role, see Hou Shaokui.

4. Liu's use of "embodied memory" and "archival memory" follows Taylor 19–20.

5. Important recent work has turned to *yinpeixiang* as a database and an illustration of medium-scale quantitative methods in theater historiography (Liu, "Quantitative Visualisation"). *Yinpeixiang* can, for instance, be used to chart the shifts in liberality and restriction vis-à-vis traditional repertoire in the early years of the PRC (465–70), quantify the preponderance of role-type divisions in *jingju* repertoire in the PRC (473), and illustrate the elements of continuity and of disruption in *xiqu* transmission (471–72), but these uses are likely to be of greater interest to the specialist than to the undergraduate student.

6. For what he terms the "religious afterlife" of Guan Yu, including its interaction with theater and narrative, see Ter Haar, especially 77–80 and 128–40.

7. No present performance practice is a direct descendant of a performance tradition that might have been used to perform the script in Guan Hanqing's time. Few scripts that provide the basis in *kunqu* repertoire have such an early pedigree, since repertoire largely derives from longer Ming and Qing *chuanqi* (传奇; "marvel play") scripts rather than from *zaju*. For the relationship between the various editions of Guan's text, the *kunqu* stage version, and versions as performed in other genres of *xiqu*, see Li Xiaobin 82–92. For an English translation of the two earliest editions with a preface that traces the distinction between surviving Yuan and Ming editions of the play, see Idema and West 236–95.

Works Cited

Evans, Megan. "Chinese *Xiqu* Performance and Moving-Image Media." *Theatre Research International*, vol. 34, no. 1, 2009, pp. 21–36. *Cambridge Core*, https://doi.org/10.1017/S0307883308004215.

Haar, Barend J. ter. *Guan Yu: The Religious Afterlife of a Failed Hero.* Oxford UP, 2017.

Hou Shaokui. "Lecture 9: 'Sword Meeting' ('Daohui' 刀會) from *Single Sword Meeting* (*Dandaohui* 單刀會)." Translated and annotated by Chao Guo. Kunqu *Masters on Chinese Theatrical Performance*, created by Yip Siu Hing, edited by Josh Stenberg, Anthem Press, 2022, pp. 241–65.

侯永奎 昆曲《单刀会》[*Hou Yongkui kunqu* Dandaohui; *Hou Yongkui* Kunqu Single Sword Meeting]. Performed by Hou Yongkui and Hou Shaokui, 2000. *YouTube*, uploaded by Chen Gaoyuan, 9 June 2017, www.youtube.com/watch?v=HjRRlubHTH0.

Hunter Gordon, Kim. *Contesting Traditional* Luzi *("Choreographic Paths"): A Performance-Based Study of* Kunqu. 2016. U of London, PhD dissertation.

Idema, Wilt L., and Stephen H. West, editors. *Battles, Betrayals, and Brotherhood: Early Chinese Plays on the Three Kingdoms.* Hackett Publishing, 2012.

Keane, Michael. "Cultural Policy in China: Emerging Research Agendas." *International Journal of Cultural Policy*, vol. 6, no. 2, 2000, pp. 243–58. *Taylor and Francis*, www.tandfonline.com/doi/pdf/10.1080/10286630009358123.

Lei, Daphne. *Alternative Chinese Opera in the Age of Globalization: Performing Zero*. Springer, 2011.

Li Ruihuan 李瑞环. 把音配像这一振兴京剧的好事办好——在《中国京剧音配像精粹》首发式上的讲话 ["Ba yinpeixiang zhe yi zhenxing Jingju de haoshi banhao—zai *Zhongguo jingju yinpeixiang jingcui* shoufashi shang de jianghua"; "Successfully Completing *Yinpeixiang* for the Fostering of *Jingju*—a Speech at the Launch of the *Gems of Chinese* Jingju Yinpeixiang"]. Tianjin Shi Zhonghua Minzu Wenhua Cujin Hui, pp. 1–5.

Li Shiji 李世济. 为了今人与后人 ["Wei le jinren yu houren"; "For the People of Today and Those of Tomorrow"]. Tianjin Shi Zhonghua Minzu Wenhua Cujin Hui, pp. 141–44.

Li Xiaobin 李晓彬. 关汉卿剧作的当代舞台传播 [*Guan Hanqing juzuo de dangdai wutai chuanbo; The Communication of Guan Hanqing's Plays on Contemporary Stages*]. 2010. Wuhan U, PhD dissertation.

Liu, Siyuan. "Quantitative Visualisation and Qualitative Research: The Beijing Opera *Yinpeixiang* (Video Matching Audio) Project." *The Routledge Companion to Theatre and Performance Historiography*, edited by Peter W. Marx, Taylor and Francis, 2020, pp. 456–77.

———. "Theatre Reform as Censorship: Censoring Traditional Theatre in China in the Early 1950s." *Theatre and State / Theatre and Law*, vol. 61, no. 3, Oct. 2009, pp. 387–406. *JSTOR*, www.jstor.org/stable/40587351.

———. *Transforming Tradition: The Reform of Chinese Theater in the 1950s and Early 1960s*. U of Michigan P, 2021.

Mackerras, Colin. "Chinese Traditional Theatre: A Revival in the 1990s?" *CHINOPERL: Journal of Chinese Oral and Performing Literature*, vol. 19, no. 1, 1996, pp. 79–94. *Taylor and Francis*, https://doi.org/10.1179/chi.1996.19.1.79.

Marcus, Alan S. "'It Is As It Was': Feature Film in the History Classroom." *The Social Studies*, vol. 96, no. 2, 2005, pp. 61–67. *Taylor and Francis*, https://doi.org/10.3200/TSSS.96.2.61-67.

Rahav, Shakhar. "Having One's Porridge and Eating It Too: Wang Meng as Intellectual and Bureaucrat in Late 20th-Century China." *The China Quarterly*, no. 212, Dec. 2012, pp. 1079–98. *JSTOR*, www.jstor.org/stable/23509482.

Rolston, David. *Inscribing Jingju/Peking Opera: Textualization and Performance, Authorship and Censorship of the "National Drama" of China from the Late Qing to the Present*. Brill, 2021.

Sun Yumin 孙毓敏. 我为祖国尽忠, 我为荀师尽孝 ["Wo wei zuguo jinzhong, wo wei Xun shi jinxiao"; "Fully Loyal to the Nation, Fully Filial to Teacher Xun"]. Tianjin Shi Zhonghua Minzu Wenhua Cujin Hui, pp. 183–86.

Taylor, Diana. *The Archive and the Repertoire: Performing Cultural Memory in the Americas*. Duke UP, 2003.

Tianjin Shi Zhonghua Minzu Wenhua Cujin Hui, editor. 中国京剧音配像精粹纪念文集 [*Zhongguo jingju yinpeixiang jingcui jinian wenji; Essays to*

Commemorate the Gems of Chinese Jingju Yinpeixiang *Project*]. Zhongguo Xiju Chubanshe, 2017.

Wang An-chi 王安祈. 京剧影音制作的商业、权力与政治.——以程派《锁麟囊》等剧为例 ["Jingju yingyin zhizuo de shangye, quanli yu zhengzhi—yi Chengpai 'suo lin nang' deng ju wei li"; "The Commerce, Power, and Politics of Media Production in Peking Opera—the Case of Cheng Yanqiu's 'The Lucky Purse'"]. 戏剧研究 [*Xiju yanjiu*; *Theatre Research*], no. 14, 2014, pp. 73–102.

———. "音配像"保存传统的盲点 ["Yinpeixiang baocun chuantong de mangdian"; "Blind Spots of Conserving Tradition through *Yinpeixiang*"]. 文化遗产 [*Wenhua yichan*; *Cultural Heritage*], no. 1, 2009, pp. 19–34.

Wilcox, Emily E. "Dynamic Inheritance: Representative Works and the Authoring of Tradition in Chinese Dance." *Journal of Folklore Research*, vol. 55, no. 1, 2018, pp. 77–111.

Ye Shaolan 叶少兰. 谈谈功德无量的京剧音配像工程 ["Tantan gongde wuliang de jingju yinpeixiang gongcheng"; "On the Unlimited Achievement of the *Yinpeixiang* Project"]. Tianjin Shi Zhonghua Minzu Wenhua Cujin Hui, pp. 156–58.

Yeh, Yueh-Yu. "Historiography and Sinification: Music in Chinese Cinema of the 1930s." *Cinema Journal*, vol. 41, no. 3, spring 2002, pp. 78–97. *JSTOR*, www.jstor.org/stable/1225700.

Zhou Huabin 周华彬. 历史行的记录与传播——有感于京剧音配像工程 ["Lishi xing de jilu yu chuanbo—you gan yu jingju yinpeixiang gongcheng"; "Historical Recording and Transmission—Thoughts on the *Yinpeixiang* Project"]. Tianjin Shi Zhonghua Minzu Wenhua Cujin Hui, pp. 105–12.

Additional Resources

CCTV. *YouTube* channel. Www.youtube.com/user/theateronair. Search: 音配像.

The Opera Quarterly. Vol. 26, nos. 2–3, spring-summer 2010. *Oxford Academic*, academic.oup.com/oq/issue/26/2-3.

Tianjin Guangbo Dianshitai, editor. 中国京剧音配像精粹赏析 [*Zhongguo jingju yinpeixiang jingcui shangxi*; *Appreciation of Gems of Chinese* Jingju Yinpeixiang]. Baihua Wenyi Chubanshe, 2015.

Ho Chak Law

A Reassessment of the Female Singing Voice in *Yellow Earth*

Widely known as the film that marked a new epoch of filmmaking in the People's Republic of China (PRC), *Yellow Earth* (黄土地) portrays an Eighth Route Army soldier who is assigned to collect folk songs in the surrounding areas of Yan'an—once the center of the Chinese Communist revolution—during the late 1930s. It represents music as a key element of Chinese folk culture with a visuality that at the time of its release brought a refreshing spectacle to international art cinema (Berry and Farquhar 103; T. Lu 34) while alluding to Chinese classical traditions such as the Chang'an school of scroll painting (McDougall, Yellow Earth 39). Accordingly, many aficionados of Chinese culture find *Yellow Earth* remarkable because of the way its director, Chen Kaige, and its cinematographer, Zhang Yimou, tried to "generat[e] new standards of realism at a time when socialist realism had lost its creditability [in the PRC]" (Berry and Farquhar 75).

No matter whether *Yellow Earth* is considered an autoethnography, a national allegory, or an artistic experiment (Schein 508–09), it showcases an early episode of the Chinese Communist cultural history of music in which folk songs are more than reflections of social life (Jones 5). On the one hand, the film's opening statement refers to the Loess Plateau as a piece of ancient land on which timeless *xintianyou* (信天游) melodies inspired a search for the origin of Shaanbei folk songs. On the other hand, the film's succeeding depiction of the Eighth Route Army soldier's involvement in the simultaneous preservation and destruction of Shaanbei folk songs is a directorial allusion to "what the Chinese Communist Party has always been doing" (Berry 90) with regard to its modern and politically driven treatment of Chinese folk culture. The arrangement of scenes and actions in the film is also inseparable from its music as a subject matter. Its first scene, for instance, illustrates in the style of direct cinema not only a traditional *guchui* (鼓吹; "drum and wind") band taking part in a local wedding parade but also a real-life folk singer improvising *jiuqu* (酒曲; "drinking songs") at a village wedding banquet.[1]

In this essay, I demonstrate how, for an undergraduate-level cultural history or cultural studies course on modern China, students can benefit from an ethnomusicological approach to *Yellow Earth*.[2] I explain how, through reflective learning (Brockbank and McGill 16–37),[3] students can inquire into the film's sonic, visual, discursive, and symbolic treatments of the female singing voice so as to gain a better understanding of the politics of cultural production in modern China. This explanation attests to the value of unpacking the ways *Yellow Earth* connects music with historical events as well as preexisting cultural practices and discourses; it aims to expose students to how, within and beyond narrative and visuality, *Yellow Earth* manifests the tension between preservation and destruction in modern Chinese culture.

Approaching *Yellow Earth* through the Lens of Music

Although *Yellow Earth* relies heavily on the moving image to deliver its story, Chen Kaige "had originally believed that the music and the sound effects in the film would be as revolutionary and as artistically successful as other ambitious plans for the structure and cinematography" (McDougall, Yellow Earth 45). This intriguing belief is substantiated by how Chen worked closely with the film's composer, Zhao Jiping; not only did they incorporate song lyrics into the film story, they also attempted to reconstruct "the original atmosphere of the native soil" while conveying "deep-seated implied meanings" by acoustic, musical, visual, and performative means (Zhao 20). They traveled to Shaanbei together for the preproduction fieldwork, during which they recruited He Yutang, a folk singer from the district of Ansai in Yan'an, as both an actor and an important source of music for the film (20–21).

The stylistic diversity of music in *Yellow Earth* is so remarkable that it merits classroom discussion. The film includes quasi-ethnographic depictions of vocal music, such as He Yutang's wedding banquet performance in the first scene and the *yangge* (秧歌; "rice sprout song") chorus during the call-for-rain ritual in the final scene.[4] There is also a brief, off-screen male singing voice when the Eighth Route Army soldier is introduced on-screen as the male protagonist on a mission to collect Shaanbei folk songs. Those verses that seem to be improvised by the film's three identifiable male characters (including the male protagonist) are, however, Chen Kaige's compositions. The theme song, "Song of a Daughter," probably leaves the deepest impression on the audience, as its tuneful and polished sonic presence contrasts with other sounds that mostly adhere to a naturalistic diegesis; it gives rise to the "musical moment," when music inverts the image-sound hierarchy and dictates the movements of the image and hence the structuring of space and time (Herzog 7). For instrumental music, aside from the drum and wind band that appears in the wedding parade and the *yaogu wu* (腰鼓舞; "waist-drum dance") that highlights the male protagonist's return to Yan'an from fieldwork, there are Western orchestral soundtracks based on the theme song and Chinese orchestral soundtracks based on a solo *guanzi* (管子; "double-reed pipe") melody featured in the film's opening credits.

On the whole, music carries a variety of meanings in *Yellow Earth* through its adoption of preexisting cultural codes, incorporation into the film's story, and juxtaposition with the moving image. It carries historical and ethnographic elements with support from classical film scoring conventions. It engages with different narration levels (diegetic, nondiegetic, metadiegetic, and extradiegetic) and agencies (vocal or verbal and instrumental or nonverbal) while providing sonic materials for a credible and coherent portrayal of a community (Slobin 4–5). Music is also constitutive of a contextual system that takes into account a particular history and conditions of spectatorship (Gorbman 30).

This brief assessment of music in *Yellow Earth* could give way to a fruitful discussion with students about issues such as authorship, indigeneity, cultural translation, and the role of music in PRC films during the mid and late twentieth century. That said, teachers might have concerns about how, without expertise in Chinese folk and traditional music, they could lead such a discussion satisfactorily and with confidence. To address this concern, I suggest that teachers treat *Yellow Earth* as primarily a combination of plots, sounds, and images whose meanings are subject to preexisting contextual associations in addition to particular histories and conventions of representation. I contend that such a treatment would allow teachers to approach *Yellow Earth* through the lens of music but with a focus on the reception of music under circumstances that deserve further attention.

I also recommend that teachers help students recognize the representational nuances in *Yellow Earth* through inductive justification that precedes deductive reasoning. I believe that students would understand *Yellow Earth* better if they first watch the film with a few basic guidelines that alert them to cultural assumptions they may have (about China, music, etc.). Teachers could then provide students with examples and information that show how the film is related to certain preexisting cultural forms or concurrent cultural phenomena (either of which could be covered in earlier classes) before referring to certain designated course objectives and deciding whether to guide students to examine the film's stylistic and storytelling elements. In other words, teachers could deploy a pedagogical strategy that would bring to light the transmission and mediation of meanings in *Yellow Earth* without undermining the sensorial or aesthetic experience of the film. Teachers could give students a better sense of how, while film narration situates the spectator in a position of agency, various social relations and historical conditions affect the subjecthood and hence the cinematic experience of the spectator.

In the next two sections of this essay, I elaborate on my proposed pedagogical strategy by associating the sonic, visual, discursive, and symbolic treatments of the female singing voice in *Yellow Earth* with the legacy of *dianying gequ* (电影歌曲; "film songs") in republican China and *shaoshu minzu dianying* (少数民族电影; "minority films") in Maoist China. I offer a guide for students to listen to modern China meaningfully by connecting the musical moment in *Yellow Earth*, when music dictates the visual elements of the film, with the film's various acts of fabulation that "brin[g] together archaic and contemporary, as well as documentary and fictional, elements in the production of collective modes of storytelling" (Chow 25).

The Comeback of Popular Music in *Yellow Earth*

Prior to exposing the audience to the diegesis, *Yellow Earth* uses a set of title cards to frame the film story with three pieces of information, which I translate into English as follows:

1. The Kuomintang (the Nationalist Party) took over the Eighth Route Army in the newly designated Shaanxi-Gansu-Ningxia border region as part of the Second United Front, formed by the Nationalists and Communists, against the Japanese invasion in September 1937.
2. While the Shaanbei people were being oppressed under the Kuomintang's governance, a handful of Eighth Route Army soldiers conducted fieldwork to find the origin of Shaanbei folk songs.
3. The first event in the story takes place in early spring 1939.

These title cards might invite viewers to identify *Yellow Earth* as a historically informed portrayal of a music ethnographer (Slobin 55), especially when viewers are reliant on subtitles to follow the story. Such viewers probably have no option but to trust the film director as the mediator between the world of the film and the world they perceive according to their everyday experience (Grimshaw 99). Those who have some exposure to the history of the Chinese language might be aware that these title cards manifest calligraphic, syntactic, and logographic nuances pointing to the politics of signification in the film (Yau, "*Yellow Earth*" 65). They might wonder about the rationales for putting together the antique appearance of *zhuanshu* (篆书; "seal script"); the left-to-right arrangement of lines, following the influence of European languages; and the use of *xiandai baihuawen* (现代白话文; "modern vernacular language") with *jianti zi* (简体字; "simplified characters") that were first standardized by the Chinese Communist Party during the mid 1950s. Similarly, those who know a bit about the history of the conflict between the Kuomintang and the Chinese Communist Party might take the three pieces of information provided in the title cards with a grain of salt. They might doubt both the interconnections between the three pieces of information and the accuracy of the information. There seems to be more than a single explanation for the treatment of these title cards. That said, it is worth pointing out the abovementioned issues so that students have some idea of the film's cultural specificity and representational complexity before they learn more about the film's treatment of the female singing voice and other aspects of the film's reception and representation.

Yellow Earth could be used alongside excerpts from seminal texts such as *Selections of Shaanbei Folk Songs* and "Talks at Yan'an Conference on Literature and Art" to introduce students to the early history of *geming gequ* (革命歌曲; "revolutionary songs") in Maoist China (Lu Xun Wenyi Xueyuan 1–58; McDougall, *Mao Zedong's "Talks"* 57–86). Nevertheless, students might be more curious about why the film features its female protagonist's singing voice alongside attributes ranging from repeated melodies and Western orchestral accompaniment to monologic lyrics and the nondiegetic presence of a playback singer. They might question the extent to which this female singing voice is connected to Shaanbei folk songs as well. A discussion on the film's treatment of this female singing voice is therefore more than a matter of teaching interest; it offers an opportunity for teachers to, for instance, refer to an interview with Zhao Jiping published in *People's Music* and elaborate on this female singing voice as an element inseparable from the film's context of production and representation.

Interviewed a year after the premiere of *Yellow Earth*, Zhao mentions how, after going through the film's processes of preproduction, production, and postproduction as a composer, he found the film comparable to some *yinyue pian* (音乐片; "musical films") of the Maoist period (19).[5] It is noteworthy that he identifies the film's female protagonist as a *nongcun nü geshou* (农村女歌手; "rustic songstress") characterized by her lack of maternal love, her expressions of rural village values, and her humble circumstances and unsympathetic father (20). Intentionally or not, he brings to focus the film's reference of a character archetype that originated in *Song of the Fishermen* (漁光曲), an early classic of Chinese left-wing cinema (Ma 111–12). Indeed, in the first three appearances of the film's theme song, the female vocalist's singing voice is presented in a way reminiscent of the monologic, interiorized, and musicalized *su xinsheng* (诉心声; "confession") common to Mandarin melodramas in republican Shanghai and postwar Hong Kong (Wong 12).

By asking Feng Jianxue to record the theme song with a subdued voice (Zhao 21), Zhao also adapted Feng's specialized singing style, *minzu changfa* (民族唱法; "ethnonational singing style"), for a singing voice that is somewhat relatable to Mandarin *shidaiqu* (时代曲; "pop oldies"). In the same vein, Zhao's use of Western orchestral accompaniment in the theme song reinforces a kind of gendered lyricism that is prevalent in Mandarin pop oldies but absent in music of the Maoist period. These decisions could have been driven by "an extreme thirst [among audiences] for soft and slow songs" (Baranovitch 11) since the main sources of popular music in the PRC were state-controlled film and television productions. The influx of popular songs from Hong Kong and Taiwan during the late 1970s and the early 1980s was so impactful that it led to the *Qingchu jingshen wuran* (清除精神污染; "Antispiritual Pollution") campaign in autumn 1983, approximately a year after the People's Music Press published

How to Inspect Yellow Songs, a collection of essays in which several veteran music educators and conservatory-trained composers censured these popular songs for their so-called obscenity and decadence, which were attributed to Western bourgeois and individualistic influences (*Zenyang jianbie*). Feng's presence as a playback singer for mainstream PRC films such as *Life* (人生) and *Love Hurts* (苦藏的恋情) is thus evident of Chen Kaige's initial insight into the popular appeal of film songs (McDougall, Yellow Earth 46). Actually, the theme song of *Yellow Earth* has retained its popularity for more than three decades. It has been performed in televised variety shows and rerecorded by high-profile singers such as Tan Jing and Wang Erni, who have been visible in the mainland popular music scene despite their affiliation with state-run performance troupes.

Remnants of Minority Film: Otherness, Verisimilitude, and Ethnocentrism

In another interview conducted by Michael Berry in the early 2000s, Chen Kaige recalled how the minimal plot and unvarnished imagery in *Yellow Earth* caused quite a stir when the film was first screened in the PRC, where the audience was accustomed to identifying with clear-cut characters and idyllic landscapes (Berry 89). Chen was eager to overturn the staginess and prescriptiveness he found in earlier PRC films, so as to "start paying attention to the people and the state of what it meant to be a human being" (86). For that reason, *Yellow Earth* abandons the once-conventional use of subtitles for on-screen, off-screen, and nondiegetic film songs, which open up possibilities for the audience to experience afresh the film's musical moment, when music dictates the film's visual elements.[6] Viewers who presumed the primacy of narrative continuity might have been disturbed by the distancing effect consequent to the film's abrupt suspension of Feng's singing voice near the end of the theme song's second and final occurrences in the film (Yau, "*Yellow Earth*" 64).

While teachers might be tempted to utilize a wealth of secondary sources to show students how *Yellow Earth* offered a refreshing outlook to PRC cinema, they could rather engage students in comparing the film's portrayal of the countryside and of folk music activities with the exotic sceneries and spectacles of singing and dancing characteristic of minority film, a film genre that was tasked with ethnological representation by means of on-location shooting during the Maoist period (X. Lu 373, 380; Yau, "Is China" 119). The way *Yellow Earth* commences with a quasi-emic display of Shaanbei village wedding rituals is, regardless of cinematographic differences, comparable to how *Hasen and Jiamila* (哈森与加米拉) depicts Kazakh nomadic lifestyle at the film's beginning. The natural landscape of the Loess Plateau in *Yellow Earth* is no less splendid than its Tian Shan counterpart in *Hasen and Jiamila*, while the Shaanbei drinking song is no less striking than a Kazakh love song, both of which are performed on-screen by indigenous performers in *Yellow Earth* and *Hasen and Jiamila*, respectively; all these visual and sonic elements are meant to engender a sense of ethnic authenticity through exoticism and verisimilitude (X. Lu 383–84).

Yellow Earth is also comparable to minority film for its inclusion of a male Han cadre who, representative of political authority, carries an agenda that bespeaks the disparity between the national self and the rustic other (Leung 261; Yau, "Is China" 120, 125):

Father. Mr. Official, you said last night that this trip of yours is for collecting something?

Gu Qing. I want to collect the folk songs of our Shaanbei.

Father. What folk songs—our poor local ballads?

Gu Qing. Can you sing, uncle?

Father. (*Pauses.*) Sing what? If you are not happy and not sad . . .

Gu Qing. There are hundreds and thousands of our Shaanbei folk songs. Tell me, how can you know them all and remember them all?

Father. You remember them when times are hard[. . . .] What is it for, collecting our local ballads?

Gu Qing. When we have collected the folk songs and written new words to them, we turn them over to the Eighth Route Army troops, boys and girls of Cuiqiao's age; to sing, so everyone can understand why our suffering people are living in fear and wretchedness[. . . .] Our Chairman Mao and Commander Zhu love listening to folk songs[. . . .] Our Chairman Mao doesn't just get us to sing [. . .] he also gets us to read and write[. . . .] (McDougall, Yellow Earth 216–17; *Yellow Earth* 00:34:50–00:36:50)

This male Han cadre does not lead the film story to the sort of triumphant ending typical of minority films; his encounter with Shaanbei people does not bring anyone to salvation. His grave concern with various forms of cultural repression persists, albeit in an introspective manner that mirrors the film crew's self-admitted inability and unwillingness to give a clear answer to what the future holds for Chinese culture (Berry 90). Ironically, such critique of socialist realism was officially reproved for ethnocentrism

(Yau, "*Yellow Earth*" 77), a perspective that has been noted for its disguise as a matter of *minzu tuanjie* (民族团结; "national unity") in minority film (Bulag 8–21; Zhang 83–84).

This irony might be easier for students to perceive if they compare the very end of the Tibet-themed film *Serfs* (农奴) with the first appearance of the theme song in *Yellow Earth*. Both scenes feature a "mother river" (i.e., the Yarlong Tsangpo and the Yellow River, respectively) that represents the cradle of a civilization,[7] alluding to the iconography of Chinese landscape painting while evoking a nationalistic feeling of longevity and magnificence that is also implied in the song lyrics sung on the soundtrack for each scene. These allusions are evident of an ongoing insistence on the historic greatness of Chinese civilization by many Han Chinese intellectuals and politicians (Pye 4), who know that *mingshan dachuan* (名山大川; "famous mountains and great rivers") were symbolic of both the territory and the *jiangshan* (江山; "regime") in ancient and imperial China. Both scenes also provide outstanding examples of conservatory-trained folk singers as attractions in PRC cinema between the late 1950s and the late 1980s. Tseten Dolma, the playback singer for *Serfs*, is actually a senior colleague of Feng Jianxue, the playback singer for *Yellow Earth*. They both studied under Wang Pinsu, a music pedagogue who played a pivotal role in establishing the ethnonational singing style as a synthesis of Han and non-Han Chinese folk singing and of Italian bel canto and Chinese operatic and narrative singing (Wang 68). They shared a repertoire created by a group of conservatory-trained composers who analyzed, adapted, and reinterpreted folk songs collected from Han and non-Han rural communities based on certain sinicized versions of Western music theory (*Minjian yinyue* 15; Zhao 20–21). Furthermore, Tseten Dolma and Feng Jianxue were famed for performing revolutionary songs, among which Tseten Dolma's version of "Singing a Folk Song for the Party" and Feng's version of "Soldiers Are Back" have been particularly famous.

Having achieved a classic status in the history of Chinese cinema, *Yellow Earth* is known for various stylistic qualities that distinguish itself from its predecessors. Less is mentioned in existing scholarship about how the film was influenced by modern Chinese culture in general and Maoist culture in particular. This essay demonstrates how examining the film's deployment of the female singing voice—as an attraction, part of the plot, and part of certain filmmaking conventions—could help students consider the film's cultural influences and better understand how modern China has been marked by moments of juncture and disjuncture between the past and the present.

Notes

1. Direct cinema is a style of documentary filmmaking that emerged in the late 1950s. Albert Maysles and David Maysles pioneered this style and hoped to rely on the camera's direct observation of events and subjects to unveil certain objective truths.

2. An ethnomusicological approach focuses on studying music in its social and cultural contexts. In other words, ethnomusicologists are concerned with what music is as well as what music means to its composers, performers, and audiences.

3. Brockbank and McGill define reflective learning "as an intentional social process, where context and experience are acknowledged, in which learners are active individuals, wholly present, engaging with others, open to challenge, and the outcome involves transformation as well as improvement for both individuals and their environment" (36).

4. For the social and ritualistic functions of *yangge* performances, see Holm 17.

5. During the Maoist period, musical films "included adaptations of traditional opera, dance dramas, and musica[l]" dramas (Clark 107); some musical dramas were in "a modern form which combined dialogue and songs, [and] usually dealt with more mundane stories and characters" (Clark 107–08).

6. According to Chion, "[O]*ffscreen sound* in film is sound . . . whose source is invisible, whether temporar[il]y or not. We call *onscreen sound* that whose source appears in the image, and belongs to the reality, represented therein. . . . [T]o designate sound whose source is not only absent from the image but is also external to the story world, I shall use the term *nondiegetic*. This is the widespread case of voiceover commentary and narration and, of course, musical underscoring" (73).

7. "Mother river" is a traditional way of referring to the rivers.

Works Cited

Baranovitch, Nimrod. *China's New Voices: Popular Music, Ethnicity, and Politics, 1978–1997.* U of California P, 2003.

Berry, Chris, and Mary Farquhar. *China On Screen: Cinema and Nation.* Columbia UP, 2006.

Berry, Michael. *Speaking in Images: Interviews with Contemporary Chinese Filmmakers.* Columbia UP, 2005.

Brockbank, Anne, and Ian McGill. *Facilitating Reflective Learning in Higher Education.* Open UP, 2007.

Bulag, Uradyn E. 2002. *The Mongols at China's Edge: History and the Politics of National Unity.* Rowman and Littlefield, 2002.

Chion, Michel. *Audio-Vision: Sound on Screen.* Edited and translated by Claudia Gorbman, Columbia UP, 1994.

Chow, Rey. *Sentimental Fabulations, Contemporary Chinese Films: Attachment in the Age of Global Visibility*. Columbia UP, 2007.

Clark, Paul. *Chinese Cinema: Culture and Politics since 1949*. Cambridge UP, 1987.

Gorbman, Claudia. *Unheard Melodies: Narrative Film Music*. Indiana UP, 1987.

Grimshaw, Anna. *The Ethnographer's Eye: Ways of Seeing in Anthropology*. Cambridge UP, 2001.

Hasen and Jiamila. Directed by Wu Yonggang, Shanghai Film Studio, 1955.

Herzog, Amy. *Dreams of Difference, Songs of the Same: The Musical Moment in Film*. U of Minnesota P, 2010.

Holm, David. *Art and Ideology in Revolutionary China*. Clarendon Press, 1990.

Jones, Stephen. *Folk Music of China: Living Instrumental Traditions*. Oxford UP, 1995.

Leung, Helen Hok-Sze. "*Yellow Earth*: Hesitant Apprenticeship and Bitter Agency." *Chinese Films in Focus II*, edited by Chris Berry, British Film Institute, 2008, pp. 258–64.

Lu, Tonglin. *Confronting Modernity in the Cinemas of Taiwan and Mainland China*. Cambridge UP, 2002.

Lu, Xiaoning. "The Politics of Recognition and Constructing Socialist Subjectivity: Reexamining the National Minority Film (1949–1966)." *Journal of Contemporary China*, vol. 23, no. 86, 2014, pp. 372–86.

Lu Xun Wenyi Xueyuan, editor. 陕北民歌选 [*Shaanbei min'ge xuan; Selections of Shaanbei Folk Songs*]. Guanghua Shudian, 1948.

Ma, Jean. *Sounding the Modern Woman: The Songstress in Chinese Cinema*. Duke UP, 2015.

McDougall, Bonnie S. *Mao Zedong's "Talks at the Yan'an Conference on Literature and Art": A Translation of the 1943 Text with Commentary*. U of Michigan P, 1980.

———. Yellow Earth: *A Film by Chen Kaige with a Complete Translation of the Filmscript*. Chinese UP, 1991.

民间音乐采访手册 [*Minjian yinyue caifang shouce; Folk Music Survey Pamphlet*]. Wenhua Yishu Chubanshe, 1986.

Pye, Lucian W. *The Spirit of Chinese Politics*. Harvard UP, 1992.

Schein, Louisa. "Ethnographic Representation across Genres: The Cultural Trope in Contemporary Mainland Media." *The Oxford Handbook of Chinese Cinemas*, edited by Carlos Rojas and Eileen Cheng-Yin Chow, Oxford UP, 2013, pp. 507–25.

Serfs. Directed by Li Jun, August First Film Studio, 1963.

Slobin, Mark, editor. *Global Soundtracks: Worlds of Film Music*. Wesleyan UP, 2008.

Wang Pinsu. 风格, 借鉴及其他: 民族声乐教学札记 ["Fengge, jiejian ji qita: Minzu shengyue jiaoxue zhaji"; "Style, Borrowing, and Other Issues: Notes on Ethnonational Vocal Art Pedagogy"]. 声乐艺术的民族风格 [*Shengyue yishu de minzu fengge; Ethnonational Style in Vocal Art*], edited by Guan Lin, Wen hua Yi shu Chu ban she, 1982, pp. 61–69.

Wong, Kee Chee. "Two or Three Things about Mandarin Pop." *Mandarin Films and Popular Songs: 40s–60s*, edited by Law Kar, Urban Council, 1993, pp. 18–20.

Yau, Esther. "Is China the End of Hermeneutics? or, Political and Cultural Usage of Non-Han Women in Mainland Chinese Films." *Discourse*, vol. 11, no. 2, 1989, pp. 114–37.

———. "*Yellow Earth*: Western Analysis and a Non-Western Text." *Perspectives on Chinese Cinema*, edited by Chris Berry, British Film Institute, 1991, pp. 62–79.

Yellow Earth. Directed by Chen Kaige, Guangxi Film Studio, 1984.

怎样鉴别黄色歌曲 [*Zenyang jianbie huangse gequ*; *How to Inspect Yellow Songs*]. Renmin Yinyue Chubanshe, 1982.

Zhang, Yingjin. "From 'Minority Film' to 'Minority Discourse': Questions of Nationhood and Ethnicity in Chinese Cinema." *Cinema Journal*, vol. 36, no. 3, 1997, pp. 73–90.

Zhao Jiping. 电影《黄土地》音乐创作札记 ["Dianying *Huang tudi* yinyue chuang-zuo zhaji"; "Notes on Music Composition for *Yellow Earth*"]. 人民音乐 [*Renmin yinyue*; *People's Music*], no. 9, 1985, pp. 19–21.

Shirley O. Lua

Without a Sword: Zhang Yimou's *Hero* in the Context of the *Wuxia* Tradition

The first two decades of the twenty-first century saw the rising popularity of *wuxia pian* (武侠片; "martial arts film") around the world. The appropriation of Chinese martial arts techniques for Hollywood movies such as *The Matrix* and *Kill Bill*, the martial arts film genre's accessibility through streaming websites and social media platforms that offer multilingual subtitles, and the genre's drawn-out narratives in the form of TV and web dramas are some determinants in shaping the *wuxia* attraction across continents.

One challenge in teaching *wuxia* films is to convince students to discard the yardstick of modern realism in approaching the film and to appreciate it in the context of its own lengthy tradition. *Wuxia* is categorized as fantasy fiction with its own cinematic, cultural, and sociopolitical histories. To appraise within the genre contexts does not mean limiting the film to the *wuxia shenguai* (武侠神怪; "martial chivalric-supernatural") tradition in Chinese-language cinema. Such an appraisal involves an intertextual reading with Chinese literature: classical texts such as historical annals (e.g., Sima Qian's *Records of the Grand Historian*, Ban Gu's biographies on wandering heroes), prose romances (e.g., *The Investiture of the Gods*), *chuanqi* (传奇; "tales of marvels"), *xiayi xiaoshuo* (侠义小说; "stories of chivalry"), Qing dynasty crime fiction, and modern *wuxia* fiction (e.g., by Gu Long and Jin Yong). Such investigation provides historical layers and cultural specificities to the *wuxia* film. Students are directed to identify significant themes such as honor and gallantry and to confront issues relevant to contemporary society such as political conflicts, alliances, ethnocultural disparities, and violence. *Wuxia* thus becomes a metaphor and a philosophy for the condition of humanity. More sophisticated students may even examine the *wuxia* codes to explore the creativity of their generic transformations, disclose a sociopolitical reading, or contemplate how the film refunctions to meet the concerns of its era. In its imaginative remaking of the *wuxia* genre, a film "simultaneously 're-functions' both the form and content of its source text so as critically to address the changed cultural and political circumstances of its own time" (Brooker 114).

In a course on Chinese cinema or a China-related humanities course, viewing the film *Hero* (英雄) is an enriching cinematic and philosophical experience for students. Parts of a module on *Hero* were conducted for international relations students in my course Chinese Culture through Cinema and for liberal arts students in my course Fantasy Fiction at De La Salle University. The proposed procedure described in this essay is a reworking of the original module. The complete module probably takes nine hours, exclusive of film screenings, and can be redesigned for online learning. Below is a sketch of my pedagogical procedure interspersed with viewpoints of *Hero* as a *wuxia* film.

Preparation and Mise-en-Scène Analysis

Before the film screening, I ask students to assess their own generic literacy through a short reflective writing exercise in which they list what *wuxia* movies and dramas they have seen and whether they like them. I ask them to be as specific as possible in citing the reasons for their likes or dislikes. This way I can ascertain if they have an adequate knowledge of *wuxia* and if there is a need to cover a historical survey of the genre and its primary conventions. Most students have seen a Jackie Chan, Jet Li, or Donnie Yen film, and a few might be familiar with web dramas such as *The Legend of the Condor Heroes* (射雕英雄传), or the *xianxia* (仙侠; "fantasy martial arts") subgenre, which includes films such as *The Untamed* (陈情令).

Hero situates its story during the Warring States period. The character known in the film as Nameless (Jet Li) works as a county prefect in the Qin kingdom. A Zhao native, Nameless seeks vengeance for his parents, who were slain by Qin soldiers. He cultivates a unique sword-fighting skill called "Kill within Ten Paces" (00:58:47). Through stratagems and determination, he secures the swords of the three most wanted assassins in Qin, gains entry to the palace, and meets the king of Qin (Chen Daoming).

After screening the film, I begin by rectifying the film's mistranslation of a dialogue between the king and Nameless. This is the scene where the king throws down his sword to Nameless, who takes it, pretends to stab the king but actually spares the king's life by touching him only with the sword's handle. The English subtitles in the film's theatrical release give this translation of Nameless's last words: "Your Majesty, your visions have convinced me that you are committed to the highest ideal of ultimate swordsmanship. Therefore I cannot kill you. Remember those who gave their lives for the highest ideal: peace. No more killing" (01:21:05).[1] I point out to the class that the original dialogue in Mandarin is worded differently and suggest a more appropriate translation: "King, I must stab you with this sword. Stabbing you with this sword will cause many to die. But you will live. For those who perish, please remember, King, the highest level of attainment." A slight difference in translation bears significance, for it alters the tone of the character's utterance and the meaning of the situation. My suggested translation affirms Nameless as a *wuxia* hero and questions the assumption that Nameless has been won over by the king's ambition to unify the warring kingdoms. This subtitle mistranslation might account for the backlash Zhang Yimou received from critics in the United States, many of whom derided him for his "paean to authoritarianism" (Orr) and "glorification of ruthless leadership and self-sacrifice on the altar of national greatness" (Hoberman) and dismissed the cineaste's repeated denial of any intended political layering in the film.

Our class investigation starts off with an inquiry-based method. I encourage the students to raise questions about the film's particulars that baffle them, and I ask them the following questions: Why didn't Nameless kill the king? Who is really the hero in the film? What does *tianxia* (天下; "All under heaven") refer to (01:15:52)? Students even have basic genre concerns about why the characters are able to leap across rooftops, fly over water, and shield themselves against hundreds of hurtling arrows and whether these abilities represent superpowers. These questions are set aside for discussion later.

I then guide the students to approach a scene or two using the formalist method of close viewing and mise-en-scène analysis.[2] Students, as film viewers, must learn to go beyond the narrative content and see the nuanced language of moving images, the material relations of image and sound. Alexandre Astruc remarks, "[M]ise en scène . . . [is] a certain way of extending states of mind into movements of the body. It is a song, a rhythm, a dance" (267). The obsessiveness of certain critics in approaching a Zhang Yimou film as if it were a propaganda pamphlet obscures the principle that film is first and foremost an amazing art form, an experience of aesthetic wonder for the spectators. In *wuxia*, the finest scenes are those showcasing *wushu* (武术; "martial prowess") through a masterful arrangement of stylized combat—a careful choreography of movement in space and space in movement—supplemented by lighting design, production sets, and the film's color palette. We choose to examine the lake scene in *Hero*, which depicts an elegant sword fight between Nameless and Broken Sword (Tony Leung; 00:52:29–00:55:43). As the scene is replayed, I instruct the students to pay attention to the cinematic details (e.g., visual composition, kinds of shots used, movement of the swordsmen, colors, sound effects, and music) and to describe them in writing. I encourage them to use metaphorical language to bolster their descriptions (e.g., "the scene is like a lovely landscape painting" or "like a ballet staged on water," and "the lake is a clear mirror"). A few students volunteer to read aloud their descriptions, and we reflect on how these details work together to fashion a unified spectacle of splendor.

Genre Analysis

This mise-en-scène analysis paves the way for the class to undertake a genre analysis, as I direct students to identify *wuxia* conventions and stylistic features in the lake scene. The students pinpoint *wuxia* feats such as flying, striding on water, and swords clashing in mid-air. Some students, still clinging to the realist benchmark, express disbelief over these abilities, calling them "unrealistic." I reiterate that a *wuxia* film is not a realist mode of storytelling. If time suffices, the teacher can segue to a discussion on realism in cinema. Realism attempts to approximate reality through the aesthetic treatment of its subject matter (e.g., authentic architecture, natural environment). Despite its historical setting, *wuxia*'s main concern is not to be verisimilar to a particular era and culture but to create a secondary world, an alternate universe with fictional characters and milieu.

A short discussion of *wushu* helps the students understand that the prowess displayed in *Hero* has Daoism as its philosophical, and spiritual source. Nameless and Broken Sword have cultivated their *wushu* to a high degree by developing *neigong* (內功; "internal power") and *qinggong* (轻功; "skill of lightness"). They slice the water with their blades, and a deep-rooted inner force propels them as they leap and fly. Other *wushu* abilities such as *dianxue* (点穴; "vital point strikes") have their origins in Chinese medicine. In *wuxia*, nature can become a weapon. Nameless and Broken Sword fling water drops like missiles at each other. We also raise the question of a swordsman's honor: Nameless voluntarily loses to Broken Sword because his sense of honor prevents him from thrusting his sword at an opponent whose back is turned. Students also find other *Hero* sequences exhilarating: for instance, the match between Nameless and Sky (Donnie Yen), which is a battle of minds and has an intensity reinforced by a montage of amplified sound effects such as the rhythm of raindrops, haunting sounds of a zither, quivering of blades, clashing of steel, and occasional battle cry; and the oak grove scene where Flying Snow (Maggie Cheung) agitates the leaves with her *neigong* and instigates a cyclonic attack on Moon (Zhang Ziyi) until the whole frame is showered in yellow leaves that turn a majestic red.

In *wuxia*, violence is ironically rendered in a striking manner. This predilection for kinesthetic aggression paradoxically serves as a philosophical and moral meditation. Stephen Teo asserts that "the best martial arts films are never about showing violence as aesthetic forms of cinematic beauty but in showing them *didactically* as aesthetic forms" (*Chinese Martial Arts Film* 4). To continue our genre study, I ask the students what the significance is of the sword fight between Nameless and Broken Sword, why this fight is deemed honorable, and how such violence is justified. This serves as a preliminary discussion. In the next section we delve deeper into the concept of *xia* (侠; "gallantry").

Valuable resources that outline the historical development of the genre, illuminate *wuxia* concepts, provide analyses of seminal works, or review the sociohistorical contexts of their material production include Chen Pingyuan's *The Development of Chinese Martial Arts Fiction: A History of Wuxia Literature*, Teo's *Chinese Martial Arts Cinema: The* Wuxia *Tradition*, and James Liu's *The Chinese Knight Errant*. Chen has a refreshing exegesis on the heritage of sword fighting (106–30) and an informative take on the cultural significance of vengeance (131–58), which can serve as supplementary readings for the students.

Intertextual Analysis I: Sima Qian

Next we engage in intertextual reading and cultural contextualization. *Wuxia*, like most genres, embodies the specters of its predecessors. It is a palimpsest, where texts are written over earlier texts. For instance, the dialogue between Nameless and the king, which spins off three versions (or four if we include Broken Sword's story) of how Nameless has come to possess the three swords, resonates with the classical usage of *yue* (曰; "speaks"). Classical Chinese chronicles and memoirs deploy the term *speaks* to recount an incident, depict verbal combat (a battle of wits), comment on a character, or simply move the action forward.[3] Yet the major influence on Zhang Yimou's *wuxia* films is Gu Long, an acknowledged master of modern *wuxia* novels.[4] Gu Long's writing style favors short sentences and dialogue, and his preferred narrative structure is that of a mystery with a convoluted plot and surprising twists. *Hero* follows the model of Gu Long in having a choppy mode of verbal exchange (between the king and Nameless), philosophy-loaded utterances (e.g., "unity of sword and man" and "calligraphy and sword aspire for the highest level of truth and simplicity" [01:20:05, 00:28:25]), varied presentations of the same incident, and intricate plotting. A viewer who knows the many *wuxia* fictions and films would discern *Hero*'s act of speaking back to the Chinese classics and modern *wuxia* forms and join in the invigorating circuit of recognitions. Thus, *Hero* is an homage to the *wuxia* masters by a postmodern cinephile.

To limit our intertexts, we focus on *Records of the Grand Historian*, by Sima Qian of the Han dynasty, and film adaptations of Gu Long's fiction. We read selections from *Records*, particularly on the wandering gallants, the assassins, and Emperor Qin (Sima Qian, *Records: Han Dynasty II* 409–18 and *Records: Qin Dynasty* 35–84, 167–78). Using close reading, we attend to details about personae, situations, and contexts. We discuss the concept of *xia* and mull over the character of the assassin Jing Ke as a *xiake* (侠客; "gallant person"). Sima Qian writes, "As for gallant citizens (*xia*), although they do not always do what is right, their word can be trusted. They keep all their promises, honor all their pledges, and hasten to rescue those in distress regardless of their own safety" (Szuma Chien 429). These gallants are commoners, dressed in plain clothes and eating simple meals. They are the "knights of the lanes and byways, who, though they had no such advantages, were so upright in conduct and careful of their honour that their reputation was known all over the empire and there was no one who did not praise them as worthy men" (*Records: Han Dy-*

nasty II 411–12). I underscore to the class that *xia* should be deemed an evolving concept, a blend of cultural imagination and histories and even of social values and the psychological concerns of the readers or viewers in response to the difficulties of their times.[5]

We analyze Sima Qian's portrayal of the king of Qin and his majestic dictum "All under heaven are of one mind, single in will" (*Records: Qin Dynasty* 124). We extract textual specifics to fashion a blueprint for the sociopolitical history of the Warring States period. The students note with interest that Sima Qian's sketches of military attacks, revolts, and massacres are juxtaposed with references to strange natural phenomena (e.g., swarms of locusts, thunder in winter, the cyclic appearance of comets, the flooding of the Yellow River, snowstorms, earthquakes, and droughts); feudal strife; and the suffering of the people (e.g., through famine, pestilence, war, and natural disasters). Such turbulence of the period conditioned the emergence of *xiake*. As an enrichment task, the students create a literary cartography of the period, mapping out, for instance, the geographic locations of the seven warring states and emplotting key events (political, social, and natural) through diagrams and graphic representations. Emplotment is a way for students to identify the particular kind of story structured by the events (White 7–11).

Intertextual Analysis 2: Gu Long

We then view clips from film adaptations of works by Gu Long. I recommend *Sword Master* (三少爺的劍),[6] and the Shaw Brothers film *Full Moon Scimitar* (圓月彎刀) for the class to detect the philosophical underpinnings of swordsmanship in *jianghu* (江湖; "world of rivers and lakes").[7] *Sword Master*, shot in 3D, has visually stunning fight scenes and lush landscapes. It raises the question of where the sword of the Third Master is as its narrative unravels the Daoist concept of being *renjianheyi* (人劍合一; "one with the sword"). Because of time constraints, the class views only the scene where Yen Shih-san speaks of the sword's soul and imagines wielding his blade against the shadowy figure of the Third Master (in a battle of the mind) while a tree god stands in the background (00:53:59–00:56:39). *Full Moon Scimitar* is a gripping mystery with plot twists. The scene viewed is the initial encounter between Ding Peng and the Third Master, the same character from *Sword Master*, at the Supreme Sword Manor (01:00:46–01:07:51). Ding Peng, thirsty for fame, challenges the Third Master, now a recluse, to a duel. He wields the full-moon scimitar, whose original owner was the Third Master. A conversation ensues in which the Third Master declares, "[T]hough I am without a sword, the spirit of the sword is in my heart. I have attained the highest level. A sword is not a sword, and I am not what I am" (01:07:08).[8] The Third Master's sword credo and way of living stems from the meditative arts of Buddhism and the Daoist path of swordsmanship.

A helpful resource on the philosophy of *xia* action—fights and heroic deeds—is Teo's *Chinese Martial Arts Film and the Philosophy of Action*. Teo invokes concepts and doctrines from ancient Chinese philosophies such as Daoism, Confucianism, Buddhism, Mohism, and Legalism, including *wuwei* (无为; "nonaction"), to examine *wuxia* such as Zhang Yimou's *Shadow* and Hou Hsiao-hsien's *The Assassin*. In *The Chinese Knight Errant*, James Liu compares the knight-errant (*xiake*) with four schools of thought—Confucians, Legalists, Mohists, and Daoists. The CGTN Documentary channel on *YouTube* has a series of videos on Chinese martial arts (with English subtitles), including a concise video titled "Taoism of Sword."

Weiqi Analogy

By this time, the students have gained a basic familiarity with the *wuxia* culture and a rudimentary knowledge of the political history of the Warring States period. They are equipped to read with confidence *Hero*'s intertextual loop. The intertexts and the contexts provide cultural specificities and layers of signification to the film. We revisit the students' initial questions about *Hero* and answer them through a chess-game reconstruction of the confrontation between the king and Nameless.

I tell the class to imagine the conversation between the king and Nameless as a game of *weiqi* (围棋; "Chinese chess"). In their aim to surround territories, each player in *weiqi* envisages the moves of the opponent and seeks to capture their stones. I show a short video demonstrating how *weiqi* is played. I ask the class to analyze the king as a chess player: How does he play? What are his strategic moves? We replay selected film sequences: the last segment of the conversation between Nameless and the king and the death of Nameless. I guide the students to attend to the audiovisual details (e.g., characters' facial expressions and movements, flickering candles, soldiers with weapons, sounds and their absence). The students discuss the actions of the king as tactical positionings and calculated moves (e.g., throwing the sword, turning his back, and loudly professing an understanding of peace). They assume that the king has attained the upper hand: he has construed that Nameless's *xiake* heart would prevent the warrior from making a killing move, and his thousand soldiers secure the palace.

I ask the class to analyze Nameless as a worthy opponent: What are his countermoves? Are they tactical? What is their significance? Why does Nameless allow himself to be a "captured stone" in *weiqi*? Through the discussion, the students should be able to perceive Nameless's final statement as a counterchallenge made by a swordsman of honor and not as an act of compliance to the king's "All under heaven" ideal (01:15:53). I guide the students to apply an intertextual reading—connecting Nameless back to Sima Qian's *xiake*, how the dramatis personae in *Records of the Grand Historian* such as Tian Guang, Fan Wuji, and Jing Ke sacrifice their lives to seal the completion of their mission. The students should be able to fathom that Nameless, likewise maintaining his *xiake* integrity, embraces the arrows of death to seal the fulfillment of the king's word.

We delve further: How do we see the king's final move? Why does he tremble and hesitate as the court officials press him to order Nameless's execution? One possible interpretation: the king is likewise bound to a code of honor. He shoulders the burden, the fulfillment of his own word—his professed realization of the highest level of attainment. Can his next move prove that he, too, has honor, that he can be a hero?

Political Analysis

How is political alliance perceived in *wuxia*? This question can be raised; however, I recommend that the teacher deliver a presentation (using slides or video) on the myth of *wulin lianmeng* (武林联盟; "martial-arts-world alliances") in *wuxia* fiction,[9] unless the students possess prior knowledge of *wuxia* adequate to comprehend and describe the realm of law in *wulin* (武林; "the martial arts world"). One conventional plot runs like this: A chieftain of a certain sect favors an alliance among various sects and clans in *jianghu* and gets himself elected as the leader of the alliance. He spearheads the eradication of so-called demonic sects that practice unorthodox martial arts, thus building a reputation for righteousness. In truth, he is a *weijunzi* (伪君子; "false gallant"), he wants total dominion over *wulin*, and his schemes are mired in avarice and evil. Selected scenes from *wuxia* dramas such as *The Smiling, Proud Wanderer* (笑傲江湖),[10] *The Untamed*, and *Word of Honor* (山河令) can be screened to assist the students in perceiving the workings of *wulin*. The teacher then leads the class back to *Hero* and asks how the myth of alliance is depicted in *Hero*. Perhaps *wuxia*'s political intentions lie mainly in its imagining of *jianghu*, a dominion with its own laws and practices, codes of chivalry, and enforcement of justice through *wushu*, where even imperial authorities fear to tread.

The *wuxia* film, with its own stylistic tools (e.g., audiovisual effects such as montage), has the capacity to transcend the limits of its narrative content (e.g., its revenge theme). Jean-Loup Bourget posits that a genre's conventionality is "the very paradoxical reason for its creativity" (467), and its high conventionality can deliver a subtly ironic commentary on sociopolitical realities. How does Zhang Yimou play with the conventions of the *wuxia* genre and reinvent it? More sophisticated students are encouraged to explore *Hero*'s generic transformations such as Zhang Yimou's inventive use of visual and rhythmic contrasts. Battle formations are enlarged to absurd proportions. Disciplined lines of warriors and the stylized synchronization of archers' movements highlight the Qin kingdom's massive military power and conjure a frigidness reminiscent of the terra-cotta warriors associated with the first Qin emperor's tomb. A vast army is mobilized just to destroy a secluded school or subdue one puny assassin.

Is *Hero*, as a *wuxia* film, concerned with issues of national identity and nation formation? Teo's chapter on *Hero* as a model of historicist *wuxia* stresses the significance of *Hero*'s combining the *wuxia* tenet of chivalry with the concept of the nation; Teo remarks that the "Fifth Generation tends to see the *wuxia* genre as historicist-nationalist" (*Chinese Martial Arts Cinema* 186, 185–92). This is a valid point but should be reconsidered in the light of the "weightiness of *wuxia* historicism" (Chan 153). The historicist-nationalist impulse appears in early *wuxia* novels such as *The Seven Heroes and Five Gallants*, in modern fiction such as *The Legend of the Condor Heroes*, and in movies such as the franchise *Once Upon a Time in China* (黄飞鸿). The "historical gravitas" of *wuxia*'s history therefore necessitates the manifestation of the historicist-nationalist specters in *Hero* (Chan 156).

Global Chinese Cinema: The Culture and Politics of Hero, edited by Gary Rawnsley and Ming-Yeh T. Rawnsley, explores through an array of multidisciplinary perspectives *Hero* as a product of China's cultural industries that opposes the forces of globalization. *Hero* appeared as a form of metacinema in the era of rejuvenated nationalism in China, when nationalist sentiments were mostly aired through social media platforms. How does China see itself? How does the world see China? Yiyan Wang's essay has an interesting segment on the myths of Chinese state origin, and *tianxia* is discussed quite extensively in the essay by Xiaoming Chen and Ming-Yeh T. Rawnsley. Despite the propensity of some of the essays to perform historiographic investigation on a work of imagination and aesthetics, some critical perspectives in the anthology can be adopted as frameworks for students to deliberate on how *Hero* has refunctioned as a global *wuxia* film to address the issues of its times.

Hero is politically controversial because it is a Chinese film. One critical challenge in teaching Chinese film is to confront ingrained preconceptions about Chinese people, such as the yellow peril and the China virus, which will invariably cast long shadows in classrooms and lecture halls across islands and continents. Teaching Chinese film is thus a bold, significant strategy of reterritorialization, an interrogation of such politics particularly in the academy in the United States. In closing, I ask the students to form group circles to reflect on and discuss the following questions, which may involve addressing preconceived notions of Chinese people: How do you perceive *xia*? What issues concerning twenty-first-century realities does *Hero* speculate on? How does the *wuxia* genre refunction to respond to the values and anxieties of its times? To approach the first question, the teacher can direct a few personal inquiries to the students: "What danger have you encountered where you wished you had been saved by someone?" "What injustices do you see in your immediate surroundings, and do you wish that a hero would appear, perhaps a *xiake* who can wield a sword to make things right?" As mentioned earlier in this essay, *xia* is a fluid concept, and aside from the interaction of cultural imagination and histories, it answers to the psychological needs and sociocultural values of the consumers of *wuxia*. What kind of *xiake* do we want in this age, in our society, and for ourselves? For the other questions, I require the students to give specific examples (e.g., personal anecdotes or current events) to concretize the issues they have identified. Students thus detect certain concerns in *Hero* as responses to the volatile forces of globalization: questions of national identity, perpetual mobility of people, political alliances, economic expansion, the mounting visibility of militarization and warfare, the pursuit of peace, technological domination, gender stratification and struggle, social injustices, ethnocultural disparities, the vanishing of heritage, and posthumanist dilemmas such as the anthropogenic impact on the natural environment.

As an enrichment activity, *Hero* can be matched with historical epics such as *The Emperor's Shadow* (秦颂) and *The Emperor and the Assassin*

(荆轲刺秦王), to allow the students to assess similar or varied images of Emperor Qin and his times. With Sima Qian's *Records* at the back of our mind, we analyze: How is Emperor Qin reimagined? What kind of sociopolitical milieu is formed? The essays in *Global Chinese Cinema* by Kam Louie and Yiyan Wang can serve as references. Again, we reflect: How do these films refunction to respond to the anxieties of their times? Students can respond in the form of an essay, as this would entail research work to figure out the specificities of Chinese history.

In summary, my pedagogical procedure is to teach *Hero* within the *wuxia* context. It requires an intertextual reading of the film with Chinese classics and other *wuxia* films and contextualization within specific sociopolitical histories and the cultural-historical practices of the genre. Suggested teaching approaches include inquiry-based methods, formalist and structuralist methods (e.g., close reading and viewing, mise-en-scène analysis, and genre analysis), lectures, discussions, reflection tasks, screenings of various films or film clips, and enrichment activities such as creating a literary cartography and performing a comparative genre analysis. I aim to assist the students in appreciating the beauty and power of film as art. I seek to make *Hero* relevant to students; thus, I invoke *xia* as an evolving concept and reflect on how *wuxia* has refunctioned in the twenty-first century to address timely issues and anxieties, individual and societal. As teachers of Chinese cinema, we plant seeds of critical cognition in students' consciousness and, by faith, believe that some transformation may take place in the mind and, some day, in history. We affirm, "[T]hough I am without a sword, the spirit of the sword is in my heart. I have attained the highest level" (*Full Moon Scimitar* 01:07:08).

Notes

1. The same English subtitles are in the DVD release of *Hero*.

2. Rutherford emphasizes teaching the concept of mise-en-scène to stimulate students to think creatively and analyze dynamically.

3. *The Chronicles of the States of the Eastern Zhou, The Chronicles of the Warring States,* and *Records of the Grand Historian* are a few examples. Their English translations are restructured prose versions.

4. Gu Long was born in Hong Kong and lived in China and Taiwan, and his real name was Xiong Yaohua. His works—including the popular novel series *The Eleventh Son, Chu Liuxiang, Lu Xiaofeng,* and *Little Li Flying Dagger*—have been adapted into films and television dramas, and their impact has been substantial within the circles of *wuxia* readers and viewers. The Shaw Brothers

studio produced exciting adaptations of Gu Long novels, including *Pursuit of Vengeance* (明月刀雪夜殲仇), *Killer Clans* (流星蝴蝶劍), and *Clan of Amazons* (陆小凤之绣花大盗).

5. Chen discusses *xia* as a fusion concept (9).

6. *Sword Master* is a remake of *Death Duel* (三少爷的劍).

7. *Jianghu* refers to the imaginary world inhabited by the martial arts characters and their sects.

8. The quotation is from the English subtitles for the film. A literal translation of the last line would read: "The sword is not a pure sword. I am not the true me."

9. I refer to Cawelti's definition of myth: "a pattern of narrative known throughout the culture and presented in many different versions by many different tellers" (499).

10. *The Smiling, Proud Wanderer* is an adaptation of Jin Yong's novel of the same name, but the most faithful adaptation is TVB HK's *State of Divinity* (笑傲江湖).

Works Cited

Astruc, Alexandre. "What Is *Mise en Scène*?" *Cahiers du cinéma: The 1950s: Neo-realism, Hollywood, New Wave*, edited by Jim Hillier, Routledge, 1985, pp. 266–68.

Bourget, Jean-Loup. "Social Implications in the Hollywood Genres." Mast et al., pp. 467–74.

Brooker, Peter. "Postmodern Adaptation: Pastiche, Intertextuality and Refunctioning." *The Cambridge Companion to Literature on Screen*, edited by Deborah Cartmell and Imelda Whelehan, Cambridge UP, 2007, pp. 107–20.

Cawelti, John G. "Chinatown and the Generic Transformation in Recent American Films." Mast et al., pp. 498–511.

Chan, Kenneth. "The Early Twenty-First-Century *Wuxia* Revival: Genre Remaking and the Hollywood Transnational Factor." *The Chinese Cinema Book*, edited by Song Hwee Lim and Julian Ward, Bloomsbury Publishing / British Film Institute, 2020, pp. 150–57.

Chen Pingyuan. *The Development of Chinese Martial Arts Fiction: A History of* Wuxia *Literature*. Translated by Victor Petersen, Cambridge UP, 2016.

The Emperor and the Assassin. Directed by Chen Kaige, Shin, 1999.

The Emperor's Shadow. Directed by Zhou Xiaowen, Xi'an Film Studio, 1996.

Full Moon Scimitar. Directed by Chor Yuen, Shaw Brothers, 1979.

Hero. Directed by Zhang Yimou, Beijing New Picture Film, 2002.

Hoberman, J. "Man with No Name Tells a Story of Heroics, Color Coordination." Review of *Hero*. *Village Voice*, 17 Aug. 2004, www.villagevoice.com/2004/08/17/man-with-no-name-tells-a-story-of-heroics-color-coordination/.

Liu, James. *The Chinese Knight Errant*. Routledge / Kegan Paul, 1967.

Mast, Gerald, et al., editors. *Film Theory and Criticism*. 4th ed., Oxford UP, 1992.

Orr, Christopher. "All about Face." *The New Republic*, 16 Apr. 2007, newrepublic.com/article/63669/all-about-face.

Rawnsley, Gary, and Ming-Yeh T. Rawnsley, editors. *Global Chinese Cinema: The Culture and Politics of* Hero. Routledge, 2010.

Rutherford, Ann. "Teaching Film and Mise-en-Scène." *Teaching Film*, edited by Lucy Fischer and Patrice Petro, Modern Language Association of America, 2012, pp. 549–72.

Sima Qian. *Records of the Grand Historian: Han Dynasty II.* Translated by Burton Watson, rev. ed., Chinese University of Hong Kong / Columbia UP, 1993.

———. *Records of the Grand Historian: Qin Dynasty.* Translated by Burton Watson, Chinese University of Hong Kong / Columbia UP, 1993.

State of Divinity. Directed by Lau Kwok-ho et al., TVB, 1996.

Sword Master. Directed by Derek Yee, Bona Film Group / Film Unlimited, 2016.

Szuma Chien. *Selections from Records of the Historian.* Translated by Yang Hsien-yi and Gladys Yang. Foreign Language Press, 1979.

"Taoism of Sword." *YouTube*, uploaded by CGTN, 13 May 2019, www.youtube .com/watch?v=fhGbTCjMcMk.

Teo, Stephen. *Chinese Martial Arts Cinema: The* Wuxia *Tradition.* Edinburgh UP, 2009.

———. *Chinese Martial Arts Film and the Philosophy of Action.* Routledge, 2021.

The Untamed. Directed by Steve Cheng and Chan Ka Lam, Tencent Penguin Pictures / NewStyle Media Group, 2019.

White, Hayden. *Metahistory: The Historical Imagination in Nineteenth-Century Europe.* Johns Hopkins UP, 1973.

Word of Honor. Directed by Gary Sing et al., Ciwen Media / Youku, 2021.

Part V

Intercultural and Comparative Approaches

Lily Li

A Comparative Approach to Lou Ye's *Suzhou River*

Modern Chinese cinema tends to draw on a wide variety of cultural sources, both Western and Asian. Among these sources, fairy tales and myths are especially vital because they embody archetypes that are intercultural and may appear in hybrid form in contemporary film. American students are often familiar with popular Western characters such as the Little Mermaid, but they seldom know the fairy-tale origins of these characters. Chinese films such as *Suzhou River* provide a good chance for students to study mermaid stories, Western and Chinese, in a comparative approach. More-over, mermaid stories in different ages and cultures seek to rethink the relationship between humanity and nature. It is therefore a very useful approach for instructors to explore the mythic or fairy-tale precedents of *Suzhou River* (苏州河) and other Chinese films to unearth the fairy tales' origins and transformations and illuminate environmental issues and problems that abide in the content and meaning of these films.

Suzhou River is set in the polluted and dilapidated waterfront of con-temporary Shanghai.[1] Meimei ("Beauty"), in her mid-twenties, performs as a mermaid in a big fish tank at a bar and is so alluring that two men fall in love with her: one of them, the narrator in the film, who is a videographer by profession, becomes her lover; the other, a motorcycle courier named

Mada ("Motor"), follows her, thinking that Meimei is his dead girlfriend Mudan ("Peony") come back to life to take revenge for his betrayal. Some years earlier, Mudan, as a naive and innocent teenager, fell in love with Mada, who was hired by her divorced-businessman father to drive her to her aunt's home whenever the father had a woman visiting. Mada was involved in kidnapping Mudan for ransom, despite his growing love for her. Betrayed by Mada, Mudan threatened to return as a mermaid for revenge and jumped into Suzhou River, together with her mermaid doll, a gift from Mada. The remorseful Mada, convinced that Mudan is dead (though she isn't), looks for her everywhere after his release from prison, believing she will come back as a mermaid, until he finds Meimei, who is identical to Mudan in appearance. However, the fact that Mudan and Meimei are not the same person isn't revealed until near the film's end, when Mada and Mudan are reunited and then drowned in the river, and Meimei comes to see their bodies.

Suzhou River has received substantial critical attention. The predominant approach taken by critics has been to identify a Western influence on the film by linking *Suzhou River* with the film noir genre (Schrader), especially Alfred Hitchcock's film *Vertigo*. Jerome Silbergeld describes *Suzhou River* as "Hitchcock with a Chinese face" and compares it with *Vertigo* (see 9–46). Examining *Suzhou River* through the lens of film noir, Hongwei Lu argues, "The film combines various aspects of film noir—aspects such as noir anxiety, negative space, moral conflicts, duality and foil characters, identity crisis, 'Liebestod' or love death—to create a world that can be seen through multiple perspectives, and it associates noir styles and themes with social concerns and social attitudes" (116). Moreover, some critics argue that the film works against its own narrative by focusing on the unreliable narrator, while others argue that the director, Lou Ye, consistently guides the narrative despite occasionally ceding authority. Alternatively, Damion Searls points out that *Suzhou River*'s true accomplishment is to do two contradictory things simultaneously: "to undercut its own intellectual paradoxes and force us to this conclusion, and to create a beautiful and moving film which speaks this truth for itself even if all the epistemological trickery goes unnoticed" (60). Finally, some scholars examine the film's production history, arguing that *Suzhou River* evokes the Chinese underground documentary film tradition because of its use of the handheld camera and its voyeuristic tone, given the perspective of the narrator-videographer (Silbergeld 121; Zhang 357).

My approach to teaching *Suzhou River* is different from the existing studies of the film. In my view, the mermaid image is the essential feature in

Suzhou River, which keeps the enigma of the double an unsolved mystery until near the end. It is the mermaid that catches students' eyes at first. This approach of tracing the figure of the mermaid in the film is a more effective way to invite students' interest and keep students more engaged. Surprisingly, few critics have paid attention to the mermaid in this film. Sean Metzger argues that the mermaid in this film constitutes the "importing [of] 'Western' femininity." Hongwei Lu perceives the mermaid as "a globalized cultural symbol of the West" (119). I would point out that the blond or golden-haired mermaid with her bright red tail and sparkling golden scales in *Suzhou River* looks quite different from the red-haired mermaid with a green tale in the Disney film *The Little Mermaid*. I argue that the visual image of the mermaid in *Suzhou River* is a cultural hybrid of the Little Mermaid in the eponymous fairy tale by Hans Christian Andersen, Rusalka from the Czech opera film *Rusalka*, and the carp fairy or carp spirit in the Chinese Yue opera film *Chasing the Carp* (追鱼; Ying Yunwei).[2]

The 1977 film *Rusalka* is a version of Antonin Dvořák's famous Czech opera *Rusalka*, written in 1900 and premiered in 1901.[3] Based on a Slavic myth, *Rusalka* was also influenced by other European versions of the mermaid tale, including Andersen's "The Little Mermaid" (Cheek 7–11). The character Rusalka is similar to Andersen's Little Mermaid, but she becomes vengeful after her lover's betrayal: now a will-o'-the wisp trapped between the human and water worlds, she lures her remorseful prince to the water and shares a fatal kiss with him; he dies happily in her embrace. This vengeful mermaid tale has become popular in China: Rusalka's romantic aria "Song to the Moon" was first sung in Chinese by the soprano Guo Shuzhen and recorded in 1959, and it has since been sung by many Chinese opera singers.

The carp fairy story, originating in a Ming dynasty play,[4] became popular in modern China when the Yue opera *Chasing the Carp* had its debut performance in Shanghai in 1956 and a film of the opera appeared in 1959 ("Yueju shiliao"). Tian Han, An E, and Kang De played an important role in revising and reviving the opera in the late 1950s (Tian 185). The opera has also been staged by Peking opera companies and companies performing many other local genres of opera. The carp falls in love with a young scholar, Zhang Zhen ("Treasure"), and transforms into Mudan's double using Daoist magic; Mudan, daughter of Premier Jin Chong ("Gold Worshipper"), is Zhang Zhen's betrothed since childhood. The now identical characters the carp and Mudan endure a trial by the famous judge Bao Gong and his double, the turtle that impersonates Bao Gong to aid the carp. Mudan's father summons heavenly warriors to kill the carp, but the carp eventually undergoes a sacrificial and painful transformation to permanently become human in order to be with Zhang Zhen.

Since Andersen's fairy tales were translated from Danish into Chinese by Ye Junjian (Andersen, "An Tusheng tonghua"), Andersen's mermaid story has been published in many different forms in China, many of which feature the illustration of the Little Mermaid with long blond or golden hair, blue eyes, and a distinctive red tail with golden scales (see the cover of Anderson, *Hai de nüer*). It is the same mermaid as in *Suzhou River*.

The enticing hybrid mermaid is also a key to the relation of the three mermaid tales to the narrative of *Suzhou River*. The mermaid's blond wig and blue eye shadow in the film mimic the appearance of Andersen's Danish mermaid and the Slavic water nymph in the myth that inspired *Rusalka*, but the mermaid in *Suzhou River* has a red lower body and tail adorned with sparkling golden scales that resemble the body of the carp spirit. Regarding the female doubling (Mudan and Meimei, both played by Zhou Xun) in *Suzhou River*, many critics relate the female double and mistaken-identity motif to the film noir tradition, especially Hitchcock's *Vertigo*. But the female doubling is not unique to the Western film tradition, as it is deployed in the traditional Chinese opera *Chasing the Carp*. The female doubles are always played by two actresses onstage but by the same actress (Wang Wenjuan) in the opera film. The operatic narrative of the female double and mistaken identity is also operative for more than two thirds of the narrative of *Suzhou River*. The carp narrative also prefigures the duality of Mudan and Meimei in *Suzhou River* because the carp in *Chasing the Carp* assumes the appearance of Mudan. Hence the doppelgänger motif of Lou Ye's film, though entirely different in its context, echoes the love theme of the carp myth. Moreover, the hybrid mermaid of *Suzhou River* reflects the influence of "The Little Mermaid" and *Rusalka* stories in the relationship between Mudan and Mada.

Tracing the figure of the mermaid in these narratives in class can lead directly to a discussion of the environmental issues presented in *Suzhou River*. The world faces unprecedented ecological crises today, such as environmental pollution, global warming, the reduction of primeval forests, and so on, because of industrialization and modernization. Ecocriticism from the 1980s to the early twenty-first century mainly focused on literature and thereafter expanded to include cinema studies, becoming eco-cinema studies. Ecocritical studies of Chinese film emerged with *Chinese Ecocinema: In the Age of Environmental Challenge* (Lu and Mi) followed by *Ecology and Chinese-Language Cinema: Reimagining a Field* (Lu and Gong). Ecocinema is defined as "cinema with an ecological consciousness," demonstrated emphatically in Chinese films and documentaries since the 1980s. The 1980s "marks the beginning of a new phase of a state-sponsored modernization campaign that has resulted in ecological problems on an unprecedented scale" in mainland China. According to Lu, Chinese eco-cinema, including *Suzhou River*, should be studied in the Chinese context (S. Lu 2). However, I contend that in the instance of films like *Suzhou River*, which involve Western or other non-Chinese elements as integral precedents, it is also important to move beyond the Chinese paradigm to fully understand and appreciate the films' full depth and import.

In sum, teaching *Suzhou River* as a love story influenced by the three mermaid background stories sets the stage for exploring the film and its mythic sources allegorically as the relationship between humanity and nature and for thereby transitioning to an ecocritical study of the love theme. Foregrounding the love story, rooted in the lore already adduced about mermaids and carp, enables the study of *Suzhou River* as ecocinema and allows for a valuable review of the fairy tales from an ecocritical perspective. The goal is to proceed from the obvious literary trope of the merwoman and her lover, reinvented in *Suzhou River* as the fatal romance of Mudan and Mada, to the environmental tragedy that resonates in the setting of the film and in its tragic ending. Instructors should use class discussion to highlight the global nature of the ecocritical issues that the film brings to the fore.

Three Mermaid Background Stories

To teach *Suzhou River* by tracing the figure of the mermaid, instructors must familiarize students with three background stories: the Danish story of the Little Mermaid, the Chinese story of the carp fairy, and the Czech story of the water nymph Rusalka. The three stories share a similar plot: the merwoman leaves the eternal water world to seek her love in the human world by giving up her identity as a mermaid, carp, or nymph. Of the three stories, two have tragic endings, and one has a happy ending. Andersen's Little Mermaid is betrayed and disappears sacrificially into the sea as foam and then becomes a spirit of the air. Rusalka is betrayed and becomes vengeful—she lures her prince to the water where she shares a fatal kiss of death with him. But the carp happily marries her devoted lover. Another major difference is that the carp fairy has a double, Mudan. The identical characters lead to comic theatrical scenes of confusion and mistaken identity.

I assign Andersen's "The Little Mermaid," the 1959 opera film *Chasing the Carp* (Ying Yunwei), and the 1977 opera film *Rusalka*. Not many students are familiar with the original Little Mermaid story. Feminist criticism of Andersen's mermaid tale may be introduced to students, as some students may be troubled by her self-sacrifice. From a feminist perspective, the mermaid story is "sentimental, misogynist, and moralizing; it shows Andersen enjoying the Mermaid's suffering and offering an oppressive mix of self-sacrifice, silence and expiation as ideals of female behavior" (Wullschlager 174). The film version of *Rusalka* that I assign has English subtitles and uses natural outdoor settings. The opera has three acts, as performed in the film. Act 1 is set in the natural world, where Rusalka falls in love with the prince, who hunts in the forest and rests near her lake. She seeks help from the witch Ježibaba to become human in order to see her love. Act 2 is set at the prince's castle, where Rusalka is betrayed by the prince, who falls in love with a glamorous foreign princess. Act 3 goes back to the natural world, where Rusalka takes her revenge on the prince. The variety of themes in this opera has led to different interpretations of the work (see Cheek 41–53).

The film *Chasing the Carp* has only Chinese subtitles, so I introduce the plotline to students and watch a few scenes with them while explaining in English. The stage performance of the opera has eight acts, as does this film. In act 1 the poor young man Zhang Zhen stays up late to study and sings to the full moon, lamenting his loneliness, which is due to his being slighted by Mudan's rich family. When he falls asleep, the carp emerges from the water and transforms into Mudan's double using her magic. Zhang Zhen and the carp disguised as Mudan fall in love with each other under the moonlight. The two Mudans are "identical in appearance but different at heart" (01:00:53):[5] they are so similar that neither the family servants nor Mudan's parents can differentiate them; however, the carp loves the young man passionately, while Mudan is indifferent to him (act 6). Acts 7 and 8 depict the carp and Zhang Zhen as devoted lovers. When she fights the heavenly warriors sent to kill her, he chases after her, determined to be with her in life or death. It is helpful for instructors to introduce the translations of two important verses sung by Zhang Zhen when discussing Zhang Zhen as a devoted lover; these verses do not appear in the film but are added in subsequent stage performances of the opera to emphasize his devotion (e.g., *Chasing the Carp* [Liu Yongzhen]). Looking for the carp all over the wilderness, he sings: "If you go to heaven, I will chase you to heaven. If you go to the underworld, I will chase you to the underworld. Determined to give up my life, I will follow you to heaven or to the underworld" (01:45:03). Later seeing the turbulent waves of water, he thinks the carp must have been killed and sings, "I, Zhang Zhen, am willing to give up my life, to share life and death with you, unseparated and unabandoned, and the two of us will die together at the bottom of the sea" (02:01:02). Zhang Zhen's devotion to the carp is in distinct contrast to the attitudes of the princes in the Little Mermaid and Rusalka stories. These scenes are directly relevant to *Suzhou River*.

Suzhou River as a Love Story

Teaching *Suzhou River* as a postmodern Chinese fairy tale or fantasy can be accomplished by comparing it with the three mermaid background stories. Mudan and Mada's relationship of love and betrayal resembles the plot of Andersen's Little Mermaid story. The female doubles and consequent mistaken identity and Mada's devotion in *Suzhou River* mirror the female doubling and the devoted Zhang Zhen in the carp story, respectively. Finally, the tragic drowning of Mudan and Mada in Suzhou River calls for comparison with the ending of *Rusalka*.

Most students will recognize that the story of the naive teenager Mudan, from her falling in love with Mada to his betrayal and to her vanishing into Suzhou River, resembles Andersen's Little Mermaid story. The mermaid doll, which Mudan takes into the water, symbolizes her mermaid identity and destiny. However, some students realize that Mudan is different from the Little Mermaid in that Mudan threatens, before jumping into the river, to come back for Mada as a vengeful mermaid.

The carp story helps to explain the main narrative of *Suzhou River*. Students need to be introduced to the contrasting political orientations and technical protocols of *Chasing the Carp* and *Suzhou River*. *Chasing the Carp*, made during the Great Leap Forward, reflects the socialist ideology of class struggle: it "praises the Carp Fairy's pursuit of pure love while it satirizes Jin Mudan's ugly spirit of preferring the rich to the poor" ("Yueju shiliao"). It is a socialist comedy, based on the socialist drama theory of the Chinese dramatist and critic Li Jianwu. According to Li, tragedy reflects flawed feudal or bourgeois society, while socialist society, because of its inherent harmony, confines itself to comedy. Li's theory became the primary view of Chinese theater in the 1960s (Tam 47). In contrast, *Suzhou River*, made by a sixth-generation filmmaker in postsocialist China, is an avant-garde film that explores the human condition from a nonofficial perspective. Moreover, *Chasing the Carp* is a polished production utilizing a variety of theatrical and cinematic techniques, whereas *Suzhou River* is a documentary-style film shot with a handheld camera and edited with jump cuts. Students will need to appreciate that while the carp film has a linear narrative that unfolds chronologically, *Suzhou River* has a nonlinear narrative with a profusion of scenes reflecting the narrator's digressive tendency and dubious reliability as a storyteller.

The mystery of the identical Mudan and Meimei in *Suzhou River* mirrors the doubling of Mudan and the carp in *Chasing the Carp*, but the audience cannot know from the beginning of *Suzhou River* whether Mudan and Meimei are the same girl or doubles. However, the audience knows from the beginning of *Chasing the Carp* that the carp is Mudan's double, hence the comic effects. Mudan's emblem of identity in *Suzhou River*, the press-on *mudan* (牡丹; "peony") tattoo on her left inner thigh, echoes the red birthmark on Mudan's left wrist in the carp film: Meimei secretly duplicates the tattoo so that she can be more like Mada's Mudan, while the carp surreptitiously duplicates the red birthmark using magic. In both cases, the secret brand makes the doubling more exact and convincing. Furthermore, as in the carp story, the doubles are identical in appearance but different at heart in *Suzhou River*. I ask students to identify the moment in *Suzhou River* when they realized that Mudan and Meimei are doubles; most students answer that they didn't know until near the end, when Meimei sees Mudan's body lying next to Mada's. However, a few students say that they accepted Mada's word: Mada claims to the narrator that Meimei is not Mada's Mudan and that Meimei only loves the narrator, a statement that leaves most students confused. But the more observant students realize that the doubles are different at heart, as in the carp story: Mada's Mudan only loves Mada, while Meimei has another lover, an arrangement that echoes Zhang Zhen's differentiating the affectionate carp from the cold Mudan. The director Lou Ye tantalizes the audience by cultivating the implicit differences and explicit visual similarities of the female doubles in *Suzhou River*. Students become very engaged when discussing how Lou Ye tantalizes the audience.

The legend of Rusalka furnishes the tragic climax of *Suzhou River*. In *Suzhou River*, Mada eventually finds Mudan, and the lovers are reunited, but they drown themselves in the polluted Suzhou River. Before their deaths, the lovers sit together silently, facing the modern skyline of Shanghai in the sunset across the river. The camera gives a close-up of an empty vodka bottle in Mada's hand—the lovers might have just shared it, as they often do earlier in the film. Then looking up to the sky, Mudan says, "Mada, take me home," and Mada silently accedes, looking down (01:09:15). Some students argue that Mada is like the scholar willing to die with the carp; however, other students point out that Mudan's threat to Mada, before Mudan jumps into the river, is bitterly resentful and that Mudan is vengeful, like Rusalka. By demanding that Mada take her home, Mudan gives Mada the command to drown them both in the filthy river, as Rusalka lures her prince to the water to share a fatal kiss with him. Mada dies as the prince does, both of them obliged to obey the fatal summons of the women they have betrayed.

Finally, students enjoy comparing two opposite views of love in *Suzhou River*, constant and cynical, represented by Mada and the narrator, respectively. Mada persistently looking for Mudan everywhere in *Suzhou River* echoes Zhang Zhen devotedly chasing the carp. The narrator's cynical view of love is initially revealed when he declares in the prologue that he does not believe in fairy tales, in direct contrast to Mada, who believes that Mudan will return as a mermaid. This difference helps to clarify Meimei's relationships with Mada and the narrator. Meimei desires to have a devoted lover like Mada and wishes that her cynical lover, the narrator, were devoted: we hear her and the narrator discuss her wishes in their conversation behind the black screen in the prologue. It is interesting for the class to discuss how the film emphasizes these contrasting views of love and how it is bookended by the black screen in the prologue and the epilogue, which address the opposing views of love.

Suzhou River as an Allegory

No one can watch *Suzhou River* without being aware of, even shocked by, the pollution, the poverty, the degraded environment of the river, and the criminal atmosphere of the Shanghai waterfront, the depiction of which constitutes an indictment of the urban underworld of postsocialist China. This entire mise-en-scène in *Suzhou River* stands in utter and ironic contrast to the enchanting natural world in all three mermaid background stories. *Suzhou River* reflects the filmmaker's concern, through the narrator-videographer's camera, about the degraded environment in China at the turn of the twenty-first century. Teaching *Suzhou River* as an allegory vis-à-vis the three mermaid stories provides students an opportunity to study *Suzhou River* as ecocinema and to revisit the fairy tales through an ecocritical approach.

Before studying *Suzhou River* in a Chinese film class, students should have learned from earlier films about Mao Zedong's socialist China—for instance, the 1958 Great Leap Forward and the Cultural Revolution—and Deng Xiaoping's economic reforms in postsocialist China. It is important for instructors to discuss how Mao's socialist revolution and Deng's economic development policy contributed to ecological issues in China (see S. Lu, "Introduction" 3–5). The historical and political background is crucial for helping students understand the modern wasteland at the Shanghai waterfront in *Suzhou River*.

When teaching *Suzhou River* as an allegory in relation to the three mermaid stories, I guide students to revisit the mermaid stories to understand certain fairy-tale elements in *Suzhou River* from an ecocritical perspective. If the class views the three mermaids as representing the natural world and the three young men as representing the human world, then all three stories can be read allegorically as the relationship between humanity and nature: the love and conflict between humanity and nature in the two European stories, and the Daoist harmony between humanity and nature in the carp story.[6] In the same vein, *Suzhou River* is an allegory of the love and conflict between humanity and nature; furthermore, the natural world, which is the home of the mermaid, has been polluted by humanity, thus her revenge against Mada constitutes an allegorical retaliation on behalf of nature.

Though it was made during the Great Leap Forward, *Chasing the Carp* advances a Daoist worldview, which advocates peace and harmony between humanity and nature. The setting of act 1 shows the harmonious human world (the study) and natural world (the pond) blessed by the heavenly world (the full moon). The full moon is also a romantic symbol of lovers together in Chinese culture, and the carp and the young scholar fall in love under the moonlight.[7] The water world, where the carp and her fellow water creatures live and practice Daoism to become immortals, is beautiful and mysterious.

Students are eager to discuss how nature is portrayed in Andersen's "The Little Mermaid," including the pristine seawater and the garden at the bottom of the ocean as well as the green woods and orchards of the human world. However, to better understand the relationship between humanity and nature in *Rusalka*, I turn to the composition history of the original opera *Rusalka* at the turn of the twentieth century. It is well known that the beauty of nature in the late-nineteenth- and early-twentieth-century countryside in what is now the Czech Republic and Slovakia inspired the opera's composer, Dvořák, and librettist, Jaroslav Kvapil. Kvapil was inspired by his memories of the lake and forest near his birthplace when he was writing the libretto for *Rusalka* in 1899. Dvořák composed the music for *Rusalka* in 1900 in his village, an environment that provided the setting of the opera. The tranquil forest and the peaceful lake nearby, later called Rusalka's lake, became the setting for the natural world in acts 1 and 3, while his relative's mansion in the village became the setting for the prince's castle in act 2 (Cheek 46). In the opera, Rusalka appears in her natural realm at the edge of the blue lake surrounded by a green forest, water side by side with earth, personified by wood sprites. Nature is represented by Rusalka, her father Vodnik (an old water sprite), and wood sprites. The 1977 film *Rusalka* faithfully reprises these settings for each act.

Nature in *Suzhou River* starkly contrasts with nature in the three mermaid stories. Students seem to enjoy comparing the image of the little mermaid (Mudan) singing at the bank of Suzhou River (00:36:22) with those of the carp fairy emerging from the lotus pond (*Chasing* [Ying Yunwei] 00:09:40; *Chasing* [Liu Yongzhen] 00:09:22) and Rusalka in her enchanting lake (*Rusalka* 00:10:46), both singing about their love for the young man and his human world. The carp fairy sings and dances and adopts Mudan's appearance to be with the man under the moonlight, while Rusalka in her beautiful pale blue gown, symbolic of her identity as a water nymph, sings her romantic aria "Song to the Moon." In both cases, the full moon is a romantic symbol of love but also of nature. In contrast, in *Suzhou River* Mudan sits on the filthy bank of the polluted Suzhou River, singing and brushing her long, blond hair and playing in the murky water with her mermaid tail. The mermaid's home has been polluted by humanity.

Suzhou River offers a particular understanding of the allegorical relation between nature and humanity. Rusalka succumbs to her accursed fate of becoming a will-o'-the-wisp and the repentant prince dies happily in her embrace. This ending signifies nature's mystical aspect, as Rusalka changes from a water nymph to a ghost, and the prince gives up his life in the service of love. In *Suzhou River*, the violent death of the mermaid (Mudan) and Mada in her polluted river denotes that nature and humanity destroy each other with no promise of redemption. Here there is no fairy-tale ending.

Both *Suzhou River* and *Rusalka* are rich in symbols of nature and humanity, and discussions of these symbols will stimulate much interest in students. In *Rusalka*, the natural elements include water (represented by Rusalka, her father, and her sisters), the earth (represented by wood sprites), fire (represented by Ježibaba's tool), and air.[8] Moreover, the symbolic meanings of the moon, the white doe, and the white rose (purity) versus the red rose (passion) can also be explored. In *Suzhou River*, the mermaid, Mudan's mermaid toy, and the peony tattoo are all associated with the natural world. Mada's Harley motorcycle; the bottle of Bison Grass Vodka; the skyline of urban Shanghai, including the Oriental Pearl TV Tower; imported Marlboro cigarettes; bare electric light bulbs; and especially the filthy Suzhou River are all adumbrations of the degenerate world of urban poverty and crime. Taken as opposing clusters of natural and decadent imagery, these symbols denote the implied contest between a once vibrant nature and a discordant civilization, a contest in which nature survives despite tragic circumstances in *Rusalka* but seems destined to ineluctable degradation and ruin in *Suzhou River*.

When teaching *Suzhou River*, I prepare the students by giving them a handout in advance to clarify the narrative and some of the techniques of the film and to alert them to the various relevant mermaid precedents that will be considered. I devote two seventy-five-minute class periods to the project. I assign Andersen's "The Little Mermaid" to be read in advance of day 1 and instruct the class to view the film *Rusalka* prior to day 2. On day 1 the students watch scenes from *Suzhou River* in class; drawn by the love story, they are eager to compare Mudan and Mada's situation to the situation in "The Little Mermaid" but are often confused by Mudan and Meimei's appearance as doubles in the film. On day 2, I usually pick out a few scenes from *Rusalka* to discuss in class and pay special attention to the scene of Rusalka singing her love aria "Song to the Moon" (00:20:20–00:23:22) and to the vengeful ending. To solve the mystery of the doubles in *Suzhou River*, I introduce the carp story using the *Chasing the Carp* and some images from the carp stage performances. When students understand *Suzhou River* as a love story combining the three mermaid stories, I guide the class to discuss *Suzhou River* as an allegory and present the three mermaid stories from an ecocritical perspective. Many students greatly appreciate my cross-cultural comparative approach to *Suzhou River* by tracing the figure of the mermaid. Examining the three mermaid stories helps resolve confusing issues while allowing students a range of options as to how to interpret the love story and the ecocritical theme in *Suzhou River*.

Notes

1. I render the characters' names in pinyin. The English subtitles in *Suzhou River* spell the names differently, such as Moudan instead of Mudan and Madar instead of Mada.

2. Other forms of cultural hybridity also exist in *Suzhou River*, such as the Oriental Pearl TV Tower (Silbergeld 29).

3. For a detailed synopsis of the opera, see Cheek 3–5; "Synopsis."

4. For more information on the history of the play, see Li Kuinan.

5. All English translations from Chinese sources are mine unless otherwise indicated.

6. For the environmental approach to *Rusalka*, see Cheek 44–45.

7. Stage performances since the film's release have used the setting of the full moon shining over the lotus pond in act 1. For more interpretations of the aesthetics and symbols in this Yue opera, see L. Li.

8. For a more detailed analysis of the natural elements in *Rusalka*, see Cheek 45–47.

Works Cited

Andersen, Hans Christian [An Tusheng]. 安徒生童话全集 一 ["An Tusheng tonghua quanji yi"; "The Complete Collection of Anderson's Fairy Tales, Vol. 1"]. Translated by Ye Junjian. 九九藏书网 [*Jiujiu cangshu wang*; *Nine Nine Collection of Books Website*], www.99csw.com/book/952/index.htm.

———[An Tusheng]. 海的女儿 [*Hai de nüer*; *The Daughter of the Sea*]. Edited by Tong ying wenhua, Sichuan Meishu Chubanshe, 2017.

———. "The Little Mermaid." Translated by Jean Hershoit. *SDU Hans Christian Andersen Center*, 19 Sept. 2019, andersen.sdu.dk/vaerk/hersholt/TheLittleMermaid_e.html.

Chasing the Carp. Directed by Liu Yongzhen, performed by Zheng Guofeng and Wang Zhiping, Shanghai Yue Opera House, 2009. *YouTube*, uploaded by user-oc3jx6sv8k, 6 Oct. 2017, www.youtube.com/watch?v=BD1bKxNz30c.

Chasing the Carp. Directed by Ying Yunwei, Shanghai Tianma Film Studio / Shanghai Yue Opera House, 1959. *YouTube*, uploaded by user-oc3jx6sv8k, 22 Apr. 2016, www.youtube.com/watch?v=6n_5zFojWt8.

Cheek, Timothy. Rusalka: *A Performance Guide with Translations and Pronunciation*. Scarecrow Press, 2009.

Li Jianwu. 社会主义话剧的戏剧冲突 ["Shehui zhuyi huaju de xiju chongtu"; "Dramatic Conflicts in Socialist Drama"]. 1960. 戏剧新天 [*Xiju xintian*; *New Horizons in Drama*], Shanghai Wenyi Chubanshe, 1980, pp. 55–60.

Li Kuinan. 鱼篮记 ["*Yulan ji*"; "*A Scholar and a Carp Spirit*"]. 中国大百科全书 [*Zhongguo dabaike quanshu*; *The Encyclopedia of China*], 20 Jan. 2022, www.zgbk.com/ecph/words?SiteID=1&ID=25457&Type=bkzyb&SubID=61238.

Li, Lily. "The Carp Fairy in the Digitalized Traditional Chinese Theatre." *Performance Arts: Research in the Age of Digital Revolution*, edited by

Kwok-kan Tam, Springer, 2023, pp. 173–202. Digital Culture and Humanities no. 4.

The Little Mermaid. Directed by Ron Clements and John Musker, Walt Disney Pictures, 1989.

Lu, Hongwei. "Shanghai and Globalization through the Lens of Film Noir: Lou Ye's 2000 Film, *Suzhou River*." *ASIA Network Exchange*, vol. 18, no. 1, Sept. 2010, pp. 116–27, https://doi.org/10.16995/ane.202.

Lu, Shelton H. "Introduction: Cinema, Ecology, Modernity." Lu and Mi, pp. 1–14.

Lu, Shelton H., and Haoming Gong, editors. *Ecology and Chinese-Language Cinema: Reimagining a Field*. Routledge, 2020.

Lu, Shelton H., and Jiayan Mi, editors. *Chinese Ecocinema: In the Age of Environmental Challenge*. Hong Kong UP, 2009.

Metzger, Sean. "The Little (Chinese) Mermaid; or, Importing 'Western' Femininity in Lou Ye's *Suzhou he* (*Suzhou River*)." *How East Asian Films Are Reshaping National Identities: Essays on the Cinemas of China, Japan, South Korea, and Hong Kong*, edited by Andrew Jackson et al., Edwin Mellen Press, 2006, pp. 135–54.

Rusalka. Libretto by Jaroslav Kvapil, directed by Petr Weigl, music composed by Antonin Dvořák. English subtitles by Jessica Rose, 1977. *YouTube*, uploaded by Jessica, 22 Apr. 2018, www.YouTube.com/watch?v=IoaeN-ppHUI.

Schrader, Paul. "Notes on Film Noir." *Film Comment*, vol. 8, no. 1, spring 1972, pp. 8–13.

Searls, Damion. "*Suzhou River*." *Film Quarterly*, vol. 55, no. 2, 2001, pp. 55–60. *JSTOR*, www.jstor.org/stable/10.1525/fq.2001.55.2.55.

Silbergeld, Jerome. *Hitchcock with a Chinese Face: Cinematic Doubles, Oedipal Triangles, and China's Moral Voice*. U of Washington P, 2004.

Suzhou River. Directed by Lou Ye, Dream Factory, 2000.

"Synopsis: *Rusalka*." *Metropolitan Opera*, www.metopera.org/discover/synopses/rusalka/.

Tam, Kwok-kan. *Ibsen, Power and the Self: Postsocialist Chinese Experimentations in Stage Performance and Film*. Novus Press, 2019.

Tian Han. 金鳞记 [*Jin lin ji*; *The Story of the Golden Scales*]. 田汉全集 [*Tian Han quan ji*; *The Complete Works of Tian Han*], vol. 9. Huashan Wenyi Chubanshe, 2000, pp. 185–242.

Wullschlager, Jackie. *Hans Christian Andersen: The Life of A Storyteller*. Alfred A. Knopf, 2000.

越剧史料: 追鱼 ["Yueju shiliao: *Zhui Yu*"; "Historical Materials of Yue Opera: *Chasing the Carp*"]. 上海越剧 [*Yueju*], www.yueju.net/api/drama_details.html?id=115.

Zhang Zhen. "Urban Dreamscape, Phantom Sisters, and the Identity of an Emergent Act Cinema." *The Urban Generation: Chinese Cinema and Society at the Turn of the Twenty-First Century*, edited by Zhang Zhen, Duke UP, 2007, pp. 344–87.

Vincent Casaregola

From Hainan to Grant Avenue: Teaching Gender Construction as Integration Propaganda in Two Films about Chinese Women

Few Americans today are familiar with the popular 1961 musical film *Flower Drum Song*, based on the 1958 Broadway musical by Richard Rodgers and Oscar Hammerstein II, which was itself based on a novel by the immigrant Chinese American writer Chin Yang Lee. Even fewer are aware of the 1961 Chinese film *The Red Detachment of Women* (红色娘子军), which was adapted into a Chinese ballet that was once performed for President Richard Nixon during his visit to China. Certainly, contemporary college students in classrooms in the United States are unlikely to know of either film, and most will also know little of the cultural contexts that allow us to understand how the two films served to further the contrasting cultural ideologies of the countries that produced them. Interestingly, both films focus on young Chinese women. While *Flower Drum Song* uses the traditional musical comedy structure to explore the immigration of Chinese people to America and their assimilation, *The Red Detachment of Women* celebrates how the Chinese revolutionary army confronted the tyranny of the old order in 1930s Hainan, China. While diametrically opposed to each other ideologically, each film attempts to justify a role for women that is ultimately shaped by men.

I teach these films in my course Chinese Screen: Representations of the Chinese and Chinese Americans in Film, which compares depictions of Chinese people in films from both countries. Both films are forms of the female bildungsroman, and they also provide excellent examples of how different manifestations of integration propaganda, defined below, can perpetuate distinctive but still patriarchal constructions of women's social roles. Each film's narrative asserts that the political structure contemporary with the film—consumer capitalism in the United States, revolutionary communism in China—provides the greatest hope of a good life and happiness for women. The China of 1961 had recently experienced a catastrophic famine resulting from the ill-conceived Great Leap Forward. In contrast, the affluent United States had just passed through the divisive fifties red scare that had reawakened long-standing hostility toward Chinese immigrants. Therefore, both films seek to reassure potentially skeptical audiences of the wisdom of a prevailing sociopolitical order. *The Red Detachment of Women* reminds the Chinese why their current revolutionary program is still necessary, especially for women, and *Flower Drum Song* expresses how Chinese American women can best fulfill themselves by adopting slightly modified versions of traditional feminine roles in a consumer society. While the American film gives female characters center stage and much control over narrative outcomes, they can take this control only by submitting to male authority in marriage. In contrast, the Chinese film shows women as active combat soldiers but only after they are liberated by a male savior figure and submit to male-dominated military authority. Despite the ideological differences, each film attempts to reinscribe some form of patriarchy.

My course attempts to guide students through an exploration of how cinematic representations of the Chinese and Chinese Americans often perpetuate long-standing racist misconceptions. At the same time, it also helps students to examine how, since the later 1960s, Americans have been able to view the works of filmmakers from Hong Kong, Taiwan, and mainland China, which have expanded and complicated American views of Chinese people. Still, as events during the COVID-19 pandemic have demonstrated, many Americans persist in holding stereotypical, often racist images of the Chinese and of other Asians, regardless of the more recent opportunities to broaden their perspectives through film.

This essay examines how teaching comparative historical analysis of Chinese and Chinese American films can generally help American students understand and critique American prejudices. The essay also focuses attention on gender representation in *Flower Drum Song* and *The Red Detachment of Women*. Among the pedagogical approaches used in this unit are in-class discussions, where students argue both for and against each of the film's ideological messages by assuming the perspectives of filmmakers and critics. Students may also evaluate how each film manifests in its distinct cultural setting Laura Mulvey's concept of the "male gaze" (11). In a course that compares many different films representing China, the Chinese people, and Chinese Americans, this two-film segment helps to integrate comparative cultural analysis with the critique of traditional gender roles.

Setting the Films in the Larger Course Context

I developed my course Chinese Screen: Representations of the Chinese and Chinese Americans in Film along historical lines, and it begins with a brief history of Chinese immigration to the United States during the mid-nineteenth century, through the period of the exclusion acts and the so-called yellow peril narratives, continuing into the twentieth century, through World War II and the Cold War and into the present. Students first view Arthur Dong's documentary *Hollywood Chinese*, which carefully examines the history of racism in Hollywood's representations of the Chinese. Dong also details the ways in which female Chinese characters in Western films are portrayed as various stereotypes, especially the mysterious Asian femme fatale or the submissive sexual object. We then view 1930s films that illustrate classic stereotyping, including one of the Charlie Chan films starring Warner Oland (e.g., *Charlie Chan at the Opera*) and *Daughter of the Dragon*, an early Fu Manchu film. We analyze both the positive stereotype of the detective Charlie Chan and the negative stereotypes of the mysterious and deadly Chinese villain Fu Manchu and his femme fatale daughter, Ling Moy. Since both films feature Oland, an American of Swedish ancestry playing a Chinese character, we also examine the chronic problem of yellowface depictions. We highlight these casting issues further as we study the 1937 film version of Pearl S. Buck's 1931 novel *The Good Earth*. Although both the novel and the film portray the Chinese, especially the main characters of Wang Lung and O-Lan, in a positive if sentimental way, the film uses white actors in the lead roles. The major star Paul Muni was cast as Wang Lung, and despite the possibility of casting the increasingly popular Anna May Wong as O-Lan, the studio bowed to social norms and instead selected the German émigré

Luise Rainer for the role. While the casting problem is obvious, the construction of gender roles in the film may be more important. In both the novel and the film, O-Lan is depicted as a classic earth mother, tied integrally to the land and sacrificing herself for the needs of her family and her sometimes unfaithful husband. Both Buck and the filmmakers celebrate this stereotype suggesting that women must "keep calm and carry on" in the face of multiple disasters (such as drought, famine, relocation, and civil unrest) and a combination of chronic male arrogance and indifference. The film's production history illustrates how even well-intentioned narratives fall prey to stereotypes built into the studio system, but even the novel perpetuates a central role for women that reduces them to little more than loyal, long-suffering slaves. For all these films, class discussions and student essays further explore the details of both casting and gender roles.

Subsequently, we examine examples of missionary-narrative films, in which white people from England, Europe, or America come as salvific figures for the Chinese who, while portrayed sympathetically, are shown to be in need of both spiritual and cultural salvation. The 1944 film *The Keys of the Kingdom*, based on the A. J. Cronin novel, tells of Father Francis Chisholm, an aging Scottish Catholic priest whose unorthodox methods have brought the scrutiny of his diocese upon him. The story is told mostly in flashback and depicts Father Francis's many years in China as a missionary, where he had improved both the spiritual and the material lives of his congregations. Similarly, *The Inn of the Sixth Happiness*, from 1958, starring Ingrid Bergman, is based loosely on the true story of British missionary Gladys Aylward, and it perpetuates the narrative of the white savior, in this case one particularly concerned with children during the devastating Japanese assault on China. This film also portrays Chinese people as noble and long-suffering but desperately in need of help from Western cultures, which are depicted as more advanced.

At this point in the course we contrast *Flower Drum Song* and *The Red Detachment of Women*, where the Chinese characters are, unlike in the films just discussed, central to the narratives. While *Flower Drum Song* reaches us through both a stage and film musical adaptations, the original story comes from Lee's novel. Admittedly, *Flower Drum Song* provided an unprecedented breakthrough in the representation of Asians to a popular American audience, yet the film still demonstrates many of the chronic problems in representations of the Chinese on American screens. This film celebrates the personal freedom that comes with adapting Chinese identity to American cultural norms, assuming that assimilation into American consumer culture is the ultimate goal of all immigrants. The female characters are depicted as especially interested in becoming wives to beloved men, and it is through marriage that they will also obtain the material benefits of consumerism. In contrast, *The Red Detachment of Women* is a Chinese film that centers on the Chinese of Hainan during the 1930s, depicting their struggles against brutal local landlords who have material support from the Kuomintang. The film is an unabashed propaganda piece that depicts characters in broad strokes as being either loyal, self-sacrificing communists or corrupt and cruel figures of the old order of political and economic oppression. Indeed, at times the narrative has an almost Robin Hood–like quality because it describes a hardy band of female communist soldiers in the countryside working to overcome their evil overlords. Released in 1961, this film's more problematic issues grow from its overt propagandistic celebration of the Communist Party at a time when China was reeling from the famine caused by the Great Leap Forward. Additionally, while celebrating the emancipation of women from traditional gender roles, the narrative still depends heavily on the figure of a male savior to initiate and promote that emancipation. Cultural propaganda of one kind or another lies at the heart of both films, and in its own way, each film includes the message that women should submit to cultural norms and to male authority. These issues form the centerpiece of class discussion as we enter the second half of the term and begin to view films made by Chinese or Chinese American filmmakers.

During the term's second half, we first examine the inexpensive chopsocky films from the later 1960s and early 1970s that made Bruce Lee into a cultural icon. Despite their poor production values but because of their low costs, these films were distributed widely by American studios hungry for new revenue. As an unintended consequence, the studios brought American audiences a range of films with powerful, central male characters who were Chinese and played by Chinese actors. We move next to the rise of Chinese American filmmakers and to the fifth generation of filmmakers in China. During the 1980s, when China was under the party leadership of Deng Xiaoping, breakthrough films by directors like Chen Kaige and Zhang Yimou offered more complex and less propagandistic narratives to Chinese audiences, and their films gradually became available to American audiences through art houses and college festivals. Over the same period, Chinese American directors like Wayne Wang were beginning their careers. Interweaving the examination of these later Chinese and Chinese American films, the course explores how American racist and stereotypical assumptions were challenged through a range of new films in a variety of genres and forms. Smaller independent American works like Wang's 1982 *Chan Is Missing* and larger studio productions like his 1993 version of the Amy Tan novel *The Joy Luck Club* offered distinctive views of Chinese American experiences from Chinese American writers and filmmakers while demonstrating that these experiences were by no means monolithic. Students also compare gender construction in the Chinese American family saga of *The Joy Luck Club* and in similar family narratives from China, such as Zhang Yimou's *Red Sorghum* (红高粱), *To Live* (活着), and *The Road Home* (我的父亲母亲). We conclude the course with two documentaries from the new century, *Up the Yangtze* (沿江而上) and *Last Train Home* (归途列车), that explore personal family struggles against the backdrop of economic development and growing economic inequality in twenty-first-century China. In both films gender issues, especially regarding the life experiences of teenage girls, are central to the narrative.

By the course's end, students have explored a range of films from the 1930s through the 2000s, and in the process they have analyzed how such films have shaped America's understanding of Chinese and Chinese American identity in terms of nationality, race, and gender. The course helps students develop a broader and deeper awareness of the complex cultural experiences of these groups while also emphasizing the chronic racism and hostility faced by the Chinese in America.

Two Films and Two Contexts for Integration Propaganda

The philosopher and cultural critic Jacques Ellul provides a useful guide to the workings of propaganda in a range of cultural settings, demonstrating that, whatever the purpose behind such discourse, the ultimate effects are not positive. His concept of "agitation propaganda" (often shortened by journalists in the 1960s to *agitprop*) refers to efforts to arouse a populace to commit to a cause. The parallel strategy is "integration propaganda," a subtler but equally important tool for controlling populations, in this case by reassuring them that accepting the prevailing social norms is their best road to a happy and successful life—integration propaganda is therefore "the propaganda of conformity" and is a kind of tranquilizer in contrast to the more obvious stimulant of agitprop (74).

My course presents *Flower Drum Song* and *The Red Detachment of Women*, at least in part, as examples of integration propaganda. In each film, the narrative tries to assure audiences that the dominant cultural norms—American individualism and market capitalism and Chinese collectivist Marxism, respectively—are the fundamental paths to the good life. Moreover, these films focus heavily on how female characters achieve self-awareness and personal empowerment by embracing the established normative cultural roles. While those roles are different in each film, they are still limiting and made dependent on male authority.

Though less well-known today, *Flower Drum Song* was a breakthrough film in 1961 because it told a story about Chinese and Chinese Americans and used mostly actors of Asian backgrounds. Two of the leads, James Shigeta, as Wang Ta, and Miyoshi Umeki, as Mei Li, were ethnically Japanese though playing a Chinese American and a Chinese immigrant, respectively—a fact that alienated some Chinese American viewers. Also, Madame Liang (Wang Ta's aunt) was played by Juanita Hall, an African American actor already known for playing a Melanesian character in *South Pacific*—an example of Hollywood's belief that a nonwhite actor might play any ethnicity or race. Still, a story drawn from a Chinese American novel that places the Chinese and Chinese American characters at the center of the drama broke new ground for both Broadway and Hollywood.

The narrative itself perpetuates other kinds of stereotypes in its representation of the female characters and in the way it resolves conflicts by having those characters not only accept but also embrace traditional roles. The two major female characters are Linda Low, a nightclub singer fully assimilated into American consumer culture, and Mei Li, a recent immigrant who has just arrived in the United States (illegally, as a stowaway on a ship) to complete a marriage contract. Linda is the commercially emancipated American woman whose identity is found in what she buys and what she is given, such as the car that the nightclub owner Sammy Fong provides. Additionally, as a nightclub entertainer, Linda displays herself as a kind of product for sale through her suggestive costume and performance style, especially when she sings "Fan Tan Fannie" (00:14:12–00:15:18). In contrast, Mei Li represents a traditional Chinese woman—obedient to her father and willing to accept the marriage that family elders have arranged. Thus, we have two distinct but consistent stereotypes of Chinese women: the sexually provocative entertainer and the submissive, obedient daughter and wife. Throughout the film, each character develops by adopting some of the qualities of the other. Linda, who loves Sammy, is tough-minded and hard-edged on the surface, but she is still on a campaign to get Sammy to marry her to fulfill her romantic dreams. Likewise, Mei Li has come over to marry Sammy because of a marriage contract arranged by his mother and Mei Li's father. This new development complicates Linda's plans, and so Linda encourages Wang Ta's infatuation withher in order to make Sammy jealous and so motivate him finally to propose. Sammy in fact does love Linda, despite his resistance to commitment. The additional complication comes with Mei Li's emerging attraction to Wang Ta and the interest of Ta's father, Wang Chi-Yang (Benson Fong), in having his son marry a traditional Chinese woman. Such plot complications are the essence of romantic comedies as far back as Shakespeare's *A Midsummer Night's Dream* and even the much earlier Roman plays of Plautus and Terence.

As the story develops, several scenes and musical numbers emphasize the various aspects of assimilation and consumption. Perhaps the clearest example is when a negligee-clad Linda, in an apartment that looks like a photo spread from a magazine, sings "I Enjoy Being a Girl" (00:34:20–00:38:21). Situated among the various stylish pieces of furniture and other interior decor, she herself is on display, as if in an advertisement. The song celebrates all the aspects of female attractiveness that make men focus their gaze on women, and Linda shamelessly reveals how much that attention pleases her (a classic illustration of Laura Mulvey's thesis about the male gaze). Parallel to this scene is the later performance of the song "Sunday," a duet by Linda and Sammy that celebrates how, if they were married, they would enjoy the pleasures of their day off together (01:44:40–01:51:08). Here we see that Linda, though certainly materialistic, is still concentrating on the traditional role of the American wife in a middle-class household. In contrast, Mei Li has much to learn in order to assimilate into American culture, but she develops a growing sense of her own identity and agency as the film progresses. Still, though she personally rejects the idea of an arranged marriage, she finds that she must go through with it as planned. It is only when she discovers, through a television drama, that undocumented immigrants are denied certain rights that she conceives of the plan to declare herself an undocumented immigrant.[1] Her declaration, which she makes at the wedding ceremony, allows her to marry Wang Ta instead of Sammy, and also for Linda to marry Sammy (02:08:15–02:08:50). By undertaking the very American activity of consuming knowledge from popular television, Mei Li demonstrates her assimilation into consumer culture. Linda is already an assimilated, card-carrying consumer. Both women have developed into the roles they hoped for—wives to the men they have decided to love—in a typical ending for an American comic film.

Theirs is a bildungsroman that positions women as becoming consumers of products and popular culture in order to achieve the dream life of marriage. Likewise, it shows that Chinese Americans can assimilate most fully by adopting and embracing the values of consumer culture. While these women demonstrate individual agency in pursuing their goals, that agency serves merely to position them under the control of the forces of consumerism and the traditional authority of husbands. Thus, the film becomes a work of integration propaganda that attempts to assure Chinese Americans that the road to assimilation is paved with purchase receipts, as well as to assure Chinese American women that the traditional role of wife and mother, perhaps dressed up and decorated with the latest clothes and decor, will lead them to personal fulfillment.

Few films can be as different from *Flower Drum Song* as *The Red Detachment of Women*. Whereas the former is set in San Francisco in the early 1960s, the latter is set in Hainan in the 1930s, when the Communist Party was contending with the Kuomintang under Jiang Jieshi (Chiang Kaishek). The film tells the story of Wu Qionghua (Zhu Xijuan), a young woman enslaved by a cruel landlord, Nan Batian (Chen Qiang), who has killed her father. Though subjected to various tortures, Wu still resists Nan Batian, even attempting an unsuccessful escape. Only with the arrival of Hong Changqing (Wang Xingang) is she able to gain her freedom. Hong is a Communist leader traveling in disguise as a merchant, and he convinces Nan Batian to let Wu accompany him. Afterward, he reveals his true identity to Wu and encourages her to join the women's detachment to fight against the landlords.

From here, the narrative takes on many of the features of the military bildungsroman, a narrative of the progress of young recruits, sometimes resistant and sometimes enthusiastic, as they proceed through training and into combat. Often there is a cycle of mistakes and failures before a recruit develops the necessary discipline and focus to be an effective member of the team. Having joined and trained with the women's unit, Wu Qionghua goes on patrols, and she causes a mission to fail when she disobeys orders not to engage because she cannot resist the temptation to fire on Nan Batian. Back at the camp, she is disciplined and learns her lesson—this rebellion is the people's struggle and not her personal vendetta. The battle between the Communist forces and Nan Batian's group, reinforced by Kuomintang units, seesaws back and forth. At one point, covering the retreat of Communist forces, Hong Changqing is wounded and captured. From afar, Wu Qionghua witnesses his brutal execution, which he endures bravely. This fills her with new resolve and commitment. Eventually, the Communist forces capture Nan Batian. When he tries to escape, he is finally killed, and the detachment continues its struggles to free the people from the control of landlords and the Kuomintang.

The Red Detachment of Women certainly espouses women's empowerment, and it rejects the traditional roles of women in Chinese society, encouraging them instead to take on the same responsibilities as men. At the same time, the narrative suggests that women cannot save themselves from oppression. The party representative, a heroic male, must come to the rescue of Wu, and he must also guide and tutor her as she proceeds with her development as a member of the unit and the party. Party authority dominates, and higher party authority is ultimately male despite the party's supposed support for women. The case of Jiang Qing, Mao Zedong's widow, comes to mind. Briefly at the pinnacle of power after Mao's death, she and the members of the Gang of Four were ultimately toppled from power, arrested, and tried. In her defense, she claimed that she was "Chairman Mao's dog," in other words, the obedient servant of the male master (Roberts 289). *The Red Detachment of Women* shows women gaining agency and authority but only when accepting the discipline of a party that is still led by idealized male figures.

In exploring these films, the class discusses and debates how they portray women and how the female characters achieve agency in some respects while still having to acquiesce to some extent to traditional male authority. In both films, students find a narrative that asserts that women must embrace the prevailing values of the dominant culture if they are to enter into and fulfill their roles in society (the focal outcome of any bildungsroman). Linda Low in *Flower Drum Song* demonstrates a great deal of independence and willfulness, but her energy is still directed toward achieving a traditional role as Sammy Fong's wife and the assurance of middle-class, material comfort in a consumer society. Mei Li follows her heart to be with the man she loves, and to do so, she breaks away from the traditionally passive role of Chinese women, gaining agency in devising her own way out of the arranged marriage. Yet she does this only to seek a new acceptance as a wife in the American mode. In *The Red Detachment of Women*, Wu Qionghua and her female comrades all escape the domination of the oppressive male landlords. Yet they do so only under the guidance of a party whose leadership is male and whose immediate heroic figure is the salvific and self-sacrificing male party representative

Hong Changqing. Again, we see a narrative of integration propaganda directed at Chinese audiences in the wake of a horrific famine caused by the Great Leap Forward. Some Chinese did, at least secretly, question the wisdom of their party leaders at this time, and therefore the film encourages viewers to remember how bad things were before Communist rule and to recognize that the best way forward is to accept party policy and leadership. While the party encourages women to go far beyond prior limited gender roles, it does so in a context where the ultimate image of leadership, Mao, is an omnipotent and omniscient male figure, and his subordinates are also principally male. *Flower Drum Song* addresses American audiences exhausted from the paranoia and xenophobia of McCarthy-era, red-scare politics, reassuring them that no political conflict is so severe that it cannot be overcome by shared consumerism. Ultimately, Ellul's theory of integration propaganda serves well in helping students to analyze and critique both films and to understand how each, in its time and place, encouraged women to accept without question the powers that be and their values. Carefully examining these two films in tandem allows students to explore gender construction and cultural propaganda in a cross-cultural context and to compare representations of Chinese people and Chinese Americans.

My course Chinese Screen evolved at a time when relations between China and the United States were far more positive. Even as recently as the first decade of the new century, China and America may have seemed tough economic competitors, but both were committed to advancing the global economy that benefitted each. During the past ten years or so, Xi Jinping's leadership has brought China to a much more aggressive international posture economically, politically, and even militarily. Likewise, the US administration of Donald Trump actively fostered the kind of racist xenophobia that had previously led to so much hostility to both immigrants and foreigners periodically throughout the country's history. The growing tensions came to a head during the COVID-19 pandemic, with increasingly dire consequences. My course attempts to illustrate the history of anti-Chinese racism in the United States while also acknowledging some of the chronic internal problems in China that its fifth-generation filmmakers tried to address. The course's goal is for students to realize just how much we must learn if we are to overcome a history of bias and stereotypes and how studying the historical patterns presented in films about the Chinese or Chinese Americans can help to achieve that learning.

Note

1. Unfortunately, the television drama uses an ethnic slur that Mei Li repeats awkwardly at the wedding ceremony, declaring her undocumented status. While the original slur is offensive on its own, particularly to Latinx viewers, the way Mei Li is positioned in the scene, as the Chinese immigrant awkwardly using an American idiom, is also offensive, particularly to Asian Americans. At the same time, this entire plot device is contrived, straining credibility even in the registers of musical comedy.

Works Cited

Buck, Pearl S. *The Good Earth*. 1931. Pocket Books, 1958.

Chan Is Missing. Directed by Wayne Wang, New Yorker Films, 1982.

Charlie Chan at the Opera. Directed by H. Bruce Humberstone, starring Warner Oland, 20th Century Studios, 1937.

Cronin, A. J. *The Keys of the Kingdom*. Little, Brown, 1941.

Daughter of the Dragon. Directed by Lloyd Corrigan, performances by Anna May Wong and Warner Oland, Paramount Pictures, 1931.

Ellul, Jacques. *Propaganda: The Formation of Men's Attitudes*. Translated by Ronald Kellen and Jean Lerner, Vintage Books, 1973.

Flower Drum Song. Directed by Henry Koster, performances by James Shigeta, Miyoshi Umeki, and Juanita Hall, Universal International, 1961.

The Good Earth. Directed by Sidney Franklin, performances by Paul Muni and Luise Rainer, Metro-Goldwyn-Mayer Studios, 1937.

Hollywood Chinese. Directed by Arthur Dong, Deep Focus Productions, 2008.

The Inn of the Sixth Happiness. Directed by Mark Robson, performance by Ingrid Bergman, 20th Century Fox, 1958.

The Joy Luck Club. Directed by Wayne Wang, Buena Vista Pictures, 1993.

The Keys of the Kingdom. Directed by John M. Stahl, 20th Century Fox, 1944.

Last Train Home. Directed by Lixin Fan, Zeitgeist Films, 2009.

Lee, Chin Yang *The Flower Drum Song*. Farrar, Straus and Cudahy, 1957.

Mulvey, Laura. "Visual Pleasure and Narrative Cinema." *Screen*, vol. 16, no. 3, autumn 1975, pp. 6–18, https://doi.org/10.1093/screen/16.3.6.

The Red Detachment of Women. Directed by Xie Jin, Shanghai Film Studio, 1961.

Red Sorghum. Directed by Zhang Yimou, Xi'an Film Studio, 1987.

The Road Home. Directed by Zhang Yimou, Beijing New Picture Distribution / Sony Pictures Classics, 2000.

Roberts, J. A. G. *A History of China*. 3rd ed., Palgrave Macmillan, 2011.

South Pacific. Directed by Joshua Logan, written by Paul Osborn, 20th Century Fox, 1958.

Tan, Amy. *The Joy Luck Club*. G. P. Putnam's Sons, 1989.

To Live. Directed by Zhang Yimou, Samuel Goldwyn, 1994.

Up the Yangtze. Written and directed by Yung Chang, Zeitgeist Films, 2007.

**Elaine Chung

Chinese Remakes
of South Korean Films

In the United Kingdom, the majority of undergraduate degree programs in Chinese studies are housed in schools or departments of modern languages (ML), which were founded originally to teach modern European languages and cultures. In the past decade the discipline has been in crisis, as a number of universities have closed their European language programs because of the sharp fall in student enrollments (Bawden). To optimize teaching staff resources and reinvigorate the curricula, many ML departments across the country have introduced courses with "a strong comparative or transnational dimension" (Hutchings and Matras). The University of Liverpool Press also launched the book series *Transnational Modern Languages* in 2020 to promote "a model of Modern Languages not as the inquiry into separate national traditions, but as the study of languages and culture and their many interactions" ("Transnational Modern Languages").

At my university, the Chinese program is established in the School of Modern Languages. All undergraduate students in the school, regardless of their majors, must take two full-year so-called transnational and national courses. In each course, students spend some weeks together in lectures on grand concepts and theories that are supposedly applicable to different national contexts, and then students split into groups for classes on topics directly related to the (national) area they specialize in. The teaching experience I share in this essay comes from the transnational and national course Cultures in Context. At the beginning of the course, Chinese studies students first attend school-wide lectures on cultural theories (such as by Matthew Arnold, Ernesto Laclau, Pierre Bourdieu, Richard Hoggart, and Raymond Williams) before attending my lectures on Chinese cultural products, including films.

This transnational turn in ML education undoubtedly encourages students to think "beyond the monolingual frame and invites practices of decolonization and diversification" (Burns and Duncan). However, in practice, it can also pose new challenges to the teaching of Chinese studies in the historically Eurocentric field of ML. The transnational theories introduced in the earlier sessions are, somewhat unavoidably, Western theories. So when students move from the transnational to the national material, they can be easily led to embrace a binary between Western theory and non-Western applications of theory. Moreover, the division of transnational and national classes may also bring about an unconsciously essentialist understanding of Chinese culture as a homogenous national culture.

In other words, this context of ML education requires teachers of Chinese studies to, first, bridge the transnational and national course material for students, guiding them toward a productive dialogue between the presumed universality of Western theories and the lived experience of Chinese cultures, and, second, remind students of the plurality and transnationality within the umbrella of Chinese cultures. I delineate in this essay how I incorporated and addressed these objectives in a class on transnational Chinese cultures by using the circuit-of-culture framework as a theoretical tool and Chinese remakes of South Korean films as texts. I first explain the rationale behind the use of this concept and set of materials before reflecting on their application in the classroom.

Reading Films with the Circuit of Culture

To avoid students' uncritical application of Western theories, it has been crucial for me to introduce the idea of dewesternization in my classes and in other higher-education teaching activities in which non-Chinese and Chinese theories intersect. The process of dewesternizing or decolonizing academic knowledge, however, does not mean a flat denial of the usefulness and applicability of Euro-American theories, which in turn may contribute to a false division between Western theory and so-called pure

Asian theory. Instead, this process requires that theories derived from Western societies must be interrogated and contextualized before being applied to explain other local realities (Glück). Thus, I pay attention to involving students in a productive dialogue between cultural theories and Chinese texts.

The circuit of culture is a theoretical framework devised by a group of cultural studies scholars at the Open University and published in *Doing Cultural Studies: The Story of the Sony Walkman* (Du Gay et al.). This framework suggests that to analyze a cultural text or artifact adequately, one must look into the five processes it must go through: representation, production, consumption, regulation and identity. One should first question how a cultural product creates meaning (representation). If the framework is applied to the study of a film, one can examine how the story is presented through the arrangements of mise-en-scène, cinematography, editing, and sound. In addition, one should also look into the industrial structure that determines the story's meaning (production). In a commercial filmmaking system, one should examine how the investors, production companies, and directors intended to profit from their targeted audiences. The framework then leads to the realm of consumption, which concerns how a film is received by viewers from different social backgrounds (identity). In addition, it is vital that one scrutinize various formal and informal constraints on cultural production (regulation), including laws, institutionalized systems, cultural norms, and expectations.

As these five processes combine to form a circuit, they are equally important, closely intertwined, and continually overlapping (Du Gay et al. 4). Underlying this emphasis on interconnectivity is the concept of radical contextuality, which is also named "the heart of cultural studies" (Grossberg 9). This concept advocates that one must consider as much contextual information as possible to see how a cultural text is surrounded, interpenetrated, and shaped by a network of forces. In short, the framework facilitates students' holistic and contingent understanding of the notion of culture.

While we can use the circuit of culture to analyze a wide range of texts, this essay underlines its use in guiding undergraduate students to read Chinese remakes of South Korean films. When making sense of the cultures of others, we often return to what we are familiar with, and I have found that students in my classes often comprehend a new Chinese film by making reference to European and Hollywood films. Therefore, an exercise comparing a Chinese film to a South Korean film can enable students to move beyond the default East/West binary and view China through the lens of inter-Asian referencing (Iwabuchi). They can then develop a sensitivity to cultural similarities, differences, and convergences within the so-called Confucian cultural sphere in East Asia.

Case Studies: *The Big Shot* and *Twenty Once Again*

Putting the ideas above into practice, I selected *The Big Shot* ("大"人物) and *Twenty Once Again* (重返 20 岁) as class materials. They are remakes of the South Korean films *Veteran* (베테랑) and *Miss Granny* (수상한 그녀), respectively. Among the many Chinese remakes of Korean films, they are the most commercially successful (both earned more than 360 million yuan at the Chinese box office). Since their original versions were also highly profitable, in South Korea, these cases allow us to explore how and why the storylines could attract moviegoers in both countries.

The Big Shot tells of the face-off between Sun Dasheng, a hot-headed police officer, and Zhao Tai, the young but psychopathic and murderous CEO of a powerful corporation. As the main hero of the story, Sun overcomes all obstacles and puts Zhao in prison. *Twenty Once Again* is about a seventy-year-old grandmother. It begins with her serendipitously entering a mysterious photo studio and being transformed back into her twenty-year-old self by an unknown force. She decides not to tell her family but to pursue her unfulfilled youthful dream of being a pop singer. But in realizing that her now-magical blood can heal her ill grandson, she chooses to save him at the end of the film, even though donating her blood means that she will return to her seventy-year-old self. Except for relocating the story to a Chinese context, each film closely follows the South Korean original. I required students to watch either pair of films before class and to identify the differences between the two versions. English subtitles are available for all four films and have been quoted below.

Representation

I began the class by inviting the students to share their observations. Most of them quickly pointed out some obvious additions of Chinese cultural elements in the Chinese remakes. For example, *Twenty Once Again* replaces Audrey Hepburn with Teresa Teng, a Taiwanese singer who has been extremely popular in mainland China since the late 1970s, as the female protagonist's idol. Also, instead of hanging out in a café frequented by elderly patrons, the protagonist's favorite pastime becomes playing mah-jongg.

Likewise, in the opening scene of *The Big Shot*, we can see a group of gangsters worshipping Guan Yu, a deified historical figure that symbolizes loyalty in Chinese cultures, but this figure is not in the original Korean film. Students also suggested that the films characterize their protagonists differently. For instance, they noted that the grandmother in *Twenty Once Again* looks more elegant after her magical rejuvenation and that the police officers in *The Big Shot* behave in a more comic manner.

Although students spotted meaningful differences in the remakes in terms of their representation of Chinese culture, they could hardly give in-depth explanations for these differences. After hearing their initial findings, I introduced the circuit of culture as a theoretical framework and asked them to reinterpret their observations from the four other processes described in the framework.

Production

The consideration of each film's production context enables students to read the two remakes as part of a broader industry trend. Chinese and South Korean filmmakers have established a strong collaborative network since the early 2000s, allowing the Chinese film industry to rely on its Korean counterpart to refine its genres, themes, storylines, and technical skills (Yecies). Furthermore, the global success of South Korean cinema in the past decade has further boosted the demand for Korean film practitioners in China. In this light, we can explain why a good number of South Korean films were remade in China (at least ten since 2015) and why many of these remakes involve Korean creative personnel who worked on the originals (e.g., Ahn Sang-hoon, who produced the Korean film *Blind* [블라인드] and its Chinese remake, and Ahn Byeong-ki, who rewrote the Korean film *Bunshinsaba* [분신사바] into a Chinese film series). Simply by checking the closing credits, students can notice the strong presence in the Chinese remake *Twenty Once Again* of Korean filmmakers who worked on the original film, *Miss Granny*. CJ E&M, the Korean company that sold the script of *Miss Granny* to a Chinese studio, was also the coproducer of *Twenty Once Again*. Similarly, a representative from CJ E&M, which distributed *Veteran*, was one of the executive producers of *The Big Shot*.

From July 2016, the diplomatic relationship between China and South Korea rapidly deteriorated after the South Korean government agreed to host an American antimissile system. As a result, South Korean media products, including Chinese-Korean film coproductions and Chinese films that cast Korean stars, disappeared in China overnight because of the

Chinese government's de facto ban and the rise of anti-Korean nationalism in the country (Wang). Nonetheless, Chinese remakes of Korean films, including *The Big Shot*, are still being made and released. Although their plots came from Korea and some of the remakes were even coproduced with Korean companies, they are officially recognized in China as domestic films.

Having provided the above information, I then asked students whether they think the two remakes are Chinese films and why. In the field of Chinese film studies, there has been a call for replacing the term *Chinese cinema* with *transnational Chinese cinemas*. The latter accentuates the fact that many Chinese films nowadays have coproducers and draw funding and personnel from different countries and regions (Berry). Therefore, when the students raised various criteria for determining what nation a film belongs to, I took the chance to engage them in the current theoretical debates surrounding transnational cinemas. But when engaging students in these debates, instructors have to remind them to use the transnational paradigm critically rather than just describe a film as transnational or not. The discussion on production context should focus on how filmmakers are caught up by various forces when they try to work across national borders (Higbee and Lim).

Consumption and Identity

The four films discussed in this essay are commercial films targeted at a mass audience. As they all generated high box-office revenues in their respective domestic markets, it is safe to say that Chinese and South Korean audiences identify with the films' main storylines. Hence, I invited the students to explore the social factors contributing to the shared cultural tastes. For example, the popularity of *The Big Shot* and *Veteran*, which tell the story of a lower-class hero bringing a wicked rich man to justice, may imply that class inequality is a heated issue in both Chinese and South Korean societies, possibly as a result of the compressed modernization experienced in both countries. Meanwhile, we can attribute the high domestic box-office figures for *Twenty Once Again* and *Miss Granny* to the growth of neoliberal feminist or postfeminist sensibilities in China and South Korea (Yu), as both films celebrate the heroine's regained youth, feminine beauty, and professional success while foregrounding the character's gender role in the family.

Students can use their prior knowledge about China and South Korea to complete the task of exploring the social factors in the films' success. In

Veteran the antagonist, Jo Tae-oh, is the third-generation heir of a powerful conglomerate, which represents a strong reference to the chaebols, the leading family-owned conglomerates in South Korea. The chaebols, which arose in the 1970s under military dictatorship, continue to dominate the South Korean economy and are blamed for social problems like the precarious labor market, toxic meritocracy, and corruption (Rhyu). Korean media often portrays the chaebols as snobbish and tyrannical, and such representations are constantly reinforced by real-life scandals surrounding young chaebol members, such as the infamous nut-rage incident (Kim et. al.). Students therefore could easily relate *Veteran*'s domestic box-office success to the hostility against chaebols in South Korea. But the main villain in *The Big Shot*, Zhao, is the CEO of a property development company and not of a multi-industry conglomerate. Meanwhile, instead of the trade-union-protest scene in *Veteran* (00:22:37–00:25:20), *The Big Shot* has a scene showing how the thugs hired by Zhao's company demolish residential properties on land the company wants to buy (00:17:50–00:18:20). In slow motion, the camera captures the helpless, poor residents retrieving their belongings from the ruins. Students asserted that the new scene in *The Big Shot* better addresses the Chinese audience since forced evictions backed by local governments are a pressing social problem in China, given that news reports ("Amnesty") and Chinese media products about the issue, notably Jia Zhangke's films (as discussed in Schultz), are readily available in English.

On the other hand, depicting the same story about a grandmother's magical new life, *Miss Granny* and *Twenty Once Again* characterize their heroine differently. In *Miss Granny*, the heroine, despite her newly earned twenty-year-old body, continues to follow her seventy-year-old mind, proudly showing off her grandmother's fashion sense and treating everyone around her like kids. But students described her Chinese counterpart in *Twenty Once Again* as more elegant. They found not only that the Chinese heroine's looks and behavior much more closely follow the normative femininity imposed on young women but also that the remake has more romantic moments for its heroine than the original version does. Some of them went further in attributing this difference to differences in women's histories in China and South Korea. That is, in the 1960s (when the heroines were in their twenties), young women in both China and South Korea lived under patriarchalism, which, as the films tell, forced them to sacrifice their dreams and instead raise children. But the 1960s were also the height of Maoism in China, when women, in the name of gender equality, had to conform to a new socialist norm of androgyny. Arguably, it is because of this historical background that *Twenty Once Again* places a stronger focus on how a grandmother empowers herself by returning to traditional feminine beauty ideals. By examining issues of consumption and identity in these films, I was able to focus students' attention on various topics in Chinese current affairs, fulfilling the learning objective of Chinese studies in ML schools and departments to enhance students' interdisciplinary understanding of Chinese culture and society.

Instructors can take the in-class discussions on social contexts to a theoretical level by asking students to suggest theories that are useful in supporting their thoughts on the films' representations of class and gender. I let students define and, more importantly, evaluate the usefulness of the theories they introduced. For example, they identified the need to extend the theory of neoliberalism, which, in the United Kingdom context, is primarily associated with economic liberalization, to account for the role of the state in China's neoliberal policies (as addressed in the story of forced eviction in *The Big Shot*). Similarly, they reviewed the limitations of the wave metaphor of feminism—which describes stages in the feminist movement in the United States—in helping them understand the life story of the grandmother in *Twenty Once Again*. This activity of applying and critiquing theories stimulates students to reflect on the relationship between Western theories and non-Western texts and interrogate the universality of Western theories and the necessity of using those theories to translate non-Western experience into Western terms. Students should leave the classroom with an understanding of how to generalize and theorize Asian realities rather than just how neoliberal or feminist China may be (see Shih; Nonini). The exercise also helps mitigate the abovementioned risk that students might uncritically apply the theories they learned in the lectures on transnational concepts to Chinese texts they encounter in the more narrowly focused classes.

Regulation

Although students can get insights into Chinese society by analyzing the films' stories, we should remind them not to take the cinematic images simply as realities, as many other factors determine what can be represented on-screen. For example, China's notoriously strict yet opaque media censorship is a crucial institutional force that affects film contents. Given that there are no transparent and consistent criteria for the government's censorship,

I ask the students to form groups and approximate which parts of the Korean films were altered in the Chinese remakes to satisfy the censors.

Despite the focus in *Veteran* on the battle against an evil chaebol, the main hero and the police force in the film are far from perfect. The protagonist forces a criminal to hold a weapon so that he can beat up the criminal, supposedly in self-defense (00:09:20–00:10:15), and other officers are bribed by the chaebols. But these negative portrayals of the police force are not found in *The Big Shot*. In addition, unlike their Korean counterparts in *Veteran*, who cannot enter private property to make an arrest and fail to disperse onlookers at crime scenes, the Chinese policemen are much more authoritative. Also, in contrast to the individual heroism in *Veteran*, *The Big Shot* upholds the message that the Chinese party-state backs the police force. For example, the boss of the male lead reveals that he stopped the lead from investigating the case because a secret investigation is being conducted by an anticorruption unit from the central government, a moment in the film that implicitly promotes Xi Jinping's massive anti-corruption campaign (01:25:00–01:26:25). The boss in the original Korean film restrains the protagonist only because he dares not confront the chaebol (*Veteran* 01:19:32–01:20:40). Moreover, while only the CEO and a few people surrounding him are prosecuted at the end of *Veteran*, the happy ending of *The Big Shot* shows that the Chinese government has uprooted the entire interest group behind the forced evictions and unlawful land sales. Finally, students noticed a disclaimer before the closing sequence of *The Big Shot*, which states, "Chinese police successfully cracked down on 514 triads and 2993 criminal organizations in 2018" (01:41:13). From all this evidence, the students concluded that *The Big Shot* is obliged to portray China as a place of law and order thanks to the reliable police force and the morally perfect government leadership.

Although *Twenty Once Again* and *Miss Granny* do not deal directly with any sensitive social issues, we can also perceive that the different endings are a result of censorship. In the closing scene of *Miss Granny*, the grandmother, returned to her seventy-year-old body, discovers that one of her elderly friends has become a young man, rejuvenated by the magical photo studio she visited. The film then ends on an ambiguous note: the grandmother's fantastical voyage may take place once again. Much of this room for imagination, however, was axed for the Chinese remake. Not only was that scene removed, but in the middle of the end credits for *Twenty Once Again*, one of the actors reappears and speaks directly to the audience:

"Bye! There are no bloopers" (02:06:05). One can only speculate on the factors leading to this change, but it is not unreasonable to attribute it to the censorship of fantastical media by the Chinese government, which has accused time-slip television dramas of distorting national history and issued a ban on them in 2011.

Although many students imagine film censorship in China as an airtight system that ensures that every Chinese film is propaganda for the party-state, the fact is that media censors in postsocialist China must balance political control and market interests (Ng). This complexity offers room for filmmakers to maneuver: *Twenty Once Again* is still a fantasy story despite the disclaimer at the end, and *The Big Shot* still touches on the sensitive topics of the wealth gap and corruption. Therefore, by interpreting how the Chinese screenwriters change the Korean plots based on their understanding of and negotiation with the censors, students can develop an ability to think beyond the dichotomy of oppression and resistance.

Finally, it is also worth mentioning to the students that the absence of a motion-picture rating system in China also forces filmmakers to adapt the Korean films to make them friendly to viewers of all ages. *The Big Shot* has significantly fewer violent scenes depicting the assaults committed by the CEO than does *Veteran* (which is classified for viewers fifteen and older by South Korea's rating system). Meanwhile, to ensure that diverse Chinese audiences can clearly understand the storyline, *The Big Shot* tends to present its story more straightforwardly. For example, in remaking the scene of a police operation against a foreign triad, *The Big Shot* puts captions on the screen that list the targets' names and the crimes they committed (00:12:10–00:13:19). In another example, when the hero in *Veteran* is about to strike the villain in public, the camera intercuts close-ups of the hero's face and the mobile phones of onlookers, indicating his fear of being blamed for using excessive force (01:55:04–01:55:17). In the equivalent scene in *The Big Shot*, viewers can hear a voice from the crowd—"he cannot do this even though he is a policeman!" (01:36:50)—that explicitly informs viewers what the male lead is worrying about. With these findings, students see how state regulations that are not directly related to political censorship can also influence the content and style of films made in China.

One of the greatest difficulties of teaching with films is to move students beyond their intuitive reactions to the text and toward a more complex view informed by history and theory (Turim 64). Hence, the teaching and learning activities presented in this essay are designed to raise students' awareness of the dynamics between text, context, and theory. The pedagogical value of these activities, as demonstrated, lies in the following aspects. By analyzing the films in terms of the five processes suggested in the circuit-of-culture framework, students can grasp the importance of contexts when reading a text. They ultimately gain from this analysis a holistic understanding of culture, but the emphasis on context also draws students' attention to broader social, economic, and political issues relating to China, serving the main objective of courses in area studies, which is to teach about a geographic, national, or cultural region through an interdisciplinary lens. When students unravel the sociopolitical connections between China and South Korea revealed by the remakes, they can learn to approach Chinese cultures from a comparative and transnational angle and, by extension, become capable of critically discerning the concepts of national cinema and culture. As Western theories still dominate the increasingly transnational curricula in ML schools and departments, I highlight the importance of developing students' reflexivity about the use and usefulness of such theories in interpreting Chinese film texts. While the lesson plan presented in this essay is situated in the context of teaching Chinese studies within the disciplinary framework of ML education in the United Kingdom, its emphasis on contextual study, comparative analysis, and inter-Asian referencing should be handy for the teaching of Chinese cultures in other higher education settings.

Works Cited

"Amnesty: China Forced Evictions in 'Significant Rise.'" *BBC News*, 11 Oct. 2012, bbc.com/news/world-asia-china-19894292.

Bawden, Anna. "Modern Languages: Degree Courses in Freefall." *The Guardian*, 8 Oct. 2013, www.theguardian.com/education/2013/oct/08/modern-foreign-language-degrees-axed.

Berry, Chris. "What Is Transnational Cinema? Thinking from the Chinese Situation." *Transnational Cinemas*, vol. 1, no. 2, 2010, pp. 111–27.

The Big Shot. Directed by Bai Wu, Firework Entertainment, 2019.

Burns, Jennifer, and Derek Duncan. "Transnational Modern Languages: A Handbook." *Liverpool University Press Blog*, 20 July 2020, liverpooluniversitypress.blog/2020/07/20/transnational-modern-languages-a-handbook.

Du Gay, Paul, et al., editors. *Doing Cultural Studies: The Story of the Sony Walkman*. Sage, 1996.

Glück, Antje. "De-westernization and Decolonization in Media Studies." *Oxford Research Encyclopedia of Communication*, Jon Nussbaum, editor in chief, Oxford UP, 20 Dec. 2018. *Oxford Research Encyclopedias*, https://doi.org/10.1093/acrefore/9780190228613.013.898.

Grossberg, Lawrence. *Cultural Studies in the Future Tense*. Duke UP, 2010.

Higbee, Will, and Song Hwee Lim. "Concepts of Transnational Cinema: Towards a Critical Transnationalism in Film Studies." *Transnational Cinemas*, vol. 1, no. 1, Jan. 2010, pp. 7–21.

Hutchings, Stephen, and Yaron Matras. "Modern Languages: Four Reforms to Reclaim the Future of Our Discipline." *Times Higher Education*, 26 June 2017, www.timeshighereducation.com/cn/blog/modern-languages-four-reforms-reclaim-future-our-discipline.

Iwabuchi, Koichi. "East Asian Popular Culture and Inter-Asian Referencing." *Routledge Handbook of East Asian Popular Culture*, edited by Koichi Iwabuchi et al., Routledge, 2016, pp. 24–33.

Kim, Rebecca Chunghee, et. al. "The Korean Air Nut Rage Scandal: Domestic versus International Responses to a Viral Incident." *Business Horizons*, vol. 61, 2018, pp. 533–44.

Miss Granny. Directed by Dong-hyuk Hwang, CJ Entertainment, 2014.

Ng, How-wee. "Rethinking Censorship in China: The Case of *Snail House*." *Chinese Television in the Twenty-First Century: Entertaining the Nation*, edited by Bai Ruoyun and Geng Song, Routledge, 2015, pp. 87–103.

Nonini, Donald M. "Is China Becoming Neoliberal." *Critique of Anthropology*, vol. 28, no. 2, 2008, pp. 145–76.

Rhyu, Sang-young. "Chaebol." *The Oxford Handbook of South Korean Politics*, edited by JeongHun Han et. al., Oxford UP, 2021, pp. 120–35.

Schultz, Corey Kai Nelson. "Ruin in the Films of Jia Zhangke." *Visual Communication*, vol. 15, no. 4, 2016, pp. 439–60.

Shih, Shu-mei. "Towards an Ethics of Transnational Encounter; or, 'When' Does a 'Chinese' Woman Become a 'Feminist.'" *Differences: A Journal of Feminist Cultural Studies*, vol. 13, no. 2, 2002, pp. 90–126.

"Transnational Modern Languages." *Liverpool University Press*, liverpooluniversitypress.co.uk/topic/book-series/transnational-modern-languages?target=titleSearch. Accessed 1 July 2023.

Turim, Maureen. "Teaching Feminist Film Theory; or, Women and Film." *Teaching Film*, edited by Lucy Fisher and Patrice Petro, Modern Language Association of America, 2012, pp. 76–94.

Twenty Once Again. Directed by Leste Chen, CJ E&M Film Division, 2015.

Veteran. Directed by Ryoo Seung-wan, CJ Entertainment, 2015.

Wang, Linbin. "The Korean Wave's Rocky Road in China." *The Diplomat*, 28 Jan. 2023, thediplomat.com/2023/01/the-korean-waves-rocky-road-in-china/.

Yecies, Brian. "The Chinese–Korean Co-production Pact: Collaborative Encounters and the Accelerating Expansion of Chinese Cinema." *International Journal of Cultural Policy*, vol. 22, no. 5, Oct. 2016, pp. 770–86.

Yu, Su-lin. "The Rise of the Neoliberal Chinese Female Subject in *Go Lala Go*." *CLCWeb: Comparative Literature and Culture*, vol. 20, no. 6, 2018, docs.lib.purdue.edu/clcweb/vol20/iss6/.

Part VI

Film in Chinese Language Courses

Jin Liu

An Integrated Approach to Teaching Chinese Language and Culture through Film

A full-fledged undergraduate curriculum in a Chinese program in the United States generally consists of a four-year language sequence and literature and culture courses taught in English. In such a curriculum, there is a common divide between language courses in Chinese and culture courses in English. Language courses usually prioritize improving students' skills in reading, writing, speaking, and listening, thus leaving culture as the weakest component of most language courses. Moreover, if we use the three *p*'s (products, practices, perspectives) framework constructed by the National Standards in Foreign Language Education Project in 2006, then it becomes clear that both the cultural products and behavioral practices of a target culture are "derived from the philosophical perspectives that form the world view of [that] cultural group" (*Standards Foreign Language Learning* 47). As Oxana Dema and Aleidine Moeller argue, this "re-conceptualized approach to culture shifted the focus of teaching culture to a study of *underlying* values, attitudes, and beliefs, rather than simply learning about cultural products and practices" (79; emphasis added). However, as pointed out by Genelle Morain, the underlying cultural perspectives "pose the greatest difficulty in understanding" for L2 (second language) learners in the target language (36). Moreover, it is important to avoid teaching culture in a singular form that reduces a group to simplistic, stereotypical ideas or that implies that all people who speak the target language share the same worldview. In this regard, the cultural courses taught in English are usually more intellectually challenging, informed, and sophisticated, but they have their own limitations. By largely excluding language learning, such courses cannot meet the needs of students who want to integrate their learning of the subject and the language. As language and culture learning are inextricably linked, it is important for L2 students to understand different cultures "on [their] own terms" and to gain "new, 'insiders' perspective[s]" (*Standards Foreign Language Learning* 47, 49).

For students to achieve both goals—not only to improve language skills, but also to enhance and broaden their understanding of Chinese culture, philosophy, history, and society—an integrated approach is called for to bridge the language-culture divide. This essay illustrates this new approach by using my content-based, advanced course Chinese-Language Cinema at Georgia Tech as an example. After giving a brief description of the course, I use two films, *Shower* (洗澡) and *Ip Man* (叶问), as examples to show how to integrate the teaching of both language and culture, in particular the Daoist and Confucian philosophies. Film proves to be a powerful and effective medium to facilitate the learning of Chinese philosophy, whose metaphysical, abstract concepts are usually difficult for American students to comprehend. In *Shower*, the protagonist, Lao Liu, epitomizes the Daoist virtue of water in the saying *shang shan ruo shui* (上善若水; "the highest virtue is like water"), while in *Ip Man*, the eponymous character embodies the core Confucian concept of *ren* (仁; "humaneness") and the golden rule of Confucianism, *ji suo bu yu, wu shi yu ren* (己所不欲勿施于人; "do not do to others what you do not want done to you"). Moreover, Bruce Lee's martial arts philosophy on water and the episodes from Lee's *Enter the Dragon* (龙争虎斗) about the art of fighting without fighting can serve as a smooth transition between the two films. Throughout the course, the students are engaged in an intellectually challenging educational experience and are able to simultaneously enhance their linguistic and cultural competences.

Course Overview and Structure

This advanced course is offered primarily to college students who have learned Chinese for three or four years as well as heritage learners at a similar level. The course objectives are twofold: first, to utilize Chinese films as authentic texts to further sharpen students' Chinese language skills by helping students learn more vocabulary, grammar points, idioms, classical and literary expressions, street slang, proverbs, and other written and spoken registers at the advanced level; and second, to advance students' intellectual growth and sharpen their critical thinking skills so they can examine issues associated with Chinese culture, history, and society from an intercultural perspective and with an open mind. To meet these goals, the films for this course should be not only aesthetically sophisticated and thought-provoking but also appropriate and suitable for language learning. I carefully selected the following films: *Shower*, *Ip Man*, *In the Heat of the Sun* (阳光灿烂的日子), *Kungfu Hustle* (功夫), *White Haired Girl* (白毛女), *The Lovers* (梁祝), *Chungking Express* (重庆森林), *Secret Love in Peach Blossom Land* (暗恋桃花源), *The Soong Sisters* (宋家王朝), *To Live* (活着), and *The Wandering Earth* (流浪地球).[1] This cohort of films covers a variety of genres: urban melodrama, martial arts film, historical epic, costume drama, comedy, socialist period classic, and science fiction.

Taking a student-centered approach, this course emphasizes self-motivated learning through watching films. Students are required to watch each film with English subtitles in advance of class and submit a sheet containing a list of ten to fifteen words they recognize, a list of ten to fifteen words they have just learned, and at least two discussion questions that reflect a careful viewing of the film and an effort to analyze it. Students are encouraged to write discussion questions in Chinese, but some English is allowed, especially when they are expressing complicated thoughts and ideas. Collating the students' lists, the instructor will come up with a list of key vocabulary and expressions and provide guidance on pronunciation, their meanings in English, and example sentences for about thirty words. This list will be the focus for language instruction in class and the film quiz, and there are eight to ten quizzes in total. Moreover, a major part of the class is dedicated to film discussion and analysis, primarily conducted in Chinese. To facilitate discussion, the instructor organizes the students' questions under different categories and themes, indicates who asked what, and shares the list of questions before class. As a result, the students feel that their questions and opinions are recognized and seriously considered, and this feeling enhances their motivation, sense of responsibility, and participation in class. A wide range of issues and topics are discussed throughout the semester, such as Daoist and Confucian philosophies, Bruce Lee's martial arts philosophy, unreliable narrators, cross-dressing characters, identity politics, propaganda art techniques, gender and nation, the traditional imperial examination, and film elements and techniques including mise-en-scène, montage, cinematography, sound, music, and so on. After each film discussion, two to three questions are posted, and students choose one to write about in their response essays of roughly four hundred to five hundred Chinese characters. Students also have an opportunity to do an oral presentation in Chinese on a suggested topic and work on a group project to analyze episodes from a film.

Teaching *Shower*

A representative work of the so-called new urban cinema, the film *Shower* is set in Beijing in the late 1990s and revolves around the relationships between a father, Lao Liu, who runs a traditional public bathhouse; his elder son, Daming, a middle-class businessman who visits back from Shenzhen; and his younger son, Erming, who is mentally ill and stays with Lao Liu running the business. A major thematic concern in the film is the conflict between tradition and modernity in the urban transformation of contemporary China, characterized by massive demolition and the relocation of people.

For this film, I compile a vocabulary list that includes approximately thirty-five words. One of the key expressions that the students need to learn is *shang shan ruo shui*. Different from most of the other new words and expressions, which the students can learn from the film dialogue, this expression obscurely appears on the calligraphy frame hanging on the wall in one of the film's settings (*Shower* 00:05:16; see fig. 1). I bring the students' attention to the important Daoist philosophical concept contained in this expression, which celebrates the weak, the insignificant, and the humble. I introduce chapter 8 of Laozi's *Daodejing*, where this saying originates, and we go over both the original text in Chinese and the English translation by Colin Ronan: 上善若水。水善利万物而不争, 处众人之所恶, 故几于道 ("The highest good is like that of water. The goodness of water is that it benefits the ten thousand creatures, yet itself does not wrangle, but is content with the places that all men disdain. It is this that makes water so near to the Way [Dao]" *Laozi* 20; Ronan 94). Ronan further explains, "Water is yielding, it takes the shape of whatever container it fills, it seeps through invisible crevices, and its mirror-like surface reflects all Nature. Great rivers and seas gain their kingship over the lesser streams by being lower so that the streams flow into them: so, too, the sage, to be above the people, must speak as though he were lower than they are."

Figure I. A still from the film *Shower* showing the obscure appearance of the phrase *shang shan ruo shui.*

Afterward, the students are guided to identify and discuss the character in the film who best represents the highest virtue of Dao, Lao Liu. When we discuss how Lao Liu's humble, low-status job is initially looked down on even by his elder son, I show the students a short clip in which Lao Liu vents out his frustration to Daming after Erming goes missing ("Erming"; *Shower* 00:27:10–00:29:15). I integrate language learning here, referencing the language notes and exercises from the booklet edited by Zhang Li and Chen Tianxu. The students review the grammar structure of potential complements in *kanbuqi* (看不起; "to look down on"), the adverbs *juran* (居然; "unexpectedly") and *genben bu* (根本不; "not at all"), and learn new four-character idioms such as *zhi zu chang le* (知足常乐; "being contented makes one always happy"). In a similar manner, I guide students to study and review the episodes about how Lao Liu helps Jinshui improve his relationship with his wife, how Lao Liu tacitly protects He Zheng from the bullying of the gangsters, and how he settles the trivial falling-outs of his elder clients. Set in Beijing, the film has a strong local flavor, and the dialogue features distinctive colloquialisms and slang such as *jinrge* (今儿个; "today"), *qiajia* (掐架; "quarrel, fight"), and *suanni youzhong* (算你有种; "to have guts" or "to be plucky"). I will compare these colloquial terms with their more standard equivalents, which students are already familiar with, to help them identify the difference between spoken and written registers and between the Beijing dialect and standard Mandarin. Besides learning language, the students will gain a better understanding of how Lao Liu enjoys being lower than others and is always willing to help others without claiming credit, boasting, or showing off. Lao Liu epitomizes the Daoist virtue of water, and the expression *shang shan ruo shui* appears again when he dies (*Shower* 01:03:20).

While Lao Liu embodies traditional Daoist philosophy, his death and the demolition of his traditional bathhouse symbolize the demise of traditional culture in its confrontation with modernization. I invite the students to analyze the characters of the new generation, Daming, Erming, and Miao Zhuang, and their relationships with modernity and tradition. For Daming, I ask the students to pay special attention to changes in his clothing and position as he showers or bathes; for Erming, I guide the students to ask about the symbolism of his psychological illness and inability to articulate his thoughts, as this character is caught between the cracks of tradition and modernity (including the Maoist version of socialist modernity, exemplified by Erming's use of the revolutionary word *xisheng* [牺牲; "die a martyr's death"]. And for Miao Zhuang, I point out the fact that he always showers while singing the Neapolitan song *O sole mio*, but his westernization and modernization would be impossible without the nourishment of traditional Chinese culture, which is symbolized by water. After the discussion, I give students three questions to choose from for their response essay:

1. 老刘和两个儿子的关系如何? 电影是怎么表现的? 大明从开始到结束有什么变化? 电影又是怎么表现他的变化的?

   How does the film show the relationship between Lao Liu and his two sons? How does it cinematically depict Daming's changes throughout the film?

2. 谈一谈"水"在这个电影中的象征意义。"上善若水"什么意思? 在这个电影里谁是"上善若水"的最好例子? 为什么? 电影中出现两个插曲-陕北缺水和西藏的圣湖, 它们和影片有何关系?

   Please discuss the symbolism of water in this film. How do you understand the meaning of *shang shan ruo shui*? Which character best personalizes this concept and why? How would you relate the two episodes (the water shortage in northern Shaanxi [*Shower* 00:49:30–00:55:17] and the holy lake in Tibet [01:26:40–01:28:23]) to the rest of the film?

3. 《洗澡》这个电影想要传达什么主题? 你怎么看待传统和现代的关系?

What major theme does the film convey? What is your opinion on the relationship between tradition and modernity?

The short essay assignment not only helps improve the students' writing skills in Chinese by applying the words just learned from the film but also works as an effective way to check on students' engagement with class discussion and understanding of the film (see the appendix for an example student essay).

Bruce Lee's Philosophy of Water

After teaching *Shower* and before teaching *Ip Man*, I use Bruce Lee as a transition. I would start by showing the clip "Bruce Lee: Be Like Water" and Lee's 1964 screen test ("Bruce Lee"; see, particularly, 01:45–02:20) for the students to develop a sense of Bruce Lee's martial arts philosophy and metaphor of water. Some group activities can be incorporated here, such as having students work in pairs to translate or paraphrase the following two paragraphs of Lee's speech from English into Chinese:

> Empty your mind; be formless, shapeless, like water. If you put water in the cup, it becomes the cup. . . . Water can flow or water can crash. Be water, my friend. ("Bruce Lee: Be Like Water")

> The best example of Kungfu would be a glass of water. Because water is the softest substance in the world, but yet it can penetrate the hardest rock . . . Water is also insubstantial. By that I mean you cannot grasp hold of it. You cannot punch it or hurt it. So every kung fu student is trying to do that: to be soft like water and flexible and adapt itself to the opponent. ("Bruce Lee" 00:01:51–00:02:20)

After the students start to identify some Daoist components in Bruce Lee's martial arts philosophy, it will be natural for the instructor to introduce chapter 78 from the *Daodejing*—天下莫柔弱于水, 而攻坚强者莫之能胜 ("In all the world, nothing is more supple and weak than water; yet nothing can surpass it for attacking what is stiff and strong"; *Laozi* 193; my trans.)[2]—as well as the alternative thinking in Daoist philosophy, which prefers the weak over the strong, the yielding over the assertive, and the foolish over the wise. We then move to the beginning scene of Bruce Lee's classic film *Enter the Dragon*, in which Lee reports to his Shaolin master about his understanding of martial arts. I show students the English and the Chinese versions of the short clip respectively ("Beginning"; "Wo"; *Enter* 00:02:30–00:03:45). Besides language study, the students will discuss and interpret what Lee says, including "the highest technique of martial art is no technique. . . . I don't hit; it hits by itself" (*Enter* 00:02:50–00:02:53; 00:03:40–00:03:45). Here I relate Lee's words to the Daoist concept of *wuwei* (无为), which is perplexing to many students and is often misunderstood as passive nonaction. As the interdependence and mutual transformation of all opposites is a common theme in the *Daodejing*, *wei* and *wuwei* constitute a dialectical binary in which one element is embedded in the other and one can change into the other, and hence the Daoist saying *wuwei er wu bu wei* (无为而无不为; "do nothing and nothing is not done"). Therefore, *wuwei* should be more accurately interpreted as "act without acting" or "act without a particular intentionality or deliberate, goal-oriented thought or action." This Daoist philosophy is vividly illustrated in another short clip from *Enter the Dragon*, in which Lee states that his style of martial arts is the art of fighting without fighting ("Art"; *Enter* 00:32:05–00:33:45). Here I also introduce the related concept of *buzheng* (不争; "noncontention"), highlighted in chapter 22 of the *Daodejing*: 夫唯不争, 故天下莫能与之争 ("because [sages] do not contend, no one in the world can contend with them"; *Laozi* 58; my trans.). In the art of war, the best general wins without combat, and in the martial arts, the best fighter never has to fight. This type of wisdom is especially valuable for developing students' mental health in a highly competitive society.

Teaching *Ip Man*

The film *Ip Man* is based on the life events of the Wing Chun grandmaster Ip Man, who was also the teacher of Bruce Lee. As the first film in the four-installment *Ip Man* series, the 2008 film depicts the life of Ip Man in his hometown in Foshan before and during the Second Sino-Japanese War. It involves the protagonist's relationship with his family, his townspeople, the challengers from north China, and the Japanese colonizers.

Just as I highlighted the key expression *shang shan ruo shui* in the film *Shower*, I include *ren* (仁), discussed below; *rujia* (儒家; "Confucianism"); and *tui ji ji ren* (推己及人; "treat others as you would like to be treated") in the list of key terms and expressions for *Ip Man*. In class, I show a clip from the film that features Ip Man's voice-over, and we go over the original line in Chinese and the English translation:

> 武术虽然是一种武装的力量，但是我们中国武术是包含了儒家的哲理。武德也就是"仁"，推己及人，这是你们日本人永远都不会明白的道理。因为你们滥用武力，将武力变成暴力去欺压别人，你们不配学我们中国武术。("Rujia"; *Ip Man* 01:35:01–01:35:21)

> Although martial arts involve the use of armed force, Chinese martial arts are Confucian in spirit. The virtue of martial arts is *ren*. You Japanese will never understand the principle of treating others as you would yourselves, because you abuse military power. You turn it into violence to oppress others. You don't deserve to learn Chinese martial arts.

I intentionally leave the key Confucian concept of *ren* untranslated before introducing some most important passages on *ren* in the *Analects* of Confucius (*Lunyu*): *ren* as love in chapter 12, line 22, *ren* as 克己复礼 ("to subdue oneself and return to propriety") in 12.1, and *ren* as the five virtues of 恭 ("reverence"), 宽 ("generosity"), 信 ("truthfulness"), 敏 ("diligence"), and 惠 ("kindness") in 17.6. Moreover, the character *ren* consists of two components, one being the human radical and the other radical meaning "two." Sharing the same pronunciation as the character for "person" (人), *ren* is essentially about one's relationship to others. Therefore, the golden rule of Confucianism is *ji suo bu yu, wu shi yu ren* in *Analects* 12.2 and 15.24. After teaching about the multifaceted meanings of *ren*, I ask students how they would translate this term into English. They translate it variously as benevolence, love, humaneness, humanity, compassion, and sympathy. Next I guide students to analyze how Ip Man is depicted as *junzi* (君子; "a Confucian gentleman") and how he embodies *ren* when interacting with others. The students will then have a better understanding of the many questions they raised when watching the film: Why doesn't Ip Man want to teach his fellow townspeople in the beginning? Why does he use a feather duster to fight with the Northern challenger, Jin Shanzhao, who wields a sword? Why does Ip Man respond to the Japanese general Miura's question "What's your name" as "I'm just Chinese"? (01:01:12; my trans.). Because Ip Man personalizes Confucianism and Chineseness in this film, his victory over Miura in their duel is not just a triumph of Wing Chun over karate but also an assertion of the superiority of cultivated Chineseness over dehumanized Japaneseness in the context of the Japanese invasion.

In teaching specific clips, I combine instruction in language and culture in a holistic manner. In a scene that features *qiecuo* (切磋; "fighting in a friendly way"; "Qiecuo"; *Ip Man* 00:07:15–00:07:35), the students work

Figure 2. A still from the film *Ip Man* showing a Confucian couplet hanging in Ip Man's house.

in pairs, play the roles of Master Liao and Ip Man, and practice new words such as *bicibici* (彼此彼此; "be no better than" or "you too!"), *huoyi henduo* (获益很多; "benefit greatly"), and *ganjibujin* (感激不尽; "incredibly grateful"). They also learn how Ip Man is depicted as a cultivated Confucian gentleman in this scene, which shows a common couplet about honoring one's family through one's work and word: 承家事业辉堂构, 经世文章裕栋梁 (*Ip Man* 00:07:34; fig. 2). For a scene featuring *qiecuo* between Ip Man and his friend Wu Chilin, students transcribe the dialogue, add subtitles, and dub the dialogue when I play and mute the clip ("Gong"; *Ip Man* 00:14:46–00:16:34). As Wu talks about the dialectic between *fang* (防; "defense") and *gong* (攻; "offense") as in 攻中有防, 防中有攻, 攻不离防, 防不离攻 ("in an attack there is defense, in defense, there is attack; there is no defense without attack, and no attack without defense"; "Gong" 00:00:29; *Ip Man* 00:15:16), I connect this speech with what Bruce Lee says about the dialectic between *jin* (进; "forward") and *tui* (退; "back") in the film *Enter the Dragon*: 以退为进, 以进为退 ("When the opponent expands, I contract; when he contracts, I expand"; 00:03:32). In learning the language, the students simultaneously reinforce their understanding of the Daoist philosophy that all opposites are interdependent and interpenetrating and can transform from one to the other. Moreover, from the feminist perspective, Ip Man's softer, feminine-oriented Wing Chun fighting style, which defeats the harder, masculine martial arts such as Miura's karate and Jin Shanzhao's northern kungfu, better embodies Bruce Lee's philosophy of being like water than does Lee's own meticulously constructed image of shirtless, bloodied, and violent masculinity in *Enter the Dragon*. In a sense, the filmic Ip Man combines both Confucian and Daoist features.

After finishing the discussion of *Enter the Dragon* and *Ip Man*, I give students the following two questions for their response essay.

1. 请谈一谈李小龙的武术思想。为什么他觉得武术最好的例子是水？武术最高的境界是什么？

   Please discuss Bruce Lee's martial arts philosophy. Why did Lee think that the best example of kungfu is water? What does he think is the highest technique in martial arts?

2. 电影中叶问的武术思想跟李小龙的有什么异同？在电影中，叶问说："武术虽然是一种武装的力量，但是我们中国武术是包含了儒家的哲理。武德也就是'仁'，推己及人，… 你们不配学我们中国武术。" 你是怎么理解这段话的？在电影中，叶问是怎样处理"己"和"人"的关系的？哪些情节体现了叶问的儒家哲理？

   Compare the martial arts philosophies of Bruce Lee and Ip Man. How do you understand Ip Man's line in *Ip Man* about *ren* and Confucian wisdom ("Rujia")? How does Ip Man deal with his relationships with others? Discuss scenes from the film in your response.

As teachers of Chinese as a second language increasingly recognize the importance of developing cultural competence along with linguistic proficiency, this essay proposes a new holistic approach to integrate instruction in language and culture in order to simultaneously enhance students' multiple competences. As one student wrote in the course feedback, "It wasn't just a Chinese language course! I learned a lot about Chinese history and culture. I even got to participate in class discussions for which I didn't always know how I felt in English, let alone Chinese, so that was a really cool experience for me." Moreover, incorporating language components on the syllabus enables the class to explore aspects that would be missed in film courses taught in English. Therefore, this integrated approach is able to bridge the language-culture gap in class instruction and create more intellectually challenging and culturally enriched learning opportunities for language students.

Notes

1. Some critically acclaimed films were not included in the course, such as Ang Lee's *Crouching Tiger, Hidden Dragon*, because of its quasi-literary language, and Jia Zhangke's films and other independent films that are rendered in regional dialects. For more about the course, see Liu.

2. Unless otherwise indicated, translations from Chinese sources are mine.

Appendix: Sample Essay

The following essay (reproduced with permission) was written by a student, Rachel Hu, who chose to respond to the second prompt for the film *Shower*, about the symbolism of water in the film. This student does well in demonstrating both language use and cultural understanding in the essay. She not only makes an effort to use new idioms such as *zhi zu chang le* and *mang li tou xian* (忙里偷闲; "to take a short break from the busy schedule") but has also absorbed the class discussion about the Daoist philosophy of water. Moreover, she makes her own observation that Daming's real change in *Shower* begins when the character helps his father repair the roof damaged by rain; in other words, it is water, once again, that changes Daming.

在这部电影里水对每个人物的象征意义不一样。最基本的方面是在澡堂子里面各人用水洗澡的方法马上让你看出他是比较现代的还是比较传统的人。电影的第一个镜头就是何正在高技术的淋浴里用五分钟忙里偷闲洗个澡。这个水是快速而不愿意耽误时间，很像现代人的生活习惯。那对大明来说水代表他的变化，尤其是他从现代思想到理解他爸爸的看法。他刚回家的时候他也站着快快洗澡，急着买票回深圳。大明真的开始改变的刹那就是他帮老刘在雨中修屋顶的时候。你可以说是大自然的水把他改变了。因为暴雨和老刘生病，他很快找回了原来在北京的生活，到最后他也跟老刘和二明一起泡澡。

如果水代表大明的变化，那水代表二明的感情。二明一辈子在澡堂子里长大，天天在那里工作和跟老刘生活。大明的水总是雨，但是二明的水就是水管子。他每天用水管子装清水池的水和打扫澡堂子。他只需要有水就会知足常乐，因为水让他感觉很自在。在电影里有三次二明用水管子表达他的感情。第一个是在售票处外面的草地玩水，可以说这是为了跟大明沟通，他很高兴哥哥回家了。第二次是苗壮唱歌的时候，二明用水传给他安全的感觉。最后一次是人来拆澡堂子他用水管子做武器，把人挡在门外，代表他的哀痛。

老刘和水的象征意义跟他的儿子们是不同的。水没在代表，而是他代表水。上善若水的意思是说最好的人会像水一样，不怕自己做事情帮每个人。老刘常常在澡堂子里做两种服务，一边给客户澡堂子的服务，另外是帮社区的服务。比如说，虽然他安排了鸳鸯浴，改善那对夫妇的关系，可是他没有跟大家讲他做的好事。这就是上善若水的行为。

大明和二明的妈妈是从黄土高原来的。她的故事让我们看到干旱的地方水是珍贵的，每一滴水都要爱惜。这样，水也代表家庭的爱心，爸爸和儿子的关系不好的话非常难过。电影里的奶奶说那湖水不但能洗净身子，还可以洗净自己的灵魂，治百病。老刘去世以后澡堂就变成一种圣湖，让大明和二明慢慢地继续生活前进。

Works Cited

"The Art of Fighting without Fighting." *YouTube*, uploaded by sailingling1, 27 Jan. 2020, youtu.be/XAvvp0gkUiA.

"The Beginning of *Enter the Dragon* (English Soundtrack)." *YouTube*, uploaded by sailingling1, 26 June 2023, youtu.be/uPPspZeu7NM.

"Bruce Lee." *YouTube*, uploaded by Synai Rockz, 25 Aug. 2017, youtu.be/uOE3P7kDdg0.

"Bruce Lee: Be Like Water." *YouTube*, uploaded by MAX ASSOCIATES, 12 July 2013, youtu.be/APx2yFA0-B4.

Chungking Express. Directed by Wong Kar-wai, Jet Tone Production, 1994.

Dema, Oxana, and Aleidine Moeller. "Teaching Culture in the Twenty-First Century Language Classroom." *Touch the World: Selected Papers from the 2012 Central States Conference on the Teaching of Foreign Languages*, edited by Tatiana Sildus, Crown Prints, 2012, pp. 75–91.

Enter the Dragon. Directed by Robert Clouse, Warner Brothers, 1973.

二明丢了 ["Erming diule"; "Erming Goes Missing"]. *YouTube*, uploaded by sailingling1, 21 Aug. 2016, youtu.be/3nEbn-n_xFs.

攻中有防 ["Gong zhong you fang"; "There Is Defense in an Attack"]. *YouTube*, uploaded by sailingling1, 8 Sept. 2016, youtu.be/JPb_360B4P8.

In the Heat of the Sun. Directed by Jiang Wen, China Film Co-production, 1995.

Ip Man. Directed by Wilson Yip, Golden Harvest, 2008.

Kungfu Hustle. Directed by Stephen Chow, Columbia Pictures Film Production Asia, 2003.

老子 [*Laozi*]. Translated and Annotated by Rao Shangkuan, Zhonghua Shuju, 2016.

Liu, Jin. "Chinese-Language Cinema." *Jin Liu*, sites.gatech.edu/liu/chin-4031-chinese-language-cinema/.

The Lovers. Directed by Tsui Hark, Golden Harvest, 1998.

论语译注 [*Lunyu yizhu*; *An Annotated Translation of the* Analects]. Translated by Yang Bojun, Zhonghua Shuju, 2017.

Morain, Genelle. "A Perspective on Cultural Perspectives." *Bringing the Standards into the Classroom: A Teacher's Guide*, edited by Marcia Rosenbusch, 2nd ed., Iowa State U, 1997, pp. 35–37.

切磋 ["Qiecuo"; "Fighting in a Friendly Way"]. *YouTube*, uploaded by sailingling1, 24 Jan. 2019, youtu.be/p0vs7x_GYmc.

Ronan, Colin. *The Shorter Science and Civilisation in China.* Vol. 1, Cambridge UP, 1978.

儒家 ["Rujia"; "Confucianism"]. *YouTube*, uploaded by sailingling1, 24 Jan. 2019, youtu.be/ErmFab6bH-A.

Secret Love in Peach Blossom Land. Directed by Stan Lai, Performance Workshop / Long Shong Pictures, 1992.

Shower. Directed by Zhang Yang, Imar Film, 1999.

The Soong Sisters. Directed by Mabel Cheung, Golden Harvest, 1997.

Standards Foreign Language Learning in the Twenty-First Century. National
    Standards in Foreign Language Education Project, 2006.
To Live. Directed by Zhang Yimou, ERA International, 1994.
The Wandering Earth. Directed by Frant Gwo, China Film Group, 2019.
White Haired Girl. Directed by Shui Hua and Wang Bin, Changchun Film
    Studio Group, 1950.
《卧虎藏龙》开头 ["*Wo hu cang long* kaitou"; "The Beginning of *Crouching Tiger
    Hidden Dragon* (Chinese Soundtrack)"]. *YouTube*, uploaded by sailingling1,
    24 Aug. 2016, youtu.be/LkkCQO82zbc.
Zhang Li 张莉 and Chen Tianxu 陈天序, editors. 中国电影欣赏:《洗澡》[*Zhongguo
    dianying xinshang*: Xizao; *Watching the Movie and Learning Chinese*: Shower].
    Beijing Language and Culture UP, 2008.

Jingjing Cai and Su-I Chen

Developing Film-Based Teaching Materials for an Advanced Chinese Class

As film plays an increasingly integral role in the digital culture of students' lives outside of the classroom, the use of target-language films in language courses at all levels has become common. Films provide rich resources for language skill training. Researchers have identified many positive outcomes of using films in language classrooms, including motivating and sustaining students' interest in the target language (e.g., Garn; Harrison), providing real-life examples of pragmatic language use for students to apply appropriately in various contexts (e.g., Hekmati et al.; Kabooha), and enhancing students' awareness of contemporary social issues and intercultural competencies (e.g., Hughes; Ning).

However, research has shown that films are mainly used as supplementary material in language classes, suggesting that their pedagogical potential has not been fully explored (e.g., Hertel and Harrington; Kalra). Most language instructors do not primarily base their classes on films for a variety of reasons. First, films do not present language elements in accordance with the progression of difficulty in a typical sequence of language acquisition. Moreover, films are not systematically organized to align with specific learning objectives. In addition, the tremendous time and effort required for selection and preparation of appropriate film segments and teaching materials are a challenge for most language teachers.

In this essay we challenge this trend by investigating the use of films as primary materials in a fourth-year Chinese course with the goals of improving the language skills of students and developing their knowledge of contemporary Chinese social issues. The impetus to develop film-based teaching materials arose from a perceived lack of engaging film-based textbooks for our students. In particular, we observed that numerous innovations reported in studies of teaching Chinese language through films have not found their way into film-based textbooks, causing a mismatch between available materials and our course goals. We decided to bridge that gap, first by surveying existing film-based Chinese language textbooks and reflecting on their suitability for our course and then by identifying the essential components of film-based teaching materials based on our experience and students' feedback. As a report of our study, this essay includes a review of existing textbooks, a description of the process of designing and implementing teaching materials, a report of students' feedback on their use, and a conclusion about the pedagogical potential of using films as primary materials for language acquisition.

Survey of Film-Based Textbooks

We reviewed two popular types of film-based language textbooks—film-script-based and adapted-narrative-based—to examine their suitability for advanced Chinese language instruction given the course goals of improving language skills and developing students' knowledge about contemporary Chinese social issues: *Lens on China* (影像中国), *Learning Chinese through Movies* (看电影学汉语), *Watching the Movie and Learning Chinese* (中国电影欣赏), *China in Movies* (电影看中国), and *Learning Chinese through Film* (看电影学汉语). *Lens on China* is adaptive-narrative-based, whereas the other textbooks are film-script-based. *Lens on China* focuses on ten films and provides one or two adapted narratives and scene descriptions for each film. The adapted narratives introduce the plot and the film's social context, and the scenes described are crucial to the theme of the film. These well-written adapted narratives and descriptive summaries are used in place of the film scripts, which lack the formal language appropriate for language instruction. Moreover, while film scripts do not present progressively more difficult language learning points, the adapted narratives and the scene descriptions are carefully written to align with a typical sequence of language acquisition. However, lacking authentic film scripts as teaching materials makes *Lens on China* less attractive to language learners, who tend to find scripts the most enticing and valuable components of film-based materials.

In contrast, *Learning Chinese through Movies* features script-based dialogues from seven films, with no adapted narratives or descriptive sections. The film scripts render the textbook suitable for learners seeking authentic materials for audiovisual and oral exercises. Although the film scripts make this book engaging, its lack of sufficient grammatical explanations and exercises and absence of adapted narratives or scene descriptions written in formal language make it inadequate as a primary text for an advanced language class.

Watching the Movie and Learning Chinese is an engaging script-based series of textbooks, each of which focuses on a single film. Each volume centers on what the series authors define as cultural elements of the film discussed, elaborating on each point in both English and Chinese, which makes the series desirable for self-learners pursuing further contextual understanding. However, each volume's focus on a single film limits the teacher's options for selecting appropriate film segments for language instruction.

China in Movies is a script-based book series that combines appreciation of Chinese films with the teaching of social and cultural context. Volumes in this series are the only textbooks under review that feature bilingual learning materials throughout and can be used as readers in non-language-focused courses. Nevertheless, these books are designed for the general study of films, not for intensive language learning.

Learning Chinese through Film is written entirely in Chinese. This script-based textbook features twenty films but focuses largely on background information about actors, directors, and awards, which might be less engaging to students than learning about the films themselves.

In sum, we find that the surveyed textbooks are inadequate in one or more of the following aspects: language exercises, grammatical explanations, and dialogue in realistic contexts. None, therefore, is ideal for university students who want to enhance and consolidate their Chinese language proficiency and expand their understanding of contemporary Chinese social and cultural issues through the study of Chinese films.

Materials Design: An Overview

After the review, we designed film-based materials tailored to our students' needs that combined the advantages of the aforementioned textbooks while avoiding their inadequacies. The course was designed for fourth-year Chinese language students whose proficiency levels ranged from high intermediate to low advanced. Over two consecutive semesters, we used six narrative and three documentary films to introduce students to a variety of Chinese societal issues. These films were used as primary materials (table 1), and no textbooks were adopted.

At the initial stage of materials design, we conducted a survey of students' favorite film topics. The survey revealed that students preferred films about social issues (the most popular topic), youth drama and science fiction (tied for second-most popular), and historical events (third most popular). Our film selections therefore largely reflected the following preferences: the films should be easily accessible—meaning that they have English subtitles and are available through common online streaming

Table 1. Film list

Film	Genre	Related topics	Language features	Sources
Please Vote for Me	Documentary	Elections, democracy	Political, formal	YouTube, Kanopy
Our Shining Days	High school romance	Animation, comics, and games subculture, Chinese versus Western music	Slang, classical Chinese	Netflix
Young Style	Drama	College entrance exam, puppy love	Slang, formal	YouTube, Dailymotion
Lost, Found	Drama	Gender, social class	Legal, formal	YouTube
Hello, Mr. Billionaire	Comedy	Charity versus greed	Business, legal	Amazon Prime Video
A Young Patriot	Documentary	Youth culture, nationalism	Political	YouTube, Dailymotion
Dying to Survive	Drama	Social justice, medical system	Legal, formal	Amazon Prime Video
The Wandering Earth	Science fiction	Humanity and nature, artificial intelligence, hope for human survival	Media, science, and engineering	Netflix
A City with Zero New Cases of COVID-19	Documentary	Pandemic, life in quarantine	Medical	YouTube

platforms—represent a variety of film genres, address diverse social issues in contemporary China, and provide a wide range of language uses (e.g., formal and informal registers, Mandarin, and other dialects).

Films were arranged according to the level of language difficulty, the complexity of the topics, and their relatability to students' interests and experiences. For example, *Please Vote for Me* (请为我投票) was the first film because it is set in an elementary school and because the language is relatively easy for students. *The Wandering Earth* (流浪地球), a science fiction film, was placed toward the end of the course packet because the theme of human survival in the distant future is comparatively abstract and less relatable to students. *A City with Zero New Cases of COVID-19* (南京抗疫现场), a minidocumentary about coping with the sudden outbreak of the pandemic, was chosen for its currency and to familiarize students with vocabulary and social issues highly relevant under the conditions caused by the pandemic.

Materials Design: Structure and Content

After selecting the films, we designed a course packet based solely on the scripts of four films, which we transcribed: *Please Vote for Me, Our Shining Days* (闪光少女), *Young Style* (青春派), and *Lost, Found* (找到你). After using the course packet for a semester, we found that, while students preferred learning from film scripts that feature native speakers' natural expressions, some considered such scripts unchallenging because they were limited to simple structures and often lacked formal uses of the language. We also found that using film scripts alone does not advance students' mastery of grammar because there is no systematic progression of grammatical difficulty in the scripts.

Reflecting on students' feedback, we designed a new course packet for the second semester, covering five films: *Hello, Mr. Billionaire* (西虹市首富), *A Young Patriot* (少年小赵), *Dying to Survive* (我不是药神), *The Wandering Earth*, and *A City with Zero New Cases of COVID-19* (see Cai and Chen, "Film-Based Course Packet Samples"). This course packet includes adapted narratives, or storyline summaries, which provide a comprehensive description of the film and incorporate focal vocabulary and sentence structures for language practice, and two dialogues from each film script to center discussion on the major topics of the film. The rationale for this new design was that the adapted narrative supports formal language learning, and the dialogues provide exposure to authentic language use. The adapted narratives and dialogues are supplemented with the following elements to reinforce in-depth learning: pre-viewing questions to prepare students for film viewing and in-class discussion, exercises to consolidate students' understanding of the film and its social topics, a grammar section and review exercises to reinforce students' mastery of grammar, and task-based activities for students to practice the language in authentic contexts.

Teaching *Dying to Survive*

The revised packet includes materials to be read alongside a viewing of each of the five films. We screened each film in its entirety to give students an extensive viewing experience, and we used selected film clips with the course packet for in-depth language and culture teaching. Below, we use *Dying to Survive* as an example to illustrate how the reading packet was used along with the film in the classroom.

Dying to Survive is a 2018 Chinese drama about how the owner of a small drugstore, Cheng Yong, smuggles into China a cheap Indian generic drug for leukemia and saves innumerable cancer patients. This unit was taught in ten class hours, with eight class hours dedicated to instruction and two hours allocated for assessment (Cai and Chen, "Application" 105). Before the first class, students viewed the entire film and prepared to discuss it based on pre-viewing questions about scenes in the film, which we designed in lieu of providing a summary of the film in order to engage students cognitively with the film and the issues it presents.[1]

Pre-viewing Questions for *Dying to Survive*

1. 吕受益是谁? 他为什么要找程勇帮忙?

   Who is Lü Shouyi? Why does he ask Cheng Yong for help?

2. 程勇是谁? 他一开始为什么不愿意走私仿制药? 后来为什么又愿意了?

   Who is Cheng Yong? Why isn't he initially willing to smuggle the generic drugs? Why does he later change his mind?

3. 程勇的卖药五人团有哪些人?

   Who is in Cheng Yong's five-member drug-selling group?

4. 程勇退出五人团后为什么又回来了?

   Why does Cheng Yong come back after leaving the group?

5. 这部电影反映了中国社会中什么现实问题?

   What real problems in Chinese society are reflected in this film?

In the first class, students discussed the primary characters and the theme of the film. In the following two classes, students used the adapted narrative to summarize the storyline and discuss Cheng Yong's contribution to health insurance reform. Students were expected to recognize the social issues behind the story and to use new lesson-specific vocabulary and grammar patterns in class discussion. See the following breakdown of topics for the first eight class hours.

Hour	Topic
1	Warm-up: the pre-viewing questions
2	Narrative 1: the five-member team of characters and the story
3	Narrative 2: the social issues reflected in the film
4	Dialogue 1: the conflicts between the police and the patients
5	Dialogue 2: Cheng Yong's sentencing
6	Extensive reading of a film review
7	Interviewing outside sources and reporting the results in class: students' opinions of medical issues in China as depicted in the film
8	Writing and delivering a speech

After studying the adapted narrative, the students learned two script-based dialogues, which for two class hours immersed them in simulated real-life contexts for language use. The first dialogue, between a patient and a police officer, was selected for students to learn about the hardships of cancer patients and a dilemma of law enforcement in a community context. The dialogue demonstrates the conflict between the patients, who have to break the law to survive, and the police officers, who have to arrest the drug smugglers while knowing that they are the only saviors for the patients (*Dying to Survive* 01:22:04–01:24:15). The second dialogue—a courtroom exchange between, on one side, the defendant Cheng Yong and his attorney and, on the other side, the attorney of the pharmaceutical company—was selected to spark a debate on the balance between sentiment and law in a formal context. Cheng's attorney pleads for a lesser sentence for his client on the grounds of his good intentions and altruistic behavior. The opposing attorney, on the other hand, claims that Cheng must be severely punished for his violation of international intellectual property law, which has resulted in the pharmaceutical company's significant financial loss and a flood of counterfeit drugs nationwide (*Dying to Survive* 01:45:41–01:49:30). Before each class, students viewed the clips featuring the dialogues and completed a set of postviewing questions.

Postviewing Questions about the Courtroom Dialogue

1. True or False:

    a. 根据诺瓦公司律师的陈述, 是诺瓦公司, 而不是印度仿制药救了慢粒白血病人。

       According to the statement by the lawyer for the pharmaceutical company Nova, it was Nova's drug, not the Indian generic drug, that saved the leukemia patients.

    b. 根据程勇律师的陈述, 程勇没有触犯法律法规。

       According to the statement by Cheng's lawyer, Cheng did not violate any law or regulation.

    c. 根据程勇的陈述, 法庭怎么判他都接受。

       According to Cheng's statement, Cheng accepts the verdict, whatever it may be.

    d. 根据法庭的判决, 程勇的行为是为了救人而非盈利, 应给予一定程度的理解, 所以只判有期徒刑两年。

       According to the court's ruling, a degree of understanding should be given to Cheng because his action was intended to save people, not to make a profit. Hence, he is sentenced to only two years in prison.

2. Match items in the left and right columns to form verb+object structures:

   触犯 to violate   有期徒刑 a fixed term of imprisonment
   宣布 to declare   法律法规 laws and regulations
   判处 to sentence to   判决结果 a verdict
   导致 to cause   假药泛滥 the proliferation of counterfeit drugs

3. Highlight the crime or crimes that Cheng Yong committed, according to the court verdict:

   销售假药罪 selling counterfeit drugs
   杀人罪 homicide
   走私罪 smuggling
   盗窃罪 theft

4. Short answer question:

   如果你是程勇, 你会冒犯法的危险帮患者买仿制药吗? 请说明原因 (100 字左右)。

   If you were Cheng Yong, would you violate the law to buy generic drugs for patients? Please explain your reason (in about one hundred words).

In class, the instructors played the clips again and explained the usage of key words and sentence structures. Students then assumed roles in the dialogues and argued for their positions on each controversy presented in the film, using lesson-specific vocabulary and grammar patterns. The purposes of this activity were for students to view an issue from different perspectives, to cultivate their critical thinking skills, and to apply appropriate registers in formal and informal linguistic contexts. To consolidate their in-depth learning with the adapted narrative and dialogues, students were assigned task-based exercises, including writing an essay, engaging in a dialogue, and delivering a formal speech.

A Double-Layered Design

We believe that the design for an effective film-based language class should include double-layered multimedia input: that is, extensive input consisting of entire films and supplementary readings and intensive input consisting of analysis of selected film clips. Films provide rich visual and audio inputs that include action, mise-en-scène, dialogue, captions, music, and sound effects to immerse students in cinematic contexts that emulate real life, making them meaningful communicative input for language and culture learning (VanPatten). Our course packet, which included the adapted narratives, dialogues, vocabulary, grammar, and task-based exercises, effectively bridged the film's input and students' language output. With the scaffolding provided by learning vocabulary and grammar through the adapted narratives and dialogues, students were able to perform task-based assignments successfully. In this section we discuss how we complemented the intensive-input design (a close examination of and practice with focal vocabulary, sentence structures, and discourse conventions) with an extensive-input approach (vicarious culture immersion and cultivation of a feel for the pragmatics of language use) and the rationale for doing so.

One student considered that spending two hours watching a film was a difficult time commitment in addition to other homework. Nevertheless, we found that viewing entire films and watching film clips were equally important for learning language through film. Viewing entire films provided an experience of sustained language and cultural immersion, while watching selected film clips with guiding materials supported in-depth language training. While the latter introduced new words and sentence patterns to students, the former provided a wide base of language reinforcement. By encountering new vocabulary and grammar from the film *Dying to Survive* in a variety of contexts, students learned how to extend their Chinese language use in contextually appropriate ways. According to William Holden, intensive learning can lead to better student performance in extensive learning (305–06). Cağrı Tuğrul Mart also argues that "the combination of extensive and intensive reading leads to substantial proficiency gains in [the] language learning process; while extensive reading aims at fluency, intensive reading aims at accuracy" (85). Our surveys, discussed below, revealed that most of our students agreed with these claims.

In addition to assigning complete films, we designed extensive reading activities to supplement intensive learning. In experiment 1, students were required to select and read one film review from the social media website *Douban* after viewing an entire film and to post their comments before the first class. However, this extensive reading assignment with minimal teacher involvement did not go well because students were overwhelmed by the numerous film reviews on *Douban*.

Accordingly, in experiment 2, we replaced this unsuccessful practice with two guided extensive reading practices to facilitate reading fluency. First, we selected and adapted one film review based on students' proficiency level: for example, in the *Dying to Survive* unit, a film review defending the legal rights of the pharmaceutical company and exploring the meaning of the film's Chinese title (*I Am Not the God of Medicine*), which students skimmed and scanned for a general understanding of the review before in-class discussions (Andreja). Second, we selected a subset of reviews for each film and marked their difficulty levels, for example, six film reviews of *A Young Patriot*; each student selected one and applied skimming, scanning, and predicting strategies to determine the theme of the review, which they then described in a written summary and in-class sharing. The first reading practice adds another perspective to the existing viewpoints in the film and motivates students' in-depth discussion. The second practice trains students to summarize main arguments and share their selected reviews with classmates. As the students select different readings, this sharing broadens their understanding of both the film and its related social issues.

Student Surveys

We conducted two student surveys, one at the end of each semester. The surveys had two parts: part 1 focused on students' interest in and motivation for using films as primary materials, and part 2 focused on film selection, the use of subtitles, materials design, and the extensive readings. Thirty students participated in the surveys.

All the students responded positively to using films as primary materials in language classes. First, the films captured and sustained their attention during the learning process. Second, the fascinating storylines of the films enhanced their interest in learning Chinese. Third, the films presented authentic language use in realistic contexts, which they learned and imitated while being immersed in the films' intricate settings and sounds. Fourth, providing bilingual subtitles with the selected dialogue clips helped students improve their reading and listening comprehension. Finally, the films proved valuable for facilitating students' understanding of cultural phenomena and bridging language and culture learning.

The surveys revealed that our students paid particular attention to the nonverbal elements in the films (i.e., mise-en-scène, cinematography, editing, and music and other nonverbal sounds), suggesting further benefits of films for learning about and connecting to the target culture. For example, our students were intrigued by the frequent classroom scenes in the film *Young Style*, in which Chinese students preparing for the Chinese National College Entrance Examination are surrounded by stacks of books on their desks. Our students found these scenes relatable to their own experiences of applying to college. Such imagery helps students participate substantively in discussions of issues in contemporary Chinese society and culture.

The majority of students were not concerned about the length and genres of the assigned films; whether a film was a two-hour feature film or a minidocumentary did not significantly affect their motivation and interest. However, students preferred films with meaningful and engaging themes, a realistic and relatable storyline, clear representation of social issues, and a blend of educational and entertaining content. Therefore, we recommend that teachers review films with diverse themes and survey students before finalizing their course syllabi to ensure that the selected films are in line with students' interests.

Several studies support the idea that L1 subtitles (which are in the students' first language) help students remember and understand the story more than do L2 (target language) subtitles or not having subtitles (Napikul et al. 110). Paula Winke and colleagues reveal that learners used L2 subtitles to increase their attention, improve processing, reinforce previous knowledge, and analyze language. For pedagogical purposes, we had students first watch entire films with L1 (English) subtitles for comprehension and then watch clips with L2 (Chinese) subtitles for language learning. However, our survey showed that students preferred having bilingual subtitles in English and Chinese over monolingual subtitles or no subtitles. Students commented that listening to and reading Chinese at the same time could help them learn new words and improve Chinese listening and reading skills, but Chinese subtitles alone were insufficient to aid their comprehension. All the students reported that bilingual subtitles improved their recognition of Chinese characters, all but one student found that subtitles enhanced their listening comprehension and overall understanding of the story, and half of the students responded that the subtitles helped them recognize sentence structures. Only one student commented that subtitles do more harm than good because they deprive students of listening practice. Students' strong preference for bilingual subtitles could be related to the need to accommodate a wide range of proficiency levels in the class.

A majority of the students responded positively to the second course packet's inclusion of an adapted narrative and two dialogues for each film. They reported that the adapted narratives, by summarizing the plot and emphasizing the main themes of the film, pointed them in the right direction for understanding the film and prepared them for class discussion. Moreover, they found the language used in the adapted narratives appropriate for their current proficiency levels and a good model for formal language learning. They also appreciated that the language used in the selected dialogues represented a diverse range of registers and accents in real-life contexts and provided them with simulated immersive learning experiences.

Some studies suggest that teachers should facilitate students' extensive reading and listening activities (Hitosugi and Day; Stoller). We did this by selecting a limited number of film reviews suitable for students' proficiency levels. Our survey results confirmed a positive connection between teachers' involvement and students' performance in extensive reading practices. Students indicated that the reading strategies introduced by the teachers in guided extensive reading practices helped them read articles slightly above their usual proficiency levels.

The purpose of our study was to explore the potential of films and related study materials as primary texts in an advanced Chinese language class. Our findings support the use of two viewing practices to maximize the effective use of films: viewing film clips for intensive learning (i.e., a close examination of and practice with focal vocabulary, sentence structures, and discourse conventions) and viewing entire films for extensive learning (i.e., vicarious cultural immersion and cultivation of a feel for the pragmatics of language use). Our findings do not support such practices as the exclusive use of film scripts, which often lack the language complexity needed as input for advanced language learning, and the exclusive use of story summaries, which lack dialogue that students can imitate and apply in real-life situations. We suggest that, to achieve the goals of a language course, film-based teaching materials should use film scripts and the films themselves to fully capture the elements of language used (i.e., register, accents, dialects, and idioms) and adapted narratives that progressively incorporate greater linguistic complexity.

This study represents a preliminary effort to empirically examine the efficacy of using films as primary materials in an advanced Chinese language class. Future researchers might investigate the use of films as primary versus secondary materials with designs that enable comparison of the two approaches. Further studies might also focus on students at different levels of proficiency. In particular, the present study has shown that advanced students found effective the inclusion of adapted narratives and dialogues in the course packet. However, whether the adapted-narrative component is effective at beginning levels, in which most textbooks provide dialogues as learning materials, has yet to be explored.

Note

1. See Herron et al. for the importance of pre-viewing questions in facilitating students' video comprehension.

Works Cited

Andreja. "A Pharmaceutical Researcher's Countless Thoughts and Anxieties While Watching *Dying to Survive.*" *Douban*, 8 Aug. 2018, 9:00 a.m., movie .douban.com/review/9498742/.

Cai, Jingjing, and Su-I Chen. "The Application of Films in Advanced Chinese Language Courses: A Cooperative-Collaborative Learning Model." *Journal of Technology and Chinese Language Teaching*, vol. 11, no. 1, 2020, pp. 84–113, www.tclt.us/journal/2020v11n1/caichen.pdf.

———. "Film-Based Course Packet Samples." emailsichen.wixsite.com/cai-chen.

A City with Zero New Cases of COVID-19. Directed by Ryo Takeuchi, Hezhimeng Culture Communication, 2020.

Dying to Survive. Directed by Wen Muye, Dirty Monkey Films Group, 2018.

Garn, Rimma. "Teaching the Five CS with Cinema." *Journal of the National Council of Less Commonly Taught Languages*, vol. 12, no. 1, 2012, pp. 37–71.

Harrison, Lucia Guzzi. "Foreign Films in the Classroom: Gateway to Language and Culture." *Journal of College Teaching and Learning*, vol. 6, no. 8, 2009, pp. 89–94, www.clutejournals.com/index.php/TLC/article/view/1118/1102.

Hekmati, Nargess, et al. "Movie-Generated EFL Writing: Discovering the Act of Writing through Visual Literacy Practices." *International Journal of Language Studies*, vol. 12, no. 2, 2018, pp. 51–64. *ERIC*, files.eric.ed.gov/fulltext/ED581474.pdf.

Hello, Mr. Billionaire. Directed by Yan Fei and Peng Damo, Slinky Town Pictures / Fun Age Entertainment / Starry Entertainment / New Classics Media, 2018.

Herron, Carol, et al. "Do Prequestioning Techniques Facilitate Comprehension of French Video?" *The French Review*, vol. 72, no. 6, 1999, pp. 1076–90. *JSTOR*, www.jstor.org/stable/399503.

Hertel, Tammy Jandrey, and Stasie Harrington. "Promoting Cultural and Linguistic Competence with Documentary Film in Spanish." *Hispania*, vol. 98, no. 3, 2015, pp. 549–69. *JSTOR*, www.jstor.org/stable/24572753.

Hitosugi, Claire Ikumi, and Richard R. Day. "Extensive Reading in Japanese." *Reading in a Foreign Language*, vol. 16, no. 1, 2004, pp. 20–30. *ERIC*, files.eric.ed.gov/fulltext/EJ689101.pdf.

Holden, William R., III. "Extensive Listening: A New Approach to an Old Problem." *Journal of the Faculty of Humanities*, U of Toyama, vol. 49, 2008, pp. 299–312.

Hughes, Haning Z. "China through the Lens: Teaching Chinese Language and Culture through Film." *Dimension*, 2019, pp. 42–56.

Kabooha, Raniah Hassen. "Using Movies in EFL Classrooms: A Study Conducted at the English Language Institute (ELI), King Abdul-Aziz University." *English Language Teaching*, vol. 9, no. 3, 2016, pp. 248–67.

Kalra, Rusma. "The Effectiveness of Using Films in the EFL Classroom: A Case Study Conducted at an International University in Thailand." *Arab World English Journal*, vol. 8, no. 3, 2017, pp. 289–301.

Lost, Found. Directed by Lü Yue, Huayi Brothers Media / Shanghai Film Group TV Series Production / Bad Rabbit Film / Haining Yixian Film Culture, 2018.

Mart, Cağrı Tuğrul. "Combining Extensive and Intensive Reading to Reinforce Language Learning." *Journal of Educational and Instructional Studies in the World*, vol. 5, no. 4, 2015, pp. 85–90.

Napikul, Supakorn, et al. "The Effects of Film Subtitles on English Listening Comprehension and Vocabulary." *International Journal of Applied Linguistics and English Literature*, vol. 7, no. 6, 2018, pp. 104–11.

Ning, Cynthia. "Engaging a 'Truly Foreign' Language and Culture: China through Chinese Film." *Educational Perspectives*, vol. 42, 2009, pp. 29–35.

Our Shining Days. Directed by Wang Ran, Edko Films, 2017.

Please Vote for Me. Directed by Chen Weijun, Steps International, 2007.

Stoller, Fredricka L. "Viewing Extensive Reading from Different Vantage Points." *Reading in a Foreign Language*, vol. 27, no. 1, 2015, pp. 152–59.

VanPatten, Bill. "Film and Language Acquisition." *Hispania*, 2015, pp. 391–93.

The Wandering Earth. Directed by Guo Fan, China Film Group, 2019.

Wang, Jing, and Xi Tian. *Lens on China*. Hong Kong UP, 2020.

Wang, Xianghui, and Wenqing Yu. *Watching the Movie and Learning Chinese*. Beijing Language and Culture UP, 2009.

Wang, Xiaoling. *Learning Chinese through Film*. Shanxi Normal U General Publishing, 2005.

Winke, Paula, et al. "The Effects of Captioning Videos Used for Foreign Language Listening Activities." *Language Learning and Technology*, vol. 14, no. 1, 2010, pp. 65–86.

Yan, Li. *China in Movies*. Foreign Language Teaching and Research Press, 2011.

A Young Patriot. Directed by Du Haibin, 24 Images, 2015.

Young Style. Directed by Liu Jie, Hubei Huanggang Radio and Television Digital Media / China Film / CCTV-6 Program Centre, 2013.

Zhao, Yunhui, and Xiaoyu Liu. *Learning Chinese through Movies*. Beijing World Publishing, 2011.

Part VII

Multidisciplinary Approaches

Seio Nakajima

Teaching Chinese Independent Cinema through the Cultural-Diamond Framework

This essay outlines pedagogical tips on teaching Chinese film in sociology and related courses by putting to work the "cultural diamond" framework presented by the sociologist Wendy Griswold (Griswold and Carroll xiv). The cultural diamond consists of four corners—cultural object, social world, creator, and receiver—which are connected by six lines (fig. 1). "[A] complete [sociological] understanding of a given cultural object requires understanding all four points and six links" (Griswold and Carroll 16). In illustrating sociological pedagogy, I focus on Chinese independent cinema—defined broadly as relatively low-budget films, including both fiction and documentary, that target a relatively small group of audiences interested in the Chinese equivalent of art-house cinema.

In teaching Chinese film sociologically, an instructor can encourage students to go beyond the simplistic notion that a film is an objective

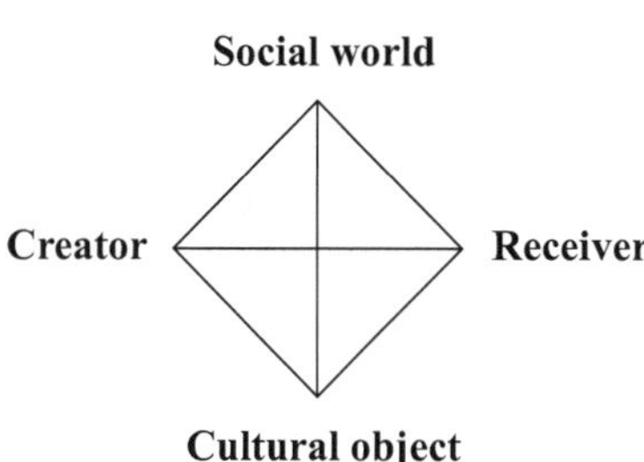

Figure 1. The cultural-diamond framework. Adapted from Griswold and Carroll, p. 15, fig. 1.1.

287

reflection of social reality. Chinese independent films provide valuable resources for understanding the realities of Chinese society. For example, documentary films by the Chinese New Documentary Film movement (described in C. Berry et al.) vividly depict people's lives at the grassroots. However, even documentary films, not to say fiction films, have cinematic conventions for production that strongly influence their representations of reality.[1]

The points and links in the cultural diamond are closely related to each other, and hence an effective pedagogy would include multiple points and links, if not the entire diamond. Because this essay focuses on sociological pedagogy, which emphasizes the inputs from creators and receivers as well as from the social world, I zero in on three subsections of the diamond. First, I examine the link between the social world and the cultural object (in this case, film) to show the potential and limitation of the reflection view of film and society. Second, I discuss the links between the social world, creator, and cultural object by examining the social conditions that have enabled the emergence of independent filmmakers and their works in China. Third, I describe the links between the social world, receiver, and cultural object by tackling how independent films are exhibited and watched by audiences and under what kind of circumstances. Fourth, in addition to the three subsections I expand the cultural-diamond framework by exploring transnational dynamics affecting Chinese independent films. Fifth, I extend the time horizon of the framework by discussing historical changes.[2] Last, I present a key pedagogical takeaway of this essay.

A caveat is in order at this point. The cultural-diamond framework should not be treated as a rigid explanatory theory that presupposes answers. As I illustrate below, the framework does not assume a priori causal primacy of any of the four points and six links. Instructors are encouraged to treat the cultural diamond as an open-ended framework that provides students with possible foci when they examine social and cultural contexts within which Chinese films are embedded. The framework is flexible enough to be used in conjunction with a variety of theories, to be chosen by instructors and students.

The Link between the Social World and the Cultural Object

How can we understand Chinese society by watching Chinese independent films? Although an instructor needs to encourage students to go beyond treating a film as an objective reflection of social reality, a close reading of a film text in relation to the social world is often quite valuable for sociological learning. Let me illustrate the pedagogical utility of teaching the social world–cultural object link by allegorically analyzing the film *Frozen* (极度寒冷), directed by Wang Xiaoshuai, who used the pseudonym Wu Ming for the film.[3]

Qi Lei, the film's protagonist, is a young, struggling artist who lives under the bleak social atmosphere of Beijing after the 1989 Tiananmen Square protests. He murmurs, "Each day, life is a major strain on me. I get very agitated. At day's end, I'm completely exhausted."[4] Qi Lei becomes increasingly attracted to the idea of death and stages a performance of his own suicide, in which he melts blocks of ice with his body and dies of hypothermia. "He calls this protest against the coldness of society 'Funeral on Ice' (冰葬)" ("*Frozen* Plot").

The film's opening blacked-out screen lasts for more than one minute, during which only the film production credits appear in a white gothic font without any sound. Then, as the ominous music composed by Roeland Dol begins, a voice-over introduces the film as follows: "The story is based on a real event. On 20 June 1994, on the eve of the first day of summer, a youth crowned his brief career as a performance artist with his own suicide. Nobody could say what his motives had been. But it did make people wonder: Is a life too high a price to pay for a work of art?" As the voice-over tells us, it is impossible to determine the real motive of his suicide. However, if we carefully watch and interpret the film, an allegorical reading is possible. In the film, the constraining political power of the party-state is represented as a psychiatric institution where Qi Lei is taken by his girlfriend and an artist friend for a medical examination. The scene is quite gloomy, with two broad-shouldered doctors in white coats taking away the patient. A twist in the story is that the doctors mistake Qi Lei's artist friend as the patient to be treated. Even though the friend repeatedly shouts out that Qi Lei is the patient and not him, the self-proclamation is completely ignored. The misrecognition allegorically reveals a comedic but deep disappointment of Qi Lei's generation of Chinese youth, who hope to at least be suppressed because of their true identities and not because of a mistake. This allegorical reading reveals that anyone outside of the system—including avant-garde artists like Qi Lei and his friends—is considered abnormal and has to be reeducated and rehabilitated within the government-approved rules and institutions.

Moreover, we can glean the economic logic in the representation of Qi Lei's brother-in-law, who lives with Qi Lei and his sister. After learning that Qi Lei has suicidal tendencies, the brother-in-law sneaks into Qi Lei's room and attempts to steal his paintings. Found out by his wife (i.e., Qi Lei's sister), the brother-in-law justifies his action: "Qi Lei is so confused. I must save some paintings for him. I've heard if a painter becomes famous, the price soars. The dealers know that Qi Lei becomes famous one day." Reprimanded by his wife, the brother-in-law returns the paintings, but the scene shows the increasingly prevalent logic of the market economy and of commercialism, which encroaches on artistic autonomy.

The film *Frozen* presents us with the possibility that there exist three contradictory logics surrounding artistic endeavors in contemporary Chinese society. First is the political logic, the purpose of which is to legitimize the rule of the party-state. Second is the economic logic, which involves being successful commercially in an increasingly competitive market economy. Third is the logic of artistic autonomy, or the freedom to pursue art for art's sake independent of the logic of politics and the logic of economics. If we further extend the allegorical reading, we could argue that Qi Lei reflects the director Wang Xiaoshuai, who has pursued the autonomous logic of art independent of political encroachment and commercial pressure. This argument could be buttressed by the fact that the director produced the film by hiding his real identity.

At this point, however, an instructor can encourage students to think critically about the potential pitfalls of this sort of reflection theory and to explore more complex relationships between the film text and the social context of production and consumption by referring to other points and links in the cultural-diamond framework. The instructor can assign published interviews with the director on the production context of *Frozen* (e.g., M. Berry 162–80) and discuss the possibility that Wang Xiaoshuai might have used a pseudonym not simply to avoid interference from the government in the making of the film but to allow him to continue with his next independent film production. At the time of the release of *Frozen*, he was preparing for another film and was negotiating with the state-owned Beijing Film Studio about its production. Indeed, Wang Xiaoshuai was able to produce the film, *So Close to Paradise* (扁担姑娘), with the state's official approval (in the form of a *gongying xukezheng* [公映许可证; "public exhibition permit"]) through the Beijing Film Studio, although the process of getting the film through the censors took three full years, after which it was completed and finally released (see M. Berry 162–80). In sum, although an instructor can encourage students to understand Chinese society through allegorical readings of independent films like *Frozen*, students should also examine the broader social contexts of production and consumption, as I examine below.

The Links between the Social World, Creator, and Cultural Object

How did the political, economic, and social conditions in the early 1990s enable the emergence of Chinese independent cinema? An instructor may teach students about the processes through which broader political-economic conditions—such as the deepening of economic reforms, urbanization, and attendant social issues in China in the late 1980s to the early 1990s, together with the introduction of new technology such as digital videos (DVs)—enabled the emergence of Chinese independent filmmakers, who began to produce innovative works in the 1990s.

Most Chinese independent film directors came into filmmaking after the fifth-generation directors had established their global reputations. These independent film directors, often known as the sixth generation, received their training at the Beijing Film Academy in the late 1980s and the early 1990s, when the academy had fully recovered from the Cultural Revolution. They are also called the "urban generation" of film directors since in their films they deal with the issue of rapid social change and the social problems that emerged in China's urban areas in the 1990s (Z. Zhang). Jason McGrath aptly summarizes the characteristics of the directors:

> [T]he Sixth Generation was said to be interested in the present rather than the past, quotidian life rather than historical melodrama, and gritty urban geography rather than scenic rural settings. Another important distinction, however, was that the Fifth Generation, for all their artistic daring and occasional trouble with the Communist authorities, had made their signature early achievements within the state studio system, while many in the Sixth Generation were making films entirely independent of that institutional structure. ("Urban Generation" 168)

An instructor can assign readings that provide biographical information on a few selected sixth-generation filmmakers (e.g., M. Berry) and can ask students to discuss how individual cases coincide with or diverge from McGrath's generational description above in order to understand the potential strengths and weaknesses of discussing Chinese film directors in terms of a "generational lineup" (Y. Zhang, "Directors" 58).

Wang Xiaoshuai, examined earlier, is a director of fictional films, and on the documentary film front, an instructor can introduce Wu Wenguang, who directed *Bumming in Beijing: The Last Dreamers* (流浪北京), which depicts the world of young Beijing artists struggling to express their artistic identities in the stifling atmosphere of the period after the 1989 Tiananmen Square protests. Although Wu is usually not considered a member of the sixth generation—whose key works are narrative feature films—there is a clear "echo" between the New Documentary Film movement and the sixth generation (Reynaud), in terms of their "postsocialist realism" (McGrath, "Independent Cinema"). Hence Wu is considered to be one of the first key figures in the independent film movement in China. As Lin Xudong points out, "It is interesting to note that all of [Wu's] documentaries, in some way or another, got their start through China Central Television, the massive state-controlled media organization." Because of the strengthening of censorship and control after the Tiananmen Square protests, many of the programs in production—including *The Chinese* (中国人) and *Tiananmen* (天安门)—had come to a halt. "Despite this setback, one of the writer/directors of *The Chinese*, Wu Wenguang, using resources garnered from his work on that project, continued to gather footage for an independent documentary of his own. It was from this footage that he selected the material that would eventually become his film *Bumming in Beijing: The Last Dreamers* (1990)." The influence of the social world can be detected in Wu's *Bumming in Beijing*: the film's five subjects are young artists living in a community in a suburb of Beijing. Chris Berry incisively observes:

> They were dropouts, something that was only becoming possible in the People's Republic with the development of a non-state sector in the 1980s. In the socialist system every Chinese was assigned a "unit," which was responsible for providing a job, housing, education, health care, and so on. Opting to live outside this system was thus impossible. Doing so, as these artists did in the 1980s, promised liberation from the monolithic state structure. But it was difficult to get by because the private sector was very much in an embryonic state. ("Wu Wenguang" 134)

Technologies such as DV played a crucial role in independent documentary productions. As only a few people, such as Wu Wenguang, had access to the expensive equipment owned by television stations, the genesis of the whole generation of independent documentary filmmakers was shaped by more accessible audiovisual technology, including personally affordable DV cameras, personal computers, and editing software. One of the people involved in the Chinese New Documentary scene explained this point to me in an interview, noting that DV cameras first appeared in Beijing around 1997, when directors began buying them, and that filming with DV cameras and editing film on a personal computer could be done relatively cheaply, especially as the equipment became more affordable over time.[5]

At this point, the instructor can ask students what inputs from the social world, other than human actors, may have influenced the production of Chinese independent films. Readings can be assigned from the collection *DV-Made China* (Zhang and Zito), which discusses the impact of DVs on Chinese independent film, and from *China's iGeneration* (Johnson et al.), which details the impact of information technology on independent filmmaking. In particular, as students today are familiar with short video-making and sharing platforms such as *TikTok* and *Bilibili* (Nakajima "Sociability"), as well as other social-networking platforms that have video-sharing functions, instructors can invite students to discuss how the popularization of audio-and-visual based social networks may transform the landscape of independent filmmaking. For example, the documentary film director and poet Qin Xiaoyu "released an announcement on micro-blogging platform Sina Weibo, asking users to send him clips recording their own lives on Feb 9, a randomly picked day" in 2020 amid the COVID-19 pandemic. The shooting of the film *One More Day* (一日冬春) "was completed in a single day on Feb 9, thanks to contributions from over 5,000 'filmmakers,'" who used cell phones and other devices to shoot their videos (K. Wang).[6]

The Links between the Social World, Receiver, and Cultural Object

How do the consumers of independent films also participate in constructing the world of Chinese independent cinema? Since most of the films in the independent film category are made outside the institutional production system, they cannot be commercially distributed and exhibited in China. However, there are still people—receivers—who watch and discuss these films inside China.

For example, I have examined independent film club activities and film festivals through sociological ethnographic fieldwork in Beijing. In the social spaces of consumption, a surprising degree of variation exists in terms of the orientation of receivers, that is, audiences of Chinese independent films. Some audiences emphasize their political defiance of the state, while others try to sustain independent filmmaking and consumption as a commercially viable, if not lucrative, business. Yet others focus on artistic expression and appreciation. Furthermore, some audiences combine some of these orientations. I have argued that these different positionings of consumers are very much related to the social world the organizers and the participants are located in—including their educational background and biographical trajectories (Nakajima, "Film Clubs").

In these consumption spaces, discussions and interpretations of the film works by the audiences are also diverse. At a symposium on Chinese independent documentary film organized by a film club, discussions and debates were held on the history of Chinese documentary; the distinction between objectivity and subjectivity, or nonfiction and fiction, in documentary films; the relationship between filmmakers and audiences; ethical issues in documentary filmmaking; and the impact of the state and politics on Chinese documentary films (Nakajima, "Watching").

In the 2010s, some pioneering studies emerged about Chinese film festivals (Berry and Robinson). Relying on but developing broader scholarship on film festivals, these works elucidate the unique dynamics of Chinese film festival circuits, including those where independent films circulate. For example, Bao Hongwei discusses the history of the Beijing Queer Film Festival. Ma Ran examines grassroots Chinese independent film festivals. Film festival studies are an essential attempt at understanding the links between social world, receiver, and cultural object in the cultural-diamond framework.

Last but not least, the development and availability of technologies such as VCD, DVD, and more recently Blu-ray discs, as well as HD, Full HD, 4K, and 8K formats, provide opportunities for consumption for Chinese independent film audiences. By assigning readings on the subject (e.g., Nakajima, "Chinese Film Spaces"), instructors can encourage students to discuss how technologies and other nonliving things, as nonhuman actors in the social world (Cerulo), shape independent film consumption in China. In addition, students should be encouraged to discuss the political potential of technologies such as DVDs and other digital formats, as their portability and ease of duplication may have enabled the distribution and exhibition of politically sensitive independent films (as discussed in Nakajima, "Re-imagining").

Transnational Dynamics

How are transnational dynamics influencing the world of Chinese independent cinema? The preceding discussions of the cultural-diamond framework have focused on the domestic dynamics within the People's Republic of China. However, students should understand that the diamond's borders transgress the borders of nation-states. For example, as is well known, Jia Zhangke's films have been financed by production companies abroad, including those in France, Japan, and South Korea. His films have been popular on the international film festival circuits and art-house film scene and watched by audiences worldwide, including academics and film critics. In other words, the creators and the receivers extend beyond the borders of mainland China. Moreover, some independent filmmakers from the mainland are now based outside China—for example, Ying Liang, in Hong Kong, and Zhu Rikun and Wang Wo in the United States. Some Chinese independent films are also set outside of the mainland—Jia Zhangke's *Mountains May Depart* (山河故人) was shot in China and Australia.

Some, if not all, of these transnational dynamics are made possible through technologies. The availability of portable DV cameras made it possible for creators to travel abroad and shoot films with relative ease. Digital films can be downloaded or streamed on the Internet. Once in cyberspace, cultural objects such as films may easily transgress the borders of nation-states, although some governments, such as mainland China's, limit the flow of digital information.

Historical Changes

How has Chinese independent cinema changed with the passage of time? Many, if not all, of the filmmakers who have been working outside the system have also made films with official exhibition permits, especially since the 2000s, when the world of Chinese film began to industrialize after China joined the World Trade Organization in 2001. For example, Zhang Yuan, who shocked the world of Chinese independent cinema with his *Beijing Bastards* (北京杂种), has made films with official approval, including *I Love You* (我爱你), *Green Tea* (绿茶), *Little Red Flowers* (看上去很美), *Dada's Dance* (达达), and *Beijing Flickers* (有种). Moreover, some of these filmmakers' productions are no longer small in scale. After Lou Ye was banned from filmmaking for two years for screening his *Suzhou River* (苏州河) at the International Film Festival Rotterdam without official approval ("Banned Chinese Director"), his first government-approved film, *Purple Butterfly* (紫蝴蝶), features the Chinese film stars Zhang Ziyi and Li Bingbing as well as the Japanese star Nakamura Tōru. Jia Zhangke's *The World*—the director's first film to receive official approval—was made "with a major national investor, the Shanghai Film Corporation (formerly the Shanghai Film Studio), which allowed Jia to operate with a significantly higher budget, giving him access to more resources, a much larger number of extras, and the ability to shoot in more exclusive locations" (Richler 13).

However, students must understand that the historical changes are not necessarily unidirectional or teleological. For example, after Lou Ye directed *Purple Butterfly* in 2003 within the system, he encountered political problems surrounding his film *Summer Palace* (颐和园). The film depicted the lives of two lovers against the background of the 1989 Tiananmen Square student protests. The film competed for the Palme d'Or at the 2006 Cannes Film Festival, but Lou was banned from making films for five years since *Summer Palace* was sent to the festival without official government approval (Musetto). Lou returned to filmmaking in 2009, before the lifting of the ban, with *Spring Fever* (春风沉醉的夜晚), but this was possible only because he registered the film as a Hong Kong–French coproduction in order to avoid the censors (Elley).

A key pedagogical takeaway of this essay is for instructors to lead students beyond an approach that exclusively focuses on the relationship between the social world and its cultural objects—the vertical line in figure 1—though it is sensible for instructors to use film to understand social phenomena of interest in sociology and related social science courses. As I show above, we can use a film—such as Wang Xiaoshuai's *Frozen*—to understand the atmosphere of the social and cultural world in the period immediately following the Tiananmen Square protests. However, as I emphasize, films are representations—not reflections—of society, because they are shaped by various inputs from humans (creators and receivers) as well as nonliving things (e.g., digital technology) in the social world. Instructors need to guide students to gain insights on all the corners and links of the cultural-diamond framework—not just on the link between the social world and the cultural object—and to obtain a comprehensive sociological understanding of Chinese independent cinema.

Notes

1. See, for example, the "performative turn" in Chinese New Documentary films as a mode of representation (Q. Wang).

2. Transnational dynamics and historical changes are briefly suggested in the original cultural-diamond framework; see Griswold and Carrol's discussion on "mediated transnationals" (160) and on historical changes in "identity politics" (168). Both aspects are crucial in understanding a rapidly transforming Chinese independent cinema that increasingly has transnational inputs in production and consumption.

3. *Frozen* is available on DVD. The analysis here draws and expands on Nakajima, "Film as Cultural Politics," especially 160–62.

4. English subtitles for *Frozen* are quoted in the essay.

5. The interviewee spoke to me on condition of anonymity, on 26 May 2004, in Beijing.

6. See Chan for more information on the film project.

Works Cited

"Banned Chinese Director Heads to Palestinian Territories." *The Guardian*, 28 Mar. 2007, www.theguardian.com/film/2007/mar/28/news1.

Bao Hongwei. "Queer as Catachresis: The Beijing Queer Film Festival in Cultural Translation." Berry and Robinson, pp. 79–100.

Berry, Chris. "Wu Wenguang: An Introduction." *Cinema Journal*, vol. 46, no. 1, 2006, pp. 133–36.

Berry, Chris, and Luke Robinson, editors. *Chinese Film Festivals: Sites of Translation*. Palgrave Macmillan, 2017.

Berry, Chris, et al., editors. *The New Chinese Documentary Film Movement: For the Public Record*. Hong Kong UP, 2010.

Berry, Michael. *Speaking in Images: Interviews with Contemporary Chinese Filmmakers*. Columbia UP, 2005.

Bumming in Beijing: The Last Dreamers. Directed by Wu Wenguang, 1990.

Cerulo, Karen. "Nonhumans in Social Interaction." *Annual Review of Sociology*, vol. 35, 2009, pp. 531–52.

Chan, Hiu Man. "One More Day: China's MeDoc Launches Citizen Documentary Project During Coronavirus Outbreak." *UK-China Film Collab*, 2 Sept. 2020, www.ukchinafilm.com/elemeet-one-more-day/.

Elley, Derek. "Helmer Lou Ye Is at It Again—This Time with Lashings of Gay Sex—in the Five-Way Ensembler 'Spring Fever.'" *Variety*, 13 May 2009, variety.com/2009/film/markets-festivals/spring-fever-1200507113/.

Frozen. Directed by Wu Ming [Wang Xiaoshuai], Another Film Company / Creative Workshop / Hubert Bals Fund, 1995.

"*Frozen* Plot." *IMDb*, 2023, www.imdb.com/title/tt0125279/plotsummary. Accessed 10 Apr. 2021.

Griswold, Wendy, and Christopher Carroll. *Cultures and Societies in a Changing World*. 4th ed, Sage, 2013.

Johnson, Matthew D., et al., editors. *China's iGeneration: Cinema and Moving Image Culture for the Twenty-First Century*. Bloomsbury Publishing, 2014.

Lin Xudong. "Documentary in Mainland China." *Documentary Box*, vol. 26, Aug. 2005, www.yidff.jp/docbox/26/box26-3-e.html.

Ma Ran. "Regarding the Grassroots Chinese Independent Film Festivals: Modes of Multiplicity and Abnormal Film Networking." Johnson et al., pp. 235–53.

McGrath, Jason. "The Independent Cinema of Jia Zhangke: From Postsocialist Realism to a Transnational Aesthetic." *The Urban Generation: Chinese Cinema and Society at the Turn of the Twenty-First Century*, edited by Zhen Zhang, Duke UP, 2007, pp. 81–114.

———. "The Urban Generation: Underground and Independent Films from the PRC." *The Chinese Cinema Book*, edited by Song Hwee Lim and Julian Ward, Palgrave Macmillan, 2011, pp. 167–84.

Musetto, V. A. "Epic Full of Love and Naked Truth." *New York Post*, 18 Jan. 2008, nypost.com/2008/01/18/epic-full-of-love-naked-truth/.

Nakajima, Seio. "Chinese Film Spaces: The Social Locations and Media of Urban Independent Screen Consumption." *Continuum*, vol. 28, no. 1, 2014, pp. 52–64.

———. "Film as Cultural Politics." *Reclaiming Chinese Society: The New Social Activism*, edited by You-tien Hsing and Ching Kwan Lee, Routledge, 2009, pp. 159–83.

———. "Film Clubs in Beijing: The Cultural Consumption of Chinese Independent Films." Pickowicz and Zhang, pp. 161–208.

———. "Re-imagining Civil Society in Contemporary Urban China: Actor-Network-Theory and Chinese Independent Film Consumption." *Qualitative Sociology*, vol. 36, no. 4, 2013, pp. 383–402.

———. "The Sociability of Millennials in Cyberspace: A Comparative Analysis of Barrage Subtitling in *Nico Nico Douga* and *Bilibili*." *China's Youth Cultures and Collective Spaces: Creativity, Sociality, Identity and Resistance*, edited by Vanessa Frangville and Gwennaël Gaffric, Routledge, 2020, pp. 98–115.

———. "Watching Documentary: Critical Public Discourses and Urban Chinese Film Clubs." C. Berry et al., pp. 117–34.

One More Day. Directed by Qin Xiaoyu, 2021.

Pickowicz, Paul G., and Yingjin Zhang, editors. *From Underground to Independent: Alternative Film Culture in Contemporary China*. Rowman and Littlefield, 2006.

Reynaud, Bérénice. "Dancing with Myself, Drifting with My Camera: The Emotional Vagabonds of China's New Documentary." *Senses of Cinema*, no. 28, Oct. 2003, www.sensesofcinema.com/2003/feature-articles/chinas_new_documentary/.

Richler, David. "Cinema, Realism, and the World According to Jia Zhangke." *Canadian Journal of Film Studies*, vol. 25, no. 2, 2016, pp. 6–38.

So Close to Paradise. Directed by Wang Xiaoshuai, Beijing Film Studio / Beijing Jin Die Yingshi Yishu / Beijing Pegase Cultural Communication Centre / TV and Art Production, 1998.

Wang, Kaihao. "A Day to Remember." *China Daily*, 27 Feb. 2020, global
.chinadaily.com.cn/a/202002/27/WS5e5700efa31012821727a9b4.html.
Accessed September 26, 2021.
Wang, Qi. "Performing Documentation: Wu Wenguang and the Performative
Turn of New Chinese Documentary." Y. Zhang, *Companion*, pp. 299–317.
Zhang, Yingjin, editor. *A Companion to Chinese Cinema*. Wiley-Blackwell, 2012.
———. "Directors, Aesthetics, Genres: Chinese Postsocialist Cinema, 1979–
2010." Y. Zhang, *Companion*, pp. 57–74.
Zhang, Zhen, editor. *The Urban Generation: Chinese Cinema and Society at the
Turn of the Twenty-First Century*. Duke UP, 2007.
Zhang, Zhen, and Angela Zito, editors. *DV-Made China: Digital Subjects and
Social Transformations after Independent Film*. U of Hawai'i P, 2015.

Corey Kai Nelson Schultz

Phenomenological Approaches to Teaching Chinese Film

This essay examines a phenomenological approach to teaching Chinese film and is based on a module I designed and taught for a second-year film studies undergraduate degree program at a British university from 2015 to 2019. Titled Contemporary Chinese Cinema, the module focused on Chinese films created since 2000 by analyzing how this period of transition in mainland China has been reflected, explored, symbolized, and constructed in film. The central idea of this module was to use selected Chinese films from a variety of genres as entry points into examining this dynamic period of massive social and economic change while building a larger contextual comprehension of how this era has been experienced, translated, and evoked through film.

The module began with Raymond Williams's theoretical concept of "structures of feeling" (133)—feelings that concretize around a particular time, place, and social group that are captured and evoked in art and culture—and considered how film records and evokes these feelings in ways that are specific to the medium and the viewers' experiences of the medium. Starting from this theoretical paradigm, the module introduced the methodology of phenomenology—the analysis of experience—with the hypothesis that a phenomenological approach to film analysis can make studying Chinese films more accessible to students outside China (or make other foreign films accessible outside their cultural sphere of influence) by examining not only the content of the films but the viewer's experience of them; this makes foreign films less foreign by focusing not solely on understanding or decoding them but also by considering the viewer's phenomenological experience of them as a mode of analysis.

In this essay, I first briefly outline the methodology and philosophy of phenomenology and its pedagogical uses. Then I describe the module, examining its content and theoretical foundation before explaining the material covered in the first lecture, the phenomenology exercise in the seminar that followed, and the ways these elements informed the module's first written assessment.

Phenomenology

Phenomenology is, as Vivian Sobchack describes it, "both a philosophy of science and a research procedure" (*Address* 26). It is defined as "the study of phenomena, where a phenomenon is anything that appears to someone in their conscious experience" (Gill 74) and is examined from the point of view of that person (87). Additionally, phenomenology is described as "a *practice* . . . by which one discovers and celebrates one's own immersion in a flux of experience that is the true source of all that we come to know and believe regarding the world" (Churchill 9). One of the main theoretical pioneers of phenomenology was Edmund Husserl, who in *Logical Investigations* advances a methodology that describes "the essence of experiences" (Gill 74). This methodology was developed further by his student, Martin Heidegger, who in his monograph *Being and Time* examines "the human experience of being" (Gill 75–76). Since then, the study of phenomenology has grown to include many different submethodologies that are used in a variety of disciplines, including psychology, education, health sciences, and film. Maurice Merleau-Ponty became one of the main pioneers of phenomenology's use in film studies, and in his text *Phenomenology of Perception* he argues that phenomenology is an embodied experience, not just the domain of the mind or of cognition. Phenomenology has since become a well-developed methodology in film studies among scholars who examine the experience of film. As Jenny Chamarette argues, "Films are objects and moments of experience in addition to being objects of and for interpretation," a perspective that encourages scholars to think abstractly as well as engage with films as phenomena (3).

The literature on using phenomenological approaches to classroom learning stresses how phenomenology-based exercises make theory more accessible for students, help them develop analytical skills and new ways of thinking, foster a student-centered learning environment, and can create supportive peer-led learning communities. First, a phenomenological approach makes film theory—which for some students, is a foreboding topic—more accessible; as Daniel Yacavone argues, phenomenology "describ[es] human experience in its immediate concreteness, without bringing secondary or extraneous interpretations to bear" (161).

Second, a phenomenological approach encourages students to develop their analytical skills by reflecting on their experiences, composing written summaries of these experiences, and interpreting these experiences for their analysis. Scott Churchill argues that phenomenological approaches urge students "to think, to apply their own intelligence to a challenge (rather than juggling others' ideas and definitions, or trying to tell the teacher something he seems to want to hear)" (8), and it is believed that phenomenological methodologies encourage students to focus their attention on experience (Halling 1). Phenomenological practices also offer new ways of analyzing and thinking about films by drawing viewers' attention to the "immediate sensory and expressive features of films" and thus encouraging viewers to examine them "as perceptual objects instead of, or in addition to, cognitive, narrative, and cultural-ideological ones" (Yacavone 159). Phenomenology is seen as an open methodology in that the experience of the experience, not preconceived notions of phenomena, are supposed to drive the analysis; as Sobchack writes, "phenomenology generates not only an *experiential* but also an *experimental* methodology that begins with a commitment to the openness of its object of inquiry, rather than to any *a priori* certainty of what that object already 'really' is" ("Phenomenology" 436). It is also argued that phenomenological approaches encourage students "to reflect on 'where they are' psychologically when they are viewing the film" (Churchill 3). Listing several different exercises for his students to test the methodology, Churchill explains that "[t]ogether, these situations constituted for us 'ways of experiencing' that were grounded in the lifeworld and thus provided an 'existential phenomenological' starting point for our reflections . . ." (6).

Third, phenomenology is a methodology that is student-centered. Steen Halling argues that by having students choose topics they are interested in, describe their own experiences, and then examine these experiences in further detail, "the phenomenon truly becomes a 'partner' in their research endeavour" (4). In this way, the phenomenological approach is an example of student-centered learning as well as active learning that has the potential to increase student engagement.

Finally, it is theorized that sharing individual experiences in a group setting, such as a seminar, "brings forth responses of respect and openness from other group members" (Halling 4) and can increase "appreciation for the interpretations of others" (Greenberg et al. 131). Although initially based on personal experience, a phenomenological approach also encourages students to consider the experience of others, as such experience is a "starting point for our encounter with others; . . . it is our starting point for our encounters with works of art, for our encounters with other cultures, for our encounters with all symbolic universes of meaning" (Churchill 9). Thus, by engaging students on a personal level and having them share with the larger group, phenomenological approaches to learning have the potential of developing a collaborative student learning community.

The Module

Contemporary Chinese Cinema was an optional second-year undergraduate module in a three-year film studies program. Since my research specialty is contemporary Chinese film, this module was also designed to promote research-led teaching at the university. The central idea of this module was to use selected films from a variety of genres (e.g., documentaries, art films, and action films) as an entry point into examining the dynamic period in mainland China since 2000 while building a larger contextual comprehension of how massive change in this period has been experienced, translated, and evoked through film. Topics included rural-urban migration, urban dislocation, the rural-urban divide, and the uses of history and myth. The students were mostly from the United Kingdom, and, although they were vaguely familiar with Chinese history because it had briefly been covered in their secondary education, China was largely unknown to them; thus, each week's lecture contained information about the nation's sociohistorical and political contexts and how they connected to the week's themes.

In the module, I also wanted to introduce other methodologies and theories for analyzing film that would complement the overall film studies program. Existing modules in the degree program focused on such areas as film history, representational analysis, and industry studies, but there were no extant modules that addressed the film-viewing experience. Thus, this module introduced a new approach by examining the emotional dimensions of film through phenomenology. Furthermore, it was the first module in which students could write their own essay questions. To emphasize the student-centered aspect of the class, I selected films from a focused date range not only because the range covered a period of fast-paced and dramatic change in China that had been recorded in film but also because the range was contemporaneous for the students; as I reminded them, these films were made during their lifetimes, and I hoped that this fact would lead to increased student engagement.

Like other modules, this one included a weekly lecture, film screening, and seminar. Students were supposed to attend all of these components as well as complete the week's assigned reading before the seminars. The first lecture introduced the module and its perspective of studying film through emotion. It began with a quick overview of the main historical events in twentieth-century China and the development of Chinese film before focusing on the sixth generation of filmmakers (whose films were the focus of the module) and their sociohistorical context in what is called the reform era, from roughly 1979 to the present. We discussed this era; how it was named after the economic reforms that Deng Xiaoping instigated in 1978 and 1979, when the nation began to shift from a socialist planned economy to a market economy; and how this era became known as postsocialist—not because the era came after socialism, since the nation is a socialist republic still led by the Chinese Communist Party, but because, according to Chris Berry, "the forms and structures of the modern (in this case socialism) persist long after faith in the grand narrative that authorizes it has been lost" (116). We discussed the sixth generation further, examining their aesthetics, such as the use of documentary film styles and cinema verité, as well as their focus on marginalized groups and everyday life, and I highlighted the ways we would examine this generation's films throughout the module.

Next, we discussed Raymond Williams's notion of "structures of feeling" (133), which Williams defines as "a particular quality of social experience and relationship, historically distinct from other particular qualities, which gives the sense of a generation or of a period" (131). According to him, different classes and generations can have differing structures of feeling, and he stresses that these can be multiple sets of feelings that can contradict or support one another. Furthermore, Williams argues that the concept is especially relevant to cultural products (such as films) because they often are the first indicators that a new structure of feeling is being formed (133). Thus, the concept is a philosophical approach as well as a methodology for analyzing feeling and affective experience.

After introducing phenomenology and Williams's structures of feeling, we then examined the representation of the Three Gorges Dam in Chinese visual culture during this first lecture. We began with screenshots from the film for that week, the international-award-winning *Still Life* (三峡好人),[1] and examined the film's focus on ruin and destruction, specifically the scenes in which buildings are being torn down to make the area navigable after it is flooded because of the dam's construction. During the lecture, I suggested that the destruction of the area can be seen as a metaphor for the destruction of Maoist-era Chinese society during the present period of economic reform and how the film captures this geographic, economic, and social transition as it is being experienced by the film's characters. To make this point further, I contrasted images from the film with propaganda posters from the Maoist period that were sourced from *Chinese Posters*, the website of the Chinese Posters Foundation, which includes the collections of Stefan Landsberger of Leiden University and the International Institute of Social History in Amsterdam. These posters glorify modernization and industrialization and usually feature construction, smokestacks, and powerful machinery, forming structures of feeling that are optimistic and patriotic. In one poster, Mao Zedong waves from the center of the frame, and in the background industrial development progresses at full throttle—represented by exhaust billowing from smokestacks, cranes constructing a dam, and a speeding locomotive—while the foreground features the products of agriculture (Ding Hao et al.). I juxtaposed this confident imagery with the scenes of ruin and destruction in the film and its representation of a population forcibly uprooted by the dam project and left to wander the nation for precarious survival.

At the conclusion of the lecture and before the screening, the students were given the following viewing instructions: "During the screening, jot down your thoughts, impressions, and feelings. Afterward, reflect on your experience of the film. How did you interpret the film? What does your experience mean to you?" After the screening, the students prepared for their seminars.

Readings on Phenomenology and Aesthetics

For every week's lecture and seminars, students were supposed to prepare in advance by completing the assigned reading, and this week's readings were designed to enhance the lecture's focus on phenomenology and aesthetics. Readings for this week included Bill Nichols's auto-ethnographic account of experiencing a foreign film festival and self-reflection on making sense of the films' aesthetics, as well as Jerome Silbergeld's text questioning the reductiveness of locating a single aesthetic style for Chinese film. These two articles complemented each other, in that the first describes the process of meaning making through phenomenology, while the second stresses the importance of avoiding stereotypes through generalizations.

In his article "Discovering Form, Inferring Meaning," Nichols examines his experience attending an Iranian film festival, a national cinema that he had previously had little knowledge about, and analyses his process of creating meaning from that experience. He begins the article by querying, "How do we encounter cinemas, and cultures, not our own?" (16), and he describes such cinematic encounters as anthropological experiences where viewers hear unfamiliar languages and witness unfamiliar cultures (17). He argues that during the encounter with foreign, hitherto unseen national cinemas, film festivalgoers are "discovering form, inferring meaning" about a culture or nation that they are unfamiliar with and thus use the discovery to "make sense" of these experiences (18). Referencing Clifford Geertz's text "Deep Play," in which Geertz analyzes his personal experience of making sense of a Balinese cockfight, Nichols draws an analogy between tourists and film festivalgoers: both seek the meaning of something made by someone in another culture. Regarding the film festivalgoer's motivation, he writes, "Like the tourist, we hope to go behind appearances, to grasp the meaning of things as those who present them would, to step outside our (inescapable) status as outsiders and diagnosticians to attain a more intimate, more authentic form of experience" (19). However, he cautions that, "[l]ike the ethnographer, we may know full well that the pursuit of intimate knowledge and authenticity is illusory." (20). Yet Nichols's account allows us to reflect on and analyze our experiences and to use this reflection and analysis to examine these experiences further.

In his examination of the films he saw during the Iranian film festival, Nichols summarizes them as having similar aesthetics, including long shots and long takes, but notes that they seem to lack close-ups, hyper-emotional music, montage, or "expressive uses of lighting, gesture, posture, mise-en-scène, camera angle, or camera movement." After making these assessments, he reflects further and describes this reflection and analysis as a deliberate cognitive process, noting that as one begins to identify stylistic elements of an unfamiliar national cinema, one remains aware that one's assumptions about style may be faulty (23). Nonetheless, as a methodological approach, the development of these assumptions may be described and examined in order to produce evidence. This approach is similar to a constructivist view of learning, in which "social knowledge is created and recreated in the personal knowledge of the learner" (Kolb and Kolb 7). The engaged festivalgoer will use their own prior knowledge to make meaning—namely, a thesis about why a national cinema uses particular visual styles. This process makes the films, which earlier may have appeared unknowable, seem more familiar. Thus, "[l]ike the tourist, we depart with the satisfaction of a partial knowledge, pleased that it is of our own making" (Nichols 27).

This article was chosen because it is a reflective account of making meaning through experience. I stressed to students that its purpose was not to indicate whether Nichols had made the correct interpretation of Iranian cinematic aesthetics but rather to show a scholar explaining their methodology. This text on interpreting a national cinema's film aesthetics was contrasted with Silbergeld's text "Cinema and the Visual Arts of China." After reviewing essentialist claims about Chinese aesthetics, Silbergeld challenges the supposition that there is a typically Chinese aesthetic in contemporary Chinese film and warns against generalizations that create stereotypes of what stylistic elements Chinese films ought to have. Although he does list tropes in art films by the sixth generation of Chinese film directors, such as "suppression of dramatic impulse," "appreciation of emptiness and stillness," and "minimal camera movement" (403), he notes that many Chinese filmmakers have also studied the studio arts and may have been influenced by them (406). He concludes by arguing that "what Chinese film shares with the other Chinese visual arts is a body of cultural reference, of content and context, both historical and contemporary. Such references, which often explain the filmmakers' stylistic and thematic choices, work best when specific and take us beyond homogenizing generalizations about style" (413).

Phenomenology Exercise

During the seminar, we began by analyzing how the cinematography explored space and emotion in *Still Life* and helped create structures of feeling. In small groups, the students reflected on their experience of the film, hypothesizing about the structure of feeling that the film evoked.

The purpose of this exercise was to engage the students in in-depth textual analysis as well as encourage them to examine their own experiences of viewing the film and sharing these experiences with their fellow students in order to begin the creation of a supportive learning community.

The seminar exercise began with the following quote by Chamarette: "Presence to the cinematic moment is not only the primary temporal mode of the cinematic encounter but also the emergent moment of interpretation. When I first encounter a work of cinematic art, I rely on my perceptions and bodily sensations, and on my capacity to recognize those perceptions, before I begin to build a form of interpretation" (36). After we discussed this quote, I showed the students an abridged version of Suzan Kozel's exercise "How do you do a phenomenology?" (53–54):

> Notice the present moment and "suspend the flow of thought."
>
> Notice the sensations of your body, including "what you see, hear, and touch," temperature, and your awareness of space.
>
> "Describe what you experienced" but do not "worry about style, grammar, or relevance" in your description. Your note-taking may immediately follow the experience or occur after "an interval." Do not allow so much time to pass that your recollection is dulled.
>
> "Re-examine your notes with an eye for what seems significant." "[S]et yourself the task of further research into ideas that relate to your experience."
>
> Write your document, choosing your "voice, style, and audience. Decide on the balance between concrete sense description and reference to abstractions (i.e., cultural or theoretical ideas). Decide whether the document will be critical in tone, or sensual, or investigative."

We then watched the film's opening scene, when one of the protagonists is traveling on the ferry. Students were asked to concentrate on the scene and its effect on their senses. Afterward, they discussed their reactions in small groups and used this discussion to develop their ideas further.

Next we discussed the readings by Nichols and Silbergeld and considered how film makes meaning in ways that are specific to the medium and its many elements, such as image, sound, movement, and color. Since the readings discuss the aesthetics of Chinese art, including the cinematic qualities of handscrolls, which require the viewer to manually unroll them in order to view the artworks in their entirety, students were given a traditional Chinese handscroll to experience. For most of the students, this was the first time they had interacted with this art form in this way, and they were asked to examine their engagement with the scroll—how it was rolled, the physical limitations of its viewing, and its textures, smells, and sounds. My aim was to use this experience of the unknown to make them curious about learning further. Then we analyzed the film's so-called scroll shots, thus connecting the aesthetics of the two media and students' phenomenological reflections on their engagement with these two art forms. This was an active-learning exercise that took a student-centered approach by using elements of experiential learning. The exercise also broke down barriers in that students were not being tested on knowledge that they had read or been told about but on knowledge that they had made themselves during this experience.

Assignment

I had hoped that the abovementioned exercise would help students prepare for their mid-semester assignments on film analysis and that they would use their experiences to generate ideas that they then could develop into a thesis or argument for the first assignment. The first assignment was a one-thousand-word report in which students were required to perform a close textual analysis of a Chinese film that was produced in the People's Republic of China after 2000 and that had not been screened in class. They were required to use at least three scholarly sources about the film, examine one or two scenes from the film, use close textual analysis to scrutinize how these scenes elicit a particular emotional reaction, and create an argument as to the larger significance of this emotion and what it might mean. As second-year students, they were still perfecting their skills in researching and writing about films, and to help them learn film studies terminology, I had them refer to the Yale University website *Yale Film Analysis*. This assignment was their first opportunity to write their own essay questions, and I used the abovementioned exercise to help guide them. In asking students to develop their own questions, I endeavored to have them think deeply about their experience, the film, and the theories that they were learning in class and to have them use these three elements to inspire their written work. Finally, they were invited to test their ideas with their fellow students during the seminars in order to receive further formative feedback before their assignments were submitted (see Schultz).

This assignment was not about finding the right interpretation; rather, it was about using the experience of film viewing to generate ideas and create an argument that was informed by scholarly literature. As such, phenomenology was a fitting methodology to use for this first assignment; as a methodology, its aim is "to transform lived experience into a textual expression of its essence—in such a way that the effect of the text is at once a reflexive re-living and a reflective appropriation of something meaningful: a notion by which a reader is powerfully animated in his or her own lived experience" (Van Manen 36).

During the four years in which I taught this module, I was nominated every year for a student engagement award and won the Most Engaging Lecturer Award in 2017. Student evaluations included the following comments: "engaging seminars/lectures which helped form ideas"; "as someone with no prior knowledge of this topic, the lectures made the module very accessible"; "seminars were really useful, particularly the discussion and interactive activities (scroll, etc.)"; and "seminars . . . create a space of intellectual freedom where ideas are not forced out of students, but rather through ideas bouncing off each other." Overall, I found the work that the students submitted to be very high-quality; they engaged well with the films they analyzed, and they appeared excited to discuss their film experiences. From the student feedback as well as the work being submitted, I discovered that students responded readily to phenomenological approaches to Chinese film and that phenomenology, as both a methodology and a theory, was accessible to students, helped them improve their analytical skills, and produced good work.

Note

1. *Still Life* is widely available online (e.g., on *Amazon*) and is subtitled in a range of languages.

Works Cited

Berry, Chris. "Getting Real: Chinese Documentary, Chinese Postsocialism." *The Urban Generation: Chinese Cinema and Society at the Turn of the Twenty-First Century*, edited by Zhen Zhang, Duke UP, 2007, pp. 115–34.
Chamarette, Jenny. *Phenomenology and the Future of Film: Rethinking Subjectivity beyond French Cinema*. Palgrave Macmillan, 2012.
Churchill, Scott D. "Teaching Phenomenology by Way of 'Second-Person Perspectivity.'" *The Indo-Pacific Journal of Phenomenology*, vol. 12, 2012, pp. 1–14.

Ding Hao et al. "Turn China into a Prosperous, Rich and Powerful Industrialized Socialist Country under the Leadership of the Communist Party and Chairman Mao!" 1954. *Chinese Posters*, chineseposters.net/posters/e13-866.

Geertz, Clifford. "Deep Play: Notes on the Balinese Cockfight." *Myth, Symbol, Culture*, themed issue of *Daedalus*, vol. 101, no. 1, winter 1972, pp. 1–37. *JSTOR*, www.jstor.org/stable/20024056.

Gill, Michael. "Phenomenology as Qualitative Methodology." *Qualitative Analysis: Eight Approaches for the Social Sciences*, edited by Margaretha Järvinen and Nanna Mik-Meyer, Sage, 2020, pp. 73–93.

Greenberg, Katherine H., et al. *The Phenomenological Heart of Teaching and Learning: Theory, Research, and Practice in Higher Education*. Routledge, 2019.

Halling, Steen. "Teaching Phenomenology through Highlighting Experience." *The Indo-Pacific Journal of Phenomenology*, vol. 12, 2012, pp. 1–5.

Heidegger, Martin. *Being and Time*. Translated by Joan Stambaugh, State U of New York P, 1996.

Husserl, Edmund. *Logical Investigations*. Translated by J. N. Findlay, Routledge, 2001. 2 vols.

Kolb, David A., and Alice Y. Kolb. *The Kolb Learning Style Inventory 4.0: A Comprehensive Guide to the Theory, Psychometrics, Research on Validity and Educational Applications*. Experience Based Learning Systems, 2013.

Kozel, Susan. *Closer: Performance, Technologies, Phenomenologies*. MIT Press, 2007.

Merleau-Ponty, Maurice. *Phenomenology of Perception*. Translated by Donald A. Landes, Routledge, 2012.

Nichols, Bill. "Discovering Form, Inferring Meaning: New Cinemas and the Film Festival Circuit." *Film Quarterly*, vol. 47, no. 3, 1994, pp. 16–30.

Schultz, Corey Kai Nelson. "Transforming Pedagogies: Adapting Art School Peer Group Design Critique (the 'Crit') for the Humanities." *Practitioner Research in Higher Education Journal*, vol. 14, no. 1, 2021, pp. 41–49.

Silbergeld, Jerome. "Cinema and the Visual Arts of China." *A Companion to Chinese Cinema*, edited by Yingjin Zhang, Blackwell, 2012, pp. 400–16.

Sobchack, Vivian. *The Address of the Eye: A Phenomenology of Film Experience*. Princeton UP, 1992.

———. "Phenomenology." *The Routledge Companion to Philosophy and Film*, edited by Paisley Livingston and Carl Plantinga, Routledge, 2009, pp. 435–45.

Still Life. Directed by Jia Zhangke, Shanghai Film Studio / Xstream Pictures, 2006.

Van Manen, Max. *Researching Lived Experience: Human Science for an Action Sensitive Pedagogy*. Althouse Press, 1990.

Williams, Raymond. *Marxism and Literature*. Oxford UP, 1977.

Yacavone, Daniel. "Film and the Phenomenology of Art: Reappraising Merleau-Ponty on Cinema as Form, Medium, and Expression." *New Literary History*, vol. 47, no. 1, 2016, pp. 159–86.

Yanshuo Zhang

Visualizing Ethnic Minorities in Multicultural China

Even though China is home to fifty-five ethnic minority groups spanning every corner of its enormous landmass, very few courses offered in North American university classrooms focus exclusively or primarily on China's ethnic minorities. A quick glance at university course offerings in the United States, particularly in Asian studies and Chinese studies programs, will reveal that, while many social and historical aspects of China are covered (such as urbanization, legal and gender issues, and China's socioeconomic transformations), ethnic minority cultures are rarely mentioned in course titles.

This current lack of attention to teaching about China's ethnic minority cultures stands in stark contrast to the scholarship, especially Western-language scholarship, about China's *shaoshu minzu* (少数民族; "ethnic minorities") that has been developing in different academic fields: for example, the groundbreaking volume *Chinese Women Writers on the Environment: A Multi-ethnic Anthology of Fiction and Nonfiction*, published in 2020 (Isbister et al.). This volume, one of the first translated anthologies of multiethnic Chinese women's writing, showcases the literary achievements and life trajectories of many marginalized ethnic minority writers of contemporary China. The next year Xiao Pélissier published her five-hundred-page French-language study of women's literature in Xinjiang. More than just a conventional study of minority literary works, Pélissier's book investigates the various narrative modes and linguistic practices of minority writing in Xinjiang. She attends to the ethnographic, aesthetic, autobiographic, and collective narratives of Xinjiang, surveying writers from Uyghur, Kazakh, and other ethnic backgrounds.

Beyond the field of literature, Chinese ethnic minorities have long been subjects of study in anthropology and history in Euro-American scholarship. The postreform era of the 1990s and 2000s, in particular, witnessed a golden period of American anthropologists visiting China's ethnic minority regions and generating pivotal studies about the Miao, the Yao, the Yi, the Tibetans, the Hui, and many other ethnic groups in China (e.g., Schein, *Minority Rules*; Litzinger; Harrell and Li; Yeh; Gladney). These anthropological studies are important in examining the non-Han groups' relationship to modernizing China, unveiling the socioeconomic and cultural life of ethnic minorities as central aspects of understanding China in a period of change.

Western academia's engagement with China's *shaoshu minzu* cinema also has a rich history. Yingjin Zhang's seminal 1997 article "From 'Minority Film' to 'Minority Discourse:' Questions of Nationhood and Ethnicity in Chinese Cinema" argues that "the 'minority film' genre in mainland Chinese cinema and the 'minority discourse' in Chinese cinema criticism destabilize such analytical categories as 'ethnicity,' 'race,' and 'nation-state'" (1). Indeed, Chinese films by or about ethnic minorities usually produce discursively complex spaces where notions of ethnicity, race, and the nation-state are contested and even redefined. Furthermore, Rey Chow's notion of film as ethnography and the primacy of visuality in translating and constructing cultures in the postcolonial world (176–95) reveals the convergence between anthropology and film: films often serve as visual ethnographic accounts to understand non-Western cultures, particularly during our modern era of global cultural encounters.

In recent years, American anthropologists have endeavored to theorize about the relationship between ethnography and film in China. For instance, Louisa Schein has written about "ethnographic representations across genres" both in and beyond the conventional feature-film genre, touching on videos and media productions created by minority villagers in the Miao areas of Guizhou ("Ethnic Representation" 1). Similarly, Jenny Chio has been engaged in experimental ethnographic filmmaking and has theorized about "observational cinema" and "sensory ethnography," attending to the sensorial dimensions of film in challenging the authority of "thick description" as an established methodology practiced by professional anthropologists (30). In my own interdisciplinary study of the Qiang ethnic group of Sichuan, I have uncovered how documentary filmmaking efforts made by minority players, such as local cultural entrepreneurs, are foregrounding indigenous worldviews in combatting the rampant commercialization and commodification of ethnic villages in southwest China (Yanshuo Zhang 423–27).

Given the growing multidisciplinary scholarship on China's *shaoshu minzu*, there is fruitful potential in teaching about multicultural China and cultivating students' interdisciplinary sensibilities through this subject matter. As we have seen, the study of ethnic minorities cannot be neatly encompassed within a single disciplinary angle, be it literature, anthropology, or film studies. Rather, the study of ethnic minorities as both historical categories and living cultural communities requires students and teachers to think outside of the convenient disciplinary categories: students and teachers need to push the boundaries of knowledge by synthesizing insights and methodologies from various disciplines. As such, research into the undertaught subject of China's diverse *shaoshu minzu* affords students and teachers unparalleled opportunities to tap into the fascinating world of multiculturalism and interdisciplinarity.[1]

In this essay, I discuss how I have taught Chinese ethnic minority films in the context of interdisciplinary approaches in the humanities. To open up the space of discursive invention and be inclusive of different parties involved in filmmaking, I use *ethnic minority films* to refer to films both about and by the ethnic minorities in China, produced both strictly within China and through transnational collaborations between Chinese and Western artists. In addition to full-length films, I also discuss other film-like media productions, such as music videos and China Central Television's New Year galas. These media productions are an indispensable part of minority cultural imagination in China. Even though the geographic focus of my essay is on China, I hope that the experiments and methodological insights generated from my teaching will be widely applicable in the humanities.

I am keen on incorporating film into three key areas of pedagogical practice. First, I challenge students to think about the question of genre by choosing films that cross or blur conventional genre boundaries, such as commercial versus arthouse cinema, propaganda versus creative cinema, and feature film versus documentary film. In doing so, I cultivate students' abilities to critically engage with humanistic inquiries by redrawing the boundaries of established knowledge. Second, I place film within a broader teaching repertoire of visual culture that includes painting and photography instead of isolating film as a singular artistic lens through which to understand China. In doing so, I encourage students to form critical habits to think in cross-disciplinary ways and to question the epistemological and disciplinary silos in academia. Finally, I juxtapose film texts with other nonvisual texts, such as literary texts, to help students make sense of the narrative contours and discursive landscapes of cultural production as a whole. In this essay, I discuss how these three key factors play out in my teaching, using examples of texts, student work, and the dynamic processes of producing knowledge in the classroom and other spaces of student-faculty interactions.

Destabilizing Genre Boundaries

The focus on genre has been a tried-and-true method in the teaching of humanistic disciplines in North America, particularly literature and film. Literature courses tend to be organized around national or regional boundaries, period, and the dichotomy between fiction and nonfiction, a dichotomy that has bled even into creative writing programs' course offerings. In film studies courses, periodization and regional focuses also prevail, and the teaching of genre conventions and genre history seem to be a heavy focus in many film studies courses. While there is tremendous merit in teaching about genre as a crucial way to guide students into the world of artistic creation, little attention seems to have been paid to how different genres speak to and enrich each other.

In my teaching of Chinese ethnic minority films, I challenge students to think across and beyond genres to make sense of the multifaceted and highly fluid spaces of artistic creation. While traditional genre studies is valuable in helping students understand established authors and canons, cross-genre teaching and learning acknowledge the voices and perspectives of emerging artists and marginalized communities. Such artists and communities may defy and often consciously contest genre conventions and the structures of power that have created canonical genres. For this reason, teaching across and beyond genres offers both a conceptual and a practical tool for teachers interested in teaching about marginalized, unconventional, and other multifaceted communities that are reflective of our multicultural global society.

In my course Imagining China from the Borders: The Literary, Artistic, and Ethnic and Racial Borderlines of China, I choose film texts that do not conform to neat genre conventions but straddle multiple genres or genre possibilities. As one of the very few American university courses to focus exclusively on China's ethnic minority groups, Imagining China from the Borders provides students with a historical lineage of understanding how the geographic and cultural margins of China have been front and center in both China's national imagination and the multicultural exchanges between China and the world.

The first half of the course focuses on the historical interactions between the Sinitic and nomadic groups in and around China. Instead of choosing a film that was exclusively produced in China, I selected the 2007 film *Mongol: The Rise of Genghis Khan*, directed by the renowned Russian director Sergei Bodrov. *Mongol* was a transnationally produced film that involved an extensive crew of four hundred people, including three hundred Chinese and one hundred Russians. Moreover, the production included German, Japanese, and Ukrainian extras. Produced with funds from Germany, Russia, Kazakhstan, and the United States, *Mongol* was mainly shot in Kazakhstan and Inner Mongolia ("*Mongol*"). The film's expansive transnational production process makes the film a rich text for students to use in deciphering the nature of cross-ethnic interactions and conflicts in premodern China and inner Asia. Despite the film's potential for engaging with discussions of transnational politics, major American reviews regarded *Mongol* as merely a commercial film and a blockbuster filled with alluring spectacles, calling it "quite grand, quite exotic," "stunning," "breathtaking," and "fun" (qtd. in "Critic Reviews"). Two of my students did a brilliant presentation that questioned the mainstream discourse about the entertaining features of *Mongol* and illuminated the problematic but also fascinating transnationalism embodied in this film.

For my Imagining China from the Borders class, I assigned a team presentation project that encourages students from different academic and cultural backgrounds to collaborate and present on course materials. The assignment was not just a conventional close-reading exercise but required students to do some outside research to form their own articulations and interpretations of the course materials. Students were required to both historize and contextualize the materials that they were presenting on by bringing outside sources, such as primary sources and historical information, into their oral presentations. The two students who presented on *Mongol* went beyond expectations, as they marshaled visual, musical, and cinematic materials to help the class understand this film not simply as an entertaining blockbuster but as a multifaceted site of transnational interactions. The student presenters started by relaying information about the international cast and production team of the film: the Japanese actor Asano Tadanobu plays the historical character Temujin (who would later become Genghis Khan), and the Chinese actor Sun Honglei plays his fictional sworn brother and rival. The presenters also pointed out that the movie was filmed in Inner Mongolia rather than in Mongolia itself, as the Mongolian nationalist sentiments around the national hero Genghis Khan made it harder to film in Mongolia. The students carefully examined the politics of transnational collaboration in the filmmaking industry and the cultural sentiments behind filmmaking by deconstructing the genre conventions of *Mongol.*

The semihistorical and semifictional nature of *Mongol* also makes it a productive text for investigating questions of cultural representation and cultural myth. In class, we viewed short clips of the film to lead the discussion beyond a formal analysis of the film language to a consideration of various aspects of cultural representation. For example, we analyzed how Mongol music, such as throat singing, became a perpetual undertone that permeated the auric space of the movie, creating a myth of the Mongols' cultural continuity. Most interestingly, we discussed how the fictional sworn brother of Temujin, played by a Chinese actor, symbolized the historically fraught relationship between Chinese and Mongol cultures. When paired with academic readings, such as Uradyn E. Bulag's *The Mongols at China's Edge*—which explores historical and contemporary interactions between ethnic Mongols, the Chinese state, and Mongols in other parts of the Eurasian world—the teaching of the movie became much more elevated than a film analysis: it became a multimedia, transhistorical moment of understanding interethnic relations and cultural politics in a global context.

If the teaching of *Mongol* speaks to the transnational politics of Chinese ethnic minority issues, then another film I used, *Erma's Wedding* (尔玛的婚礼), exemplifies the complex nature of negotiating minority identity and modernization in contemporary China. In recent years, there has been a vibrant scholarly discussion about the emergence of an indigenous discourse in Chinese minority communities (e.g., Hathaway; Luo; Yanshuo Zhang). Indigenous discourse shifts attention away from how minority regions have been transformed by processes of modernization to how minority groups have come up with creative ways to reinvent their identities in the face of China's developmental agendas. *Erma's Wedding* serves as an excellent example for students to explore the struggles and hopes of ethnic minorities as they reimagine who they are in twenty-first-century China.

Somewhat similarly to *Mongol, Erma's Wedding* provides a fertile ground for students to investigate questions of cultural interactions and cross-cultural representations when analyzed outside of the conventional genre categories. This film was a coproduction between a renowned ethnic Han filmmaker, Han Wanfeng, and scholars and communities of the Qiang ethnic group of Sichuan. The film tells the story of Erma, a young Qiang woman who is courted by and decides to marry a Han teacher who teaches English in her village. As Erma and her fiancé plan for their wedding, a clash arises: while Erma yearns for a traditional Qiang-style wedding that involves the entire community and colorful and elaborate ceremonies, her fiancé prefers a Western-style wedding to please his aunt, a local official. The film unveils the cultural conflict faced by the Qiang villagers, who are caught between the lure of a modern lifestyle promised by the Han teacher and his aunt and the desire to preserve their ancestral ways. Instead of offering a simple answer, the film presents two competing and contradictory endings: in one ending, Erma succeeds in persuading her fiancé to have a Qiang-style wedding; in an alternative ending, the Han teacher manages to get Erma to agree to a Western-style wedding. In the second ending, the bride impatiently rides the bus to the county seat for what she perceives to be a dull, stern wedding ceremony.

In my teaching of the film, I engage students with the cinematic discourse of "docufiction" to unpack this artistically and thematically complex film (Deppman 188). Docufiction is a new film genre that contests the boundaries between the real and the imagined. Open to presenting ambiguity and the multiple perspectives of a society in flux instead of offering a definitive and coherent narrative, docufiction has been mobilized by many of China's contemporary filmmakers in making statements about contemporary China. The two endings of *Erma's Wedding* are a telling example of how ethnic identities are imagined in competing and contradictory ways in this docufictional film. Furthermore, in class we analyzed a five-minute clip to understand the cultural dilemmas of minority communities under the sway of social development (1:21:12–1:25:37). This clip came from the first ending of the film and represents a traditional Qiang wedding. From emotional singing parties to sending away the bride to the solemn shamanistic blessing ceremonies, and from cheerful ritual dances performed by male members of the village to the poignant sound of the Qiang flute, this clip is a comprehensive exhibition of many aspects of traditional Qiang culture. Students were able to quickly point out the visual politics of representing ethnic cultures by analyzing not only the realist and documentary style of this clip but also how ethnic cultural elements are imagined and artistically displayed. With my guidance, the class discussed how this clip exemplifies a documentary style of auto-ethnography—the painstaking efforts of presenting many aspects of Qiang culture embody the filmmakers' desire to visually exhibit and preserve the diverse cultures of China and to reveal the vulnerability and tenacity of indigenous lifeways under the threat of modernization. On the other hand, the strong fictional dimension of the movie tantalizes the audience with the romantic tension of a couple caught between two worldviews. Indeed, at the end of the clip, we see that while the bride takes delight in the shamanistic ritual blessings of her wedding, the groom is completely stupefied, looking confused and afraid in what to him is the strange world of Qiang cultural symbolism.

Without either its documentary or its fictional dimension, the film would fall flat as what some critics might call a clichéd cross-cultural love story. Yet by seeing beyond the conventional genre categories that might get attached to the film and by attending to the cultural politics behind the film's visual representations, my class was able to use this film as a kind of textbook to understand the cultural dilemmas experienced by *shaoshu minzu* in contemporary China.

By destabilizing the boundaries between documentary and fictional films, commercial and artistic films, I am able to use ethic minority film as a powerful tool to cultivate students' critical capacities to understand ethnic representation and cross-cultural politics in China and Asia more broadly. Most minority-themed films involve multiple parties in their production, multiple sites of imagination, and multiple perspectives and worldviews. The question of genre becomes enriched and expanded if we contextualize it within the rapidly transforming multiethnic Chinese society, where ethnic minority artists deploy multifaceted cinematic styles and themes to express minority identities as creative and dynamic imaginaries rather than as stereotypical and static images.

Interdisciplinary Learning: Film and Visual Culture

In this section, I shift the focus from discussing the aesthetic and social dimensions of ethnic minority film to the intertextuality between film and other visual genres. Students in the twenty-first century are exposed to all kinds of media productions on a daily basis. The vast majority of students are users of social media and regularly produce social media and other media content themselves. The goal of my multimedia teaching is to shape students into critical and responsible consumers and producers of media by helping them understand the interconnections and crosscurrents of the multimedia world they live in.

Many discipline-specific critical concepts can be taught with an interdisciplinary and multimedia approach in order to drive students to make unexpected discoveries. One of the core concepts I teach in my Imagining China from the Borders course is ethnography. Rather than treating ethnography simply as the invention of modern anthropology, I urge students to probe into the historical lineage of ethnography in the context of premodern Chinese culture. In this course, students explored the ethnographic and visual portrayals of the non-Han tribal communities in southwestern and southern China that were first collectively identified as the Miao in Ming- and Qing-dynasty historiographical and artistic accounts. In particular, we analyzed the ethnographic sensibilities embedded in the pictorial representations of the social customs, gender relations, and natural and cultural landscapes of the various Miao communities. We used the book *The Art of Ethnography: A Chinese "Miao" Album*, translated and edited by David Deal and Laura Hostetler. Students delved into the ethnographic mode of analysis and, through close-reading exercises of the Miao albums, explored the political desire of the Ming and Qing dynasties' ruling classes to depict and govern borderland ethnic groups in premodern China. Students analyzed the production of the Miao albums' finely executed paintings and poems—produced by commissioned Confucian artists—and the albums' circulation among educated elites in China, sometimes as gifts from one official to another. Through guided exercises, students also came to see that ethnography in premodern China was not just a discursive or academic domain of representing cultural others but embodied the imperial government's administrative need to understand and rule the country's heterogenous ethnic groups. By engaging with the historically and culturally specific ramifications of ethnography, I broadened the teaching of this anthropological critical concept by applying it to history and art history.

Taking the concept of ethnography into modern China, I encouraged students to discover the shifts from premodern to modern Chinese ethnographic accounts of non-Sinitic societies in the realm of visual culture as well as the convergences between these accounts. For example, a few class periods were devoted to the visual representations of ethnic minorities at the inception of the People's Republic of China in the 1950s. I asked students to analyze, side by side, the representations of *shaoshu minzu* in political and film posters and in films. Students quickly recognized the ethnographic elements of political posters produced in the 1950s, which rendered the dresses and headwear of minority women in ethnographically realistic detail. One student insightfully pointed out that in the poster for a famous minority-themed film, *Five Golden Flowers* (五朵金花), the female protagonist wears an emerald-colored jade bracelet ("Movie Poster"), possibly a sign that the filmmakers had decided to make minority women appear more familiar to the Han audience by having them wear jade, which is a Han cultural symbol.

Students' understanding of minority-themed visual culture was greatly enhanced through exercises that helped students contextualize the production, consumption, and reception of minority-related materials beyond the film texts themselves. For the final research project, one student studied how *shaoshu minzu* are still cast in an ethnographic light in the annual Lunar New Year galas hosted by China Central Television, which portray minorities as a colorful and timeless presence in a fast-developing China. Another student explored how the ethnographic elements of minority life have been appropriated to create ethnic spectacles for tourists. By learning to engage with materials across different visual genres, students are able to transport critical concepts beyond film as they form creative habits for dealing with ideas and genre conventions across disciplines.

Perhaps my most memorable and productive moment teaching across visual genres is when I introduce students to the lived experience of minority groups of contemporary China. Because I routinely engage in ethnographic and archival research in the minority regions of southwest China, particularly in the Qiang and Tibetan regions of Sichuan, I show students my own field photographs. In recent years, because of a new wave of touristic and industrial development, many minority villagers in Sichuan have left their home villages in search of livelihoods elsewhere. In one of my classes, I showed students a group of photographs I took when I visited an old Qiang village in Sichuan. While the architectural fabric of that village remained intact, most residents had moved out. Yet one Qiang man had chosen to stay in his old home, and I photographed him looking out from his balcony. This photographic documentation of the changes in a minority village and the tenacity of one villager's attachment to his familiar lifeworld left students deep in thought. Students commented that they appreciated seeing the lived realities of minority communities beyond the spectacular and colorful representations of minority groups in mass media.

Constructing a Discursive Contour
of Cultural Production

To foster students' understanding of multiethnic politics and poetics in contemporary China, I teach nonvisual texts alongside film texts. One of the major sources of nonvisual narratives about *shaoshu minzu* is literature. The twenty-first century has witnessed a blossoming community of ethnic minority writers in China, who have been prolific in writing about minority culture, history, community life, and other personal or collective themes (Bender 70). I juxtapose *shaoshu minzu* literary narratives with films and other film-like media, such as television drama. For example, the prominent ethnic Tibetan author Alai's epic novel, whose title translates literally as *The Dust Settles* but has been published in English as *Red Poppies*, delves into the historical realities and shifting identities of Tibetan groups under the traditional *tusi* (土司; "chieftain") system. In class, I asked students to read excerpts from the novel, particularly the chapters that deal with the different cultural influences that intersected to reconfigure Tibetan identities in the early twentieth century, such as Christian missionaries and Han officials. I then showed clips from episodes of the TV dramatic adaptation of *Red Poppies*, *Chen'ai luoding*, to stage a comparative conversation about the TV drama and the novel. Whereas the novel is narrated from the perspective of the son of a chieftain, and the changes in Tibetan regions are told through the eyes of a Tibetan observer, the TV drama seems to adopt a very different perspective. The TV drama exoticizes the Tibetan regions, and the chieftain is made to show off his muscles, giving him an almost macho image. Students learned to analyze the different audiences that the novel and the drama were aiming for; furthermore, they developed a critical lens to investigate both the creative freedom and the limitations of transforming an epic historical novel into a mass-entertainment TV drama.

I also teach the film *Mountain Patrol* (可可西里), Lu Chuan's influential tale of the ecological landscape in Tibet. Like *Erma's Wedding*, *Mountain Patrol* has a strong docufictional character—the film was based on the real stories of Tibetan mountain patrol volunteers who fought against the poaching of Tibetan antelopes. The film shows photographs of an actual patrol team, and its plot involves a half-Tibetan, half-Han reporter writing down the stories of the patrol team—these elements created a wonderful opportunity for students to contemplate the question of reportage, narration, and ecology. In class, I asked students to analyze the film's representation of photographs together with the fictionalized narrative of the reporter. As with *Red Poppies*, students had exciting discussions about the power of narration, the role of the sympathetic narrator in constructing a credible story about minority regions, and the convergences and divergences between literary and cinematic narratives in *Mountain Patrol*.

Learning about China's ethnic minorities is important for teachers and students who wish to understand multicultural China and the country's place in a multicultural world. Ethnic minority films serve as an excellent source for visualizing multicultural China. Learning about these ethnic minority groups requires that teachers and students think creatively across artistic genres, critical categories, and disciplinary boundaries. The study of ethnic minorities does not have to be constrained to courses that focus exclusively on non-Han groups; rather, materials on ethnic minorities can be incorporated into many different kinds of courses on China and Asia more broadly, such as courses dealing with modernization, economic development, gender issues, and globalization. The inclusion of *shaoshu minzu* as a topic in China and Asian studies courses will add a valuable angle of multiculturalism to class discussions and enrich the courses' theoretical breadth. Teachers and students can even contest the term *multiculturalism* and discuss its special ramifications in China in a comparative global context.

For class projects, teachers can encourage students to pursue questions on multiculturalism and China from different disciplinary approaches. When students are allowed the creative freedom to pursue a question rather than simply study a genre or a subject matter, students dive into their work and form exciting and unexpected connections, breaking down the silos of academic and social knowledge in the process. It is my hope that the methodologies presented here will help teachers and students approach multicultural China from multidisciplinary perspectives. It is also my hope that teachers will apply these methodologies in other cultural and regional contexts, ushering in a new generation of humanities scholars who dare to think across and beyond conventional categories to extend the horizon of knowledge.

Note

1. Though it differs in China compared with in the West, the concept of multiculturalism is still useful when discussing multiethnic relations and cultural productions in China. Multiculturalism in any context denotes group rights and the power of representation. Ma Rong, a scholar in China, distinguishes between two types of policies for managing ethnic relations: politicization and

culturalization. Politicization refers to the making of policies that emphasize the "integrity, political power, and 'territorial' conservation of ethnic groups," whereas culturalization entails "emphasizing the cultural characteristics of ethnic groups" and "treating ethnic relations as cultural relations." (6). Similarly, the American scholar Susan McCarthy points out that multiculturalism in China implies efforts to patronize, curate, and consume minority cultures (32). We can observe that China's official ideologies and cultural practices by and large celebrate cultural diversity and ethnic difference within the national discourse of interethnic unity. China's multiculturalism is also evidenced through many regional and national journals, academic societies, and television and social media programs that present and promote ethnic literatures, languages, music, architecture, traditional craftsmanship, and other cultural aspects. I use the term *multiculturalism* with its specific connotations in China.

Works Cited

Alai. Red Poppies: *A Novel of Tibet.* Translated by Sylvia Li-chun Lin and Howard Goldblatt, Mariner Books, 2003.

Bender, Mark. "Cry of the Silver Pheasant: Contemporary Ethnic Poetry in Sichuan and Yunnan." *Chinese Literature Today,* vol. 2, no. 2, 2012, pp. 68–74.

Bulag, Uradyn E. *The Mongols at China's Edge: History of the Politics of National Unity.* Rowman and Littlefield, 2002.

尘埃落定 [*Chen'ai luoding; The Dust Settles*]. Directed by Yan Jiangang, 2003.

Chio, Jenny. "Theorizing in/of Ethnographic Film." *The Routledge International Handbook of Ethnographic Film and Video,* edited by Philip Vannini, Routledge, 2020, pp. 30–39.

Chow, Rey. *Primitive Passions: Visuality, Sexuality, Ethnography, and Contemporary Chinese Cinema.* Columbia UP, 1995.

"Critic Reviews for *Mongol: The Rise of Genghis Khan.*" *Metacritic,* www.metacritic.com/movie/mongol-the-rise-of-genghis-khan/critic-reviews. Accessed 6 June 2022.

Deal, David, and Laura Hostetler, translators. *The Art of Ethnography: A Chinese "Miao Album."* U of Washington P, 2006.

Deppman, Hsiu-Chuang. "Reading Docufiction: Jia Zhangke's *24 City.*" *Journal of Chinese Cinemas,* vol. 8, no. 3, 2014, pp. 188–208.

Erma's Wedding. Directed by Han Wanfeng, Xiaoxiang Film Studio, 2008.

Gladney, Dru C. *Dislocating China: Muslims, Minorities, and Other Subalterns.* U of Chicago P, 2003.

Harrell, Stevan, and Li Yongxiang. "The History of the History of Yi, Part Two." *Modern China,* vol. 29, no. 3, 2003, pp. 362–96.

Hathaway, Michael. "The Emergence of Indigeneity: Public Intellectuals and an Indigenous Space in Southwest China." *Cultural Anthropology,* vol. 25, no. 2, 2010, pp. 301–33.

Isbister, Dong, et al., editors. *Chinese Women Writers on the Environment: A Multi-ethnic Anthology of Fiction and Non-fiction.* McFarland, 2020.

Litzinger, Ralph. *Other Chinas: The Yao and the Politics of National Belonging.* Duke UP, 2000.

Luo, Yu. "Alternative Indigeneity in China? The Paradox of the Buyi in the Age of Ethnic Branding." *Verge: Studies in Global Asias*, vol. 4, no. 2, 2018, pp. 107–34.

Ma Rong. "A New Perspective in Guiding Ethnic Relations in the Twenty-First Century: 'De-politicization' of Ethnicity in China." *De-politicization of Ethnic Questions in China*, edited by Lizhong Xie, World Scientific, 2014, pp. 1–27.

McCarthy, Susan. *Communist Multiculturalism: Ethnic Revival in Southwest China.* U of Washington P, 2009.

Mongol: The Rise of Genghis Khan. Directed by Sergei Bodrov, CTB Film / Andreevsky Flag Film / X-Filme Creative Pool, 2007.

"*Mongol: The Rise of Genghis Khan*: Trivia." *IMDb*, www.imdb.com/title/tt0416044/trivia/?ref_=tt_trv_trv. Accessed 6 June 2022.

Mountain Patrol. Directed by Lu Chuan, Columbia Pictures / Huayi Brothers Media / National Geographic World Films, 2004.

"Movie Poster for 1959 Chinese Film *Five Golden Flowers*." 15 May 2017, en.wikipedia.org/wiki/Five_Golden_Flowers#/media/File:Five_Golden_Flowers_Poster.jpg.

Pélissier, Xiao. *Narration féminine et ethnique du Xinjiang.* Edition You Feng, 2021.

Schein, Louisa. "Ethnic Representation across Genres." *The Oxford Handbook of Chinese Cinemas*, edited by Carlos Rojas and Eileen Chow, Oxford UP, 2013, pp. 507–25.

———. *Minority Rules: The Miao and the Feminine in China's Cultural Politics.* Duke UP, 2000.

Yeh, Emily T. "Tibetan Indigeneity: Translations, Resemblances, and Uptake." *Indigenous Experience Today*, edited by Marisol de la Cadena and Orin Starn, Berg Publishers, 2007, pp. 69–98.

Zhang, Yanshuo. "Entrepreneurs of the National Past: The Discourse of Ethnic Indigeneity and Indigenous Cultural Writing in China." *positions: asia critique*, vol. 29, no. 2, 2021, pp. 423–50.

Zhang, Yingjin. "From 'Minority Film' to 'Minority Discourse:' Questions of Nationhood and Ethnicity in Chinese Cinema." *Transnational Chinese Cinemas: Identity, Nationhood, Gender*, edited by Sheldon Hsiao-peng Lu, U of Hawai'i P, 1997, pp. 81–104.

Notes on Contributors

Angie C. Baecker is lecturer in the Department of Art History at the University of Hong Kong. She is an interdisciplinary scholar of modern Chinese cultural history specializing in the socialist period, and her manuscript reexamines the Maoist fine arts project through the lens of socialist amateurism and mass art practice.

Jingjing Cai is assistant professor of Chinese at Centre College. She has published research articles, critical essays, and book and film reviews in scholarly journals (*Asian Women, Journal of Technology and Chinese Language Teaching, Chinese Literature Today*, etc.) and the popular press. Her research interests include Chinese literature, film studies, gender and women's studies, and Chinese language pedagogy.

Vincent Casaregola is professor of English and former director of film studies at Saint Louis University. His areas of interest include film and media studies, American literature and culture from 1900 to the present, and rhetorical studies. He teaches courses in ethnic American literature and in Chinese and Chinese American film. His book *Theaters of War* (2009) examines the American representation of World War II in literature and film. He has published numerous academic articles and book chapters, along with poetry and creative nonfiction. He has recently completed a collection of poetry focusing on illness and loss ("Vital Signs"), which has yet to be published, and he is at work on a scholarly monograph concerning the dark films of the 1950s.

Angie Chau is assistant professor of modern Chinese literature and film at the University of Victoria, and her current project is a transnational investigation of Chinese writers and artists in Paris during the first half of the twentieth century. Her essays on Chinese literature, art, film, and Internet culture have been published in *Modern Chinese Literature and Culture, Chinese Literature Today, Concentric*, and various edited volumes. Her research interests include contemporary Chinese literature, visual culture, pop culture, and translation.

Hongwei Thorn Chen is assistant professor in communication and Asian studies at Tulane University. His research examines nontheatrical film, media history, and the trajectories of colonial modernity in modern China. Chen has been the recipient of the Mellon International Dissertation Research Fellowship, and his writing has appeared in *Wide Screen* and *The Journal of Chinese Cinemas*.

Jasmine Yu-Hsing Chen is assistant professor in the Department of World Languages and Cultures at Utah State University. She specializes in contemporary Chinese and sinophone theater, film, media, visual culture, and literature. Her research examines how theatrical and cinematic works challenge government-promoted nationalism and how theater interacts with new media. She has published peer-reviewed articles in journals including *Theatre, Dance and Performance Training*, *Comparative Media Arts Journal*, *Journal of the Oriental Society of Australia*, *Prism: Theory and Modern Chinese Literature*, and *Journal of Chinese Overseas*. Currently, she is a member of the board of directors at the North American Taiwan Studies Association.

Su-I Chen is principal lecturer in Chinese at Clemson University. She has taught general linguistics, phonetics and phonology, Chinese language courses, and Chinese culture through films. Her research interests include Chinese language pedagogy, films in language and culture classes, and the application of technology in teaching.

Elaine Chung is lecturer in Chinese studies at the School of Modern Languages, Cardiff University, where she teaches courses on sinophone histories and cultures. Her research focuses on the transnational politics of East Asian popular cultures. Her essays on Chinese-Korean cultural relations have appeared in various edited volumes, including *The Rise of K-Dramas* (2019), *Asia-Pacific Film Co-productions* (2019), *Sino-Enchantment: The Fantastic in Contemporary Chinese Cinemas* (2021), and *Unpacking Discourses on Chineseness: The Cultural Politics of Language and Identity in Globalizing China* (2021). She has recently coedited a special issue of *Archiv Orientalni* on East Asian media comedies, which includes her article on Stephen Chow's stardom in South Korea.

Emma Clawson is a recent graduate of Utah State University who majored in global communications and minored in Chinese. She has lived in Taiwan, where she has further learned how to communicate within diverse cultures. Her research project on China's left-behind children was funded by the College of Humanities and Social Sciences at Utah State University.

Marjorie Dryburgh is lecturer in modern Chinese studies in the School of East Asian Studies, University of Sheffield. Her research focuses on memory, life writing, and the social histories of northern and northeastern China, and she has specific interests in the social effects of Japanese engagement in the region and the interplay between personal and official, and Chinese and Japanese, histories in stories of youth and education. She is the coeditor of *Writing Lives in China, 1600–2010: Histories of the Elusive Self* (2013), and her recent publications have appeared in *History Workshop Journal, Japan Forum,* and *Social History.*

Ho Chak Law is a full-time faculty member of the College of Performing Arts at the New School. His publications have appeared in academic journals such as *The Drama Review, Analytical Approaches to World Music,* and *Music and the Moving Image.* His current research interests include ecomusicology, music historiography, and sinophone media culture and performing arts.

Han Li is associate professor of Chinese in the Department of Modern Languages and Literatures at Rhodes College. She specializes in the material culture of late imperial China, contemporary Chinese cinema, and media studies. She has published in journals including *Concentric: Literary and Cultural Studies, Asia Major, Ming Studies, Journal of the American Oriental Society, ASIA Network Exchange, Traditional Dwellings and Settlement Review, Journal of Curatorial Studies, Asian Cinema,* and *American Journal of Chinese Studies.*

Lily Li is currently adjunct professor of Chinese and humanities at Eastern Kentucky University. Her critical studies of Chinese literature and film have been published in edited volumes and academic journals. She is coeditor of a forthcoming volume on diasporic Chinese literature and film. Her most recent critical study of aesthetics in digitalized traditional Chinese theater appears in *Performance Arts: Research in the Age of Digital Revolution* (2023).

Jin Liu is associate professor of Chinese language and culture at Georgia Institute of Technology. She conducts interdisciplinary research on contemporary Chinese popular culture and media culture from the perspective of language, writing, sound, voice, and music. She is author of *Signifying the Local: Media Productions Rendered in Local Languages in Mainland China in the New Millennium* (2013), which examines film, television, the Internet, popular music, and fiction in mainland China. She is coeditor of *Chinese under Globalization: Emerging Trends in Language Use in China* (2012). She has published peer-reviewed articles in journals including *positions: asia critique; East Asian Journal of Popular Culture; Journal of Chinese Cinema; Journal of New Music Research; Twentieth-Century China; Chinese Literature: Essays, Articles, Reviews; Modern Chinese Literature and Culture; Journal of Modern Literature in Chinese; Chinese Language and Discourse; Chinese as a Second Language;* and *Digital Scholarship in the Humanities.*

Shirley O. Lua is associate professor of literature and cultural studies at De La Salle University, Manila. She is a jury member of the Manunuri ng Pelikulang Pilipino, the film critics group that confers the Gawad Urian awards on the best Philippine movies of the year. She wrote *Forty-Four Cineastas Filipinos* (2011). She coedited Direk: *Essays on Filipino Filmmakers* (2018) with Clodualdo del Mundo Jr.

Seio Nakajima is professor of sociology and Asian studies at the Graduate School of Asia-Pacific Studies, Waseda University. He has conducted organizational analyses of the Chinese film industry, as well as ethnographies of Chinese film audiences and consumption. His articles include "The Genesis, Structure and Transformation of the Contemporary Chinese Cinematic Field: Global Linkages and National Refractions" (*Global Media and Communication*, 2017), "Official Chinese Film Awards and Film Festivals: History, Configuration, and Transnational Legitimation" (*Journal of Chinese Cinemas*, 2019), and "Studies of Chinese Cinema in Japan" (*Journal of Chinese Film Studies*, 2021).

Sydney Pond is a graduate student in the Communication Studies Department at Utah State University, with a focus on global and intercultural communication. Her research interests include cultural bias in efforts to alleviate global poverty, including media representations of humanitarian organizations, and mental health—specifically reverse culture shock—in returning religious missionaries.

Corey Kai Nelson Schultz is associate professor in international communications at the University of Nottingham, Ningbo, China. He is the author of *Moving Figures: Class and Feeling in the Films of Jia Zhangke* (2018) and has published in *Screen*, *Visual Communication*, *Film-Philosophy*, *Asian Cinema*, and *Celebrity Studies*.

Aleksander Sedzielarz is assistant professor in the School of English at Kean University, Wenzhou, where he teaches courses on film and literature. He was formerly Marion L. Brittain Postdoctoral Fellow at the Georgia Institute of Technology and lecturer in Chinese cinema at the University of California, Riverside. Sedzielarz is coeditor of *Transnational Crime Cinema* (2022).

Josh Stenberg is senior lecturer in Chinese studies at the University of Sydney. The author of *Minority Stages: Sino-Indonesian Performance and Public Display* (2019) and Liyuanxi: *Chinese "Pear Garden Theatre"* (2022), his research interests include *xiqu* in modern and contemporary periods, the cultures of Sino–Southeast Asian communities, and Chinese translation studies.

Zhuoyi Wang is professor of East Asian languages and literatures (Chinese) at Hamilton College. He is the author of *Revolutionary Cycles in Chinese*

Cinema, 1951–1979 (2014) and coeditor, with Ping Zhu and Jason McGrath, of *Maoist Laughter* (2019), which was a 2020 *Choice* Outstanding Academic Title. He has published in such English- and Chinese-language scholarly journals, edited volumes, magazines, and new media venues as *Arts, China Review International, Chinese Literature Today, Chinese Literature and Thought Today, Cinema and TV Culture, Illuminating Empirical Data with Theory, Literature and Art Studies, Literature and Culture Studies, Journal of Beijing Film Academy, Journal of Chinese Cinemas, Phoenix Weekly, Prism: Theory and Modern Chinese Literature, Taiwan Lit,* and *WHYNOT.*

Emily Wilcox is associate professor of Chinese studies at William and Mary. She is the author of *Revolutionary Bodies: Chinese Dance and the Socialist Legacy* (2018), winner of the de la Torre Bueno Prize from the Dance Studies Association; coeditor, with Katherine Mezur, of *Corporeal Politics: Dancing East Asia* (2020); and coeditor, with Soo Ryon Yoon, of *Inter-Asia in Motion: Dance as Method* (2024). She has published more than thirty scholarly articles and book chapters in English and Chinese and is the cocreator, with Liangyu Fu, of the University of Michigan Library's Chinese dance collection.

Hongmei Yu is associate professor of Chinese at Luther College. Her research interests are film studies, comparative literature, and contemporary Chinese culture. Her papers have been published in the journals *Modern Chinese Literature and Culture* and *ASIA Network Exchange* and in various edited volumes.

Shaolu Yu is associate professor of urban studies at Rhodes College. Trained as an urban geographer with an interdisciplinary background and participating in urban studies projects in China, the United States, and Canada, she has developed a comparative and global perspective and a mixed-method approach in her research on cities. Her current research interests include urban space and place making, transportation geography and mobility, race and ethnicity, urban segregation, and Asian urbanism. She is also interested in applying cartography and GIS in visualizing and analyzing spatial data. Her papers have been published in *The Professional Geographer, Urban Geography, Geographical Review,* and the *Journal of Transport Geography.*

Yanshuo Zhang is assistant professor of Asian languages and literatures at Pomona College. Her research centers on the creative reinvention of cultural heritage in modern China. She combines interdisciplinary methodologies crisscrossing literature, anthropology, history, and art history in her study of multiethnic China. She has published in *positions: asia critique, Prism: Theory and Modern Chinese Literature, Modern Chinese Literature and Culture, Heritage and Society,* and *Journal of Urban Cultural Studies.*

Chenshu Zhou is assistant professor in the Department of Cinema and Media Studies at the University of Pennsylvania. She is the author of *Cinema Off Screen: Moviegoing in Socialist China* (2021), winner of the Best First Book Award from the Society of Cinema and Media Studies. Her research centers on media experiences in modern and contemporary China. Her writings and translations have appeared in journals such as *positions: asia critique*, *Journal of Chinese Cinemas*, and *Chinese Literature Today*.

Ping Zhu is professor of Chinese literature and culture at the University of Oklahoma and editor in chief of *Chinese Literature and Thought Today*. She is the author of *Gender and Subjectivities in Early Twentieth-Century Chinese Literature and Culture* (2015); the coeditor, with Zhuoyi Wang and Jason McGrath, of *Maoist Laughter* (2019), which was a *Choice* Outstanding Academic Title in 2020; and the coeditor, with Hui Faye Xiao, of *Feminisms with Chinese Characteristics* (2021).